Handbook on
Corporate Fraud

Handbook on Corporate Fraud

Prevention, Detection, and Investigation

Jack Bologna
Siena Heights College
Adrian, Michigan

Butterworth–Heinemann
Boston London Oxford Singapore Sydney Toronto Wellington

Recognizing the importance of preserving what has been written, it is the policy of
Butterworth–Heinemann to have the books it publishes printed on acid-free paper, and
we exert our best efforts to that end.

Library of Congress Cataloging-in-Publication Data

Bologna, Jack.
    Handbook on corporate fraud : prevention, detection, and
investigation / Jack Bologna.
      p. cm.
    Includes bibliographical references (p.   ) and index.
    ISBN 0-7506-9243-X (alk. paper) : $69.95
    1. Fraud investigation. 2. White collar crime
investigation. 3. Corporations—United States—Corrupt
practices. I. Title.
    HV8079.F7B65   1993
    364.1'68—dc20

                                       92-12300
                                          CIP

British Cataloguing-in-Publication Data

A Catalogue record for this book is available from the British
Library.

Butterworth–Heinemann
80 Montvale Avenue
Stoneham, MA 02180

10 9 8 7 6 5 4 3 2 1

Printed in the United States of America

Contents

Preface and Acknowledgment

In operas and musical comedies, the show begins with an overture before the curtain goes up. The overture is a kind of sampler of the melodies and musical themes that will be enlarged upon when the show gets underway. So it is with this book on corporate fraud. This preface is intended to be a preview of what follows in the text.

Let me begin by confessing that I am not a world authority on corporate fraud. Corporate fraud is a vast area of study; no one can fairly claim to be a world authority. The phenomenon of corporate fraud cannot be understood without reference to such other fields of study as sociology, personal and organizational psychology, political science, economics, ethics, accounting, auditing, criminal justice, law, and history. It would take several well-rounded individuals working ceaselessly to do this subject justice.

Corporate fraud, in a nutshell, involves people in organizational settings who lie, cheat, and steal. There are, of course, many people who lie, cheat, and steal. Indeed, we probably all do or have done so. However, lying, cheating, and stealing in an organizational setting is unique in one essential characteristic: The culprit is influenced by both personal predisposition and organizational conditions that breed fraudulent behavior.

The notion that screening out potential thieves on the basis of background investigation, polygraph or psychological testing, or intensive interviewing will solve the problem of corporate fraud is somewhat naive. Clever thieves (the ones who cause the largest losses) are skillful enough to overcome these screening techniques—to say nothing of the question of the legality and ethics of the techniques themselves.

If corporate fraud is to be prevented, we must focus our attention on two factors:

1. the social psychology of fraud perpetrators, that is, their motivations
2. the control environment of the firm that employs the potential fraud perpetrator, that is, the fraud opportunities provided by nonexistent or unenforced accounting and security controls

As the old saying goes, corporations do not commit corporate fraud, people do—people who work in low-level, middle-level, and high-level positions in corporations. Accounting and security controls are not designed to inhibit high-level fraud because high-level employees can override these controls. At high levels of management, controls really consist of personal ethics. However, personal ethics can quickly be compromised when economic and competitive conditions threaten bottom-line profits, which in turn threaten pay raises, bonuses, perks, and job survival. Balancing your economic and professional survival against the interests of stockholders, creditors, suppliers, customers, employees, and competitors tends to be a one-sided argument when your neck is on the line. Weighing self-interest against "outside" interests is a short exercise for most of us when we add to our deliberations the needs, wants, and demands of our spouses and children and our current lifestyle preferences.

We can therefore conclude that corporate fraud is alive and indeed thriving today. Corporate fraud is likely to be with us for some time to come. There are no permanent remedies on the horizon. The goal is to reduce the risk of corporate fraud by decreasing both the motivations of perpetrators and the opportunities provided by the absence or weakness of controls. Reducing the risk of corporate fraud requires something else. The ethics of high-level managers must be enhanced. These individuals serve as corporate role models. If truth, justice, honesty, integrity, and fairness are important values to top managers, they become important to those who report to them because employees tend to mimic the behavior of their superiors.

I would like to thank Judith Mara Riotto for her tireless effort to turn a skeleton into a full-bodied book. Her copyediting corrections were most helpful.

Introduction

This book is a treatise on corporate fraud, that is, fraud committed by, for, or against corporations by insiders (directors, officers, employees, and agents) and outsiders (vendors, suppliers, contractors, and customers). As a matter of law, corporations act only through their directors, officers, employees, and agents. In that context, corporations do not commit crimes themselves; however their directors, officers, employees, and agents can commit crimes for them—and against them as well.

There are literally thousands of types of fraud, and millions of frauds are perpetrated every year in the United States. Indeed, fraud is the number one crime in America. All types of fraud share the common element of intentional deception, that is, lying and cheating. Frauds also share another common characteristic: a breach of trust or a violation of a trusting relationship. Illustrations of breaches or violations of trust include the following:

- The CEO of a public company deceives the stockholders by falsely representing the value of corporate assets or liabilities or the amount of income earned by the company.
- A vendor, supplier, or contractor intentionally overbills, double-bills, or substitutes inferior materials.
- A corporate employee gains legitimate access to assets but converts or embezzles them.
- A "loyal" employee covers up losses and mistakes to save the company from embarrassment.

Fraud is of epidemic proportions today in the United States and perhaps in the world. It is a by-product of a consumer society that places a premium on acquisitiveness. Individual greed replaces communal good as the major motivator. When greed becomes a dominant value, fraud takes off for the heavens—witness the savings and loan and Wall Street scandals of the eighties. Easy money and a fast return on investment became as addictive as cocaine and heroin in that decade. Indeed, they may be related phenomena. By the end of the decade, greed itself was venerated as a virtue. In the movie *Wall Street,* the character Gordon Geco told a group of future MBAs that "greed is good."

Personal freedom, property ownership for the masses, and a free market economy are what distinguish capitalism from communism. These rights, however, must be balanced with a sense of responsibility. Indeed, all rights have concomitant responsibilities. In a capitalist society, constraints must be placed on greed. Constraints may take the form of laws, professional codes of conduct, and social values. For example, while we value property accumulation, we also constrain it through inheritance and estate taxes. While we value spending for consumption, we also value thrift. Increasing consumption of goods while decreasing savings may stimulate the economy on a short-term basis, but a long-term continuation of such habits could bankrupt the nation. Greed must therefore be tempered with responsibility.

In the communist economic system, the means of production and other capital assets are owned by the state. Prices for consumer goods and services are set by the state, not by the marketplace. Personal freedom is restrained by government fiat. In the communist system, need rather than greed is the force that inspires growth and development. In Maslow's terms, survival needs are satisfied best in the communist system, and self-actualization is satisfied best in the capitalist system.

The flaw in the communist system is the assumption that needs can be satisfied more efficiently through governmental direction. However, the heavy hand of government cannot compete for efficiency with the "invisible hand" of the marketplace. A little greed goes further than a lot of need when it comes to motivating workers. If that were not true, the poor would not be poor for very long. The data of the social sciences show that poverty provides little inspiration for progress. Poverty tends to beget poverty.

The question now is whether fraud occurs with as great a frequency in the communist economic system as it does in the capitalist system. The answer may be that need provokes more fraud than greed; that is, that fraud occurs with greater frequency in the communist system than in the capitalist system. Greed can be controlled by cultural conditioning, legislation, and public opinion. Need, when unsatisfied, is sublimated. When needs are sublimated, they can be channeled into highly creative endeavors, such as lying, cheating, stealing, subterfuge, and impersonation. When I visited the Soviet Union, officials of the Ministry of the Interior confessed that fraud was rampant, what with the counterfeiting of passports and travel permits, the black market sale of goods and currencies, the falsification of production reports, the theft of government goods and supplies, and so on.

Fraud seems to exist in most societies; it is not unique to the United States. Indeed, fraud may not be as prevalent in the United States as it is in other countries, yet Americans have no reason to gloat. The situation in the United States is serious enough to warrant immediate attention.

CHAPTER 1

Crime

What Is Crime?

The word *crime* has no universal definition. In the United States, *crime* generally means an act of adult misbehavior. It is distinguished from *delinquency,* which refers to adolescent misbehavior. In the legal sense, a crime is an act or omission that is made criminal by a penal law; that is, some punishment may be meted out for its violation. The punishment can take the form of a fine, imprisonment, or both.

The main purpose of criminal law is to prevent and to deter crime. Some authorities, however, believe that punishment and retribution for harm done are also important purposes because they protect the public's interest in law, order, and civility. In that context, crime is a public wrong as well as a wrong against the person or organization harmed.

If crimes are public wrongs, torts (violations of another's property or personal rights and acts of negligence) are private wrongs. Civil suits are filed by the victims of such acts against those who committed them for damages or return of property. Some acts are both crimes and torts, and their commission can subject the violator to both civil and criminal action. Examples include assault and battery and some types of fraud.

A criminal act generally consists of an *actus reus* and a *mens rea,* which mean, respectively, a voluntary act or omission and an evil state of mind or criminal intent. Some criminal statutes, however, do not require proof of intent, for example, traffic violations and violations of certain government regulations on public health and safety.

Who Causes Crime?

Crime is largely a demographic phenomenon. It generally involves poor, undereducated, unemployed, bored young men. Given our current economic bent toward high-technology jobs for the well-educated and low-pay service jobs for the undereducated, the reduction of crime in general is a formidable challenge.

White-collar crime does not seem to be abating either. The white-collar crime rate is driven by greed rather than need, and greed is popular right now. When greed grips a society and allows self-interests to be pursued more vigorously than the common good, no net benefit accrues to society.

How Is Crime Categorized?

Crimes against persons and property are committed either overtly (openly) or covertly (secretly). Crimes against persons include murder, manslaughter, rape, and assault and battery. Crimes against property include larceny (theft), burglary (breaking and entering), and embezzlement. Crimes like fraud and deceit can be directed against people or property. Crimes against persons (violent crimes) are considered to be more serious than crimes against property. The penalties for the former are therefore greater than those for the latter.

Crimes can also be classified into those in which criminal intent is a required element of proof and those in which intent need not be proved. However, ignorance of the law is no excuse. Everyone is presumed to know the law, within certain limits.

How Is Crime Detected?

Crimes in general are uncovered on the basis of allegations and complaints filed with police authorities by crime victims and by public-spirited citizens who observe their commission. Crimes are also uncovered through the observations of police authorities themselves.

White-collar crimes like embezzlement, theft of corporate assets, and misrepresentation of financial facts are generally not observed by victims, third-party witnesses, or police at the time of their commission. In fact, white-collar criminals often use disguise, deception, cover-up, and destruction of evidence to mask their criminal activities. These crimes are not impossible to detect, however. Audit and investigative skills are needed.

CHAPTER 2

White-Collar Crime

What Is White-Collar Crime?

At the essence of a white-collar crime is a breach of trust, confidence, or fiduciary duty. Someone relies on and trusts another, to his or her economic detriment. Some illustrations of white-collar crime follow:

- A stock swindler misrepresents the value of a security.
- An advertiser misrepresents the benefits or value of his product vis-à-vis competitive products.
- A con woman feigns illness, ignorance, or a worthy cause to melt her mark's heart and loosen his wallet.
- A used car salesman shows one side of a car that isn't dented or rusted but hides the other side.
- A software vendor says her product can do everything the client wants and then some, when the software was in fact designed for one limited purpose.
- An undertaker guarantees that the burial vault will last one hundred years. (Who's going to be around to collect? Worse yet, who's going to be around to pay?)

Each of these situations involved an intentional deception or fraud directed at consumers. However, white-collar crimes can be directed against a variety of victims by a variety of victimizers, as the following shows:

Victim	Victimizer
Buyer	Seller
User	Supplier
Employee	Employer
Principal	Agent
Beneficiary	Trustee
Bailor	Bailee
Mortgagor	Mortgagee
Manufacturer	Vendor

Victim	*Victimizer*
Stockholder	Chief executive
Customer	Broker

White-collar crimes can be classified as (1) those directed against consumers and (2) those directed against employers. The latter category— corporate fraud—is the focus of this book.

White-collar crime is costly in three ways: financial loss, loss of faith in our economic and social institutions, and loss of faith in one another. Our economic system relies on trust between buyers and sellers and other parties in commercial transactions. Loss of trust adds greatly to the cost of doing business.

The Hallcrest Report II estimates that economic crime cost U.S. consumers and businesses $114 billion in 1990, or about 2% of the nation's gross national product.[1] That's a rather princely sum of money, to say the least. The authors add that businesses and citizens currently spend another $52 billion annually for security products and services to combat crime and prevent losses.

White-collar crime—including all manner of criminal fraud on the public; all criminal violations of government regulations; all employee theft, fraud, and embezzlement; and all political and commercial corruption—is a cancer in our society. Not only does it breed future generations of corrupt white-collar workers, but it also contributes to violent crimes in that injustice breeds social corruption.

Causes, Perpetrators, and Victims of White-Collar Crime

White-collar crime is caused by greed and by lax control mechanisms, which provide motive and opportunity. Control mechanisms include accounting controls (separation of duties and creation of audit trails), physical and data access controls, and management controls (supervision, work climate, and reward system).

The people most likely to commit white-collar crimes are members of the middle and upper classes who hold positions of trust, have easy access to other people's property, and have a need for economic wealth brought about by an expensive lifestyle or by personal misfortune. They often rationalize their crimes. For example, they convince themselves that the victim deserved it, that they were just getting even, or that they were just borrowing, not stealing.

Victims of white-collar crimes are people and organizations who give their confidence and trust to the unworthy. Victims do not adequately screen their victimizers or their proposals, and they easily succumb to appeals to their fear, greed, or need for self-preservation.

Detecting and Preventing White-Collar Crime

White-collar crime is a crime of stealth and deception. Trails are often destroyed, facts are distorted, justifications are concocted, and psychological pressures are brought to bear on victims to discourage prosecution. White-collar crime can be detected by auditing books and records for breaches of control, trust, and confidence and by spotting deviations from conventional accounting methods or deviations from expectations.

You can prevent white-collar crime by becoming more informed about it and by applying rules of self-protection. For example, be wary of employees who never take vacations, live beyond their means, or suffer from mood swings. Be wary of offers that sound too good to be true—they usually are.

Victims of White-Collar Crime

In 1970, Henry S. Ruth, Jr., then director of the U.S. National Institute of Law Enforcement and Criminal Justice, wrote that "the entire field of white-collar crime represents a national priority for action and research— to define the problem, to examine its many faces, to measure its impact, and to look for ways in which its *victims* can be helped."[2]

Research on white-collar crime has dealt at great length with crime victimizers. Substantially less has been written about the victims of crime. Why has so little academic and lay attention been given to the victims of crime in general and to the victims of white-collar crime and investment fraud in particular? Is it not the purpose of the law in Western societies to make whole the person who has suffered at the hand of another?

A suit for damages brought by a small investor victimized by a securities fraud sounds like a plausible and fair remedy, but recent experience suggests that victims of investment fraud get little of their principal back, much less punitive damages against their victimizers. Furthermore, by the time the small investor gets in line to sue the promoter, the promoter has dissipated assets by high living and legal defense costs. The typical return rate for small investors in such suits is about 10% of their investment, and that comes only after years of litigation. Punitive damages, even if awarded, are a hollow victory because there are no assets left. That may explain why so many of the suits brought by small investors now include the following as parties defendant: accountants, directors, officers, and anyone else within earshot of the fraud who has deep pockets.

In the United States, the next wave of lawsuits by small investors may include government regulatory agencies as parties defendant on the legal theory that the government agency carried out its regulatory activities in a negligent manner, for example, the savings and loan (S&L) regulators. Western governments may therefore have to provide investors with reasonable assurance that their regulatory machinery is state-of-the-art and that justice for all investors—large and small, institutional and individual, private and public—is a legal reality.

What does that mean? For starters, it means that regulators should know who the real losers are in investment fraud. Are the real losers the insurance companies, mutual funds, bank trust departments, and large investors? Or are they the small investors and the general public? It's probably the latter. The general public pays the freight for investment fraud in the form of higher prices, higher taxes, and lower trust in the system.

If small investors expect the trading markets in stocks, bonds, and commodities to be corrupt or rigged against small investors, they won't invest their money. They may prefer to spend what they have and live for the moment. Indeed, that may well be evident from the fact that in the United States, the savings rate is far below the averages of other Western countries.

Faith in the economic system and in its inherent fairness to all players is a prime ingredient in encouraging saving. The flight of capital when doubts exist about a government's economic viability, its political stability, or its social cohesion is evidence of that point. Indeed, political scientists today suggest that a government that cannot protect its small investors will not protect its large investors for very long.

Small investors are the last ones to know about the impending collapse of firms tainted by fraud and mismanagement. Getting out of such investments late costs them more. The following list of failed companies and near failures caused great financial harm to many small investors:

Beverly Hills S&L
Bevil, Bresler & Schulman
Cenco, Inc.
Continental Illinois
DeLorean Motors
Drysdale Securities
E.F. Hutton
Equity Funding
ESM Government Securities
Four Seasons Nursing Homes
Home State Savings
National Student Marketing Association
North American Acceptance
Old Court S&L
OPM Leasing
Penn Square Bank
Saxon Industries
Stirling Homex
United American Bank (Jake Butcher)

U.S. Financial
U.S. Surgical
Weis Securities
ZZZZ Best

What may be truly unique about these cases, in addition to the sheer size of the loss, is that in subsequent civil suits brought by shareholders and creditors, outside audit firms were joined with management as parties defendant.

Fraud is a "status" offense. Frauds committed by people of high social, economic, or political status are excused or their frauds are labeled as something less ignoble such as defalcation, financial irregularity, misapplication, or misappropriation. Important people rationalize their fraud as follows:

- Everybody's doing it.
- Boys will be boys.
- Rank has its privileges.
- It was just an innocent mistake in addition.

Ivan Boesky's three-year sentence for insider trading offers further proof that the rewards of white-collar crime outweigh the penalties. In a case that may have foretold Boesky's light penalty,[3] Edward Browder pleaded guilty to transporting $500,000 in stolen bonds across state lines and pledging them as collateral. Browder was given a 25-year prison sentence for his act. In his objection to the long sentence, he claimed to have studied one hundred similar white-collar crime cases, and he concluded, "The greater the offense against capital, the less the punishment imposed by the sentencing judge." In reviewing Browder's sentence, which Browder claimed was "cruel and inhuman," an appellate court judge reasoned, "I cannot reconcile a policy of sending poorly educated burglars from the ghetto to jail when men in the highest positions of public trust and authority receive judicial coddling when they are caught fleecing their constituencies." Browder's long sentence was not found to be "cruel" or "inhuman," but his research was certainly confirmed by the Boesky sentence. The moral seems to be this: If you are going to be a financial crook, be a big one. This moral is reminiscent of Adolf Hitler's propaganda minister, Josef Goebbels, who believed that if you're going to lie, you should tell a big one so at least part of it will be believed.

The lines are now quite clearly drawn. Fraud victimizers have money, political power, and a judicial policy of leniency on their side, and the victims of fraud have no real financial recourse. They must live with the knowledge that they have been duped, cheated, lied to, and stolen from but are unsupported by current law.

New sentencing guidelines have been implemented in the United States that set higher criminal fines for frauds of organizations in relation to the harm done to their victims. An opponent of the proposal alleges somewhat illogically that excessive fines carry social costs that are as damaging as fines that are too low. In any event, higher fines may enrich the government's coffers, but they will do little for the victims.

Facts about White-Collar Crime

For too many years now, the literature of white-collar crime has been dull, boring, and listless. This is not true of Gary S. Green's *Occupational Crime*.[4] Green's book is a synthesis of the literature on white-collar crime, and it includes a wide assortment of authorities and points of view. The book contains many interesting theories and survey results. The following are but a few:

- The public's attitude toward white-collar crime is not benign. For example, one researcher reported that 78% of a sample group believed that violations of pure food and drug laws should be given harsher punishments (p. 18).
- In another survey, 88% of respondents supported jail terms for embezzlers, 70% for antitrust violators, and 43% for false advertisers (pp. 18–19).
- As organizations grow larger, there is less control and authority over middle managers (p. 98).
- One researcher suggests that the larger an organization grows, the weaker the control exercised by top management becomes (the "law of diminishing control") (p. 98).
- We can expect more crime in organizations that have bureaucratic structures because specialization emphasizes subunit self-interest (p. 98).
- Large organizations create cultures in which compliance (loyalty) is encouraged. These organizations tend to hire people who possess values, skills, and motivations that agree with organizational goals. Loyalty is fostered by social and financial dependency (pp. 98–99).
- "Managers and executives seem to be the major sources of ethical attitudes within organizations" (p. 98).
- Males arrested for embezzlement outnumber females by about two to one (p. 205).
- The age demographics of embezzlers show that about one-third of both males and females are 22 to 29 years of age; they constitute the largest grouping of all (p. 205).
- In a 1983 survey, one-third of the respondents admitted that they had stolen from their employers during the preceding year (p. 205).
- "Morality that opposes occupational crime must be validated consistently and constantly" (p. 231).

- Enforcement of laws that punish occupational crimes is "unimpressively low" (p. 253).

The conventional wisdom in white-collar crime suggests the following:

- Psychological deterrents, physical security, and internal accounting controls are no match for a determined employee thief with access to assets and accounting books.
- Some criminal justice authorities believe that criminals reason through their crimes by weighing such factors as risk of apprehension, severity of punishment, and social disapproval against the expected rewards. Other authorities suggest that criminals do not reason through their crimes but act out of ignorance, impulsiveness, or compulsion. Others suggest that criminals become so involved in their crimes that they overweigh the rewards and underweigh the risks. In other words, criminals have one-track minds; they are so determined and so goal-oriented that they chronically err on the side of optimism. Indeed, if it were not that way, police, auditors, and investigators would catch far fewer criminals.
- Much of the literature on criminal behavior deals with the seeming irrationality of criminals; the assumption is that anyone who intentionally violates the law and risks social disapproval and punishment must be sick. That rationale stems from too narrow a point of view. White-collar criminals at least do assess the risks of apprehension, social disapproval, and punishment before they commit a criminal act. Like wise investors, they weigh both the risks and the expected rewards. To them, crime is a matter for cost/benefit analysis: a rational, utilitarian process.
- As a matter of control policy, therefore, it seems logical to maintain tight controls as a psychological deterrent. Deterrence is also a matter of cost and benefits, however. Control costs should bear some reasonable relationship to the value of the protected assets.
- White-collar crime has been variously described or defined as occupational, corporate, economic, or financial. The common characteristics of each of the so-called white-collar crimes are intentional deception (fraud, theft, embezzlement, and corruption), destruction of property (industrial sabotage), gross negligence (product liability), and failure to comply with government regulations on environmental pollution, unfair pricing practices, untrue advertising, unsafe and unhealthy products, stock fraud, tax fraud, and so on.

  The last category, or perhaps the last two, are not considered crimes by many people. They don't seem to fit the common law notion of crime, which requires both a criminal act and criminal intent. Yet, these two categories raise more public concern today than such crimes as employee fraud, theft, embezzlement, and corruption. The apparent reason for this is that violating government regulations is a crime of high-level corporate officials who should know better. High-level employee crimes are perceived to be based on economic greed, while low-level employee crimes are perceived as based on economic need. In the case of economic need, some members of the public feel the culprit is merely balancing an inequity, that is, getting even with his employer for some injustice.

- Some people are more prone to violate the law than others. By the same logic, some companies are more prone to violate the law than others, and some industries are more prone to crime than others. The tendency of individuals and organizations to violate the law has often been explored. The tendency of whole industries to violate the law has received far less coverage, yet much research in criminology supports that thesis.[5]

  Organizational criminality "arises from the emphases on performance that are both internal and external to the organization."[6] If organizational goals can't be met legally, there is a great temptation to meet them illegally. Goal attainment can be frustrated by these conditions: (1) an unrealistic forecast of economic and competitive conditions, (2) a goal that is set arbitrarily by senior management without input by lower levels of management, and (3) cutthroat competition in the industry. Cutthroat competition is more likely to occur in industries that have few barriers to entry, are made up of many small, highly competitive firms, or are dominated by organized crime elements via a corrupt labor organization. A number of industries fit the last category, for example, construction, trucking, garment manufacturing, waste disposal, and distributors of amusements such as records and video games.

- A recent survey by Melissa S. Baucus of the University of Kentucky and Janet P. Near of Indiana University concludes that large firms operating in dynamic, munificent environments are the most likely to behave illegally.[7] Firms with poor performance are not as prone to commit wrongdoing. "Membership in certain industries and a history of prior violations also increased the likelihood that a firm would behave illegally," Baucus and Near found.

- Most authorities agree that personal pathology plays no significant role in the genesis of white-collar crime.[8] Indeed, white-collar criminals are psychologically normal. They commit their crimes after a process of assessing the rewards against the risks.

- The psychological deterrence of crime is a topic on which everyone seems to be an expert, but it is not always easy to discuss. First, there is not much data on the subject. Second, the experts have been drawn into opposite political camps, so dialogue on the subject tends to be more polemic than rational. In an effort to add a little more light and a little less heat to the subject, here is a review of a few basics on psychological deterrence.

Psychological deterrence deals with fears and inhibitions that can be placed in an individual's mind to discourage the commission of a criminal act. For example, the dissemination of information on the probability of apprehension, the severity of punishment, and the degree of social disapproval works to discourage the commission of crime. Disseminating information on the consequences of being convicted of a criminal act (loss of life, liberty, property, civil rights, and social standing) also acts to discourage crime. The threat of being fired for a job-related crime is another illustration of a psychological deterrent.

Psychological deterrence is predicated on the assumption that criminals are rational decision makers who weigh both the risks and the rewards of crime before taking action. If that assumption is correct, psychological deterrents will not work for certain types of crime—for example, white-collar crime—because the rewards outweigh the risks. Worse yet, in relative terms, the more a white-collar criminal steals, the lighter the sentence.

Criminal justice data suggest that only 50% of all crimes are reported to the police and that only one of every five criminal defendants are sentenced to jail terms. In the case of white-collar crimes, these numbers may be even lower. For all intents and purposes, then, psychological deterrence of white-collar crime is mainly one of social disapproval, and there's not much evidence of social disapproval of white-collar crime.

- Criminology offers no satisfactory method of screening potential risks except in terms of the most obvious sorts of things such as a previous criminal record or evidence of a severe personality disorder. In other words, employees rarely take a job with the idea of violating the criminal law and breaching company rules. It is only later that things happen that produce that intent. These involve internal developments—the failure to obtain a desired position, for instance—or outside circumstances such as a marriage gone sour.[9]

Notes

1. William C. Cunningham, John J. Strauchs, and Clifford W. Van Meter, *The Hallcrest Report II* (Stoneham, MA: Butterworth–Heinemann, 1990), p. 31.

2. Henry S. Ruth, "Foreword," in *The Nature, Impact, and Prosecution of White-Collar Crime* (Washington, D.C.: U.S. Government Printing Office, 1970).

3. Browder v. U.S., 38 F. Supp. 1942 (D. Oreg. 1975).

4. Gary S. Green, *Occupational Crime* (Chicago: Nelson-Hall, 1990).

5. See Green, *Occupational Crime;* and Marshall Clinard and Peter Yeager, *Corporate Crime* (New York: The Free Press, 1980).

6. Green, *Occupational Crime,* p. 97.

7. Reported in Melissa S. Baucus and Janet P. Near, "Can Illegal Corporate Behavior Be Predicted?" *Journal of the Academy of Management* (March 1991): 9–36.

8. James W. Coleman, *The Criminal Elite* (New York: St. Martin's Press, 1985).

9. Gilbert Geis, *Fraud Examiner's Manual* (Austin, Tex: NACFE, 1990), pp. iv, 3.

CHAPTER 3

Fraud

What Is Fraud?

Corporate fraud is a fraud committed on behalf of or against a corporation by its directors, officers, employees, and agents.

Corporate frauds against a company include the crimes of larceny (theft), embezzlement, false pretenses, and forgery. Corporate frauds on behalf of a company include corporate tax evasion, misrepresentation of company assets or net income, false advertising, and violation of government regulations that provide penalties.

Corporate frauds can be subclassified as criminal, civil, or contractual offenses. Criminal fraud consists of the intentional misrepresentation of a material fact that causes financial loss to another. Civil fraud has similar elements, but the amount of proof required to sustain a judgment or verdict is less. A preponderance of evidence is required in civil cases; evidence beyond a reasonable doubt is required in criminal cases. In the contractual sense, fraud can be subclassified as fraud in the inducement of a contract or in the execution of a contract.

Evolution of Fraud in English Common Law

Early references to fraud in English common law define it as pretense, false tokens, or intentionally false representations that induce another to part with real or personal property or legal or equitable rights. Common law fraud was considered both a crime (a misdemeanor, as distinguished from larceny, which was a felony) and a matter for civil redress in courts of law and equity by way of contract rescission, restitution, or recovery of damages. Thus, fraud has a historical foothold in the English civil law as well as in its criminal law.

Because fraud will be presented mainly from the perspective of commercial transactions and law, some comments about commerce and law may be in order. Commerce, once it passes the barter state, relies on law. Laws are social controls evolving from conventions (customs and usages) and are designed by societies to protect the rights these societies confer on their members.

The "law merchant," from which Americans have derived many legal rules of commerce, began as a set of rules governing fair business conduct during the Middle Ages. Merchants, tradesmen, freight handlers, and brokers of goods needed some way of ensuring that their work and products would be paid for and protected from theft or conversion. Commerce could not flourish in an environment in which no trust existed between buyers and sellers. (A man's word may be his bond, but if it is reduced to writing, there is a higher level of assurance that he will, in fact, make good on his word.) Rules of contract thus evolved, including contracts of sale, of agency, of bailment, and of carriage. Because all commercial transactions could not be paid for in cash for fear of robbery, credit had to be extended. Mediums of exchange other than cash had to be designed, such as drafts (guarantees of payment) and bills of lading. Rules on negotiable instruments were created. Banking and insurance companies were formed as intermediaries to facilitate commerce and to minimize the risk of loss from such perils as robbery and shipwreck. Rules of fairness in commercial transactions were introduced into the laws of the time and were based on human experience (customs and traditions) and not necessarily on moral principles of proper conduct.

Morality and the law are separate worlds. Moral principles may influence the law or the enactment of the law, but laws have an existence of their own quite apart from morality. What is right and just legally may be far different from what is right and just morally. Morality concerns itself with individual virtue, and law concerns itself with group and interpersonal relations.

In the Middle Ages, mercantile interests had more power than consumers of goods and services. Therefore, the "law merchant" dealt primarily with how merchants should interact in business transactions with one another, "at arm's length," neither trusting nor distrusting completely. There were few rules governing how merchants should transact business with consumers other than the doctrine of caveat emptor or "let the buyer beware." The idea of fairness at that time had to do with the process of business transactions, not with the object of such transactions. Value, in the medieval mind, was subjective. "Whatever the traffic will bear" was the rule of thumb in setting prices for goods and services.

The fairness or reasonableness of the price charged for goods and services was determined at common law by the price at which an accord could be struck by a seller who was willing but under no compulsion to sell and a buyer who was willing but under no compulsion to buy. This subjective rule governing fairness in pricing articles of commerce generally holds true today. It is difficult to set precise objective limits on the value of anything. Value—the price at which goods or properties are exchanged in an arm's-length transaction—continues to be construed on a rather subjective basis, that is, on what seems to be reasonable under the circumstances or on the going price for like or similar goods in similar condition in that market area at that particular time. Courts are not inclined to impose their judgment on the value of an article as long as the parties to the transaction are on a similar footing, that is, of roughly equal intelligence, competence, and means. It is only when the value paid seems clearly unconscionable under the circumstances of the case that a court will intervene when the issue of value is raised.

Deceptions regarding the kind, character, and condition of goods, their quantity, their quality, and their ownership have historically been grounds for judicial concern and review. Misrepresentation of value, however, was generally not an actionable offense under the common law. Statements about the value of goods were seen as puffery, as expressions of personal opinion, or as subjective judgments, not as objective realities. Who knew the value of anything in an era of ignorance and illiteracy? However, willful misrepresentations about such things as the quantity of the goods (weights and measures) could be determined. Value determinations were left to philosophers and moral theologians to debate. Commerce could not flourish if arguments were raised about the value or consideration paid for goods.

Even today, unless it appears clearly unconscionable, the value of an article or the consideration paid for it is not generally a subject of great judicial concern in contract litigation. Even if unconscionable, cases turn more on the issue of competency than adequacy: anyone who overpays must be crazy, inexperienced in business, too young or too old to know better, or a victim of duress or undue influence.

From a legal standpoint, fraud can be viewed as (1) a tort, that is, a civil or private wrong in which the recovery of an asset, monetary damages, or both are sought; (2) a contract law or Uniform Commercial Code violation, in which rescission and return of money or property are sought; or (3) a criminal offense (a public wrong), for which a fine, imprisonment, or both can be imposed.

Fraud versus Fairness

Judicial constructions (definitions and interpretations of statutes) of fraud have over the years tended to hinge on the legal notion of fairness. If justice is to be accorded to the parties in a litigated matter, some criteria must be established to facilitate the disposition of the lawsuit. In tort actions involving allegations of negligence, the criteria used by judges is the so-called prudent-man rule, that is, what would an ordinary, reasonable, prudent person have done under similar circumstances? In tort and contract actions involving an allegation of fraud, the equivalent of the prudent-man rule exists in the rule of fairness or fair dealing. The theory of fairness concerns undue advantage. For example, if the seller in a sales transaction has superior knowledge, there may be an obligation to disclose such information. Business transactions operate on the legal theory that both parties, buyer and seller, are or can become equally knowledgeable about the substance of their transaction, that is, about the value, worth, or condition of the article or service being sold. Therefore, if an advantage lies with the seller or the buyer in terms of knowledge of value or condition, that advantage cannot be silently used to exploit the other party. Silence may be golden, as the proverb says, but not when it contributes to a fraud. The transaction must be conducted "at arm's length," that is, "without trusting to the other's fairness or integrity and without being subject to the other's control or overmastering influence."[1] At arm's length means "beyond the reach of personal influence or control."[2]

The legal concept of fraud relates to human interactions in social and business transactions. Social transactions that may result in allegations of fraud include situations that involve seduction, undue influence over a person making a will, or a breach of promise to wed. That aspect of fraud is not covered in this text, nor are situations involving confidence schemes like the pigeon-drop game, sleight-of-hand card tricks like three-card monte, stacked or marked decks, or loaded dice. The primary concern in this book is fraud in business transactions—the so-called corporate and management fraud—and particularly fraud involving either theft or conversion of assets by corporate personnel or financial deceptions practiced by personnel against shareholders, creditors, and regulatory authorities.

Legal Definitions

To laypeople, the words *theft, fraud, embezzlement, larceny,* and *defalcation* can be used interchangeably. The terms *breach of trust or fiduciary responsibility, conversion, false representation, false pretenses, false tokens, false entries,* and *false statements* are rarely used by laypeople because they sound more ominous and legalistic.

The word with the broadest connotations is *theft.* Most people have some sense of what the term means and implies. Even children understand the implication of "You stole my toy." Translated, that means, "You took my toy without my permission and are keeping it from me against my will."

Theft and *stealing* have become so generally understood and so commonly used that they are considered generic terms for a range of different crimes, but they are rarely used in criminal statutes. The technical charge for the kind of behavior most people think of as theft or stealing is larceny.

Larceny is usually defined as the "wrongful taking and carrying away of the personal property of another with intent to convert it or to deprive the owner of its use and possession."[3] If the taking is by stealth, the crime committed is larceny. If the taking is by force or fear, the crime committed is robbery. If the taking is by guile or deception, by false representation, or by concealment of that which should have been disclosed, the crime committed is fraud.

Fraud, then, is any kind of artifice employed by one person to deceive another. *Fraud* is a generic term, too. Because of its generic use and applications, the word *fraud* now means behavior that may be either criminal or civil. In a contractual sense, fraud may be found in the inducement of a contract or in the execution of a contract.

Embezzlement, which has not yet been discussed, is a kissing cousin of larceny and fraud. By definition, *embezzlement* is the "fraudulent appropriation of property by a person to whom it has been entrusted, or to whose hands it has lawfully come."[4] It implies a breach of trust or fiduciary responsibility.

The major distinction between larceny and embezzlement lies in the issue of the legality of custody of the article stolen. In larceny, the thief never has legal custody. He or she feloniously takes the article stolen. In embezzlement, the thief is legally authorized by the owner to take or receive the article and to possess it for a time. The thief may formulate intent to steal the article after taking possession of it or concurrently with initial possession. If initial possession and intent to steal occur simultaneously, the crime is larceny. If intent to steal occurs after initial possession, the crime is embezzlement. These hairsplitting distinctions make a prosecutor's job more difficult.

This book was not written for lawyers, teachers of English, or even psychologists. It was written for people who have the burden of ferreting out fraud and documenting its existence—regulatory agents, police officers, detectives, internal auditors, private investigators, and crime reporters. What should they know about fraud, larceny, and embezzlement?

One thing they might want to know is the definition of various types of fraud crimes. The definitions given thus far are broad and generic and cover common-law crimes, such as larceny, robbery, embezzlement, and criminal fraud.

Fraud as a Crime

The Michigan Criminal Law, Chapter 86, Section 1529, which is typical of the law in other states, defines fraud as follows:

> Fraud is a generic term and embraces all the multifarious means which human ingenuity can devise, which are resorted to by one individual, to get an advantage over another by false representations. No definite and invariable rule can be laid down as a general proposition in defining fraud, as it includes all surprise, trick, cunning and unfair ways by which another is cheated. The only boundaries defining it are those which limit human knavery.
>
> Fraud is a term of law, applied to certain facts, as a conclusion from them, but is not in itself a fact. It has been defined as any cunning deception or artifice used to cheat or deceive another.
>
> "Cheat and defraud," as the term is ordinarily used, means

every kind of trick and deception, from false representation and intimidation to suppression and concealment of any fact and information, by which a party is induced to part with his property for less than its value or to give more than its worth for the property of another. Fraud and bad faith are often synonymous, particularly when applied to the conduct of public offenders.

The essential elements to be established, in order to constitute an offense under most of the statutes relating to frauds and cheats, are:

1. An intent to defraud
2. The commission of a fraudulent act, and
3. The fraud accomplished.

Fraud as a Civil Wrong

In 1887, the U.S. Supreme Court defined *fraud* in the civil sense as follows:[5]

The burden of proof [in civil fraud cases] is on the complainant; and unless he brings evidence sufficient to overcome the natural presumption of fair dealing and honesty, a court of equity will not be justified in setting aside a contract on the ground of fraudulent representations. In order to establish a charge of this character, the complainant must show by clear and decisive proof:

First	That the defendant has made a representation in regard to a material fact;
Second	That such representation is *false;*
Third	That such representation was not actually believed by the defendant, on reasonable grounds, to be true;
Fourth	That it was made with intent that it should be acted on;
Fifth	That it was acted on by complainant to his damage; and
Sixth	That in so acting on it, the complainant was ignorant of its falsity, and reasonably believed it to be true.

The first of the foregoing requisites *excludes such statements as consist merely in an expression of opinion or judgment, honestly entertained; and again, excepting in peculiar cases, it excludes statements by the owner and vendor of property in respect to its value.* [Emphasis added.]

What Is Corporate Fraud?

Corporate fraud is any fraud perpetrated by, for, or against a business corporation. Corporate frauds can be generated internally (perpetrated by directors, officers, employees, or agents of a corporation for or against it or against others) and externally (perpetrated by others—suppliers, vendors, customers, etc.—against the corporation).

Management fraud is the intentional overstatement of corporate or unit profits. It is inspired, perpetrated, or induced by employees serving in management roles who seek to benefit from such frauds in terms of coveted promotions, job stability, larger bonuses, or other economic incentives and status symbols.

A Corporate Fraud Classification System

Corporate fraud can be classified into two broad categories: (1) those frauds or crimes that are directed against the company and (2) those frauds or crimes that benefit the company. In the former, the company is the victim; in the latter, the company, through the fraudulent actions of its officers, is the beneficiary.

Corporate fraud can therefore be classified as follows:

I. Crimes against the company
   A. Input scams
      1. Cash and petty cash diversions
      2. Cash and petty cash conversions
      3. Receivables manipulations, for example, lapping
      4. Payables manipulations, for example, phony vendor invoices, benefit claims, and expense vouchers
      5. Payroll manipulations, for example, phony employees and altered time cards
      6. Overstating inventory
   B. Thruput scams
      1. Bypassing controls in systems and application programs, for example, salami slicing, trap doors, Trojan horses, and time bombs
   C. Output scams
      1. Destroying exceptions reports and logs
      2. Stealing files, programs, reports, and data (customer lists, research and development results, marketing plans, etc.)
II. Crimes for the company
   A. Smoothing profits
      1. Inflating sales
      2. Understating expenses
      3. Not recording sales returns
      4. Inflating ending inventory
   B. Balance sheet manipulations
      1. Overstating assets
      2. Not recording liabilities
   C. Price fixing

    D. Cheating customers
      1. Short weights, counts, and measures
      2. Substitution of cheaper materials
      3. False advertising
    E. Violating government regulations, for example, Equal Employment Opportunity Commission and Occupational Safety and Health Administration regulations and environmental, securities, and tax regulations
    F. Bribing customer purchasing personnel
    G. Political corruption
    H. Padding costs on government contracts

Seriousness and Frequency of Corporate Fraud

Criminal behavior is a major concern today in all advanced countries, and the United States is no exception. If crime statistics can be trusted and are interpreted properly, the United States is experiencing an upsurge in all categories of crime, that is, crimes against persons (violent crimes) and crimes against property (nonviolent crimes). When data on white-collar crime (nonviolent, middle- and upper-class crimes) are reported, the cost is placed at anywhere from $4 to $40 billion per year. Some authorities would place it even higher. The S&L scandal alone will cost taxpayers an estimated $500 billion over the next 20 years. Forty percent of this amount has been attributed to fraud, or $10 billion a year.

Corporate frauds against and on behalf of companies are not at all uncommon. Frauds against companies by insiders and outsiders (vendors, contractors, suppliers) are considerable both in number of incidents and in dollar losses. Frauds on behalf of companies—such as corrupting customer personnel, price-fixing, deception of creditors and shareholders, selling unsafe, unhealthy, or defective products—are considerable as well. In fact, a *Fortune* magazine survey some years ago indicated that more than 10% of Fortune 1000 companies had been convicted of fraud two or more times.[6] Corporate fraud by these large, well-known, domestic and multinational firms, whose stock is publicly traded, shows significant social flaws in the character of their officers. People often expect more honesty and integrity from such firms and their officers because they are considered leaders and role models in industry.

Historically, corporate fraud has occurred with greater frequency at certain times and under certain economic and market conditions. For example, fraud on behalf of public companies increases when competition in an industry becomes intense and the general economy is in recession. Fraud against companies can also increase at such times, as employees discover that their style of living is threatened by competitive forces and economic conditions.

Causes, Perpetrators, and Victims of Corporate Fraud

The increase in crime in all general categories (personal, property, and white-collar) has been attributed to several factors:

- poverty
- unemployment
- poor education
- lack of prison space
- drug use
- political corruption
- lax law enforcement
- disintegration of the family
- loss of respect for authority
- sex and violence on television and in movies
- loss of such traditional values as honesty, loyalty, and respect for elders
- inadequate funding of schools, police, and human services

Solving any one of these problems will be difficult, expensive, and time consuming. Solving all of them will be impossible. It is likely that the crime problem will remain for some time to come.

Corporate fraud is caused not only by economic and competitive forces but also by social and political forces. If trust and honesty become less valued and winning at all costs becomes more valued in a society, corporate fraud increases.

The economic, competitive, political, and social forces that exacerbate fraud are external to corporations, but internal forces also make fraud more likely. Examples include poor internal controls, poor personnel policies and practices, and poor examples of honesty at the level of senior management. The following factors enhance the probability of internal fraud, theft, embezzlement, and corruption:

I. Inadequate rewards
   A. Pay, fringe benefits, recognition, job security, job responsibilities
II. Inadequate management controls
   A. Failure to articulate and communicate minimum standards of performance and personal conduct
   B. Ambiguity in job roles, duties, responsibilities, and areas of accountability
III. Lack of or inadequate reinforcement and performance feedback mechanisms
   A. Failure to counsel and take administrative action when performance levels or personal behavior falls below acceptable standards

IV. Inadequate support
   A. Lack of adequate resources to meet mandated standards
V. Inadequate operational reviews
   A. Lack of timely or periodic audits, inspections, and follow-through to ensure compliance with company goals, priorities, policies, procedures, and governmental regulations
VI. Lax enforcement of disciplinary rules
   A. Ambiguous corporate social values and ethical norms
VII. Fostering hostility
   A. Promoting or permitting destructive interpersonal or interdepartmental competitiveness
VIII. Other motivational issues
   A. Inadequate orientation and training on legal, ethical, and security issues
   B. Inadequate company policies with respect to sanctions for legal, ethical, and security breaches
   C. Failure to monitor and enforce policies on honesty, loyalty, and fairness
   D. General job-related stress or anxiety

Fraud can only be perpetrated by people. The people who cause corporate fraud are mainly insiders with motive and opportunity. Vendors, suppliers, and contractors can also commit fraud against corporations. Insiders, however, have easier access to accounting systems and current assets and therefore represent the greatest threat.

Victims of corporate fraud are the firms who pay too little attention to their people and to their internal controls. A blend of toughness and compassion is needed to thwart corporate fraud.

Loose cash, loose controls, and loose morals are what it takes to commit fraud. It helps if the perpetrator has no conscience, easy access to records, and easy access to assets. If he or she can't carry it off alone, there is always someone else who can be enlisted in exchange for a share in the proceeds.

Detecting and Preventing Corporate Fraud

Corporations can detect fraud by establishing good accounting and management controls. These include reporting exceptions—that is, flagging deviations from quantified goals and spotting unconventional accounting practices (misclassified entries, misplaced assets, misinterpreted policies)—and detecting oddities and anomalies in accounting practices—that is, amounts, times, places, and people that don't jibe. The seeds of fraud are planted when the unexpected becomes commonplace and the commonplace becomes unexpected.

Corporate fraud by middle- and lower-level employees can be prevented by reducing opportunities and motivations. Hiring honest people helps, but keeping them honest on the job is even more important. Keeping employees honest means not giving them a reason to steal, cheat, or lie; treating them fairly; paying them equitably; listening to them; watching for symptoms of serious behavior change; and coaching and counseling them. It also means recognizing and reinforcing good work.

For senior management personnel, corporate fraud is a matter of character weakness. Egocentricity, jockeying for promotion, and excessive greed, among other things, cause senior management people to victimize their employers. They often rationalize that their frauds benefit the company, are not illegal, contribute to the organization's survival, will not be considered unethical by their peers, or will not be discovered.

Because white-collar crime does not carry the stigma of blue-collar crime, punishments are light—usually fines, probation, or community work. The most notable of the recent white-collar convicts who served any time at all received short sentences at "prisons" that had tennis courts, weight rooms, swimming pools, and golf courses.

If the news media provided the same intensive coverage of higher class crimes as they do of lower class crimes, it might discourage the former. Sentences could also be increased as a deterrent. However, the best long-term prevention method may be to inculcate a higher standard of ethics in up-and-coming executives.

Factors that reduce the probability of internal theft, fraud, embezzlement, and corruption include these:

I. Prevention measures
   A. Internal accounting controls
      1. Separation of duties
      2. Rotation of duties
      3. Periodic internal audits and surprise inspections
      4. Development and documentation of policies, procedures, systems, programs, and program modifications
   B. Computer access controls
      1. Identification defenses
      2. Authentication defenses
      3. Establishment of authorization by levels of security
II. Detection measures
   A. Logging of exceptions
      1. Out of sequence, out of priority, and aborted runs and entries
      2. Transactions that are too high, too low, too many, too few, too unusual (odd times, odd places, odd people)
      3. Attempted access beyond authorization level

    4. Repeated improper attempts to gain access (wrong identification, wrong password)
- B. Variance reporting
  1. Monitoring operational performance levels for
     - a) variations from plans and standards
     - b) deviations from accepted or mandated policies, procedures, and practices
     - c) deviations from past quantitative relationships, for example, industry trends, past performance levels, normal profit and loss (P&L) and balance sheet ratios
- C. Intelligence gathering
  1. Monitoring employee attitudes, values, and job satisfaction levels
  2. Soliciting feedback from customers, vendors, and suppliers for evidence of employee dissatisfaction, inefficiency, inconsistency of policies, corruption, or dishonesty

Overcoming Resistance to Controls

Accountants, auditors, and security people are the most control-minded employees in any organization, as indeed they should be to properly discharge their duties. However, they often erroneously assume that the employees who must live with their control plans will accept them out of logic, rationality, and good business judgment. They feel abused and frustrated when their plans are not welcomed with open arms. Pockets of resistance develop even before attempts to implement change because all change tends to cause resistance. Change may be perceived by the employees on whom it will have a major impact as a threat to their economic security; to their power base, authority, status, job responsibilities, or work place relationships; to their time; or to the status quo. Their response to change may take several forms, depending on their level of authority:

- aggression: hitting back, for example, by sabotaging the new system or controls (most common among nonmanagers)
- projection: blaming their new difficulties on those who implemented the change or on the new ideas or devices (most common among middle managers)
- avoidance: stubbornly refusing to comply or finding ways to overcome or compromise the new controls (most common among top managers)

How do you overcome resistance to change where controls are admittedly less than adequate? It must be done very carefully. There is no recipe for defusing the anxiety over change or overcoming resistance to change. There are, however, some general rules:

- Implement changes incrementally—a little at a time—not radically.
- In the early planning or decision-making process, involve the employees or a representative group of the employees on whom the major burden of adjustment to change will be required.
- Communicate the reasons for the change, for example, cost savings, theft reduction, loss prevention, prudence, regulatory requirement.
- Focus on the benefits of the change to the organization itself and to its people.
- Relate the new controls to meaningful and accepted corporate goals.
- Don't try to control too much—the costs always outweigh the benefits.

Notes

1. Henry Campbell Black, *Black's Law Dictionary,* 4th ed. (St. Paul: West, 1968), p. 100.
2. Ibid.
3. Henry Campbell Black, *Black's Law Dictionary,* 5th ed. (St. Paul: West, 1979), p. 792.
4. Ibid., p. 468.
5. Southern Development Co. v. Silva, 125 U.S. 247, 8 S.Ct. 881, 31 L. Ed. 678 (1887).
6. *Fortune,* December 1, 1980, "How Lawless are Big Companies," p. 56.

CHAPTER 4

Management Fraud Overview

Corporate versus Management Fraud

Corporate fraud, theft, and embezzlement are commonly understood to mean lying, stealing, and cheating on the job by people in management positions.

Management fraud, in its simplest definition, is the intentional understatement of losses and liabilities and the overstatement of assets or profits. Profits can be manipulated by overstating revenues or understating costs. Revenue can be overstated by recording fictitious sales, recording unfinalized sales, recording consignments as sales, or recording shipments to storage facilities as sales. Costs can be manipulated by deferring them to the next accounting period or understating them in the current period; by such ploys as overstating ending inventories of raw material, work in process, and finished goods; or by understating purchases of raw materials.

In theory, each of these methods for overstating profits is detectable through traditional financial audit techniques, including transaction sampling, account analysis, receivables and payables confirmation, physical inventory counts, eyeball and reasonableness checks, gross profit tests, and internal control tests. In fact, few such frauds are ever discovered in the course of financial audits—at least not in the early stages of such frauds. Early-warning systems for these frauds do not exist in the classical auditor's kit bag. Auditor's tend to look at current numbers in isolation from the past or future and in isolation from the people who generate these numbers. Financial auditors want to believe in the numbers they are reviewing and to trust the people they are auditing. Both are laudable, if slightly unrealistic, objectives.

Management fraud of this type is possible because of a human need for faith and trust in numbers and people. Management fraud is also possible because accounting controls can be circumvented by senior managers. Controls are designed mainly to keep lower-level managers and employees from becoming dishonest. Senior managers are trusted more and have more authority to dispense with controls under proper circumstances. Internal and accounting controls do not prevent the possibility of fraud by senior management.

Another peculiarity of management fraud is that it usually doesn't happen in social isolation. Management fraud tends to involve a number of people; it tends to be a conspiracy. A conspiracy to commit management fraud is even more difficult to detect than an act or series of acts by any one person.

As a further complication in management fraud detection, even when discrepancies, oddities, variances, and exceptions surface, it is difficult to distinguish these things from innocent errors, mistakes, and omissions. It is also difficult to distinguish acts of fraud from acts of mismanagement or incompetence. Human error and incompetence occur far more frequently than fraud. Not all dumb people are crooks, nor are all crooks dumb people. Some crooks are rather intelligent, and management defrauders tend to fall into that category.

Signs of Management and Corporate Fraud

In almost every case of management and corporate fraud, signs of the fraud exist for some time before the fraud itself is detected or disclosed by a third party. These signs include the following:

- significant changes in the behavior of the defrauder
- knowledge that the defrauder is undergoing an emotional trauma at home or in the work place; that the defrauder is betting heavily, is drinking heavily, or has a very expensive social life or a very active sex life; or that the defrauder is heavily in debt
- audit findings of errors and irregularities that are considered immaterial when discovered
- knowledge that the company itself is having financial difficulties, such as frequent cash flow shortages, declining sales or net profits, and loss of market share
- signs of management incompetence, such as poor planning, organization, communication, and controls; poor motivation and delegation; management indecision and confusion about corporate mission, goals, and strategies; management ignorance of conditions in the industry and in the general economy

In crisis management parlance, these precipitating or predisposing conditions and events are called *prodromal,* or warning, signs. The word is derived from the Greek, in which it means "running before."

For example, when Continental Illinois National Bank came close to failure in the early 1980's, conditions existed before the bank had to be bailed out by the Federal Deposit Insurance Corporation (FDIC). One such event was the discovery by the bank's internal auditors that a bank officer, who had purchased $800 million in oil and gas loans from Penn Square

Bank, had been the recipient of $565,000 in loans from Penn Square. Was that a prodromal event? It seems so in retrospect, but Continental's top management wasn't too concerned about that kind of impropriety. It issued a mild rebuke because the officer brought in a portfolio of loans that would have earned a gross return rate of 20% if the loans had performed. In fact, most of the loans had to be written off a short time later.

Dealing leniently with management fraud when it first surfaces doesn't solve the problem, and not dealing with it promptly when it is fully uncovered may be quite costly in terms of the financial loss and the loss of corporate image. A company may be able to insure against the financial loss, but the damage to the image of the company and its products and services may be irreparable. This is particularly true if the company is in the financial services business, where faith, confidence, and trust in the industry and institution are the critical factors of success.

Additional Signs of Fraud

As any second-year accounting student knows, profit can be "juggled" in a few ways: (1) by delaying the recording of expenses, (2) by recording sales that are not yet finalized, and (3) by overstating ending inventory. In fact, these are the favorite techniques of profit-center managers who are determined to make their budgets come true in feast or famine. The budget review process, however, is designed to thwart the latter sort of financial trickery. Budget reviews are supposed to keep the players honest. The give and take of budget reviews generally ends with some sort of compromise between boss and subordinate on expectations for revenue, costs, profits, and capital expenditures.

In hard times, bosses tend to bargain harder and compromise less, if at all. In good times, bosses generally split the difference or at least are more generous in the terms they impose on subordinates. The strategy that smart subordinates use to win these annual contests changes with economic conditions. In good times, expected revenue is understated, and expenses are overstated. In poor times, expected revenue is overstated, and expenses are understated.

The spate of Securities and Exchange Commission (SEC) actions against major companies provides evidence of these deceptions. Profit-center managers manipulated their operating data to hide losses, to report numbers their bosses wanted to hear, or even to enhance their own bonus awards. The companies involved include McCormick, PepsiCo, Ronson, J.W. Thompson, Saxon Industries, AM International, and H.J. Heinz.

Both the profit-center manager and his or her superior at corporate headquarters have a financial stake in the unit's profitability. Success may bring not only personal pride, but also larger paychecks for both. There is thus a dual temptation to cheat a little: the superior does not look too deeply into the subordinate's report numbers, and the subordinate manipulates the numbers so they come out "right."

Ferreting out financial reporting frauds is not as simple as it may seem. The players are a rather sophisticated lot, and they often know as much about the accounting rules as the auditors do. Although internal controls are designed to keep the game honest, internal controls can be bypassed or overridden by higher authorities. Controls are designed to keep honest people honest. Dishonest people are rarely discouraged or thwarted by even the best controls. In an environment in which executive compensation is based on short-term results, both senior management and middle management have an economic incentive to alter operating data. The proper audit perspectives should, therefore, not be shortsighted. If the auditor looks only at short-term figures, fraud is not likely to surface.

Financial auditing, as distinguished from fraud auditing, concentrates on the present: on the adequacy of internal controls and on the reliability, validity, and mathematical accuracy of today's entries. Such a narrow focus doesn't provide a historical perspective. Reasonableness tests, when not related to past relationships and trends, don't provide enough insight. This is why fraud auditing looks beyond, behind, and before current transactions. Fraud auditing concerns itself much more with the past than the present.

Although there are few fixed relationships in accounting data, there are some to which fraud auditors should pay particular attention, for example, the past relationship of sales to cost of sales, of sales to accounts receivable and accounts payable, and of sales to bank deposits. The fraud auditor seeks evidence of receivables lapping, inventory overstatement, check-kiting, and phony invoices for merchandise and services. A fraud audit should therefore contain a trend analysis of these items as well as the relationship of sales to freight out, sales to purchases, and purchases to freight in. Use these items for dollar and percentage trend analysis. Volume measurements might also make interesting studies, for example, sales in terms of unit volume, pounds of raw materials in versus pounds of finished goods out, and their relationships to sales, purchases, and inventory.

Because of the seasonability of most businesses, a month-to-month comparison may not be too useful for a fraud audit. However, a consistent build-up of receivables balances or payables balances discovered through a month-to-month aging process may sometimes highlight a current fraud. An inventory build-up inconsistent with sales volume may also be symptomatic of fraud or mismanagement. A long-term build-up of inventory that is inconsistent with sales increases is a sign of fraud. The same is true with respect to receivables build-ups, payables build-ups, and deposit volume decreases. These items should be plotted on a year-to-year basis for reasonableness testing.

CHAPTER 5

Characteristics of Fraud-Prone Organizations

Internal Environment

Organizations are not by their nature fraud prone. They may become so as a result of environmental and interpersonal pressures. For example, poor economic conditions or predatory practices in an industry in which an organization competes may threaten its profitability. If performance bonuses are tied to profits, an incentive or motive is created to misrepresent the true state of the organization's financial affairs. At the interpersonal level, executives with profit-center responsibilities may overstate their financial results to curry favor with their bosses or to compete with their peers for topside attention.

The following list of characteristics of fraud-prone organizations is based on the author's 40 years of experience in fraud auditing and investigation.

1. Top management is nontrusting and autocratic; focuses on profits and economic rewards on a short-term basis; is ambivalent about social issues; and is hostile toward the equitable interests of customers, stockholders, employees, creditors, and competitors.
2. Financial and operational planning and internal communication are poor.
3. Company loyalty, employee morale, and work motivation are poor.
4. High turnover exists among senior managers, outside auditors, and outside counsel.
5. Persistent cash flow shortages exist.
6. The company has a waning line of products or services and devotes little effort to research and development.
7. The company is in a highly competitive industry known for predatory practices.
8. Internal controls are absent, weak, or loosely enforced.

9. Employees are hired without consideration for their honesty and integrity.
10. Employees are poorly managed, exploited, abused, or placed under great stress to accomplish financial goals and objectives.
11. Management models are corrupt, inefficient, and incompetent.
12. The entire industry has a history of corruption.
13. The company has fallen on bad times; that is, it is losing money or market share, or its products or services are becoming passé.
14. The company has a corporate culture in which social values are obscure and in which profit and economic incentives are the only motivators.
15. The company has failed to establish, communicate, and enforce a code of corporate ethics.
16. The company creates strong and authoritarian management controls but does not monitor them for compliance.
17. Complaints from customers, stockholders, employees, and vendors are ignored.
18. Management overrides of internal controls are not monitored.
19. Litigation against the firm by regulatory authorities, vendors, customers, creditors, and competitors abounds.

Auditors use a technique they call red flags for spotting transactions that may be symptomatic of fraud. While there are literally hundreds of such red flags, the following items are fairly representative. Remember, these items are not *evidence* of fraud but merely indicators thereof.

1. Cash flow is diminishing.
2. Sales and income are diminishing.
3. Payables and receivables are increasing.
4. Inventory and cost of sales are increasing.
5. Income and expense items are continually reclassified.
6. Suspense items are not reconciled.
7. Suspense items are written off without explanation.
8. Write-offs of accounts receivable are increasing.
9. Journal entries are adjusted at year end.

Many accounting frauds start out as small in amount and insignificant in terms of impact on financial statements. However, they have the potential of becoming large and significant through repetition if not discovered early. Perpetrators of accounting fraud therefore tend to rationalize their crimes as vital to the survival of the firm. They believe that deceiving stockholders and bankers, for example, are not serious offenses, but mere management deceptions, on the order of white lies morally.

The following are "little" management deceptions that can become "big" frauds:

- booking sales before they are finalized
- delaying necessary repairs and maintenance
- not making adequate provision for doubtful accounts receivable
- capitalizing expenses that should have been charged to the current year
- acquiring another company whose current profits are high and consolidating its income with the firm's income at year's end
- selling an asset that has appreciated in value to enhance earnings
- accepting goods or merchandise on consignment without adding the liability to the balance sheet or the goods to the cost of sales
- keeping the books open beyond the year end
- closing the books before the year end
- deferring expenses or income
- inflating ending inventory
- creating "slush funds" where profits are accumulated for lean years

As small accounting frauds multiply through repetition, they become more and more obvious and difficult to cover up. In time, they surface during normal audit activity by internal and external auditors, but they surface in a number of other ways, too. The following list may provide some insight thereon:

- oral complaints by friends, spouses, co-workers, vendors, suppliers, contractors, customers, and competitors
- intelligence gathered by security and law enforcement professionals
- suspicions reported by security and law enforcement professionals
- detected systems-control violations
- internal operational and financial audits
- external audits
- accident

Classic Characteristics of Embezzlers

Embezzlement is another form of accounting fraud. Records are generally altered or destroyed to cover up missing funds or other assets. Embezzlers tend to have a number of unique characteristics that distinguish them from executives who perpetrate accounting frauds. The following list specifies the major distinctions between embezzlers and other white-collar criminals:

1. They usually work their crimes alone.
2. They tend to be compulsive; for example, they gamble, abuse alcohol or drugs, overeat, or spend money freely (their own and that of their employers).

3. They work themselves into favor by using their compulsiveness on the job; that is, they work quietly, they work hard, and they work long hours (when no one knows what they are doing).
4. They rationalize their thefts by thinking they are merely "borrowing."
5. They tend to be recidivists; that is, they repeat their crimes.
6. They exploit weaknesses in internal controls to cover their embezzlement.
7. They have ready access to cash or its equivalent on the job.

Embezzlers do not tend to be the kind of criminals who commit one large theft and then retire. They start out stealing small sums to feed immediate economic needs. They also tend to deliberate on their illegal acts and formulate both a rationalization for their theft and a scheme to carry it out. In designing a scheme, they go through a process of reasoning. For example, embezzlers may ask themselves the following questions:

1. What are the weakest links in this system's chain of controls?
2. What deviations from conventional good accounting practices are possible in this system?
3. How are off-line transactions handled, and who can authorize such transactions?
4. What would be the simplest way to compromise this system?
5. What control features in the system can be bypassed or overridden by higher authorities?
6. How can I introduce a fake debit into this system so that I can get a check issued or get my hands on cash?
7. What transaction authorization documents are easiest to access and forge?

Checklist of Vendor Frauds

While the major threat of fraud, theft, and embezzlement is from internal sources (management and nonmanagement personnel), there are external threats as well, predominantly vendors, suppliers, and contractors. A listing of their frauds would include the following:

- false weights, counts, and quality representations
- double billing
- full billing for partial shipments
- diversion and conversion
- intentional overpricing and extension errors
- corruption of purchasing employees
- conspiring with employees to overlook shortages

Checklist of Customer Frauds

Vendors are not the only sources of external threats to organizational assets. Customers also bear some scrutiny. They may engage in the following deceptions:

- falsification of credit worthiness
- false claims for refunds, discounts, returns, and allowances
- corrupting sales and credit department personnel
- conspiring with employees to ship unbilled merchandise
- threatening lawsuits for spurious damage or liability claims

Checklist of Competitor Frauds

Competitors too may pose an economic threat. Their frauds, thefts, and acts of corruption may take the following forms:

- predatory sales, advertising, and pricing practices
- theft, conversion, or appropriation of technology, trade secrets, proprietary information, patents, and copyrights
- employee pirating
- commercial slander
- hostile takeover
- low-balling contract bids
- corrupting customers

Computer-Related Frauds

A current form of accounting fraud often involves computers. Computer-related accounting frauds and embezzlements are growing. Proving such cases is a complex process. An articulation of some basic facts about computer-related fraud is therefore in order.

1. They are generally committed by people with appropriate skills in computer operations, programming, and auditing.
2. Frauds are committed by exploiting weaknesses in internal controls.
3. They are committed to satisfy economic, egocentric, ideological, or psychotic needs.
4. Computer-related frauds can be executed at any of the three stages of processing, that is, input, thruput, output.
5. The most common computer-related frauds uncovered are those executed in the input stage, where false, forged, or altered data are entered.
6. The most common accounting applications subverted by computer criminals are accounts payable, payroll, and benefit or expense claims.

CHAPTER 6

Assessing the Threat of Corporate Fraud

Outside versus Inside Threats

The threat of fraud against a corporation can be assessed in terms of the most likely culprits. That is, one might look at outsiders versus insiders or at the levels of insiders: high-level, middle-level, and low-level personnel.

Insiders clearly pose a greater threat of fraud than outsiders because their access to assets and records is more immediate. Outsiders have at least one more barrier to get through to commit their frauds. Outsiders often attempt to enlist insiders as willing or unwitting accomplices. Although they make initial detection more difficult, conspiracies make prosecution easier if one conspirator can be turned against the others.

The Outside Threat

Outsiders who represent a high threat of fraud are people and organizations who have an existing relationship with the victim company, that is, customers, vendors, suppliers, contractors, and service providers like property owners, maintenance and janitorial personnel, insurance agencies, advertising agencies, consultants, law firms, accounting firms, utilities, and repairers. Middle-level and low-level employees may be bribed to cover up or overlook these frauds. On the other hand, insiders in purchasing may extort money or property from outsiders. Customers may also enlist the aid of personnel in sales, accounting, or credit to carry out their frauds.

The Inside Threat

With respect to the insider hierarchy, it is reasonable to assume that since high-level personnel have the greatest amount of power and authority, they pose the most significant risk. They can bypass, waive, or override internal controls. They have total access to funds and records, and their actions usually go without internal challenge. External auditors, however, do have a measure of control if the company's stock is publicly traded. The most egregious offenses by high-level personnel are the deception of outside auditors and the fraud foisted on investors and creditors.

The concept of risk deals with the frequency and severity of events that cause losses. Fraud in books of account is one such event. Fraud in books of account depends on two factors: (1) the adequacy of internal accounting controls and (2) the honesty of the people who maintain custody over assets and accounting records.

Although dishonest high-level personnel pose the most serious threat of fraud because they have the greatest opportunity to commit it and cover it up, their motive to commit fraud may not be as great as employees at middle-management and lower levels. Motives for the commission of internal corporate fraud include economic need, greed, egocentricity, and differing values and beliefs. Jealousy, envy, spite, and revenge can also precipitate fraud.

High-Level Fraud

It might seem plausible that, because senior managers have adequate incomes, social status, economic power, and authority, they would tend to be more honest. Although this is generally true, senior managers are also under more pressure to perform. Today, performance is a short-term concept. An executive can compromise the future profitability of the firm and still be revered by stockholders because his or her decisions favor immediate profit, not long-term growth.

In addition to immediate profit, stockholders expect that profits will continually grow at exponential rates, regardless of the season and the general economy. These pressures cause senior managers to develop "slush funds" or to create "profit banks," practices that may not have been originally intended to defraud but that, over a period of time, tend to corrupt the accounting system and accounting personnel as well as top-level and middle-level managers. Some of the more celebrated corporate fraud cases of the past decade or two involved "slush fund" frauds, for example, H.J. Heinz and McCormick Spices.

Stockholder expectations of continuous growth also lead to the practices of recording sales that are not finalized, keeping the books open beyond the end of the fiscal year, and recording consignments as sales. Inflating ending inventories is another favored technique to enhance profits.

Low-Level Fraud

Low-level fraud usually takes the form of such crimes as larceny (theft of corporate funds and proprietary information), embezzlement (theft of entrusted assets), corruption (bribe-taking), sabotage (surreptitious damage to corporate assets), and the unauthorized accessing of assets or data (computer browsing, hacking, cracking).

The motivation of high-level managers may be economic greed, but at lower levels the motivation more often than not is economic need. The need arises from expensive hobbies and lifestyle, alcoholism, drug abuse, gambling, and family illness. The motive must be matched with opportunity, that is, access to cash and accounting records. Because the act involves a breach of trust, the culprit may rationalize the theft as borrowing and may even intend to pay it back. Invariably, however, conditions go from bad to worse, more funds are taken, and the amount of each theft begins to escalate. In time, the loss becomes great enough to capture the attention of managers, internal auditors, or external auditors. This is the classic case of embezzlement: a trusted employee with a private financial problem that can be resolved by a small breach of trust and a rationalization.

Middle-Level Fraud

Middle managers are caught in the middle of events and conditions in large corporations today. Accordingly, they suffer the most stress. They must pass on the bad news from top management to lower levels and the bad news from lower levels to top management. Their own jobs are often in jeopardy because high-level managers look to reduce costs by replacing middle managers with computers or younger executives who do not require large salaries and expensive perks.

The motive for fraud from middle managers is based on revenge for their embarrassment or loss of status or identity. They retaliate by stealing, sabotaging, or whistle-blowing. Whistle-blowing is a form of retaliation and is not a fraud in itself.

Threat Assessment Tool for Corporate Fraud

While no scientifically derived study of the incipient causes of corporate fraud has ever been published, the conventional wisdom among fraud auditors suggests the traits of top management and the environmental conditions below may bear on the probability of fraud in a given corporate environment. The author has converted those assumptions into the checklist that follows. It could make a useful tool in assessing the threat or risk of corporate fraud.

I. On a scale of 1 to 10, where 1 = low and 10 = high, how does the firm's top management rate overall with respect to the following criteria:
   A. Honesty/truthfulness   ____
   B. Openness/candor   ____
   C. Intelligence/competence   ____
   D. Rationality/logic   ____
   E. Diligence/industriousness   ____
   F. Generosity/compassion   ____
   G. Imagination/daring   ____
   H. Ambition/drive   ____
   I. Wisdom/maturity   ____
   J. Sense of responsibility   ____
             Total   ____

II. On a scale of 1 to 10, how well does the firm's top management do the following:
   A. Communicate and coordinate _____
   B. Plan and budget _____
   C. Control expenses _____
   D. Motivate subordinates _____
   E. Conceive new product and market opportunities _____
   F. Respect the rights of employees _____
   G. Respect the rights of shareholders _____
   H. Respect the rights of customers _____
   I. Respect the rights of suppliers _____
   J. Respond to community needs _____
   Total _____

III. On a scale of 1 to 10, how strong are the following internal control measures?
   A. Audit trails _____
   B. Separation of duties _____
   C. Protection of current assets _____
   D. Protection of information resources _____
   E. Protection of fixed assets _____
   F. Ethical standards _____
   G. Recruitment standards _____
   H. Internal audit function _____
   I. Data security function _____
   Total _____

IV. Respond "yes" or "no" to the following questions.
   A. Does the industry have a history of corruption or predatory practices? _____
   B. Has the company fallen on bad times; that is, is it losing money or market share? _____
   C. Has much litigation been brought against the firm by regulatory authorities, vendors, customers, creditors, or competitors? _____
   D. Is the cash flow diminishing? _____
   E. Are sales and income diminishing? _____
   F. Are payables and receivables increasing? _____
   G. Are inventory and cost of sales increasing? _____
   H. Are income and expense items continually being reclassified? _____
   I. Are suspense items reconciled? _____
   J. Are suspense items written off without explanation? _____
   K. Are write-offs of accounts receivable increasing? _____
   L. Are many journal entries adjusted at year end? _____
   M. Are sales booked before they are finalized? _____
   N. Is the provision for doubtful accounts adequate? _____

O. Are expenses that should have been charged to the
current year capitalized?   _____

P. Are goods and merchandise received on consignment
added as a liability to the balance sheet and to cost
of sales?   _____

Q. Are the books kept open beyond the year end?   _____

R. Is ending inventory inflated?   _____

S. Are "slush funds" created to bank profits for lean
years?   _____

Vital Signs of a Fraud-Free Business

Although fraud can occur in any organization, some organizations
appear to be more susceptible than others. Most studies of accounting fraud
dwell on conditions that exist in enterprises that are fraud-prone—the red-
flags theory of fraud auditing.

The red-flags theory suggests that fraud-prone organizations can be
diagnosed as such by applying certain experiential rules of thumb. These
experience-based rules of thumb include those listed in the previous section.

If it is true that some organizations are more susceptible to fraud than
others, then the reverse must also be true: some organizations must be less
prone to fraud than others. What do these organizations have in common?
They manage all their resources well. More particularly, their vital signs
show them to be viable, and they will likely continue in business for some
time. The following characteristics describe organizations that are most likely
to survive in business and are less likely to be victims of accounting fraud:

Financial Resources

- The company is profitable and has a positive cash flow.
- The profit trend is upward.
- There is ready access to new capital for growth and expansion.
- The company has good fiscal controls and good accounting and
internal controls.
- The sales trend is upward.
- The cost trend is downward.

Human Resources

- The company hires competent ethical employees and has a low
turnover.
- Employees have high morale, are highly productive, highly innova-
tive, and loyal.

Administrative Resources

- The company plans and budgets well.
- It applies the latest technologies to its production, marketing, finance, personnel, and administrative functions.
- It documents its policies and procedures, and implements and monitors its performance against its plans, policies, and procedures.
- The company has satisfied customers and reliable suppliers.
- It develops new products and markets as competition and economic conditions require or warrant it.
- The company has a good public image and produces good products.

Information/Technological Resources

- The company has ready access to data bases that supply accurate, complete, and concise information on economic, competitive, legal, regulatory, political, social, and technological threats, risks, and opportunities.
- It places high value on and protects its proprietary information.
- The company maintains state-of-the-art familiarity with all developments in its industry and with its products and markets.
- It develops innovations in its manufacturing and distribution functions.

Predicting Corporate Fraud

The capitalist system operates on the general theory that the pursuit of private interests (profit, income, property accumulation) creates public benefits—that is, satisfies human needs like food, clothing, shelter, education, and health care. A large measure of the success attributed to this system comes from its ability to balance public needs against private greed. The system is therefore said to have a self-correcting mechanism, or the "greed index." When the greed surpasses need, some force (economic, political, or social) must intervene either by natural reaction or by planned intervention.

If greed prevails over need, some form of regulation may be required; for example, antitrust enforcement efforts are enhanced, new consumer rights laws are passed, or consumers boycott the products of greedy producers. When need prevails over greed, consumer spending is reduced, thus requiring measures that provide economic incentives, such as lower taxes, lower prices, lower interest rates, unemployment compensation, and job creation efforts.

The greed index helps to explain what happens in the macro-economic environment, and it has micro-economic implications as well. A business organization, for example, has its own greed index. When greed prevails over need, organizations may become corrupt and exploitative. In the process, employees also become infected because they tend to mimic the behavior of their employers. At such times, corporate fraud becomes commonplace.

What characteristics distinguish an organization smitten with fraud? Fraud-prone organizations show certain signs. One type of sign is the red flag: an indicator that internal controls are not what they ought to be, for example, poor audit trails, failure to separate duties, and nonexistent policies on ethical behavior. Another sign is the diminution in social values in an organization, for example, how highly does management value truth, honesty, fairness, and justice? Is the trend upward or downward? If the trend is downward, fraud may be just around the corner. If the trend is upward, companies should go easy on expenditures for control, trust employees more, and take more risks.

How can a company measure changes in organizational values? These values are qualitative conditions, not quantitative ones, but the greed index can help. A company should periodically take stock of how highly its people value such personal qualities as truth, honesty, fairness, justice, loyalty, compassion, cooperation, assumption of responsibility, diligence, competence, and self-esteem.

A company can circulate a questionnaire every six months that asks employees to rate on a scale of 1 to 10 the importance of these personal qualities. There will be no comparison base for the first survey. After that, however, the company can make comparisons and determine whether employees are more committed to these values than before.

How to Select Honest and Productive Personnel

The liquid and long-term assets of a firm are no longer kept in cash drawers or underground vaults. Indeed their form, shape, and substance have changed substantially. Assets are now kept in the form of electronic impulses on computer tapes and disks. People who can access such impulses can convert them into cash very quickly.

During the era of manual accounting and data processing, few people had access to the most valuable assets of an organization. Today, unless strictly controlled, literally thousands of employees in large organizations can access an organization's assets. The defenses against this threat are the traditional ones: tight internal controls (separation of duties and audit trails); physical security (barriers to entry); information security (software access controls; electronic data processing (EDP) audit controls; identification, authentication, and authorization controls; encryption of sensitive data during transmission or storage); and personnel security (selection of honest employees).

The latter is not as easy as it has been made to seem by providers of investigative services, polygraph examinations, and paper-and-pencil tests. Honesty depends on who defines it and in what environment it is applied. Honesty is accordingly situation-specific.

To a typical employer, honesty is a characteristic of someone who values the property rights of others; believes in truth, justice, and trusting relationships; and who honors loyalty, obedience, and efficiency. Intelligence, sobriety, and emotional stability also count. Can these characteristics be measured, tested, or otherwise determined? They *can* be weighed but within certain limits of accuracy and application.

Psychological testing tools for the selection of personnel have been available at least since World War I when tens of thousands of service members had to be processed (tested, trained, and placed) in a short period of time. Arguments about the validity and reliability of these tests have raged ever since. Critics have complained that they often demean the test-taker or invade his or her privacy, but what are the alternatives? Background investigations are expensive and even more intrusive. Polygraph examinations are intimidating and of questionable validity, reliability, and legality for use in pre-employment screening. Judging applicants by eye can lead to selections based on prejudice or subjectivity. Interviewing can be a more objective technique if the questions posed are relevant to on-the-job success, are properly addressed and interpreted by the interviewer, and are free of personal bias.

Screening applicants for employment serves several purposes:

   I. Screening matches an organization's assessed present and future human resource needs with applicant skills, competencies, and growth potential.
      A. Skills can be confirmed through
         1. Verification of educational achievements and previous work experience
         2. Aptitude testing
         3. Proficiency testing
      B. Growth potential can be confirmed through
         1. Vocational interest testing
         2. Achievement orientation testing
  II. Screening matches an organization's values, beliefs, attitudes, and management style with an applicant's values, beliefs, attitudes, and style.
      A. These characteristics can be confirmed through
         1. Personality testing
         2. Attitude testing
         3. Projective testing
         4. Style compatibility testing
         5. Verification of moral suitability through reference, credit, and criminal history checks and honesty testing techniques, such as polygraph examinations and integrity tests

Most of the objections raised about testing have centered on the second goal of applicant screening. As conditions of employment, the so-called suitability and compatibility tests are much maligned because they deal with human characteristics and frailties and are seen as invasions of personal privacy that have little to do with technical competency and may lead to discrimination on the basis of subjective criteria or personal characteristics that are not job-specific. Critics suggest that the criterion for employment should be whether the applicant possesses the necessary skills, job knowledge, and experience to get the job done, regardless of the applicant's sex, race, ethnic background, personal values, attitudes, beliefs, lifestyle, or management-style preferences.

In fact, both of the goals of applicant screening have weaknesses. Instruments designed to test vocational interests, motivational orientation, personality, values, style preferences, and honesty can all be manipulated by wary test-takers. Aptitude tests (general intelligence, mechanical abilities) and proficiency tests (work knowledge) are often so crude, general, or non-specific that achievement scores bear little relationship to on-the-job success. One might therefore question the benefit of any of these tests. With federal and state employment, fair credit, and privacy legislation and the need for validation studies of job-specific characteristics, who needs the grief of potential litigation?

These sentiments and concerns have caused many personnel recruiters, at the behest of their legal departments, to abandon almost all forms of personnel testing and other screening procedures—such as educational, employment, credit, or reference checking—and to rely instead on interviewing techniques. However, even interview techniques are subject to the same laws, rules, and regulations. Improperly worded questions about age, race, sex, marital status, credit standing, criminal history, and even height and weight can lead to litigation or charges of discriminatory hiring practices.

If the goals of pre-employment screening are reducing turnover, reducing training costs, and increasing worker output, it is assumed that applicants will always be plentiful; that they will be well-equipped intellectually, emotionally, and in terms of skills to do their jobs adequately with a minimum of training; and that their own motivation will cause them to rise in the hierarchy of the firm. How real are these assumptions? Do they stand the test of current experience?

The United States is approaching a new era in which shortages of applicants with special skills will continue and in which selection may become a matter of seizing anyone with enough credentials to pass minimum standards. It will be a seller's market. Therefore, personnel *development,* not *selection,* will become the primary goal. More time and money will be spent on training and development than on recruitment and selection.

Even in this new era, testing will have a place, but it will be for the purpose of identifying training and development needs for career counseling and for the whole process of human resource planning. What testing tools will be most appropriate? One tool will not be enough. A battery of tests will be needed to evaluate aptitude, vocational interests, proficiency, achievement orientation, and personality characteristics.

The hiring decision should not be made on the basis of any one or all of these tests. The test results merely provide a competent interviewer with some insight into the applicant's probability of on-the-job success, that is whether a proper fit exists between the employer's current long-term human resource needs and the applicant's abilities, interests, experience, character, and so on. Depending on the nature of the job and the employer's business, additional checks may be required regarding employment and character references, and credit and criminal history. The latter checks should be deferred until psychological tests have been completed, and the applicant should be informed that such checks will be undertaken to ensure that, should employment be offered thereafter, the probability of a successful fit will be enhanced.

Japanese employers who set up shop in the United States are very careful in their employee selection criteria. They realize that on-the-job success depends a great deal on employee personality characteristics that are compatible with Japanese management practices, for example, team work, quality consciousness, loyalty, and dependability, among other things.

Creating an employment environment that satisfies the needs of employers and the needs of employees (stable employment, good wages, fair profits) is no simple task. Some Japanese firms spend about 14 hours interviewing and testing each applicant for employment and the testing tools they use are American ones. The Japanese often make better or more consistent use of these tools than the Americans do.

American employers have not relied heavily on the use of psychological testing tools because they are concerned about their cost, validity, reliability, and legality in this era of litigiousness and equal employment rights. These concerns have not inhibited the Japanese, however. They start with a better understanding of what it takes to be successful in their organizations, and that knowledge helps them to design their own success formula for recruitment.

CHAPTER 7

Landmark Cases in Management Fraud

"Crime in the suites," or corporate fraud, is a phenomenon that mystifies laypeople. Why would anyone with a huge salary and all the perks one could imagine become involved in crime? Why jeopardize all that security and prestige for a few more dollars? It cannot be need, so it must be greed—or so laypeople think—but that is not always the case. The celebrated corporate frauds described in this chapter have some common threads.

H.J. Heinz Case

Heinz has been a household name for quality food products for about a hundred years. The company has been well managed, profitable, and socially responsible. In the late seventies, however, it received much unfavorable publicity for what appeared to be a minor financial flaw. Some of its profit-center managers had engaged in accounting irregularities. They had understated sales, overstated some expenses, and deferred other expenses to the next year. These practices reduced their unit's profits and created a "cushion" for the next year's slush fund so they could meet the profit goals imposed by company headquarters. The total of these profit manipulations was quite small ($8.5 million) compared to the overall sales ($2.4 billion). However, the annual sales and profits were not as reported to the Internal Revenue Service (IRS), the SEC, and the stockholders.

The disclosure of these irregularities resulted from an antitrust suit brought by Heinz against Campbell Soup. In its discovery efforts, Campbell found evidence that Heinz's advertising agency was billing for services that had not yet been rendered. When a Heinz executive was questioned about the matter, he pleaded protection under the Fifth Amendment (self-incrimination). The antitrust suit was settled shortly thereafter, but the disclosure caused personnel from Heinz's headquarters to launch an investigation into the accounting practices of several subsidiaries.

Because the corporation is highly decentralized, headquarters personnel claimed that they were unaware of the lower level wrongdoing. Headquarters monitored the lower levels through budget forecasts of sales and expenses and an incentive compensation plan that benefited managers who met the high end of their profit goals. The watchword was consistent growth in profits. Top management personnel were committed to that goal, and indeed the company's earnings did consistently rise; 1978 marked the 15th consecutive year of record profits.

Heinz's senior management was not necessarily derelict here. The company had an explicit policy that prohibited its divisions from having any form of unrecorded assets or false entries in its books and records, and Heinz didn't measure short-term performance alone. The top 19 officials, including division general managers, had long-term incentive plans in addition to the one-year plan.

In a nutshell, the situation initially centered around income transferal aided and abetted by vendors who supplied invoices one year for services not rendered until the next year. When that wasn't enough, false invoices were submitted one year and then reversed the following year. The amounts involved did not have a material effect on the company's reported profits.

What can be learned from this case? First, exerting pressure for continuous growth in profits may well foster improper accounting practices, particularly when coupled with an incentive compensation plan that rewards and reinforces continuous growth on the high side. Second, autonomous units with independent accounting capabilities may be tempted under these circumstances to manipulate performance data.

Strangely, the problem at Heinz began in 1974 when it appeared that profits in the Heinz USA division would exceed those allowed by the wage and price controls in effect at the time. World headquarters sought a way to reduce the division's profit. Losses in commodity transactions did not reduce profits enough, so the division prematurely booked $2 million in advertising services. Instead of treating the expense as a prepaid item, it charged it off immediately. Despite the division's lowered profits, world headquarters decided the division had achieved its goal, and Heinz paid the relevant bonus.

By 1977, the following practices evolved at the Heinz USA division:

- Year-end shipments were delayed to justify invoicing them in the following year.
- When some customers complained about the delays, the shipments were made, but shipping and invoice documents were misdated.
- Credits from vendors were not recorded until the following year.
- "Income management" became a way of life. One employee was given the task of maintaining private records to ensure the recovery of amounts paid to vendors on improper invoices.
- The practice of delayed shipment and prepaid billing permeated the division down to the departmental level to ensure that departmental budgeted amounts were met.
- Ten separate vendors supplied improper invoices.

- Other questionable tactics to manipulate income included inflated accruals, inventory adjustments, commodity transactions, and customer rebates.

McCormick Spice Case

In the early 1980s, the SEC alleged that McCormick inflated reported current earnings by deferring the recognition of various expenses and increased reported revenues by accounting for goods ready for shipment as current sales even though they were not shipped until later. These irregularities occurred in autonomous divisions and involved a number of employees in middle-management positions. These employees believed that the improper practices were the only way to achieve the profit goals set independently by a distant, centralized corporate management. Several employees claimed to view their activities as a "team effort" for the benefit of the company. There was no evidence that corporate funds were diverted for the personal benefit of any McCormick employee. (See SEC vs. McCormick & Co. Inc.; Civil Action No. 82-3614, D.D.C. 1982.)

AM International Case

In the AM International case, the SEC alleged that AM grossly overstated its operations' results, assets, and shareholders' equity, understated liabilities, and misstated changes in financial position.

How did AM International accomplish this? Inventory losses were deferred, and ending inventory overstated; books were kept open after cutoff dates to increase reported sales and earnings; sales were recorded although products were not shipped; sales were inflated by deliberate double-billing; operating leases were recorded as sales; allowances for losses were arbitrarily reduced without any basis whatsoever; sales were recorded when products were shipped to branch officers and a public warehouse—not to customers; accounting policies were changed to increase earnings without any disclosure of the changes in policy; known errors that increased earnings were ignored; intercompany accounts were out of balance, and the differences were arbitrarily reclassified as inventories; known inaccuracies in books and records were neither investigated nor resolved; costs of sales were manipulated; fixed assets were not depreciated; expense accounts were understated; and accounts payable were simply not recorded.

The organizational environment described in the AM complaint seems very unhealthy. For example, following are two excerpts from the Commission's complaint:[1]

> During the course of the 1980 fiscal year, AM International's financial position deteriorated and its management then applied increasing pressure on the division to meet performance goals. Such pressure

consisted of, among other means, threatened dismissals, actual dismissals, and character attacks on certain of the division's senior management to middle-management. These pressures were motivated, in part, by the desire of AMI to have a public offering of its securities in the fall of 1980 and the belief that a pre-tax profit of $10 to $12 million for the 1980 fiscal year was necessary in order to proceed with the offering.

In response to the pressure . . . various divisions . . . engaged in widespread and pervasive accounting irregularities . . . in order to present results of operations which conformed to budget performance objectives. Throughout the 1980 fiscal year, AMI's corporate headquarters learned of many instances of accounting irregularities employed by its divisions. Despite this knowledge, AMI continued to pressure its divisions to meet projected operating results. (See SEC vs. A.M. International, Inc., Civil Action No. 83-1256, D.D.C. May 2, 1983, Litigation Release No. 9980, February 27, 1984.)

U.S. Surgical Case

The SEC's complaint in U.S. Surgical alleged that the company

- issued falsified purchase orders to vendors who in turn submitted false invoices so that Surgical's reported cost for parts was decreased and its reported cost of materials was improperly capitalized by over $4 million
- shipped significant quantities of unordered products to customers and recorded them as sales
- improperly treated shipments on consignment to its dealers, sales representatives, and certain foreign entities as sales, resulting in a cumulative overstatement of income by over $2 million
- improperly failed to write off assets that could not be located or had been scrapped, and capitalized certain operating costs as overhead, increasing earnings by millions of dollars
- improperly capitalized approximately $4 million of legal costs, purportedly for the defense of certain patents, when those costs did not relate to the defense of patents but were recurring operating expenses (See SEC vs. U.S. Surgical Corp., Civil Action No. 84-0589, D.D.C. 1984, Litigation Release No. 10293, February 27, 1984.)

Equity Funding Case

The Equity Funding fraud began in 1966 with a simple overstatement of assets. Earnings continued to be inflated each year thereafter. By the time the case became a matter of public knowledge in 1973, the fraud had taken on gigantic proportions:

- Assets had been overstated by more than $100 million
- Fictitiously funded loans to policyholders totaled $62.3 million
- Fictitious commercial paper totaled $8 million.
- In 1972, Equity Funding listed assets of $737.5 million and a net worth of $143.4 million. The subsequent investigation and audit showed actual assets to be worth $488.9 million and actual net worth to be a negative $42 million.
- Over two hundred insiders were aware of some aspect of the fraud before its exposure.
- Thousands of fictitious insurance policies were generated by company computers.
- Stock certificates were counterfeited in the company's print shop.
- Before the dust settled, 22 former officers of the company and three auditors were indicted on charges of mail fraud, stock fraud, filing false financial statements, interstate transportation of counterfeit securities, and illegal wiretapping.

Other Management Fraud Cases

Since 1982, the author has published a monthly newsletter that focuses on financial fraud, fraud auditing, and investigative accounting. The newsletter is called the *Forensic Accounting Review*.[2] Some of the more significant incidents of accounting and corporate fraud reported therein include the following:

September 1982: Datapoint Corp., a San Antonio computer manufacturer, was the subject of a stockholder's suit that claimed that the firm misrepresented its financial data by engaging in a warehousing and brokerage scheme to inflate sales. Customer orders were booked in advance as sales by some of Datapoint's marketing representatives to achieve sales goals. This later resulted in an "unusually high level of returned products," according to the firm's CEO.

October 1982: Saxon Industries, Inc., and three former executives were cited by the SEC for falsifying company records. The Commission charged that the officials created fictitious inventories of $75 million by listing additional inventory after the physical count was completed, by programming the company's computers to automatically add inventory, and by transferring fake inventories from one division to another.

December 1982: Fallout from the insolvency of Saxon Industries, Inc., continued to raise questions about the competence and integrity of both senior management of the firm and its Business Products Division in Miami Lakes, Florida. For example, fictitious inventories of copier parts amounting to $65 million were alleged. Phantom inventory items and phantom warehouse locations were allegedly fed into the company's computerized inventory accounting system, until the ending inventory was satisfactory. Inflated sales and understated expenses were also alleged to be part of the year-end adjustments made to the Business Product Division's general ledger. Some data processing and accounting personnel were allegedly given bonuses of $2000 or more for their efforts in carrying out the alleged fraud. (In 1985, the former president of Saxon Industries pleaded guilty to fraud charges stemming from a scheme to inflate profit.)

December 1982: In an administrative proceeding, the SEC took action against Ronson Corporation for the accounting practices followed by a former Ronson subsidiary in California, Ronson Hydraulic Units Corp. (RHUCOR). For a period of five years prior to 1980, RHUCOR understated its expenses and recorded as sales products that had not been shipped. These tactics resulted in an overstatement of profits by the subsidiary and were allegedly committed to meet the unit's profit goals. Arbitrary increases were also allegedly made to the unit's monthly ending inventory to overstate profits for the period. Ronson settled the charges with the SEC by neither admitting nor denying them, and the corporation agreed to report accurately in the future.

January 1983: PepsiCo, Inc., was sued by two shareholders who alleged that the company had filed false and misleading financial statements as a result of irregularities in its overseas operations. The irregularities resulted in $92.1 million in overstated earnings over a five-year period and overstated assets of $79.4 million. Also joined in the shareholder class-action suit were 15 of PepsiCo's current and past directors and its outside auditors. PepsiCo itself made the irregularities known after it conducted its own investigation into the matter. Internal controls have since been tightened, and 12 employees of the foreign subsidiary were terminated.

August 1984: In the first case of its kind, the SEC charged a supplier firm with aiding a customer company to violate federal securities laws. In a civil suit, the SEC charged that the Barden Co., a Danbury, Connecticut, supplier of surgical equipment, assisted U.S. Surgical Corp. of Norwalk, Connecticut, by providing it with false invoices that allowed the company to capitalize costs that should have been expensed. Robert P. More, a Barden vice-president, confirmed to U.S. Surgical's auditors that the false invoices were correct. Barden and More have consented to a court order barring them from further violations of the securities laws, but they neither admitted nor denied the SEC's charges.

September 1984: Stauffer Chemical Co. of Westport, Connecticut, was sued by the SEC in a civil action that alleged that Stauffer overstated its 1982 earnings by $31.1 million. According to the SEC, Stauffer effected consignments of some of its agricultural chemicals to its dealers and reported the consignments as sales in 1982 rather than sales in 1983. Earnings were therefore understated for 1983 but overstated for 1982, the SEC charged. Stauffer settled the suit without admitting or denying the SEC charges.

What these cases share in common is a flaw in the design of the compensation plans of the firms mentioned. Compensation plans that are based on short-term projections of revenue and profit can corrupt the judgment of those responsible for achieving those goals. The business environment is neither chronically good nor chronically bad. Business tends to be cyclical. Therefore, a compensation plan that arbitrarily imposes revenue and profit goals for awarding bonuses may create a work environment in which cheating (fudging the numbers) becomes an accepted practice.

Auditor Liability and Undetected Fraud

In testimony before the House Subcommittee on Oversight and Investigations in 1986, John Shad, then chairman of the SEC, reported the following facts about the financial reporting system in the United States:

- There are 11,000 publicly owned companies that file reports and registration statements with the SEC.
- During the previous three years, the SEC took action against one hundred issuers or their employees for disclosure violations. In 43 other cases, the SEC took action against public accountants for "alleged misconduct."

Shad continued, "The Commission's primary concern, of course, is with fraud that materially impacts the public financial reports of registrants. While the Commission has been unable . . . to quantify the nature and impact of such fraud, it is clear that fraudulent accounting or disclosure practices, however isolated, can cause substantial harm to investors, creditors and others."

In *United States vs. Arthur Young & Co.,* the Supreme Court tried to define professionalism in the accounting profession in the loftiest terms. In a unanimous decision, the Court stated[3]

> By clarifying the public reports that collectively depict a corporation's financial status, the independent auditor assumes a *public* responsibility *transcending any employment relationship* with the client. The independent public accountant performing this special function owes *ultimate allegiance to the corporation's creditors and stockholders,* as well as to [the] investing public. This "public watchdog" function demands that the accountant maintain *total independence from*

the client at all times and requires *complete fidelity to the public trust.* To insulate from disclosure a certified public accountant's interpretations of the client's financial statements would be to ignore the significance of the public accountant's role as a *disinterested analyst charged with public obligations* [emphasis added].

The Court later states

It is therefore not enough that financial statements be accurate; the public must also perceive them as being accurate. Public faith in the reliability of a corporation's financial statements depends upon the public perception of the outside auditor as an independent professional.

For a further reminder of just how serious the problem of audit failure and fraud has been, consider this historical flashback. The following incomplete list contains 95 public companies and regulated financial institutions in the United States. In these cases, stockholders, creditors, or regulatory authorities alleged that audit failures by major certified public accountant (CPA) firms occurred during the past 15 years.[4] The audit failures consisted mainly of the issuance of "clean" financial statements shortly before an insolvency claim was made or where accounting errors or irregularities (frauds) went undetected for some time. In many instances, the CPA firms were later sued for negligence by stockholders or creditors of the companies and institutions. In a few instances, regulatory agencies censured the public accountants.

Alexander Hamilton
Allied Artists
Amcor, Inc.
AM International
AMPEC Securities
Ampex Corp.
Banker's Trust
Barnett Mortgage Trust
Beverly Hills Savings & Loan
Bevil, Bresler & Schulman
Cabot, Cabot & Forbes Land Trust
Capital Mortgage Investments
Cartridge TV
Cenco, Inc.
Chase Manhattan Mortgage & Realty Trust
Chromalloy American
Chronar Corp.
CI Realty Investors

Citizens Mortgage Investment Trust
CNA Financial Corp.
Columbia Pictures
Commonwealth Savings & Loan
Consolidata Service
Continental Illinois National Bank
Continental Mortgage Investors
Datapoint Corp.
DeLorean Motors
Digilog, Inc.
Diversified Industries
Drysdale Government Securities
E.F. Hutton
Equity Funding & Subs.
E.S.M. Government Securities
Falstaff Brewing
Fidelco Growth Investors
Firestone Tire

First Penn Mortgage Trust
Fisco, Inc.
Flight Transportation Corp.
Four Seasons Nursing Homes
Geico
Geo-Tek Resources
Giant Stores
HNC Mortgage & Realty
International Bank (Mercantile)
International Controls
Investors Funding Corp.
Itel Corp.
Jewelcor, Inc.
J. Walter Thompson
Lykes Corp.
Marine Midland Corp.
Marsh & McLennan Co.
Mattel, Inc.
McCormick & Co.
National Student Marketing
   Corp.
North American Acceptance
Northwest Conference of United
   Methodist Church
Oak Industries
Old Court Savings & Loan
Omega-Alpha
Omni-Rx
OPM Leasing
Penn Life

Penn Square Bank
PepsiCo
Punta Gorda Isles
Reliable Life & Casualty
Republic National Life
Reserve Insurance
Rockwood National
Sa Com Co.
Saxon Industries
SCA Services
Security National (Hempstead)
Sharon Steel
Standard Life Corp.
Stauffer Chemical Co.
Stirling Homex
Tidal Marine
Tiffany Industries
Uniroyal, Inc.
United American Bank
U.S. Financial Corp.
U.S. Realty Investments
U.S. Surgical Corp.
Weis Securities
Westgate Cal
Westinghouse Electric
Wheatheart, Inc.
W.T. Grant
WUV's Restaurants
Zale Corp.

Notes

1. SEC vs A.M. International, Inc., Civil Action No. 83-1256 D.D.C. May 2, 1983.

2. The *Forensic Accounting Review* is published monthly by Jack Bologna, c/o Computer Protection Systems, Inc., 150 N. Main St., Plymouth, Mich. 48170.

3. United States v. Arthur Young & Co., 465 U.S. 805, 104 S.Ct. 1495, March 21, 1984.

4. Not all of the public accountants were found to be negligent in these cases. Some cases may have been frivolous in nature.

CHAPTER 8

Detecting Employee Embezzlement and Corruption

Embezzlement

Embezzlers steal $4 to $6 billion a year from their employers, masters, and principals, yet their thefts are rarely detected. Even when thefts are detected, embezzlers are rarely prosecuted, and when they are prosecuted, their criminal sentences are very light.

The crime of embezzlement generally consists of the fraudulent misappropriation of the property of an employer, principal, or master by an employee, agent, or servant to whom possession of that property has been entrusted. Typically, embezzlement occurs when the embezzler gains initial possession of property lawfully but subsequently misappropriates it. In this respect, embezzlement is different from larceny, which is committed when property is taken without the owner's consent.

By way of accounting and audit controls, embezzlers are discouraged from breaching their employers' trust through fear of detection and fear of punishment. Embezzlement can be detected through several techniques: (1) the traditional control concepts of separation of duties and audit trails; (2) periodic financial and operational audits; (3) the gathering of intelligence on the lifestyles and personal habits of employees; (4) allegations and complaints by fellow employees; (5) the logging of exceptions to prescribed controls and procedures; (6) the review of variances in operating performance expectations (standards, goals, objectives, budgets, plans); and (7) the intuition of the embezzler's superiors.

Embezzlers are not "hit-and-run" criminals like swindlers. Their thefts often go on for years, and they often get larger over time. The size of the theft eventually gives the embezzler away. Even a neophyte auditor can detect an embezzlement in its later stages.

Each embezzler has a pattern of theft that is somewhat unique but will be discernible to an experienced fraud auditor. These patterns include the following: an account category that gets an inordinate amount of "padding" to cover up the loss; a particular step in the audit trail procedures that is often bypassed, circumvented or overridden; a favorite customer, supplier, or contractor whose account balance is manipulated; and an input document that is often fabricated, counterfeited, or forged. Most long-lasting embezzlement schemes are found after discovery to be very simple. The truly complicated schemes surface very quickly.

Fraudulent pattern recognition is the unique skill of trained and experienced fraud auditors. Current efforts to design audit software that duplicates this skill with artificial intelligence are the best hope for stemming the tide of computer-related embezzlement.

How Embezzlement Surfaces

Information concerning an act of employee embezzlement initially surfaces in one of several ways:

1. An accounting discrepancy, financial irregularity, questionable transaction, or asset loss is detected in the course of a routine internal, external, operational, or compliance audit.
2. A complaint or allegation of misconduct is made by corporate insiders, that is, the employee's peers, subordinates, or superiors.
3. A complaint or allegation of misconduct is made by corporate outsiders, for example, suppliers, contractors, customers, or competitors; police, security, or regulatory officials; or friends, associates, or relatives of the employee.
4. There is a notable change in the behavior of the culprit.

An accounting or financial discrepancy noted by an auditor does not by itself make a *prima facie* case. Often, the auditor only knows for sure that an adjusting journal entry may be required or that financial statements may need to be corrected. However, the discrepancy should not be allowed to stand without follow-up action.

Discrepancies and questionable transactions discovered by auditors should be brought to the immediate attention of higher authorities in audit, general management, legal, and security positions. Complaints or allegations of employee theft or fraud from insiders or outsiders should be brought to the immediate attention of corporate security and legal departments. If audit support is needed, that function should also be advised.

Some embezzlers who fear discovery attempt to make their fraudulent entries appear normal by standard control criteria. That is, the amount must be within established limits, the entry originator must be authorized, the account classifications must be proper, the place and time of the transaction and the transacting parties must be appropriate, and the subject matter of the transaction must be plausible given the needs of the business. This is asking a lot from a typical defrauder, so many of them bypass the accounting system completely if they can. They take the money or other things of value without subverting the accounting system to cover it up. Other embezzlers sell assets for full value, alter the document of sale to a lesser value for a fabricated reason, and then pocket the difference. Others find clever ways to manipulate weaknesses in the accounting and control systems so that their embezzlement appears to be within the bounds of the weak standards, policies, procedures, and exceptions criteria. Finally, some defrauders exploit not just weaknesses in controls but absences of control. More frauds probably occur in environments where controls are absent than where controls are weak.

Fraud auditors tend to look for implausible entries, that is, entries that seem too high, to low, too frequent, too rare, or too irregular in volume or entries made at odd times, by odd people, or at odd places. Defrauders know this, and they try to dodge those control devices by creating entries that fit within the exceptions or are designed to throw auditors off the scent, such as small errors intended to distract auditors from the fraudulent entries.

To cover their activities, for example, embezzlers typically create misinformation, destroy information, suppress information, or use rationalizations if the authenticity or accuracy of an entry is challenged. They dream up stories that can justify their entries and thereby create a form of "plausible deniability."

If you were to program a computer to audit for the possibility of fraud, you would first provide a mechanism that enabled the system to screen out people who are not authorized to have any form of access. Then you would layer the legitimate users according to their job responsibilities and information needs; that is, you would assign access rights by security level. Next, to protect the system from legitimate users who might exceed their authority, you would provide a mechanism that allowed the system to audit its users for security violations, that is, those who access information that they have no right or need to know. Technologies now exist that can accomplish these control objectives relatively well.

However, when you move into the realm of fraud prevention controls, you are left with monitoring individual system users according to their profile of legitimate uses, that is, their defined program and file access rights and privileges and their prespecified and expected transaction characteristics. You would then monitor them either continuously or on a sampling basis for deviation from security standards, acceptable accounting practices, and other control criteria, like transaction amount, timing, frequency, volume, mathematical accuracy, and modification of programs, files, and logs.

Common Embezzlement Techniques

Cash disbursement embezzlement is the most common fraud in books of account. This type of embezzlement involves the creation of fake documents or false entries in some category of expense—for example, purchases, accounts payable, or payroll—usually in the form of a phony invoice from a phantom supplier or a faked time card from a phantom employee. The fabricated purchases may be for merchandise, raw materials, supplies, parts, rental of property, service contracts for repairs, maintenance, janitorial or temporary help, insurance, travel and entertainment, benefits, and so on. However, fabricating the purchase of raw material and merchandise is difficult to accomplish because the costs of manufacture and sale are closely scrutinized by top management. If the fabricated purchases are for services or supplies, the fraud is easier to execute and conceal. These expenses are not monitored as closely as costs of manufacture and sale. Good controls require the separation of duties and clear audit trails, yet in the era of computerized accounting, particularly with respect to small firms, duties may be merged, and audit trails may not exist.

Cash disbursement fraud is very common in small firms with one-person accounting departments or in companies in which separation of duties and audit trails are weak or nonexistent. The computerization of small firms will exacerbate the disbursement fraud problem because business owners are less skeptical about data generated by computer. They must rely on the honesty of their accounting employees because the cost of added controls seem prohibitive. With lessened controls, disbursement fraud increases. Worse yet, if audit trails are flawed, legal accountability is flawed. If accountability cannot be legally established, there may be no way to prove criminal fraud, theft, or embezzlement.

Cash receipts fraud is also common. The classic cash receipts fraud involves the lapping of cash or accounts receivable; that is, the embezzler "borrows" from today's sales or receipts and replaces them with tomorrow's sales or receipts. This fraud requires the creation of false data, false reports, or false entries.

There are other noteworthy types of receipts fraud. *Skimming* is holding out or intercepting some of the proceeds of cash sales before any entry is made of their receipt. This is also called *fraud on the front end*.

Another cash receipts fraud can be generated by the issuance of fake credits for discounts, refunds, rebates, or returns and allowances. Here, a conspiracy may be required with a customer who shares the proceeds of the fake credit with an insider.

Cash is certainly not the only asset stolen or embezzled by insiders. Besides cash, the assets most vulnerable to such risks are tools, supplies, equipment, finished goods, raw materials, and proprietary information. As a general rule, assets are vulnerable when they are lightweight, easy to dispose of, and valuable. Theft or embezzlement of such assets may involve false entries, counterfeit or forged documents, and alteration or destruction of records to conceal the crime.

Among other noncash assets that may be vulnerable to theft, fraud, and embezzlement are assets that appear to have little value, such as waste, scrap, and obsolete products. Few people know the true value and true amount of these assets, and few controls exist for their transfer, removal, or disposal. Any revenue they generate is treated as a windfall by senior management. If the real value is twice what the books say, only a handful of warehouse clerks know it.

Proving Criminal Intent in Embezzlement Cases

Without a full, voluntary confession, proving criminal intent in cases of white-collar crime is a formidable challenge to the skills and patience of investigators and auditors because evidence of intent is usually circumstantial. Direct proof rarely exists showing that a defendant "knowingly" or "willfully" violated larceny, embezzlement, fraud, bribery, or income-tax laws. Criminal intent must be inferred from other facts, such as the defendant's education, training, experience, and intelligence; sophistication in the ways of business, finance, or accounting; past actions and past contradictory statements; tacit admissions; efforts to conceal or destroy evidence; evidence of subornation, perjury, or obstruction of justice; and evidence of the conversion of funds to the defendant's own use.

Defense lawyers in criminal cases often direct their whole defense to the issue of criminal intent because it is so difficult to prove. In the era of modern business, criminal intent is also very complex, and reasonable doubt can be created by a clever attorney. How then do investigators go about the task of proving intent beyond a reasonable doubt?

As stated previously, evidence of education, experience, training, intelligence, and sophistication in the ways of business, finance, and accounting may bear on the issue of generalized intent, that is, knowledge, willfulness, and evil motive. However, some laws have specific intent requirements. Burglary, for example, requires the breaking and entering into the residence of another in the nighttime with the intent to commit a felony (the theft of property). Larceny is the taking and carrying away of the personal property of another with the intent of permanently depriving the owner of its use.

Now consider the hypothetical example of a bookkeeper-embezzler who uses an accounts receivable lapping scheme. The bookkeeper has at least a limited right to access certain assets of his employer and the responsibility to make certain entries in the business records of the firm. In need of money for the payment of a gambling or speculation debt, high living, or family medical problems, the bookkeeper decides to "borrow" $1000. A customer's check is received, payable to the company. The bookkeeper opens the mail, finds the check for $1000, and substitutes it for $1000 in the cash drawer, intending to make an entry crediting the receipt to customer A's account the next day when another $1000 check is expected from customer B. Customer B's check is then used as the basis for covering customer A's account. The subsidiary ledger accounts of customers A and B may properly reflect their current balances because no entry debiting cash and crediting the control account for customer A's payment was made. An audit could disclose the discrepancies in accounts receivable and in the cash drawer at this point, so the bookkeeper might take an additional step to conceal the embezzlement. If he can access a credit memo form and can pretend authority to issue it by a forgery, customer A's account could be written off fictitiously as a discount, a rebate, an allowance, or even a bad debt. This effort at concealment would bear on the issue of intent and could be used to rebut the bookkeeper's defense of lack of intent to embezzle.

This evidence alone, however, may not be enough to convict the bookkeeper of embezzlement. Nor would evidence of high living, gambling, speculation, or family expense prove intent per se. However, this evidence would provide a motive for embezzlement and would be admissible for that purpose.

Evidence of the improper entries alone does not prove intent either. The bookkeeper may claim in defense that his intention was not to permanently deprive his employer of the money, but just to "borrow" it.

Evidence of this kind of "borrowing," however, implies or infers an intention to breach a fiduciary responsibility. This could help to prove criminal intent for embezzlement, if not larceny. In and of themselves, these pieces of evidence may not be enough to convict, but when strung together, they might. For example, the following facts may prove intent beyond a reasonable doubt:

1. The bookkeeper is educated, trained, and experienced in accounting.
2. The bookkeeper has a fiduciary responsibility to keep and maintain records in a timely and accurate manner.
3. The bookkeeper has been employed by the company in that capacity for five years and knows the company's accounting policies, procedures, and controls and how to make proper entries.
4. The bookkeeper's living expenses exceed his income by several orders of magnitude.
5. The bookkeeper was fired from two previous jobs when large amounts of money in his custody were found missing.
6. The lapping scheme went on for three years, and the bookkeeper kept a running tab on his "borrowings." He now claims the running tab proves his intention to repay. However, in a barroom conversation a year ago, he told an acquaintance that the company could be "stolen blind" by a clever thief because its controls were so weak.
7. When the cash drawer was counted during the fraud audit and investigation, there was a check from the bookkeeper to the company for a large sum of money that was used to balance the drawer. It equaled the amount of the embezzlement for the current year.
8. Evidence exists of the concealment of documents, the destruction of records, forged and counterfeited documents, false statements, and the solicitation of false testimony.

When these facts are added together, a judge or jury may reasonably conclude that the defendant did indeed formulate criminal intent.

Investigating Internal Corruption Charges

Very few large firms are totally free of some form of employee corruption by vendors, suppliers, service providers, or contractors. In most instances, the considerations taken or offered are of nominal value, for example, free tickets, lunches, dinners, and Christmas gifts. Company policies sometimes discourage even these minor demonstrations of gratitude for past business.

What happens when allegations or suspicions of large-scale corruption begin to surface? The handling of these events by personnel departments has not been particularly good. Playing at the investigative business by amateurs can cause many problems. Employee morale and trust can be shattered. Unsubstantiated charges can bring on lawsuits for defamation, illegal firing, false arrest, invasion of privacy, and so on. Evidence that may support the charges can often go uncollected or be mishandled. Confrontations with the suspected employee can be staged before the allegations are even documented or verified.

The following tips may help you investigate internal corruption charges:

- Qualify the source of the allegations; that is, check on the source's identity, credibility, knowledgeability, and reliability.
- Determine whether the source knows the information first-hand (personal knowledge) or whether it has been passed on by another (hearsay).
- Determine the motives of the source (revenge, spite, jealousy, pique, money).
- If the source demands money before disclosing details—beware. Don't "front" money until verifiable information has been given and has been confirmed through independent means (other credible witnesses or documents).
- Qualify all further information about the alleged corruption; that is, verify and corroborate the charges through other independent sources and documents.
- Never take disciplinary action without a complete record of the corruption allegations, including the identity of the source of the allegations and his or her written account of the allegations (an oral account is not enough).
- Confirm the allegations through documents and the testimony (written and subscribed to) of other knowledgeable witnesses.
- Approach the vendors, suppliers, or others alleged to be involved; elicit their response and enlist their cooperation.
- Interview the suspected employee to seek his or her version of the situation. (For example, did the vendor make the offer or did the employee solicit the vendor?)

Should the investigation and audit be done with inside resources, that is, company security personnel, in-house counsel, and an internal auditor? If they are trained and experienced, yes. If not, you would be better served by going outside to a reputable and experienced private detective agency, legal firm, and audit firm.

Data Base Research for Investigators

Thirty years ago, investigating financial fraud was a time-consuming and tedious chore. Researching credit data bases and public records in that manual era exhausted investigators. In Detroit during that period, investigative accountants with the IRS, the FBI, and other agencies had to start their real estate ownership searches by referring to the grantor-grantee index. Once the list of buy-sell transactions was compiled, they moved to the deed libers, and made appropriate notes or copies. From the deed libers, they moved to the mortgage filings and discharges, liens, and *lis pendens* files. Investigators could sometimes calculate the value of a specific sale of real estate by determining the amount of the federal tax stamps placed on the deeds.

Today, an investigator does not have to leave home to do this kind of research. A new on-line ordering feature introduced by Mead Data Central, Inc., gives LEXIS/NEXIS subscribers quick, easy access to public records filings from any jurisdiction—state or local—in the United States. With the LEXDOC® feature, subscribers can electronically place an order for a manual search or for certified or uncertified copies of public records filings. The LEXDOC feature allows users to order searches for or copies of a variety of public documents, including articles of incorporation, certificates of good standing, annual reports, Uniform Commercial Code (UCC) filings, tax liens, judgments, and pending suits. LEXIS customers can order any number of documents from any state or local jurisdiction in the United States in a single session.

Technical Advisory Service for Attorneys (TASA) provides attorneys, insurance companies, and government agencies with information on independent experts for case evaluation, litigation preparation, and testimony. TASA's data base includes information on nearly 15,000 experts in 4000 categories. Being listed in the data base is one way to make yourself known as a CPA expert witness. For more information on how to be listed, contact Technical Advisory Service for Attorneys, 1166 DeKalb Pike, Blue Bell, PA 19422-1844. The telephone number is (215) 275-8272.

Martindale-Hubbell, which has provided the legal profession with information on lawyers and law firms for more than a century, has released the Martindale-Hubbell Law Directory on compact disk read-only memory (CD-ROM). It is accessed through a personal computer with a compact-disk drive. The CD-ROM format enables users to access, in a matter of seconds, detailed information on the 700,000 lawyers, law firms, and banks, services, and suppliers to the legal community contained in the Martindale-Hubbell Law Directory.

Private investigators are now developing their own on-line network via an electronic mail (E-mail) connection. The originator of the Investigator's On-line Network (ION) is Leroy E. Cook, 6303 South Rural Road, Suite 1, Tempe, AZ 85283. His telephone number is (602)730-8088. ION uses packet-switched electronic mail to keep subscribers abreast of information sources. Cook feels that, without sufficient knowledge, investigators have no choice but to take a chance when ordering information from brokers. ION enables subscribers to

- communicate with five hundred on-line investigators throughout the United States and other countries
- learn about information sources and providers helpful to the investigative business
- learn about on-line data retrieval
- reduce advertising and marketing costs through a cooperative marketing program

To access ION, subscribers need a computer, a Hayes-compatible modem, a telephone, and a communication software package. The ION directories of subscribers and providers are available on hard copy and on disk for investigators who do not have modems.

CHAPTER 9

Auditing and Investigating Corporate Crime

Crime Detection

In U.S. law enforcement, most investigations of crime are not initiated by detectives. Most investigations by police authorities follow the receipt of complaints from victims or allegations of criminal acts witnessed or otherwise discovered by members of the general public. Self-initiated investigations of crime by police authorities are usually based on information and belief that a crime has been committed, is being committed, or is about to be committed. Information and belief can be predicated on the fact that police authorities have observed or witnessed a criminal act or have in their possession sufficient knowledge of an actual or potential crime to warrant an investigation. Information and belief can also be predicated on other factors:

- knowledgeable, credible third parties (witnesses, criminal confederates, paid informers)
- knowledge acquired by the police themselves based on education, training, and experience (sometimes referred to as *intuition*)
- knowledge acquired by police based on surveillance and observations
- knowledge acquired by the systematic gathering of intelligence on the activities of criminal organizations and habitual crime perpetrators
- research on crime, criminals, and criminal organizations

Crime is defined generally as a public wrong, a human act or omission that is made punishable by public law. According to law, a crime, therefore, must meet several requirements:

1. There must be a validly enacted law that provides for criminal sanctions (fine, imprisonment, or both) if the law is breached. The law must be made generally known.
2. There must be a perpetrator—someone who has, in fact, violated the law.

3. The perpetrator must have sufficient legal and mental capacity to understand the nature of his or her act.
4. The violation must become known to a law enforcement officer by his or her own faculties and resources or by some third party (a victim of the breach, a witness to the breach) or someone otherwise knowledgeable about the breach (a confederate of the violator, a paid or unpaid informer).

The work of the detective then is to document the violation of the law with evidence and to gather that evidence in such a manner that the suspect's legal rights are not transgressed. Evidence may consist of confessions given freely by violators, statements from witnesses who observed the criminal act or were its victims, and physical things that relate to the crime, for example, means, instruments, and fruits of the crime, weapons, tools, written documents, clothing, and money.

The first step in the process of crime investigation is to determine whether a crime has in fact been committed. Has a criminal law been violated? If so, what specific law? Who is the violator? Can the violator's identity be established? Is the violator of sufficient legal capacity to respond to or be held accountable for criminal charges? What evidence of identity and violation are available? Can this evidence be gathered legally? Is this evidence legally sufficient to support the charge or violation?

A step-by-step process or checklist of criminal investigation can be set forth in terms of a procedural logic:

I. A putative criminal act is reported, discovered, or discerned.
   A. Is the act, in fact, a violation of a criminal law?
   B. If so, what specific law or laws?
   C. When was the act committed (statute of limitations)?
   D. Where was the act committed (jurisdiction, venue)?
   E. How was the act committed (*modus operandi*)?
   F. Who committed the act (legal capacity)?
   G. How can the perpetrator be identified and located (arrest, search, and seizure)?
   H. Why was the act committed (motive, intent)?
II. What evidence links the criminal act to the suspect?
   A. Are witnesses to the criminal act available?
      1. Are these witnesses legally competent, credible, and willing to testify?
      2. Can they positively identify the suspect?
   B. Are documents available to prove the charge?
      1. In whose legal custody are these documents?
      2. Will these documents be surrendered voluntarily, or will judicial processes be required (subpoena)?
      3. Do the documents speak for themselves, or will they

require a foundation for their introduction (public versus private records)?
4. Are the documents kept in the regular course of trade or business?
5. Are the documents original or copies (best evidence)?
C. Are tools, means, instruments, and fruits of the crime available?
1. How were these acquired? (Incident to arrest? Execution of search warrant? Voluntarily submitted? Found at the crime scene? Discovered by accident?)
2. Have these items been marked, identified, and kept in a secured place? Has their transfer been recorded with date, person, and purpose (chain of custody)?
3. Has the suspect been arrested? (With or without a warrant?)
III. Was the suspect advised of his or her rights?
IV. Was the suspect searched?
A. Incident to arrest?
V. Was any incriminating evidence found on the suspect or in the immediate area of the arrest?
VI. Was the suspect interrogated?
A. Was the interrogation before or after the suspect was advised of his or her rights?
VII. Did the suspect make any admissions of guilt?
A. *Res gestae* statements?
VIII. Did the suspect make a confession?
A. Was it voluntary?
B. Were any oral promises made of leniency?
C. Any promises of intercessions with prosecutorial or judicial authorities?
D. Any other assurances?

What Fraud Investigators Need to Know

What does a fraud investigator need to know about law? At a minimum, a fraud investigator should know the following:

- the nature and sources of substantive and procedural law, constitutional law, the common law, and criminal and civil law
- the distinctions between crimes that are *mala in se* (evil in of themselves; morally wrong) and *mala prohibita* (made wrong by law or prohibited by law, but not necessarily evil or morally wrong, for example, traffic violations)
- the distinctions between criminal and civil law, between crimes and torts, and between federal and state crimes

- the elements of a crime and a tort
- the distinctions between criminal fraud and civil fraud
- the elements of criminal fraud and civil fraud
- the Constitutional principles that apply to criminal investigations, both procedural and substantive, particularly as they relate to probable cause, search and seizure, arrest, identification, interrogation, self-incrimination, the right to counsel, due process, and equal protection
- the rules of evidence with respect to such things as burden of proof; presumptions; relevancy, materiality, and competence; judicial notice; and hearsay exceptions, for example, admissions, statements against interest, spontaneous declarations (*res gestae*), expert opinion, official records, business records, best evidence, chain of custody, and privileged communications

Substantive Law

There are three sources of substantive law in the United States: (1) statutes and ordinances enacted by federal, state, and local legislative bodies and regulations promulgated thereunder; (2) state and federal constitutions; and (3) the so-called common law or case law (previous opinions of state and federal courts of appeal). Criminal and civil laws are derived from substantive law.

Procedural Law versus Substantive Law

Procedural law deals with the manner in which substantive laws are passed, administered, and enforced, that is, according to due process and equal protection standards as set forth in the U.S. Constitution. For example, a criminal law that has vague or ambiguous language may be ruled unconstitutional as a matter of substantive due process. Criminal laws must be clear and understandable so that people can know in advance that a particular act or inaction may be punishable as a crime. However, an action or inaction alone, without criminal intent, may not be punished as a crime. Intent (*mens rea*) is a required element in most crimes; that is, crimes that are *mala in se*. Crimes that are *mala prohibita* usually don't require proof of criminal intent. The mere commission of the act voluntarily or the failure to act when required may be enough.

Rules of Evidence

In a broad sense, *evidence* is any type of proof perceptible by the five senses and legally presented at a trial to prove a contention and induce a belief in the minds of the court or jury. Any of the following might be introduced as evidence: the testimony of witnesses, records, documents, facts, data, or concrete objects. In weighing testimony, the court or jury may consider such things as the demeanor of a witness, the witness's bias for or against the accused, and the witness's relationship, if any, to the accused. Evidence can be testimonial, circumstantial, demonstrative, inferential, and even theoretical when given by a qualified expert. Evidence is simply anything that proves or disproves any matter in question.

In the Anglo-American tradition, witnesses, other than experts, generally cannot testify about probabilities, opinions, assumptions, impressions, generalizations, or conclusions, only about things, people, and events they saw, felt, tasted, smelled, or heard firsthand. Even those things must be legally and logically relevant. *Logical relevancy* means that the evidence being offered must tend to prove or disprove a fact or consequence. Even if logically relevant, a court may exclude evidence if it is likely to inflame or confuse a jury or consume too much time. Testimony about the statistical probability of guilt is considered too prejudicial and unreliable to be accepted.

Evidence can be direct or circumstantial. *Direct evidence* proves a fact directly; if the evidence is believed, the fact is established. *Circumstantial evidence* proves the desired fact indirectly and depends on the strength of the inferences raised by the evidence. For example, a letter properly addressed, stamped, and mailed is inferred to have been received by the addressee. Testimony that a letter was so addressed, stamped, and mailed raises the inference that it was received, but the inference may be rebutted by testimony that it was not.

Some evidentiary matters considered relevant and therefore admissible are

1. the motive for a crime
2. the ability of the defendant to commit the specific crime
3. the opportunity to commit the crime
4. threats or expressions of ill will by the accused
5. the means of committing the offense (possession of a weapon, tool, or skills used in committing the crime)
6. physical evidence at the scene linking the accused to the crime
7. the suspect's conduct and comments at the time of arrest
8. the attempt to conceal identity
9. the attempt to destroy evidence
10. valid confessions

The *materiality rule* requires that evidence must have an important value to a case or prove a point in issue. Unimportant details only extend the trial. Accordingly, a trial court judge may rule against the introduction of evidence that is repetitive or additive (that merely proves the same point in another way) or that tends to be remote although relevant. Materiality, then, is the degree of relevancy. The court cannot become preoccupied with trifles or unnecessary details.

Competent evidence is evidence that is sufficient, reliable, and relevant to the case and is presented by a qualified, capable, and sane witness. Competency differs from credibility. The question of competency arises before the court considers the evidence given by a witness. Credibility refers to the witness's veracity. Competency is for the judge to determine; credibility is for the jury to decide.

Judicial notice is the process by which a judge—on his or her own motion and without the production of evidence—recognizes the existence of certain facts that bear on the issue on trial. For example, the judge may elect to judicially notice that a state law on a certain subject exists; that mixing oxygen and hydrogen in a certain combination will produce water; or that July 4, 1990, fell on a Wednesday.

The *best evidence rule* deals with written documents proffered as evidence. The rule states that if the contents of a document are at issue, if the original has been destroyed, or if it is in the hands of an opposite party and not subject to legal process by search warrant or subpoena, then an authenticated copy may be substituted. Business records and documents kept in the ordinary course of business may also be presented as evidence even when the person who made the entries or prepared the documents is unavailable.

Photocopies of original business documents and other writings and printed matter are often made to preserve evidence. These are used by investigators so that the original records needed to run a business are not removed and so that, in the event of the inadvertent destruction of the originals, a certified true copy of the document is still available as proof. The certified copy may also be used by investigators to document their case reports. At trial, however, the original document—if still available—is the best evidence and must be presented. In this context, *best evidence* means the original, not a copy or substitute.

To introduce *secondary evidence,* one must explain satisfactorily the absence of the original document to the court. Secondary evidence is not restricted to photocopies of the document; it may consist of testimony of witnesses or transcripts of the document's contents. Whereas the federal courts give no preference to the type of secondary evidence, the majority of other jurisdictions do. Under the majority rule, testimony (*parol evidence*) will not be allowed to prove the contents of a document if there is secondary documentary evidence available to prove its contents. However, before secondary evidence of the original document may be introduced, the party offering the contents of the substitute must have used all reasonable and diligent means to obtain the original. Again, this is a matter to be determined by the court.

When the original document has been destroyed by the party attempting to prove its contents, secondary evidence will be admitted if the destruction was in the ordinary course of business, or by mistake, or even intentionally, provided it was not done for any fraudulent purpose.

The *burden of proof* in a criminal case is the burden of the state to prove the guilt of the accused beyond a reasonable doubt. In civil litigation, the burden of proof is on the plaintiff to prove the case by a preponderance of the evidence, which is somewhat less than proof beyond a reasonable doubt. In a criminal case, then the prosecution produces evidence beyond a reasonable doubt on each element of the crime, to the point where a *prima facie* case has been made, the defendant can be convicted unless he or she accepts the burden of going forward and introduces evidence that tends to challenge or controvert the prosecution's evidence.

Presumptions and Inferences

A *presumption* is a rule of law, statutory or judicial, by which the finding of a basic fact gives rise to the existence of a presumed fact until the presumption is rebutted.[1] A presumption, therefore, shifts the burden of going forward with evidence to the other side to rebut it, but it doesn't shift the burden of proof.

The *presumption of innocence,* on the other hand, is not a presumption at all. It merely means that in a criminal case, the state has the burden of proving each element of a crime beyond a reasonable doubt. The defendant, therefore, has no burden to prove him- or herself innocent.

An *inference* is a derived truth, that is, a process of reasoning from other facts that have not been controverted. In essence, an inference is a deduction or conclusion.

Other Rules of Evidence

The *chain of custody rule* requires that when evidence in the form of a document or an object (means or instrument) is seized at a crime scene or as a result of a subpoena *duces tecum* (for documents) or is discovered in the course of a fraud examination, it should be marked, identified, inventoried, and preserved. The evidence must be maintained in its original condition, and a clear chain of custody must be established until the evidence is introduced at trial. If gaps in possession or custody occur, the evidence may be challenged at the trial on the theory that the document or object introduced is not the original or is not in its original condition and therefore is of doubtful authenticity.

For a seized document to be admissible as evidence, the prosecutor must prove that it is the same document that was seized and that it is in the same condition as it was when seized.

The rule prohibiting the introduction of *privileged communications* at a trial is based on the belief that it is necessary to maintain the confidentiality of certain communications and that the protection of certain relationships is more important to society than the possible harm resulting from the loss of such evidence. The rule covers only those communications that are a product of a protected relationship. Legal jurisdictions vary as to what communications are protected. The following are some of the more prevalent privileged relationships:

1. attorney-client
2. husband-wife
3. physician-patient
4. priest-penitent
5. law enforcement officer-informant
6. reporter-source
7. accountant-client (not recognized in federal courts)

When dealing with privileged communications, consider the following basic principles:

1. Only the holder of a privilege or someone authorized by the holder can assert the privilege.
2. If the holder fails to assert the privilege after being notified of it and after having an opportunity to assert it, the privilege is waived.
3. The privilege may also be waived if the holder discloses a significant part of the communication to a party not within the protected relationship.
4. To be within the privilege, the communication must be sufficiently related to the relationship protected. For example, communications between an attorney and client must be related to legal consultation.

Under common law, a person cannot testify against his or her spouse in criminal trial. While they remain married, neither spouse may waive this testimonial incompetence. The confidential communications between spouses made during the marriage retain their privileged status after the marriage has been ended.

Conversations in the known presence of third parties do not fall within the purview of privileged communications. Protected communications are those that are in fact confidential or induced by marriage or other relationship. Ordinary conversations relating to matters not deemed to be confidential are not within the purview of the privilege.

A fraud examiner who needs to use evidence in the nature of communications between parties in one of these relationships should consult with counsel, especially if the evidence is crucial to the case.

The *hearsay rule* is based on the theory that testimony that merely repeats what some other person said should not be admitted because of the possibility of distortion or misunderstanding. Furthermore, the person who made the actual statement is unavailable for cross-examination and has not been sworn in as a witness. Generally, witnesses may testify only to those things of which they have personal and direct knowledge, and they may not testify to conclusions or opinions.

There are some occasions when hearsay evidence is admissible. The following are some examples:

1. dying declarations, either verbal or written
2. valid confessions
3. tacit admissions
4. public records that do not require an opinion but speak for themselves
5. *res gestae* statements, that is, spontaneous explanations spoken as part of the criminal act or immediately following the commission of a criminal act
6. former testimony given under oath
7. business entries made in the normal course of doing business

A *confession* is the acknowledgment of all the facts on which a criminal conviction can stand. An *admission* falls somewhat short of a full acknowledgment. A *statement against interest* is a prior acknowledgment of a material fact relevant to an issue now being litigated when the prior acknowledgment is at variance with the person's current claim. For example, in a tax evasion prosecution, evidence in the form of a financial statement submitted for credit or life insurance that shows a higher net worth than now claimed, may be used in evidence against the defendant.

A *res gestae statement* is a spontaneous comment made by a defendant at a time of great emotional strain, for example, at the time of arrest or at the scene of an accident. The theory is that a statement made at such a time is likely to be truthful.

The *shopbook rule* is an exception to the hearsay rule in that books of original entry kept in the regular course of business can be introduced in court by someone who has custody of them but who may not have made the entries therein. However, the custodian must authenticate the records by testifying that he or she is the custodian, that entries are original (not copies), and that the entries were made contemporaneously with the transactions described.

The *official records rule* allows the introduction of books, records, reports, and compilations kept as a regular and routine duty by a public official.

Testimony as to the *character and reputation of an accused* may be admissible under certain conditions even though it would seem to violate the hearsay rule. Such testimony may be admitted when character is an element of the action, that is, when the mental condition or legal competency of the accused is in question.

Evidence of other crimes committed by an accused is not generally admissible to prove character. It may be admitted for other purposes, however, such as proof of motive, opportunity, or intent to commit an act.

The credibility of a witness may be attacked by showing that he or she was convicted of a serious crime (punishable by death or imprisonment for more than a year) or of such crimes as theft, dishonesty, or false statement. The conviction must have occurred recently, usually within the last 10 years.

Expert testimony is opinion evidence given by a person who possesses special skills and knowledge in a science, profession, or business—skills and knowledge not common to the average person. The expert's testimony is therefore intended to assist the judge to determine a fact in question.

When an expert witness is called on to testify, the counsel must lay a foundation before the testimony is allowed. Laying a foundation means that the witness's expertise must be established before he or she is permitted to render a professional opinion. To qualify a witness as an expert, the counsel must demonstrate to the judge's satisfaction that, through formal education, advanced study, and experience, the witness is knowledgeable about the topic on which his or her testimony will bear. The testimony of experts is an exception to the hearsay rule.

Although all of the following characteristics are not necessary to qualify a witness as an expert, they are listed to provide a comprehensive view of the matter:

1. professional license, certification, or registration by a recognized professional body in the field of expertise in question
2. relevant undergraduate, graduate, or postgraduate academic degrees or a suitable background in the field of expertise
3. specialized training or continuing professional education beyond academic degrees that indicates up-to-date familiarity with the latest technical developments in the expert's subject area
4. the expert's writings and publications that display technical opinions and are available as part of the general body of knowledge in the subject area
5. relevant teaching, lecturing, or consulting undertaken by the expert that indicates that he or she is held in high professional esteem in the given subject area
6. professional associations with which the expert is affiliated
7. directly relevant prior experience that the expert has gained by undertaking similar assignments, whether as technical advisor or expert witness, in the given subject area
8. special status or access to privileged information peculiar to the case at hand that renders the individual an expert because he or she is in possession of unique facts

Financial Auditing versus Fraud Auditing

Financial auditing is intended to uncover deviations and variances from standards of acceptable accounting practice. Looking *behind* and *beyond* the transaction is what fraud auditing is all about. That perspective forces the auditor to focus on substance rather than on form. The questions the fraud auditor has uppermost in mind are not how the accounting system and internal controls stack up against American Institute of CPAs (AICPA) standards, but rather the following:

1. Where are the weakest links in this system's chain of controls?
2. What deviations from conventional accounting practices are possible in this system?
3. How are off-line transactions handled, and who can authorize such transactions?
4. What would be the simplest way to compromise this system?
5. What control features in this system can be bypassed by higher authorities?

Auditing for fraud is more of an intuitive process than it is a formal analytical methodology. It is more of an art than it is a science. As a consequence, it is difficult to teach. Skill depends on the right mindset (thinking like a thief, probing for weaknesses) and practice. Instruction at the hands of a competent mentor is important in the early development of a good fraud auditor. It is not technique that you should master; it is mental disposition, that is, doggedness and persistence. No lead and no shred of evidence are ever too small to have relevance. The fraud auditor absorbs information, organizes it in some meaningful way, and then sees what the pattern looks like.

The patterns to look for are the exceptions and oddities, the things that do not seem to fit in an organized scheme of things because they seem too large, too small, too frequent, too rare, too high, too low, too good to be true, too extraordinary, too many, too few; they involve odd times, odd places, odd hours, odd people, and odd combinations. In a word, the auditor looks for the unusual rather than the usual and then goes behind and beyond those transactions to reconstruct what may have led to them and what may have followed. (The *evidence* of fraud is more often contained in the data that precedes or follows a questionable transaction.)

What a Fraud Auditor Should Know and Be Able to Do

An effective fraud auditor should understand in some depth what fraud is from these perspectives:

1. human and individual
2. organizational, cultural, and motivational
3. economic and competitive
4. social
5. regulatory, legal, and evidential
6. accounting, audit, and internal control

The auditor should also know

7. when, where, and how fraud is most likely to occur in books of account and in financial statements
8. who is most likely to commit fraud in books of account
9. why fraud occurs
10. how to detect and document fraud

An effective fraud auditor should therefore be able to do the following with some degree of competence:

1. conduct a review of internal controls
2. assess the strengths and weaknesses of those controls
3. design scenarios of potential fraud losses based on identified weaknesses in internal controls
4. identify questionable accounts, account balances, and relationships between accounts for variances from current expectations and past relationships (historical ratios)
5. identify questionable and exceptional transactions
6. distinguish simple human errors and omissions in entries from fraudulent entries (unintentional random error versus intentional error)
7. follow the flow of documents that support transactions
8. follow the flow of funds into and out of an organization's accounts
9. search for underlying support documents for questionable transactions
10. review such documents for evidence of forgery; counterfeiting; fake billings; irregularities in serial sequences, quantity, pricing, extension, and footings; substitution of copies for original documents
11. reconstruct revenue and expense data through outside and independent sources
12. confirm asset and liability values through outside and independent sources
13. gather and preserve evidence to corroborate asset losses, fraudulent transactions, and financial misstatements
14. document and report a fraud loss for criminal, civil, or insurance claims
15. conduct a review of management, administrative, and organizational control policies, plans, procedures, and practices
16. test the organization's motivational and ethical climate

From an accounting and audit standpoint, fraud is an intentional misrepresentation of a material fact in books of account or in financial statements. The misrepresentation may be directed against organizational outsiders like shareholders or creditors or against the organization itself by way of covering up or disguising embezzlement, incompetence, misapplication of funds, theft, or improper use of organizational assets by officers, employees, and agents.

Physical custody of property, access to accounting records, and knowledge and authority to override controls are the main ingredients of fraud in books of account and in financial statements. People who have access to corporate assets, who have knowledge of the internal and accounting controls, or who hold management roles that enable them to override controls are in the best position to commit financial frauds against their companies. The threat of fraud is greatest at the level of senior management because the access to assets and the authority to bypass controls are greatest at that level. However, financial fraud is also possible among personnel with responsibility for accounting, finance, data processing, and property handling. They too may have access to accounting records and can use that knowledge and authority to compromise controls and gain access to corporate assets.

Types of Fraud

In books of account and financial statements, fraud can take the following forms:

- Adjusting journal entries that lack authorization and supporting details
- expenditures that lack supporting documents
- false and improper entries in books of account
- unauthorized use and conversion of corporate assets
- unauthorized and illegal payments
- misapplication of corporate funds
- false and fraudulent representations in financial statements with respect to profits and the value of assets
- theft of corporate assets by employees, agents, and officers
- destruction, counterfeiting, and forgery of documents that support payments
- columns of numbers that do not add up properly

A Short Taxonomy of Corporate Accounting Frauds

I. By corporate insiders
   A. Lower-level employees
      1. Cash disbursement frauds
         a) Accounts payable (phony vendor invoices)
         b) Benefit payments (phony claims)
         c) Expense account padding

B. Higher-level employees
  1. Early booking of sales
  2. Expense deferral
  3. Inventory overstatement
  4. Check kiting
II. By corporate outsiders
  A. Vendors
    1. Short shipment, overpricing, extension error, substitution of inferior grades, double-billing

Investigating Corporate Fraud

Fraud audit reminders:

Don'ts

- Don't play detective yourself.
- Don't accuse.
- Don't assume guilt.
- Don't let information leak out.
- Don't detain suspects.

Do's

- Get legal and security assistance—early.
- Get the facts—all of the facts.
- Develop the case *very* carefully.
- Verify and corroborate your data. Confirm its accuracy.
- Check your witnesses for credibility. Look for possible motives of revenge, spite, jealousy, or bias.

Interrogation Suggestions

- Don't be alone with the suspect.
- Don't threaten the suspect.
- Don't entrap the suspect.
- Don't bribe the suspect with offers of "deals" or immunity.

Fraud Auditing Summary

I. Fraud definition
  A. Civil fraud
  B. Criminal fraud
  C. Fraud versus theft and embezzlement

       1. Frauds *for* the company
       2. Frauds *against* the company
       3. Frauds *by* insiders
         a) Nonmanagement employees
         b) Management employees
         c) Senior management
         d) Profit-center directors
       4. Frauds *by* outsiders
         a) Vendors, suppliers, contractors, customers, criminals

II. Fraud elements
    A. Innocent victim
    B. Knowledgeable perpetrator
    C. Misrepresentation of a material fact

III. The Momms taxonomy
    A. Motivations, opportunities, means, methods

IV. Defrauder's motivations
    A. Economic, egocentric, ideological, psychotic motives

V. Opportunities
    A. Weakness or absence of management controls, administrative controls, internal controls

VI. Means
    A. Compromising controls or personnel

VII. Methods
    A. Input scams, thruput scams, and output scams
    B. Faking debits, footings, reconciliations, confirmations, and management information reports
    C. Phony invoices, benefit claims, and expense reimbursement

VIII. Common fraudulent schemes
    A. Disbursement frauds
       1. Accounts payable, payroll, reimbursement claims for benefits, travel expenses, petty cash
    B. Accounts receivable lapping
    C. Check kiting, raising, forgery, counterfeiting
    D. Inventory overstatement
    E. Inflating sales and assets
    F. Understating liabilities and expenses

IX. Financial auditing versus fraud auditing
    A. Mindset versus methodology
    B. Science versus art
    C. Experience versus knowledge

X. Fraud detection
    A. Discovered discrepancy versus allegation
    B. Audit versus investigation

XI. Fraud detection, deterrence, and reduction
    A. Formal controls

      1. Internal and accounting controls
      2. Security controls
        a) Access and authorization
        b) Documentation of policies
        c) Physical security
        d) Personnel security
        e) Information protection
   B. Informal controls
      1. Climate for controls
      2. Organizational stress, undue pressure for performance
      3. Corporate ethics
      4. Interpersonal trust
XII. Developing fraud scenarios
   A. Assessing control weaknesses (red flags)
   B. Identifying likely consequences of weak links in controls
   C. Discrepancies (oddities, variances, exceptions)
   D. Identifying suspects
   E. Developing a theory of the case

Accountants and Auditors as Expert Witnesses

Accountants and auditors are often called on to provide testimony in criminal prosecution where their services are used to support investigations of such crimes as financial fraud, improper accounting practices, and tax evasion. Accountants and auditors may also be used as defense witnesses or as support to the defendant's counsel on matters that involve accounting or audit issues.

Qualifying accountants and auditors as technical experts is generally not a difficult task. Questions are posed to them concerning their professional credentials, that is, education, work experience, licensing or certification, technical training, technical books and journal articles written, offices held in professional associations, and awards or commendations received.

Smart defense lawyers generally do not challenge the expertise of accountants and auditors, assuming that they meet at least minimum standards of professional competence. To do so may give the experts an opportunity to fully highlight their professional credentials and perhaps make a greater impression on the jury or judge, thus adding more weight to their testimony.

In general, accountants and auditors testify to their investigative or audit findings if called by the prosecution; if called by the defense, they may testify about the quality of the audit or the opinions expressed by the prosecution's accounting expert. The goal in this case is to create doubt in the jury's minds about the credibility or weight to be given to the prosecution's expert.

To become a "credible" expert accounting witness, you must be generally knowledgeable in your field as demonstrated by education and experience, be a member of the profession in good standing, and perhaps be recognized as an authority in the field or in some specialized aspect of the field if it is pertinent to the case at hand. There are other considerations as well in making an expert a credible witness. The following are some tips to bear in mind when testifying:

1. Speak clearly and audibly.
2. Refrain from using professional jargon.
3. Use simple terms to describe your findings and opinions.
4. Answer the specific questions asked and do not digress or volunteer more than the question requires.
5. Do not verbally fence with the defense attorney or prosecutor.
6. Look directly at the person posing the question, whether it is the prosecutor or the defense counsel.
7. Maintain a professional demeanor. Do not smile gratuitously at the judge, the jury, the lawyer who hired you, or the opposing counsel.
8. Be calm and deliberate in responding to questions. Speak neither too slowly nor too rapidly.
9. Wear conservative clothing: a gray or dark blue business suit, black shoes (shined) and dark socks, and a conservative tie properly knotted at the collar (not askew) for men; the same holds true generally for women.
10. Be well-groomed.
11. Use graphs, charts and other visual aids if they help to clarify a point.
12. Do not read from notes if you can avoid it. (The opposing lawyer may demand to see your notes, and you will look as if you rehearsed your testimony.)
13. If you have documents to introduce, organize them so that you can quickly retrieve them when asked to do so by the lawyer who hired you.
14. Do not hesitate or stammer. Quickly recover your composure when a difficult or complex question is posed.
15. Ask for a repetition or clarification of the question if you do not fully comprehend it.
16. If you do not know the answer, say so. Don't guess.
17. In cross-examination, do not respond too quickly. The counsel for your side may wish to object to the question.
18. If the judge or jury elects to ask a question, look at the judge or jury when responding.
19. Do not stare off into space, at the floor, or at the ceiling.

20. Be friendly to all sides.
21. Do not raise your voice in anger if the opponent's lawyer tries to bait you.
22. Be honest. Be honest. Be honest. Do not invent, inflate, or evade.

Qualities of Successful Investigators

The *Dictionary of Occupational Titles* (DOT), published by the U.S. Department of Labor, catalogues some 15,000 separate and distinct occupations. If it were not for this tome, many people would find it difficult to describe what it is they do at work.

There is one occupation, however, that has become so celebrated in books, in movies, and on television that everyone feels they have some expertise in it. The occupation is that of the police or private investigator. Most people have an image of a detective based on a favorite character in a book, movie, or television series, and they *think* they are experts at solving crimes.

The DOT says some of them could be successful investigators, and others are likely to fail. Following is the DOT's description of the functions of a private detective:[2]

DETECTIVE, PRIVATE EYE; UNDERCOVER AGENT: UNDERCOVER OPERATOR. Conducts private investigations to locate missing persons, obtain confidential information, and solve crimes; questions individuals to locate missing persons. Conducts surveillance of suspects using binoculars and cameras. Conducts background investigation of individual to obtain data on character, financial status, and personal history. Examines scene of crime for clues and submits fingerprints and findings to laboratory for identification and analysis. Writes reports of investigations for clients. Reports criminal information to police and testifies in court. May investigate activities of individuals in divorce and child custody cases. May arrange lie detector tests for employees of clients or witnesses. May escort valuables to protect client's property. May be employed in commercial or industrial establishments for undercover work or as personal bodyguard.

The DOT's job description for police detective is as follows:

DETECTIVE, CRIMINAL INVESTIGATION; PLAIN-CLOTHES OFFICER. Carries out investigations to prevent crimes or solve criminal cases; investigates known or suspected criminals or facts of particular case to detect planned criminal activity or clues. Frequents known haunts of criminals and becomes familiar with criminals to determine criminals' habits, associates, characteristics, aliases, and other personal information. Records and reports such information to commanding officer. Investigates crimes and questions witnesses. Examines scene of crime to obtain clues and gather evidence. Investigates suspected persons and reports progress of investigations. Arrests or assists in arrest of criminals or suspects. Testifies before court and grand jury. May be designated according to nature of crime investigated as DETECTIVE, AUTOMOBILE SECTION; DETECTIVE, HOMICIDE SQUAD, etc.

Occupational Requirements—Police Detective: Occupations in this group usually require education and/or training extending from one to over ten years, depending upon the specific kind of work. Local civil service regulations usually control the selection of police officers. People who want to do this kind of work must meet certain requirements. They must be U.S. citizens and be within certain height and weight ranges. In addition, they may be required to take written, oral, and physical examinations. The physical examinations often include tests of physical strength and the ability to move quickly and easily. To work in these jobs, persons should have the physical condition to use firearms or work on dangerous missions. Personal investigations are made of all applicants.

Most police departments prefer to hire people who have a high school education or its equal. However, some departments hire people if they have worked in related activities such as guarding or volunteer police work.

Jobs with federal law enforcement agencies usually require a college degree. For example, to be hired as a customs officer, a degree or three years of related work experience is required. FBI Special Agents are required to have a degree in law or accounting. Accounting degrees should be coupled with at least one year of related work experience.

Most management or supervisory jobs in this group are filled from within the ranks. Promotions are usually based on written examinations and job performance and are usually subject to civil service laws.

Most workers in these jobs are on call any time their services are needed. They may work overtime during emergencies. Many of these jobs expose workers to great physical danger.

Work Activities

The required work activities depend on the specific job. For example, a detective might

- set procedures, prepare work schedules, and assign duties
- direct and coordinate daily activities of a police force

- assign and supervise detectives
- investigate and arrest people suspected of the illegal sale or use of drugs
- patrol an assigned area in a vehicle or on foot and issue tickets, investigate disturbances, render first aid, and arrest suspects
- patrol an assigned area to observe illegal activities and arrest persons violating laws

Skills and Abilities

To do this kind of work, you must be able to

- understand laws and regulations written in legal language
- use practical thinking to conduct or supervise investigations
- supervise other workers
- plan the work of a department or activity
- deal with various kinds of people
- work under pressure or in the face of danger
- patrol an assigned area to observe illegal activities and arrest people suspected of violating laws
- keep physically fit
- use guns, fire-fighting equipment, and safety devices

If you are considering a career in law enforcement, the following questions may offer some guidance in assessing your interests and skills:

- Have you taken courses in government, civics, or criminology? Did you find these subjects interesting?
- Have you been a member of a volunteer fire department or emergency rescue squad? Were you given training for this work?
- Do you watch detective shows on television? Do you read detective stories? Do you try to solve mysteries?
- Have you been an officer of a school safety patrol? Do you like being responsible for the work of others?
- Have you used a gun for hunting or in target practice? Are you a good shot?
- Have you spoken at a civic or community organization? Do you like work that requires frequent public speaking?
- Have you been a military officer?
- Do you value adventure, authority, leadership, and public contact?
- Have you studied political science, sociology, or physical education?
- Do you have good eye-hand-foot coordination?
- Do you deal with people in a business-like manner?
- Do you think on your feet and use good judgment?
- Can you relate to people at all levels of society?

- Do you enjoy a variety of work and unpredictable work schedules?
- Do you work well under pressure and in dangerous situations?
- Can you function well even when specific guidelines have not been issued?
- Do you learn quickly?
- Are your math skills adequate?
- Are your verbal skills adequate?
- Are your writing skills adequate?
- Can you detect differences in forms, shapes, sounds, and colors?
- Do you take a systematic approach to your work?

Most of these questions were abstracted from occupational literature sources. As valuable as they are, these questions do not describe real-life detectives and investigators. A successful detective:

- thinks critically and logically
- makes objective judgments
- is reasonably free of bias
- works effectively as a team member or independently
- sizes up situations quickly
- responds quickly to emergencies and perilous situations
- protects information and sources
- shares information with trustworthy professional colleagues
- works long and hard on sensitive cases
- does not embarrass superiors (without just cause)
- can draw reasonable inferences and conclusions
- maintains a professional working relationship with other law enforcement, security, and intelligence agencies
- is eternally curious
- listens intently
- is not intimidating unless the situation demands it
- confirms information with independent sources
- offers no personal impressions or opinions on active cases to the media
- refers media inquiries to appropriate superiors
- has a working knowledge of the laws that he or she enforces
- has a working knowledge of constitutional limitations on authority
- assimilates information from a myriad of sources and draws logical inferences and conclusions
- is persistent, patient, and committed to deriving the truth
- separates facts from opinions, generalizations, and stereotypes
- is cool under fire from defense attorneys
- dresses appropriately to fit the requirements of varied work roles
- is enthusiastic about the work and is energetic in accomplishing the mission

- writes clear case reports that have a minimum of grammatical and spelling errors and are relatively free of jargon

Computer Theft, Fraud, and Embezzlement

Computers dedicated to business applications came into general use in 1954. One of the initial features touted by computer manufacturers—beyond the benefits of speed and the elimination of repetitious, error-prone, manual bookkeeping journalizations—was the security provided by sophisticated hardware. They claimed that employee theft, fraud, and embezzlement would be thwarted or at least minimized because of the complexity involved in committing these acts. It appeared for a time that complex hardware did indeed provide such insurance. However, although the computer made it more difficult to appropriate small sums of money, it also made it possible to steal large sums with less likelihood of discovery. Investigations of common law crimes (murder, mayhem, larceny, robbery, burglary, rape, and arson) begin with a fairly definitive statement of facts. Someone has been injured physically or financially and demands justice, that is, criminal action against the offender. Even if the offender is not known, it *is* known that a crime has been committed and against whom it was committed.

In computer crimes like fraud, larceny, and embezzlement, it is often not known by whom it was committed or, worse yet, how it was committed. The latter is often left to forensic experts. Auditing and accounting, although not considered classic forensic sciences, are useful tools in the investigation of computer-related crimes. Investigators of computer crimes must therefore have at least a general knowledge of accounting and auditing principles and techniques as well as some understanding of how computers operate with respect to recording financial transactions and financial information.

What follows is by no means an exhaustive treatment of the auditing of computerized accounting systems, but it may help you save time by directing the investigative effort to the more serious internal control weaknesses of most systems. Control weaknesses create the conditions that lead to fraud by computer, and auditing is designed to detect where such weaknesses are most likely to occur.

Accounting Systems and Auditing

An accounting system consists of records that provide detailed information about business transactions, which are called *journals,* and records that summarize account balances, which are called *ledgers.* The most commonly used journals are for the recording of cash receipts and disbursements. In other journals, sales and purchases are recorded. Ledgers can be subclassified into general ledgers—which reflect the current balance in asset, liability, revenue, and expense accounts in a summary form, that is, total debits and credits posted—and subsidiary ledgers, which reflect the specific details of transactions between the firm and its customers and suppliers, that is, accounts receivable and accounts payable. Subsidiary ledgers are kept on the basis of individual customer or vendor name.

The process of recording business transactions is called *double-entry bookkeeping*. Each transaction is divided into two parts of equal amounts: a debit entry and a credit entry. When an asset is purchased or when an expense is incurred, a debit entry is made to the appropriate asset or expense account, and an offsetting credit entry is made to a liability or revenue account. When an asset is sold or disposed of or a liability is incurred, a credit entry is made to the appropriate revenue or liability account, and an offsetting debit entry is made to an asset or expense account.

The information recording process begins with a business transaction of one of the following types: the purchase or acquisition of an asset, the incurring of an expense, the sale or disposition of an asset, or the incurring of a liability. These transactions are summarized in ledgers and result in periodic statements that assess or measure the firm's financial condition in a balance sheet and its degree of profitability in a statement of income.

An accounting system may be manually operated (handwritten entries), automated (electromechanical equipment), or computerized (electronic equipment). Some accounting systems combine the attributes of these systems.

Computerized accounting systems are designed to increase the speed with which repetitive business transactions are processed and recorded. An increase in speed is accomplished in three ways:

1. Simultaneous entries are made in journals, subsidiary ledgers, and general ledgers, thus avoiding multiple postings.
2. Unnecessary paper flow to document transactions is eliminated.
3. The number of human control points are decreased and replaced by programming controls to verify accuracy and validate expenditures.

Computerized accounting systems come in two forms: batch-oriented and on-line systems. In a batch-processing system, transactions are accumulated and entered as a group at some point in the business day or processing cycle. In on-line systems, transactions are processed as they occur. In batch processing, the controls for accuracy consist of batch totals, item counts, and hash totals. *Batch totals* are the sum of all of the amounts to be entered, that is, the total dollar amount of all of the invoices about to be entered for accounts payable processing. *Item counts* are the total number of invoices to be entered. *Hash totals*, another form of accuracy check, consist of adding up all the vendor identification numbers or payment voucher numbers before entering and then comparing the sum with the number the computer generates from the same addition while the data is being processed. If a difference exists between the hash total computed manually and the total calculated by the computer, an investigation is made to determine why more or fewer items were processed than expected. Batch totals, item counts, and hash totals are called *input controls*. They are intended to ensure the accuracy but not validity of transactions.

Validity checks involve authorization procedures established to determine whether a payment to be made is based on a legitimate claim against the company by a vendor or supplier who has actually supplied something of corresponding value. For example, in the case of a vendor who has supplied raw material for manufacturing, the steps or procedures leading up to payment are as follows:

Form	*Purpose of Document*
Purchase requisition	To limit purchasing authorities and to verify need for goods
Purchase order	To document goods ordered, quantities, quality, cost, and time of delivery
Receiving report	To verify receipt and condition of ordered goods and conformity with purchase order terms
Check voucher request	To verify accuracy of vendor invoices (quantities, pricing, and extensions)
Check	To pay for goods actually received

Validity checks are designed to accomplish these goals:

1. to separate the duties of those with property handling responsibilities and those with property recording responsibilities
2. to determine that a purchase has been approved by someone who has the authority to commit funds for purchases from an approved vendor, that the specific goods ordered were in fact received, and that the proper unit price was charged and extensions were stated correctly on the vendor's invoice
3. to provide an oversight mechanism at each step in the processing of transactions to detect errors, omissions, and improprieties in the previous step (these oversight mechanisms include the division of labor and the dual responsibility for certain transactions—that is, counter signatures, segregation of functions, dollar authorization limits, and so on—thus forcing collusion by at least two parties to effect a fraudulent transaction)

Auditors call these controls the *paper trail documentation flow*, or simply the *audit trail*. In manual accounting systems, it is possible to trace the sequence of events leading to an issued check through retained documents to determine whether the check was authorized, accurate in amount, supported by the actual receipt of the goods ordered, based on actual need, and provided for in the budget.

Computerization and automation have changed the forms of these documents. Records are still retained, but they are in electronic (magnetic impulses on tape) or microfiche form (microfilm reduction). The human controls have been replaced by control mechanisms in computer operating systems and applications programs, for example, parity checks, limit checks, echo checks, and sequencing checks.

Parity checks are controls that ensure that data initially read into a computer have been transmitted correctly to other components of the computer system. *Limit checks* are designed to flag transactions in which amounts or quantities are compared with predetermined limits or standards for such amounts or quantities. For example, if payroll checks rarely exceed $500, the payroll system can be programmed to flag any check exceeding that amount.

Echo checks are computer messages that play back a transmission to its original source for comparison. The echo check tells the transmitter of data that the data have been received as originally transmitted. *Sequencing checks* are designed to determine whether any gap in sequencing has occurred between transmissions or processing cycles of prenumbered documents such as checks, invoices, and purchase orders.

These new controls are intended primarily to assure management that the computer is processing the information, as fed into it, correctly. If incorrect data are fed in, the controls are designed to flag the transaction, order retransmission, instruct the user how to transmit properly, or log those items that seem exceptional and report them to management. However, if fraudulent messages are transmitted in proper form and amount, these controls will not detect them. Good controls discourage fraud, but they cannot prevent it.

The separation-of-duties principle and the audit trail were the main defenses against employee fraud in manual systems, and they persist in a new form today. Separation now means segregating the work efforts of computer operators from systems analysts (who design systems), from programmers (who write instructions so that the systems will operate efficiently and correctly as designed), and from people who enter data into the system. The audit trail now consists of history files, programs, flow charts, and procedures and not of supporting documents such as stock requisitions, purchase orders, receiving reports, and invoices.

In a manual system, the audit trail is made up of paper documents that support each step in a regular business transaction from requisition of goods or services to purchase, receipt of goods, and payment or from billing a customer to receipt of payment and its deposit in the bank. These paper documents are stamped with the date and time. Calculations are reviewed and approved by supervisors and authorized for processing in the next step of the transaction. Copies of the documents are kept and filed at each stage. The audit trail in a manual system is therefore quite visible.

In computerized systems, particularly in on-line systems, the audit trail is almost invisible. To gain authorization for a transaction or a processing step, a supervisor may unlock a computer terminal or a data-entry clerk may enter a password or code at the terminal. Signatures, time stamps, and initials no longer appear on source documents to prove authorization. In a manual system, paperwork accompanies a transaction from its point of origin to its end point. The paperwork literally travels with the product. In on-line computer systems, the system itself moves the product to its end point with very little human intervention.

The audit trail is used by auditors to test transactions and thereby determine whether the built-in controls are providing the checks necessary to maintain proper internal control. An effective audit trail is one that provides an auditor with the opportunity to trace or reconstruct any given transaction backward or forward from the original source of the transaction to a final total. A transaction can be traced through its entire processing cycle to see if it was entered correctly at its inception and processed correctly to arrive at its result.

Weak or Nonexistent Controls

Audit techniques involving computers are called *audit-around* and *audit-through*. The audit-around technique checks whether data entering the computer (input) matches data leaving the computer (output). Batch totals and hash totals are compared at both input and output stages. If they agree, the auditor assumes that no mistake has occurred. The audit-around technique fails because data can be manipulated while running through the computer as well as at the time of entry. The audit-through technique is more acceptable for auditing computerized accounting systems. It requires that programming logic be understood by the auditor. In the audit-around approach, the auditor is alerted to a problem only when the input total does not match the output total. If the payroll program is written so that small sums are withdrawn from each employee's check and added to the programmer's check, the auditor would not be aware of it because the total payroll amount has not changed nor has the total number of payroll checks issued. This form of fraud is referred to as *salami slicing* because a little bit is sliced off each check. The fraud does not arouse anyone's curiosity and is generally undetectable if the audit-around approach is used. This example illustrates why audits must be conducted *through* the computer. It is just as important to see what is happening inside the computer as it is to see what is happening outside it.

The logic built into accounting application programs is based on a chain of events that takes place in a normal business transaction. The logic is based on general rules and standard operating procedures (SOPs) or policies. In a well-organized, well-managed, and stable organization, these standard rules account for the majority of transactions. Exceptions or deviations are rare. In environments where crisis and chaos reign—unstable conditions, poor management, poor organization of work—transactions are handled on an ad hoc basis. Everything is an exception. There are no general rules, and in such unstable environments, opportunities for theft, fraud, and embezzlement abound. Internal controls, if they exist at all, only give the appearance or illusion of control. The absence of controls leads to fraud more often than the failure of controls. Even in reasonably well managed firms, exceptions are bound to occur. Human error alone accounts for many of these exceptions.

When computers are used for accounting, and particularly in on-line and distributed systems, the probability of error is magnified by the complexity of the system. The system's programming accommodates temporary entries such as suspense accounts (an account in which transactions reside temporarily, until they can be correctly entered), unresolved differences, unclassified expenditures, unknown vendors or payees, and inventory variation accounts. With computerized processing, data can be processed much faster than humans can correct past processing errors. Therefore, large amounts of money representing assets that have been bought, sold, or disposed of cannot be fully accounted for at any given time.

Now enter the thief. In such chaos (*chaos* is used here to denote the many items moving through the system that cannot be correctly classified yet as to expense or revenue category, or asset or liability category), even a semiliterate thief can commit fraud. The data processing department is kept so busy "plugging holes" that an ultimate system of controls is never developed. A hodgepodge of controls is the best that can be designed.

With such looseness in internal controls, a thief need not have much imagination to exploit weaknesses. If inventory postings are already running two weeks behind, no one will be the wiser if a receiving clerk on the loading dock validates a shipment as fully received when in fact it is short one or two boxes, one or two skids, or one or two barrels. Such sloppiness in work habits can lead to an even more serious problem: theft. Why not take a box home, or share the loot with a confederate (a truck driver, a receiving dock supervisor, or a colleague)? When analyzing accounts and receiving transactions, the auditor must be keenly aware that the danger of fraud lies not with normal transactions but with the exceptions, the deviations from the norm, if any exist in the environment being audited.

Investigators, too, must become aware of what is normal and abnormal in accounting systems and internal controls. Deviations from the usual course of business events represent the greatest potential threat for employee fraud because they permit the easy overriding and bypassing of controls. If thieves cannot fabricate an entire transaction, they can always fabricate an emergency or create a distraction to justify a deviation at some intermediate step in the transaction process.

Common Computer Crimes

The most common computer crimes are those in which the computer is used as a means or an instrument for effecting the crime (fraud and embezzlement) and those in which the computer is the victim of the crime (theft of information files, records, lists, and reports, and sabotage against the computer). From another perspective, computer crimes can be classified as follows:

1. *Input scams.* False, forged, and altered transactions are added to the stream of data being processed (false invoices for services or merchandise, false payroll claims, or false benefits claims).
2. *Thruput scams.* Computer programming is intentionally designed to contain hidden weaknesses (trap doors, salami slicing, Trojan horses, etc.).
3. *Output scams.* Output documents, reports, files, listings, and exceptions logs are destroyed, obliterated, suppressed, altered, or stolen.

Of the three categories, more than half of the computer crimes reported to date have been input scams that involved the submission and entry of false and fraudulent vendor invoices, expense claims, salary claims, and benefit claims. In this sense, nothing new is occurring in the world of crime. Historically, most accounting frauds have fallen into this category.

The easiest way to beat an accounting system is by creating a fake debit through a phony claim from an alleged vendor, customer, employee, or benefit claimant. The claimant is usually either nonexistent or real but not entitled to payment. Phony expense claims are made for real claimants, but they are either completely fabricated or overinflated. What is different about this form of crime today is the increasing unavailability of the phony paper documents to use as proof of the crime. The evidence now consists of electronic impulses on magnetic tape, and an investigator who is ignorant of computer systems may overlook the electronic evidence of the crime. Untrained investigators tend either to gather more electronic data than it is possible to review or to disregard the data completely and hope to gain a confession from a suspect.

Even if the suspect confesses, corroboration is required under criminal law. A theory of the crime (how it was committed) is still necessary. A broad statement of confession ("I took the money") is not enough. The investigator must reconstruct the crime from information supplied by the suspect and determine whether the method outlined by the suspect is a reasonable explanation of how the crime was committed. Supporting documentation must then be sought. Documentation might include increases in the suspect's bank accounts at the times when false claims were paid; copies of false invoices, payroll or time cards, and benefit claims; and copies of canceled checks bearing the culprit's signature or false endorsements. Although computers have made fraud detection and reconstruction more difficult, fraud can still be proved to a court's satisfaction when a confession is obtained.

When the investigator must start from scratch (there are no known suspects, only the loss is known), it is a much more difficult situation. The investigator must rely on professional assistance—a qualified audit and data-processing expert—to aid in the investigation. This assistance saves time and potential embarrassment and strengthens the case.

Computer Fraud Techniques and Countermeasures

While no classification of computer-related fraud wins the support of all auditors or investigators, a typology does help to provide perspective on the problem. The following typology is offered therefore.

I. Computer fraud techniques
   A. Input scams
      1. *Data diddling.* Changing data before or during input to the computer, that is, counterfeiting, forging, altering, or fabricating input documents. This is the most common computer scam.
      2. *Piggybacking.* A form of impersonation in which a nonauthorized person gains access to a terminal that has not been deactivated (signed off) and uses it for his or her own purposes or uses an authorized person's password code to sign on.
      3. *Imposter terminal.* Using a home computer or an off-site terminal with a telephone modem to gain access to a mainframe computer by fabricating authorization (cracking the password code) and then either intercepting data or using time on the computer free of charge.
      4. *Multiple data base manipulation.* Gaining access to one computer in a network and using that access privilege to break into other computers in the network by use of a common access code, or cracking an access protocol through successive attempts to decipher the access code and then stealing time on the computer, converting software, or manipulating data files.
   B. Thruput scams
      1. *Trojan horse.* Covertly placing instructions in a computer program so that the computer will perform unauthorized functions.
      2. *Salami slicing.* Stealing small amounts of money from a large number of sources by shaving a penny from each savings account during an interest calculation run or rounding off the mills (one-tenth of a cent) and accumulating them for transfer to a particular account.
      3. *Trap doors.* A systems programming design flaw intended to facilitate subsequent modifications or debugging. If not

edited out after the program is debugged, an unscrupulous programmer may be able to steal time on the computer or obtain data or programs without authorization.

4. *Logic bombs.* Instructions inserted in a computer operating system or program to facilitate the commission of an unauthorized or malicious act.

C. Output scams

1. *Pizza boy ploy.* Gaining access to the computer room (normally at night or on weekends when security is relaxed) by posing as a pizza delivery person or a repair technician and then stealing output reports or console logs or sabotaging the computer mainframe.

2. *Software piracy.* Stealing or copying output reports, computer files, or programs and then using them for unauthorized purposes, selling them to others (competitor firms), or offering to return them to the company for ransom.

3. *Scavenging.* Searching through the computer room's trash (old reports, operation logs, used punch cards and paper tapes, etc.) to learn enough about the system to compromise it.

II. Computer fraud countermeasures

A. Programming controls

1. One way to detect thruput scams is periodically to run the current version of a program against the original or back-up copy to determine whether any modifications or changes have been made. If the computer abuser has also modified the back-up copy, it is very difficult to determine if a program has been altered.

2. Input and output scams are easiest to detect. Thruput scams, because they take place inside the "black box," are more difficult to detect. They are less visible.

3. Good security controls are transparent. The abuser does not know he or she is being monitored or observed.

B. Data transmission security controls

1. Cryptographic transmission and data storage avoid the interception and casual perusal of sensitive information.

2. Scramblers garble the computer message being transmitted.

C. Computer and terminal access controls

1. *Passwords.* Alphabetical or numerical codes.

2. *Compartmentalization.* Restricting users to only the files and programs that they are authorized to use.

3. *Error lockout.* Shutting down the terminal's power after successive incorrect attempts to log on.

4. *Voice print recognition.*

5. *Fingerprint recognition.*
6. *Palm geometry.*
7. *Magnetic card access.*
8. *Automatic shutoff.* Occurs after transmission is completed if the operator fails to sign off.
9. *Time lock* Prevents messages from being received or transmitted at the terminal after normal working hours.
10. *Call back.* Before the user gains complete access, a phone call is made to the terminal site to verify the user's identity.
11. *Random personal information.* Before the computer allows access, it will pose random questions that are stored in its memory: "What is your mother-in-law's maiden name?" "In what hospital was your oldest child born?" "When will you celebrate your 25th wedding anniversary?" This personal information is rarely carried in a wallet. If the wallet were stolen, the thief could not use the information to impersonate the authorized user and gain access to the computer.
12. *Personal identification number (PIN).* Used in conjunction with a magnetic card that has a coded authorization. The user must present or insert both the card and the PIN (a four- or five-digit number that is committed to memory) as proof of identity.
13. *Personal signature recognition.* After logging on, the terminal operator writes his or her name with a light pen and the computer matches that signature with an authentic sample in its memory.

Accounts-Payable Scams

To make an accounts-payable scam work in a manual accounting system that has reasonably good internal controls, an employee would need to do the following:

1. Add a phony vendor to the list of approved vendors. Someone in purchasing or someone with authority to approve new vendors would have to be compromised, a new vendor authorization would have to be forged, or the approved vendor master file would have to be amended with the new name.
2. Gain access to purchase order requisition forms to fabricate a requisition and then forge the signature of someone with authority to issue such forms.
3. Issue a fraudulent purchase order. The surreptitious theft of purchase orders that have not yet been numbered sequentially would

be required, and authorization to issue the purchase order would have to be faked or forged. If purchase orders are not prenumbered, it is easier to accomplish this kind of fraud. Random numbers could be used for the purchase orders. In a computerized system, however, with proper programming controls, a purchase order with a number that is random or out of current sequence would be "flagged" as an exception. This is called a *sequence check*.

4. Fabricate a receiving report showing delivery of the goods.
5. Fabricate a vendor invoice for the amount of the goods allegedly received.
6. Fabricate an account number or expense category to be charged for the alleged purchase.
7. Issue a fabricated check requisition or check voucher.

Judging by the number of steps involved in perpetrating a fraud of this type it might be assumed that successful frauds are rare. They are not. Disbursement-type frauds are rather commonplace, and they are the most frequent of all employee frauds.

Despite what might seem like airtight control procedures, each control can be compromised or bypassed. The assumption inherent in all accounting and internal controls is that some order exists in the organization and that time is always available to process items in accordance with sound control principles. However, controls hinder processing. The payment of bills could be greatly expedited if no controls were present, so tradeoffs are continually made when backlogs develop or emergencies arise. In such circumstances, controls are compromised by the exigencies of the moment. In designing accounting and control systems, deviations from normal processing steps (deviations that permit compromises or overrides of the control procedures) are allowed. These exceptions to the general rule are what serve as the inspiration for fraud.

For example, when a critical part is necessary for the completion of a manufactured article, the purchasing department may be instructed to buy from anyone, whether approved as a vendor or not. The addition of the vendor's name to the approved vendor list may follow, not precede, the actual receipt of the part. A large order from a new customer may be so vital to the company's cash flow that normal credit checking procedures are bypassed. A large customer may demand the immediate shipment of goods, even before an invoice is properly prepared. Inventory control records may be so far behind in postings that requisitions are issued for goods that are in large supply already.

The criminal attempts to exploit these deviations or exceptions. Chaos is the criminal's stock in trade. Instead of fabricating six or seven documents, the criminal fabricates an emergency event to justify overriding or bypassing controls. For example, expenditure controls for routine purchases may be quite effective because the purchase is charged against the current year's budget. Capital expenditures come from another budgetary control—the long-range plan or budget. The signature of one person (the controller or financial vice-president) may be the only requirement for check issuance. A fabricated invoice presented to that one person may be all it takes to get an "off-line" check issued to a spurious provider of corporate services if the explanation accompanying the request is some sort of feigned emergency. The only other control might be that the amount of the check is within the check requester's capital budget and that its alleged purpose lies in an area of the business for which the check requester has responsibility.

Advice for Inexperienced Investigators

An investigator with limited knowledge of accounting should not attempt to investigate even a small fraud or embezzlement. Investigation requires a knowledge of the business, the type of fraud and its variations, the organization's internal controls, and the possible results of the fraud. What appears to be a fraud or embezzlement often turns out to be either a mistake or simple error or a Pandora's box affecting top management and outsiders. Investigators with sufficient expertise and experience can often quickly determine how deep they may need to probe, although even experienced investigators sometimes must consult legal and accounting professionals to determine to what extent an investigation is necessary.

Notes

1. VanWart v. Cook, Okla. App. 557 p. 2d 1161, 1163.
2. U.S. Department of Labor, *Dictionary of Occupational Titles* (Washington: GOP, 1992).

CHAPTER **10**

Fraud and Forensic Accounting

Forensic Accounting

Simply stated, *forensic accounting* is using accounting and auditing expertise to prove a point in a criminal or civil controversy. Forensic accounting, sometimes called *fraud auditing* or *investigative accounting,* is a skill that goes beyond the realm of corporate and management fraud, embezzlement, or commercial bribery. Indeed, forensic accounting goes beyond the general realm of white-collar crime. Forensic accounting can even be useful in homicide cases, two of which are described in this chapter. In both cases, the forensic accountants were members of the Toronto, Ontario, staff of Lindquist, Avey, MacDonald & Baskerville.

Under what conditions might forensic accounting skills be useful in a homicide investigation? Forensic accounting might be applied in homicide investigations for the following purposes:

- to analyze and determine whether a financial motive for murder exists
- to analyze financial data for clues and investigative leads
- to identify possible payments of money on a contract for murder

In determining financial motive, the accounting analysis is directed primarily toward establishing any financial benefit to the accused as a result of that person's association with the murder victim. Benefit may be shown in various ways:

- payments by the victim to the accused (for evidence of extortion)
- assets such as stocks, bonds, real estate, collectibles or antiques transferred to the accused shortly before the murder
- insurance proceeds paid to the accused as a beneficiary under a life insurance policy
- other benefits transferred to the accused such as equity in a business or a partnership interest

When analyzing the financial affairs of the victim to assist the police in the investigation, the accountant may seek to determine the following:

- the victim's business ownerships and the identity of people with whom he or she had business relationships
- whether any debts were owed *by* the victim and whether evidence exists to suggest that the victim was resisting payment on them
- whether any debts were owed *to* the victim and whether evidence exists to suggest that the debtor was resisting payment on them
- whether a financial motive can be *eliminated* as an aspect worth pursuing in the case
- whether any other motive might exist, such as a love triangle

Regina v. Serplus

In *Regina v. Serplus,* the Crown's attorney alleged that William Serplus murdered Muriel MacIntosh, with whom Serplus had lived for about two years, for the purpose of appropriating certain of her assets to his own use. Those assets included a collection of Royal Doulton figurines valued at more than $100,000, MacIntosh's private home in Toronto, with an equity of $35,000, and some pieces of jewelry.

Regina v. Kelley

In *Regina v. Kelley,* forensic accounting was used to demonstrate that the defendant, who was charged with murdering his wife, may have had a financial motive. He was the beneficiary of a $270,000 insurance policy on her life. Before her death, he had lived far beyond his means. Had it not been for the life insurance proceeds, his expensive life style would have caused his personal bankruptcy.

Until July 1980, Kelley was employed by the Royal Canadian Mounted Police (RCMP) as an undercover narcotics officer. His salary and his wife's salary totaled less than $40,000 per year, yet they lived in an exclusive high-rise apartment near Lake Ontario and leased a Porsche. After leaving the RCMP, Kelley had no known source of steady income. He borrowed heavily on credit cards and sold off assets to maintain his style of living. He invested in a number of unsuccessful business ventures. Between early 1980 and March 1981, when his wife died, his net worth declined substantially. A week after her death, Kelley flew to Hawaii with another woman. They incurred more than $100,000 in living expenses between that time and September 1981, when the insurance company paid Kelley the proceeds of his wife's policy.

One of the objectives of the Crown's attorney was to introduce documentary evidence of financial motive that would force Kelley to take the stand in his own defense. The Crown attorney and the investigating officer believe that the accounting evidence did just that. It showed that Kelley was living well beyond his means and, in the light of the other evidence introduced, suggested a motive for murder.

CHAPTER **11**

Corporate Fraud Practice Cases

This chapter provides readers with limited experience in auditing a set of practice cases that can be used for self-training and applying some of the lessons learned in earlier sections of this book.

X-Corp Credit Union Case

X-Corp is a U.S. multinational computer manufacturer. The company has very enlightened policies with respect to its personnel. It provides generous salaries and benefits and rarely lays off employees. It subscribes to a fair employment practices code and is highly regarded by the mass media for its sense of social responsibility.

One benefit it provides for its employees is a federally chartered credit union. The general manager of the credit union has historically come from the ranks of the company's middle management or finance staff. The current incumbent is the former manager of corporate administrative services.

The X-Corp Federal Credit Union has fallen on bad times since the government deregulation of financial institutions in 1978. Profits have been sagging due to large losses from loans, the high cost of funds, high general and administrative expenses, and a staff relatively unskilled in the new technologies of banking and finance.

This year, the credit union's general manager found it necessary to terminate the chief financial officer (CFO), who was a 30-year veteran of X-Corp, because he was unable to cope with all of the changes in banking laws and banking technology. The departure was amicable, however. The former CFO was given a generous early retirement bonus after waiving his rights to sue for discriminatory employment practices. He is now basking in the sun in the Cayman Islands. Because of your knowledge and experience in matters of accounting, finance, law, investigation, and criminology, you are hired as the new CFO at an annual salary of $50,000 plus a bonus if profits improve.

Scenario 1 During your first month on the job, you discover the following:

1. The accounting records are a mess.
2. There are irreconcilable differences in the general ledger to the tune of $500,000.
3. Entries related to investments are not made contemporaneously with transactions. Some entries are made months after the transaction.

Question 1 What legal, audit, or investigative action would you take?

Scenario 2 The broker through whom jumbo certificates of deposit are purchased and sold has not supplied transaction documents for all transactions and has failed to provide an accounting or confirmation of balances even after repeated requests by the outside auditor. Some of the jumbo CDs bought and sold by the credit union were issued by failed S&Ls. Although these investments are protected for up to $100,000 each, some of the CDs were of larger denominations. You do not know the current status of these CDs. The former CFO was alleged to have been trading in stocks, bonds, commodities, and futures on his own account with the same broker.

Question 2 What legal, audit, or investigative action would you take now?

Scenario 3 The former CFO had on a few occasions used a company credit card for personal expenses. When questioned, he admitted this orally and in writing and made partial restitution. The balance was paid to the credit union by its fidelity bond carrier. The loss claim was less than $2000.

Question 3 What legal, audit, or investigative action would you take now?

Scenario 4 The CFO used a personal computer with spreadsheet software to keep track of the credit union's investments in jumbo CDs and for certain other accounting applications. The data were encrypted, however, and thus far no one has been able to break the code.

Question 4 What legal, audit, or investigative action would you take now?

Scenario 5 A review of the former CFO's share-draft (checking) account at the credit union shows that he frequented a bar and made monthly payments on a condominium owned by a woman who worked for him as a data-entry clerk.

Question 5 What legal, audit, or investigative action would you take now?

Scenario 6 A review of the CFO's credit card transactions shows that he purchased a $3000 diamond ring while in Las Vegas last year.

Question 6 What legal, audit, or investigative action would you take now?

Scenario 7 An anonymous source writes to you today and says that the former CFO has a secret bank account in the Caymans and just paid $200,000 in cash for his condominium. He is also about to divorce his wife. The CFO made these comments to the source in a barroom conversation.

Question 7 What legal, audit, or investigative action would you take now?

Scenario 8 A confidential source of known reliability tells you that the former CFO lost $100,000 to a bookmaker last year. He welshed on the bet and is now being sought by a hit man.

Question 8 What legal, audit, or investigative action would you take now?

Scenario 9 After a few days on site, the audit staff of the federal regulatory agency for credit unions advises you that loan and operating losses and the mysterious disappearance of assets will eat up your statutory reserves and make the credit union insolvent—unless you can prove to their satisfaction that a bond claim for honesty and faithful performance will be presented immediately to the insurance carrier and that the claim has a reasonable chance of being paid.

Question 9 What legal, audit, or investigative action would you take now?

Emma Good Case

Emma Good is a 35-year-old divorced mother of three sons—ages 14, 9, and 7. Her former husband left her shortly before the youngest child was born and has not been heard from since. His departure was a blessing in several respects. Good no longer has to cater to his immaturity, and as a welfare recipient, she received support for her family and job training in computers. She now works at Jason Jumpers, Inc., a clothing manufacturer, as a data-entry clerk in accounts payable.

Things are not going too well for Good. Her youngest child is often sick, so she loses time from work—with no pay. Her oldest child has taken up with a group of chronic truants who roam the streets and rob people. Good thinks he is using or selling drugs, too. A year ago, Good took up with a rock musician, Blue Berry, who seems intent on making it big in the music business. He is an excellent musician but lacks the capital to buy his band new costumes, instruments, and sound and lighting equipment. He cannot afford to make demo recordings.

Berry and Good discuss his circumstances. If he could just "borrow" $100,000, he says, he could break into the music business in a big way and later pay back the principal plus interest. Good says that borrowing $100,000 from a bank is an impossible dream for them—their combined income is a little over $20,000, and they have few assets—but she thinks she might be able to "borrow" the money from Jason Jumpers. She knows that the firm's computer program for accounts payable has a weakness in controls. She can add the name of a new vendor to the master file without further approval and then order a check to be made out to the vendor. There would be a few other incidentals: stealing purchase orders and receiving reports, fabricating an invoice, filing an assumed name, and opening a bank account and post office box.

Stealing the purchase orders and receiving reports turns out to be the most difficult task, so Good changes the invoice from one involving raw materials to one involving office supplies. Jason Jumpers buys a lot of computer paper of all sorts, sizes, and descriptions, and inventory controls for it are very weak.

Good processes the phony invoice for $100,000 through her terminal, which is on-line to a computer in another state. Unknown to her, there is an additional control feature. All vendor checks in excess of $10,000 are flagged for review before mailing. For some reason, the control fails and the check is mailed. Good and Berry visit the post office several days later, remove the check, endorse it, and deposit it into the phony company's account. Before they can draw any funds, however, they are arrested based on a complaint filed by Jason Jumpers, which had discovered the fraud.

1. From a legal standpoint, what arguments, pro and con, can be made on the issue of whether Good formulated a "criminal intent"?
2. If Good were charged with mail fraud, what elements of proof would be required?
3. In conducting the investigation, a Jason Jumper security officer told an official of the bank branch where the check was deposited that Good and her oldest child were suspected of using and selling drugs. Would that be cause for liability in a slander or defamation suit? What if it were true?
4. The banker showed the Jason Jumper investigator Good's personal bank account records as a matter of professional courtesy. Is there an invasion of her privacy rights? Would your answer be the same if the investigator were a federal agent? A state police officer? How so?

5. What action—criminal, civil, or otherwise—would you recommend that Jason Jumpers take against Good? Why?
6. Could Good be charged with civil fraud, criminal fraud, or both? Under what circumstances?
7. Could Jason Jumpers recover the $100,000 in the bank account of the phony company Good created?
8. Suppose the internal control procedures of Jason Jumpers had worked and the $100,000 check was flagged and intercepted be fore it was mailed out. Was a crime committed? If so, what crime or crimes?
9. Suppose Good makes a complete and voluntary confession. Is any other evidence needed?

ABCO Case

Last year was a banner year for ABCO Co., a consumer product manufacturer that is number two in its industry. Revenue, profit, and market share reached record levels. This year's financial plan calls for a modest increase of 10% in revenue, 8% in gross profits, and 0.5% in market share to be taken mainly from the number one company, XYX Co. If those goals are reached, there will be a bonus for everyone.

ABCO's Midwest Division shared in the good fortune of its parent company last year, and this year it optimistically forecasted revenue, gross profit, and market share increases in accordance with the corporate plan. Midwest Division came through the first quarter right on target, but in the fourth month of this year, consumers spent their money on other things. Sales, profit, and market share goals were not reached. That was hard to accept at headquarters, but the problem was national. Midwest Division was admonished to move more decisively to correct the problem.

Unfortunately, in the fifth month, sales slumped again for both ABCO's Midwest Division and XYX's Midwest Division. XYZ countered with a heavy advertising and a price-slashing strategy to move its products in the marketplace. That caught ABCO's Midwest Division off guard. When sales, profits, and market share were reported to headquarters, the feedback was crude, and the implication was not so subtle: "Get your numbers to come out right, or we'll get somebody who can."

The general manager and regional director of sales for the Midwest Division called a meeting of all sales personnel and made it clear that customers had to be sold a lot of product. The goals had to be met. Without additional advertising and price cuts, however, retailers and consumers were not about to take anymore of ABCO's product. As the sixth month was coming to an end and disaster loomed on the horizon, the sales manager ordered the sales representatives who handled the biggest accounts to process fictitious sales through the accounting system to "buy some time." The fictitious sales could be reversed by credit memos in the following month.

The sales reps did as they were told but were concerned that inventory levels would give away the scheme. The sales manager reassured them.

The seventh month came, and sales were again less than predicted. The sales manager enlisted the aid of the production and warehouse managers, whom he asked to "juggle the inventory for a month" as a favor. The eighth month passed, and actual sales were still off. Inflated sales by that time came to $5 million, and now all customer accounts were being manipulated at month-end and relieved by credit memos during the following month. By year end, everyone in sales, accounting, data processing, production, and warehousing was involved in the scheme, which then involved a sales overstatement of $10 million.

ABCO's total sales are $500 million this year. You are the audit manager of the public accounting firm that does the audit of ABCO's Midwest Division. What would you do if the above information were brought to your attention before you began your audit? What if you learned about it from an employee during your audit? What if you found the errors and irregularities in the sales and inventory accounts during your audit?

CHAPTER 12

Chronology of Corporate and White-Collar Crimes: 1985 to 1990

News Summaries

The following news summaries originally appeared in the *Forensic Accounting Review,* which is published by Computer Protection Systems, Inc., Plymouth, Michigan. The months given refer to the publication date in the *Forensic Accounting Review.*

January 1985

- Ban Cal Tri-State Corp., a unit of Japan's Mitsubishi Bank, Ltd., reported that an internal investigation disclosed that a trust officer (now deceased) had defrauded the bank of about $10 million. (*Wall Street Journal,* 11/28/84.)
- Florafax International, Inc., was charged by the SEC with overstating financial results for fiscal years 1981 and 1982. The SEC alleges that the company recorded as sales, shipments of flower containers that had not been ordered by customers, thus inflating sales and earnings. (*Wall Street Journal,* 11/29/84.)
- GM fired, demoted, or forced the resignations or retirements of 20 white-collar employees because the company believed that they accepted favors from a supplier firm. GM's employee conduct guidelines prohibit the acceptance of such favors as cash payoffs, gifts, or special accommodations from vendors, suppliers, and contractors. It was alleged that the supplier provided free use of Sun Belt condominiums, hired relatives of GM personnel, provided gifts and free travel, and made cash payoffs to GM employees. (*Detroit Free Press,* 12/2/84.)

February 1985

- The former president of the Columbia Pacific Bank in Portland, Oregon, was indicted by a federal grand jury on 70 counts of bank fraud, conspiracy, and misapplication of more than $3 million in bank funds. (The bank failed in 1983.) The indictment alleges that the former president and a local real estate developer arranged a series of phony loans to conceal the fact that they were the true borrowers. (*Wall Street Journal,* 1/11/85.)

- A former Bekins Co. executive pleaded guilty to accepting kick-backs from law firms. The former senior vice-president and general counsel of the moving firm was charged with defrauding his employer of $234,000 through kickbacks, misappropriated funds, and overpayments of legal fees. He created and used a fictitious law firm to handle the kickbacks from real law firms in New York, Illinois, Texas, Florida, and Arizona. (*Wall Street Journal,* 1/22/85.)

- A top GM purchasing executive is on leave pending the completion of an investigation about an apparent gift of $1200 worth of Astroturf® carpeting provided by GM's leading supplier of tires—Uniroyal, Inc. Both GM and Uniroyal have policies against giving and receiving expensive gifts. (*Detroit Free Press,* 1/20/85.)

- Bribery is a tradition in the oil areas of the Southwest, according to the *Wall Street Journal.* Rig bosses at drilling sites are the favorite targets of bribery. Suppliers provide them with cash, liquor, prostitutes, and lavish gifts and entertainments. In some cases, officials of supplier firms and rig bosses get so "cozy" that rig bosses authorize and approve overpayments to suppliers and then split the proceeds. (*Wall Street Journal,* 1/15/85.)

March 1985

- The First National Bank of Boston, a unit of Bank of Boston, Inc., the 16th largest bank in the U.S. and a "blue blood" among domestic banks, found itself in a rare jam in February. First National pleaded guilty to a felony charge of failing to report $1.22 billion in cash transactions with foreign banks. None of the money was electronically transferred; instead, it was carried across the Atlantic in satchels on commercial airline flights. About $1.16 billion of the total transactions were between First National and Swiss-based banks. Also included among the cash transfers were cash purchases of cashier's checks by reputed members of organized crime organizations. Some of the bank's North End branch managers had exempted one alleged Mafia family member from reporting cash deposits and withdrawals because he was engaged in "legitimate" businesses that generated large amounts of currency. These exemptions are highly prized by organized crime members, particularly those in Miami who are engaged in drug trafficking. Bank examiners, however, do not make a major effort to police or monitor such exemptions. Bank of Boston officials apparently delegated the responsibility of granting such exemptions to its branch managers. (*Wall Street Journal,* 2/8/85, 2/11/85, 2/14/85, 2/15/85, 2/22/85.)

- One might wonder why the financial press was so critical of Bank of America for $37 million in mortgage loans that went sour in the fourth quarter of 1984. The first news of that loan loss hit the press in late January 1985. The implications were that the collateral that supported some loans for Texas commercial and residential developments was overinflated. By mid-February 1985, the Bank of America loss was said to have escalated by an additional $58 million, for a total loss of $95 million, from inflated collateral on real estate loans. Where the case will end is unknown at this time, but Bank of America probably was not the only bank hoodwinked by unethical real estate speculators and developers. Before it is all over, total bank losses may exceed $500 million, and as many as a dozen people may be indicted. (*Wall Street Journal,* 1/28/85, 1/30/85, 2/8/85, 2/11/85, 2/12/85, 2/14/85.)
- The former president and vice-president of Abilene National Bank of Texas were indicted for accepting kickbacks from loan applicants, falsifying bank records, and failing to report currency transactions to the Treasury Department. (*Wall Street Journal,* 2/21/85.)
- The IRS has been investigating cash transactions in about two hundred Florida banks since it discovered several months ago that the banks were awash with $6.6 billion more in cash than usual. Several of the Florida banks had also improperly exempted several suspected drug traffickers from reporting requirements. (*Wall Street Journal,* 2/19/85.)
- In addition to the Treasury Department's requirement that banks report unusual currency transactions of $10,000 or more, it will soon issue a regulation compelling gambling casinos to report such transactions. The expected effective date is 5/1/85. (*Wall Street Journal,* 2/1/85.)
- A $2.7 million embezzlement charge was made against a freight claims director by his employer, the Chessie Systems Railroads. (*Wall Street Journal,* 2/13/85.)

April 1985

- The SEC moved against an Alexander Grant partner in Fort Lauderdale, Florida. The commission charged Jose Gomez, the former AG partner, with accepting $125,000 in payments from ESM principals. Gomez was the audit partner on the ESM account. An unqualified opinion had been rendered on ESM's financial condition just before its failure. (*Wall Street Journal,* 3/21/85.)

- Accounting "gimmickry" makes many savings and loan associations appear solvent, according to a recent *Wall Street Journal* front-page review. The article, written by the *Journal*'s specialist on the accounting profession, Lee Berton, suggests that S&L "solvency" is helped by a lot of accounting legerdemain. About one-third of the S&Ls would look sick in terms of their net worth if they had to remove "goodwill" from their balance sheets. (*Wall Street Journal*, 3/21/85.)
- Forty-five large banks are seeking assurances from the Treasury Department that charges will not be pressed if they confess to reporting violations. The Treasury Department is now investigating 41 of these banks for such violations. (*Wall Street Journal*, 3/12/85.)
- E.F. Hutton & Co. received media criticism this month for allegedly accepting $13 million in small bills from a previously unknown client who turned out to be a money courier for an organized crime heroin trafficking business. The money was delivered to Hutton during a five-month period in 1982 and was carried in by the courier in gym bags and suitcases. The courier is one of 38 people recently indicted in a $1.5 billion heroin trafficking case called the *Pizza Connection*. (*Wall Street Journal*, 3/12/85.)

May 1985

- General Dynamics (GD) is facing several allegations by government auditors and investigators:
  - GD kept two sets of books on submarine contracts to conceal cost overruns.
  - GD low-balled its bids to get contracts and then charged the government for cost overruns.
  - Overruns on one submarine contract came to almost $1 billion, and GD was reimbursed for $789 million.
  - GD overcharged the Defense Department by about $244 million during the past decade. GD is the subject of concurrent investigations by the Justice Department, IRS, and SEC. (*Wall Street Journal*, 4/3/85, 4/5/85, 4/8/85, 4/10/85.)
- Joseph H. Sherick, the inspector general of the Department of Defense (DOD), reports that the department now has 750 fraud-trained criminal investigators. He wants to add four hundred more to do a better job of policing 15 million DOD contracts worth $146 billion. In 1984, DOD obtained 174 indictments and 181 convictions. (*USA Today*, 4/25/85.)
- Purchasing agents of three California defense contractors (Northrup, Hughes, and Teledyne) were indicted for accepting kickbacks from a California subcontractor. The indictment charges that the

kickbacks were usually paid in cash and amounted to about 5% of the contract award. (*Wall Street Journal*, 4/25/85.)

- Half of all U.S. mobile home manufacturers (about 45 firms) pleaded guilty to defrauding the Veterans' Administration (VA) by padding invoices for mobile homes purchased by veterans. (*Wall Street Journal*, 4/10/85.)
- A Texas businessman pleaded guilty to charges that he channeled $10 million in payoffs to two top officials of Mexico's government owned oil giant, Pemex. The bribes were paid to obtain $640 million worth of oil field equipment orders from the government officials. (*Wall Street Journal*, 4/5/85.)

June 1985

- Fraud is often seen in the behavior of selected segments of industry, but rarely has an entire industry been accused of fraud. Mobile home manufacturers and dealers have been so accused by the Veterans' Administration. The VA, which guarantees loans on mobile homes purchased by veterans, claims that manufacturers and dealers in mobile homes have padded invoices to accommodate a kickback practice whereby manufacturers returned part of the excess billings to dealers to get them to carry their lines. The excess, or "pack," allegedly resulted in an inflated price for the buyer and an inflated balance for VA financing. The VA says that it is fraud. (*Wall Street Journal*, 5/20/85.)
- The IRS reports that tax fraud is on the increase. The "tax gap"— that is, overstated deductions and credits and unreported income— will rise to $92 billion in 1986, an increase from $62 billion in 1982. If tax revenues from illegal activities like drug trafficking and gambling were added, the tax gap in 1986 would exceed $100 billion—equal to half of the current budget deficit of the United States. (*Wall Street Journal*, 5/6/85.)
- Lloyd's of London found that fraud can hit the high and mighty as well as the uninformed lower classes. About 1500 investors in a Lloyd's syndicate were recently advised that their underwriting groups sustained large losses, not only from exposures like product liability, medical malpractice, and personal injury, but from mismanagement and fraud. The losers include members of the British royal family, Middle East magnate Adnan Khashoggi, and Lloyd's own chairman, Peter Miller. Syndicate members may have to contribute an extra $25,000 in addition to their previous investment losses of about $100,000 each. Not only were underwriting losses sustained, but syndicate members were advised that about £38.9 million had been spirited away to offshore places and then used to

purchase or finance yachts, jets, and racehorses by certain of the syndicate's managers. (*Barron's,* 5/20/85.)

August 1985

- Bank fraud and embezzlement losses in 1984 reached $382 million, an increase of $100 million from 1983. (*Security Letter,* 7/1/85.)
- Four large New York banks have agreed to pay civil fines for failing to report certain currency transactions to the IRS. Chase Manhattan will pay $360,000; Manufacturers Hanover will pay $320,000; Irving Trust will pay $295,000; and Chemical Bank will pay $210,000. The banks made voluntary disclosures of the unreported transactions in March 1985. (*Wall Street Journal,* 6/19/85.)
- Bank failures continue to rise. "Problem" banks now number 987 (a new record), and 22 banks are being added to the watch-list each month. Thus far in 1985, about 55 banks have failed. By year end, 100 failures are expected. Last year, 79 banks failed, a post-Depression record. (*Wall Street Journal,* 7/12/85.)
- Congressional investigators took the Federal Home Loan Bank Board to task for failing to act expeditiously when it appeared that Beverly Hills Savings and Loan Association was headed for disaster. (The thrift was taken over by the Home Loan Bank Board in April 1985, but bank board examiners had been reporting serious problems for three years.) The Home Loan Bank Board chairman, Edwin Gray, denied any regulatory breakdown but said that his staff of 750 auditors is "severely overworked." The causes attributed to Beverly Hills S&L's downfall were questionable investments in real estate and "junk bonds," heavy reliance on brokered deposits, poor internal controls, and the auditing performance of the S&L's outside auditors. The auditing firm denies that its audit was deficient in any way. (*Wall Street Journal,* 6/19/85, 7/16/85.)

In two *Wall Street Journal* reports on July 16, 1985 (pages 1 and 6), the following critiques are made:

- While banking continues to grow, bank examiners continue to dwindle. There were 5000 examiners in 1980 but only 4400 in 1985.
- While banking becomes more sophisticated, the skills of bank examiners do not keep up. Training, education, and experience are deficient.
- Bank examinations are no longer unannounced. Banks are informed of the length and scope of the examination before the audit.
- Endless travel "burns out" bank examiners, and turnover is high.

- The quantity of audits is preferred over quality of audits.
- Bank examiners are not paid competitive salaries.

September 1985

- Big 8 CPA firms have paid nearly $180 million in out-of-court malpractice settlements in the last five years, according to the *Wall Street Journal*. This is why their professional liability insurance rates have soared this year, increasing 200 to 400% from last year. (*Wall Street Journal*, 7/26/85.)
- The Management Fraud Commission was formed by the American Institute of Certified Public Accountants (AICPA), Internal Auditors Institute (IAI), American Association of Accountants (AAA), Financial Executives Institute (FEI), and National Association of Accountants (NAA), which are all accounting-related associations. Ray J. Groves, AICPA chairman and partner in Ernst & Whinney, said, "The Commission will study management fraud in an effort to identify ways to detect and prevent such improprieties." Another major goal is to determine whether increased management fraud is the result of a decline in professionalism on the part of those responsible for financial information. That is, has deregulation unwittingly contributed to the incidence of management fraud? (*Today*, published by the Institute of Internal Auditors, July/August 1985.)
- The E.F. Hutton case gets more "sticky" with each passing month. It would not be surprising if the case becomes a cause célèbre for the U.S. Attorney General. It is beginning to look more and more like Hutton top managers played a little fast and loose with federal law enforcers and provided them with documents that did not convey the whole truth about the magnitude of the Hutton checking scheme or convey the high level of involvement of Hutton topsiders. Consider the following examples:
  - In 1981, Hutton allegedly paid $440,000 to Chemical Bank for persistent bank overdrafts. The payment was approved by a Hutton senior executive months before top managers claim that they first learned about Hutton's widespread overdraft scheme.
  - Hutton's former president asked for and received a detailed accounting of the profits earned by the Hutton branches that were most involved in "aggressive" cash management.
  - Despite many years of complaint from bankers about Hutton's aggressive cash management schemes, top Hutton managers continued to encourage such practices.
  - Hutton officials now concede that certain documents covered by a subpoena were not turned over to federal investigators until a

subsequent search uncovered them. (*Wall Street Journal,* 7/25/
85, 7/31/85, 8/2/85, 8/6/85, 8/15/85.)
• White-collar crime seems to be *leaping* forward! Take, for example, the loss claim experience of insurance companies that write
fidelity bonds to guarantee employee honesty. The Surety Association of America, a trade group to which fidelity insurance underwriters belong, provided the following data on recent direct losses
incurred by its members:

Year	Loss Claims	Percentage Increase
1979	$162 million	
1980	$178 million	9.8
1981	$213 million	19.6
1982	$283 million	32.8
1983	$318 million	12.3
1984	(Not available yet)	

October 1985

• Crocker National Bank was fined $2.25 million for failing to report
certain currency transactions totaling $3.98 billion. The fine is the
largest civil penalty ever imposed by the Treasury Department for
failure to report unusual currency transactions. (*Wall Street Journal,* 8/28/85.)
• The SEC brought suit against a former chief financial officer of
Tonka Corp., charging that he schemed with three others to defraud the company of about $2 million. Tonka funds were alleg-
edly transferred to another company for "investment" purposes.
The SEC also charged Tonka with having inadequate internal controls to avert a misappropriation of funds. (*Wall Street Journal,*
9/25/85.)
• GTE was charged in a federal criminal suit with conspiring to secure classified documents to help it prepare bids on military contracts involving electronic warfare products. (*Wall Street Journal,*
9/11/85.)
• A former divisional controller of Aydin Corp., a maker of telecommunications, radar, and electronic intelligence-gathering equipment, accused the firm of firing him because he refused to take
part in a scheme to pay $262,500 to foreign officials in exchange
for business in their country. Aydin denies the charges. (*Wall
Street Journal,* 9/13/85.)
• After many years of investigation, the former president of Saxon
Industries, Inc., pleaded guilty to charges of fraud, stemming from

a scheme to inflate earnings by overstating inventory and other accounting machinations. (*Wall Street Journal,* 9/4/85.)

January 1986

- In federal law enforcement circles, indictments, trials, and civil litigation were once deferred during the holiday period. However, December 1985 may go down in history as the peak month of white-collar crime prosecutions and civil actions for fraud. Consider the following examples:
  - Marvin L. Warner and others linked to the Ohio thrift crisis were indicted by an Ohio grand jury. (*Wall Street Journal,* 12/16/85.)
  - A fund raiser for the American Cancer Society was indicted by a New York federal grand jury in a scheme to generate $4 million in phony charitable tax deductions. (*Wall Street Journal,* 12/19/85.)
  - A former senior clerk for Kidder Peabody in New York was indicted for stealing $6 million in U.S. government securities from the brokerage house. (*Wall Street Journal,* 12/16/85.)
  - Eight current and former officials of Paradyne Corp. were indicted for conspiring to bribe officials of the Social Security Administration to obtain a contract for a computer system. (*Barrons,* 12/16/85.)
  - NASA administrator James M. Beggs, a former General Dynamics Corp. executive vice-president, was indicted for improperly charging $7.5 million in cost overruns on a defense contract. Beggs vehemently denied the charges. (*Wall Street Journal,* 12/3/85.)

February 1986

- The ESM Government Securities case continues to show external auditors in a very poor light. The former managing partner of Alexander Grant & Co. of southern Florida, already convicted of grand theft and obstruction of justice, pleaded guilty to forging the will of an ESM officer. The accountant also agreed to cooperate with federal and state authorities and to testify against other defendants in the ESM case. (*Wall Street Journal,* 1/14/86.)
- In a case related to ESM, the state official who is overseeing the liquidation of Home State Savings Bank of Cincinnati, which failed because of its dealings with ESM, has brought suit against Home State's auditors, Arthur Andersen and Co. The Ohio state S&L official alleges that the auditors did not use "due care" in certifying Home State's financial statements for 1981, 1982, and 1983.

Arthur Andersen & Co. denies the allegations and claims that it relied on audits of ESM conducted by Alexander Grant & Co. (*Wall Street Journal,* 1/13/86.)

- While Ohio was having its problems with the Home State S&L debacle, Maryland was cleaning up a mess with Old Court Savings & Loan, which crumbled in May 1985. (*Wall Street Journal,* 1/6/86.)
- A steel buyer at John Deere & Co.'s Moline, Illinois, plant was indicted by a federal grand jury for defrauding the company of $1 million. The indictment charges that steel shipments were funneled through phony warehouses, invoices were marked up, and the difference was paid to the Deere & Co. steel buyer. (*Wall Street Journal,* 1/24/86.)
- In New Jersey, federal law enforcement officials are conducting a broad investigation into payoffs and kickbacks by vendors to purchasing agents and high officials of large companies. Two former employees of Hoffman-LaRoche, Inc., have already pleaded guilty to tax fraud stemming from their acceptance of $400,000 in kickbacks from printers to whom they had referred work. (*Wall Street Journal,* 1/24/86.)
- It is becoming harder to get quotations on banker's blanket bonds, and even when a quote is made, it is likely to be 100% more than a year or so ago. Deductibles are higher, and maximums are lower too. The loss experience on banker's blanket bonds has not been good, as the following shows (*ABA Banking Journal,* January 1986):

Year	Direct Premiums Earned	Direct Losses Incurred	Loss Ratio
1984	$112,552,578	$157,568,775	140.0
1983	110,188,806	116,171,181	105.4
1982	114,721,968	95,857,600	83.6

- Bankers are not the only ones being charged by federal authorities for money laundering. In Miami last month, a federal judge ordered a CPA to pay a fine of $6,495,000 and sentenced him to 35 years in prison for laundering narcotics money. In May 1983, the defendant was arrested at the Fort Lauderdale airport carrying $5.4 million in cash, which he was about to take to Panama. (*Wall Street Journal,* 1/3/86.)

March 1986

- The IRS has a major fraud problem on its hands. A number of its Philadelphia audit staff members were recently indicted for accepting about $230,000 in bribe payments. Two local tax accountants were also indicted for making these payments. Corruption in the Philadelphia office of the IRS has been the subject of a federal investigation for over a year. An earlier indictment charged the CEO of a fashion design firm with tax evasion and bribery. (*Wall Street Journal*, 2/7/86.)

- The chairman of Interstate Cigar Co. of Boston pleaded guilty to charges that stemmed from kickbacks paid to a purchasing agent of the Stop and Shop supermarket chain. In all, some $256,000 in kickbacks were paid through a "straw" corporation under the guise of brokerage commissions. (*Wall street Journal*, 2/6/86.)
- A Merrill Lynch sales representative was arrested when one of his clients (his uncle) discovered that his account balance had been overstated by $47 million. The sales rep fabricated monthly statements to deceive his uncle into believing that his account was being managed well and that it had grown substantially. In fact, the nephew had engaged in many transactions resulting in loss. (*Wall Street Journal*, 2/18/86.)

May 1986

- A Northrup Corp. engineer was accused of setting up a bogus supplier company and recommending that Northrup award the company $600,000 in subcontracts. (*Wall Street Journal*, 2/25/86.)
- Four former G.D. Searle & Co. executives and an outside contractor were charged with defrauding Searle of $500,000 by submitting invoices from fictitious companies for payment. They allegedly split the proceeds. (*Wall Street Journal*, 3/20/86.)
- A former employee of F.W. Woolworth was indicted for defrauding the company of $2 million in a scheme in which he allegedly altered store leases and forged invoices for fictitious legal and building maintenance expenses. (*Wall Street Journal*, 4/16/86.)
- The SEC sued three former top executives of Oak Industries, Inc., for fraud and disclosure violations, charging that they caused the company to overstate its earnings for 1984. A loss of some $46 million was incurred rather than the reported profit of $4.1 million for that year. (*Wall Street Journal*, 3/28/86.)
- A scheme in which phony invoices were allegedly supplied for a fee to certain garment makers in New York caused the IRS to lose $100 million in taxes. About 170 companies joined in the scheme, which was led by a New Yorker who supplied the fictitious invoices. One garment district businessman used more than 700 of the phony invoices to justify $25 million in false expenses. (*Wall Street Journal*, 4/3/86.)
- An accounts payable clerk at Michigan Consolidated Gas Co. was

charged with issuing three checks totaling $145,373 to a fictitious contractor—her husband, who used a pseudonym. A company internal auditor discovered the alleged fraud and referred it to the FBI. (*Detroit Free Press*, 4/25/86.)

June 1986

- Fraud was everywhere in the news this past month. It made the front pages and the national network news shows. Dennis B. Levine's $12.6 million "insider" caper, Greyhound Leasing's second multimillion dollar embezzlement in two years, and the vice-chairman of the U.S. Postal Service's Board of Governors, who lined his pockets at government expense, were but three of the stories.
- The chief financial officer of Tele Video Systems, Inc., was charged by a U.S. Federal District Court Judge of defrauding his employer of $900,000 and the CEO of his employer's firm of $1.3 million, most of which he allegedly gambled away in Reno, Lake Tahoe, Las Vegas, and Atlantic City.
- A New York accountant pleaded guilty in a huge tax fraud scheme whereby fictitious trades in forward contracts (futures) for metals were used to create bogus losses that were then sold as "tax shelters." In all, $445 million in false income tax deductions were generated, with a loss to the IRS of some $250 million. (*Wall Street Journal*, 6/6/86.)
- Employees at the Defense Industrial Supply Center in Philadelphia stand accused of accepting bribes from suppliers. More than two dozen former Supply Center purchasing agents and officers of supplier firms have been convicted or have pleaded guilty to bribery charges. Supply Center buyers were alleged to have demanded 5% of contract amounts. (*Wall Street Journal*, 5/28/86.)

July 1986

- ESM Government Securities, Inc., was in the news again this month. Its former president, Nicholas B. Wallace, was convicted of conspiracy and fraud charges in a scheme to keep the firm afloat years after it became insolvent, thus enabling the company to defraud customers of more than $300 million. The scheme involved the use of the same securities as collateral for loans from multiple lenders and the falsification of the company's financial statements to conceal its operating losses. The record $300 million loss makes ESM the new landmark case in corporate fraud. The previous leader was Equity Funding at $200 million. (*Wall Street Journal*, 7/3/86.)
- In another development of the ESM case, Grant Thornton, succes-

sor to Alexander Grant & Co., ESM's former auditor, agreed to pay $50 million to 17 public bodies who had been customers of ESM. When ESM was closed by the SEC in March 1985, these public bodies incurred losses of $105 million. The settlement will allow them to recoup about 48¢ on the dollar. They previously received about 22¢ on the dollar from the U.S. Bankruptcy Court, which is administering ESM's remaining assets. (*Wall Street Journal,* 7/8/86.)

- When ESM failed, it took with it two business related S&Ls: American S&L of Miami and Home State Savings of Cincinnati. Home State's failure then led to the crisis in state-chartered S&Ls in Ohio and, shortly thereafter, to the state-chartered S&L crisis in Maryland. The Maryland crisis was brought about by the downfall of Old Court Savings and Loan. Jeffrey A. Levitt, former president of Old Court, was recently sentenced to 30 years in prison and fined $12,000 for theft and misappropriation of funds. He pleaded guilty in May 1986 to embezzling about $14 million while president of Old Court. (*Wall Street Journal,* 7/3/86.)
- As a result of the Old Court failure, Maryland is now suing a Baltimore law firm for $450 million. The state alleges that the firm engaged in malpractice when it represented Maryland's S&L insurance fund, Jeffrey A. Levitt, and Old Court simultaneously, which Maryland claims is a conflict of interest. The law firm denies any wrongdoing. (*Wall Street Journal,* 7/7/86.)
- The Federal Savings and Loan Insurance Corporation (FSLIC) filed suit against certain former officers and directors of Butterfield Savings and Loan Association of Santa Ana, California. The FSLIC seeks $40 million in the lawsuit, claiming that the defendants defrauded the thrift and violated their fiduciary duties by making imprudent loans to themselves and others and then attempting to conceal the S&L's declining net worth. The S&L was declared insolvent in 1985. (*Wall Street Journal,* 6/20/86.)

August 1986

- E.F. Hutton Group, Inc., sued a number of Texas business owners for defrauding it of $48 million in 1984 and 1985. The defendants are accused of conducting a trading scheme whereby they invested proceeds from uncollected checks to buy additional securities. Hutton is also reviewing the conduct of its own employees in the transactions under question and says it will take disciplinary action if necessary. (*Wall Street Journal,* 7/22/86.)
- In relation to Hutton's own overdrafting practices of a few years back, the SEC is about to lift a ban that barred Hutton from managing or underwriting mutual funds. The SEC stated that the firm

had been penalized enough for its past misdeeds. Hutton paid $3 million in fines and created an $8 million reserve to pay bank claims resulting from the overdraft scheme. (*Wall Street Journal,* 8/4/86.)

- The U.S. Justice Department reports that 25% of federal prosecutions now involves a white-collar crime, an increase from 20% in 1980 and 8% in 1970. (*Security World,* July 1986.)
- The former head of security at Glaxo Holding's Zebulon, North Carolina, plant was convicted of attempting to sell the formula for the company's anti-ulcer drug to a competing firm. (*Wall Street Journal,* 7/21/86.)
- In a civil suit brought by the company, a former public relations executive for Revlon, Inc., was accused of approving fraudulent invoices totaling $1.1 million from an outside printing company. (*Wall Street Journal,* 7/31/86.)
- Robert C. Bonner, U.S. Attorney at Los Angeles, California, reported that "corrupt practices are widespread and longstanding" in the defense industry. Bonner added, "Many buyers are on the take, and many suppliers are willing to make under-the-table payments." His comments were made in relation to the indictment of 19 employees of defense contracting firms for offering and accepting kickbacks. (*Wall Street Journal,* 7/25/86.)
- Litton Industries, Inc., pleaded guilty to defrauding the Pentagon of $6.3 million on defense contracts. The fraud was uncovered during a DOD audit of a Litton subsidiary in Philadelphia. False cost and pricing data were used to increase billings to the DOD. (*Wall Street Journal,* 7/16/86.)

September 1986

- Citibank and Marine Midland Bank of New York were the victims of a huge check-kiting scheme perpetrated by a transit mix cement firm in New York. Some 15,000 checks with a face value of $9.2 billion flowed back and forth between the two banks, making the scheme bigger than the E.F. Hutton kite, which involved about $4 billion. When discovered, the principal actors in the scheme made restitution. (*Wall Street Journal,* 8/11/86.)
- Prudential-Bache was allegedly the victim of an employee fraud. A former employee of the Prudential-Bache London office was accused by British authorities of fraudulently transferring $8.5 million in bonds from the London office to a Swiss bank account. The alleged scam was discovered before funds or securities were diverted from the Swiss bank account. There was some question about the adequacy of Bache's security system; the culprit allegedly realized that a transfer could be effected by way of a home

computer and a modem if the password was known. (*Wall Street Journal*, 9/3/86.)

October 1986

- A bookkeeper in the Chicago office of Domino's Pizza, Inc., pleaded guilty to embezzling $1 million from the company. She spent the funds on furs, boats, and eight trips to Hawaii. Her embezzlement put such a severe strain on the Chicago region's financial performance that employee bonuses had to be cut by 75%. How did she do it? She lapped on the company's state sales, payroll, and income taxes. When delinquency notices came in, she just threw them away. (*Detroit Free Press*, 9/20/86.)

December 1986

- Robert Richter, former vice-president and controller of Union Labor Life Insurance, pleaded guilty to wire fraud in connection with a $900,000 diversion of the insurance company's funds. (*Wall Street Journal*, 12/1/86.)
- An employee of the City of Detroit's Department of Transportation was charged with authorizing a check for $141,000 to a vendor for work that was never performed by the vendor. (*Crain's Detroit News*, 11/10/86.)
- A recent U.S. government study indicates that 80% of convicted white-collar criminals serve little or no time in jail. (*Detroit Free Press*, 11/17/86.)

January 1987

- A New York Metropolitan Transit Authority data-processing clerk inadvertently left a schedule of phantom employees on her desk. A supervisor spotted it and wondered who all the unknown people were. The resulting investigation revealed that the clerk had conspired with a temporary help agency and authorized overbillings of $10,000 per month for over a year. (*Security Letter*, 12/15/86.)

March 1987

- The Pentagon announced that it is investigating 59 of the nation's largest defense contractors for contract violations. Last year at this time, only 40 firms were under investigation. (*Wall Street Journal*, 2/23/87.)
- One defense contractor, Martin-Marietta, pleaded guilty to federal charges in a travel rebate scheme that supposedly led to inflated

billings. Martin-Marietta has a travel subsidiary that books travel for its personnel. The agency receives a commission or rebate from the hotels and airlines that get the business. Those refunds, rebates, or commissions were allegedly not passed on to the Defense Department. (*Wall Street Journal,* 2/18/87.)

- The state banking commissioner of Oklahoma was suspended by the governor for allegedly using inside information to determine when to sell shares in a troubled bank. The bank had been under the commissioner's supervision, and he allegedly personally held or controlled 50,000 shares of the bank's stock. The commissioner claims that he placed his bank holdings in a "blind trust" when he took office, but the governor says he continued to control the disposition of assets in the trust, for which his wife served as trustee. (*Wall Street Journal,* 3/11/87.)
- Exxon Corp. says many forged Exxon bonds are circulating in European capital markets—about $19 million worth. Exxon and Morgan Guaranty, its agent, are investigating the matter. The bonds are zero coupon notes of Exxon Capital Corp., issued in 1984 and due November 15, 2004. (*Wall Street Journal,* 3/9/87.)
- In another matter of foreign intrigue, Volkswagen AG claims that it incurred a foreign exchange loss of $259 million due to fraud. VW has not publicly identified either inside or outside culprits in the scheme, but it is investigating the matter and has filed criminal charges against unidentified outsiders for fraud, breach of trust, and forgery. (*Wall Street Journal,* 3/11/87.)

April 1987

- A record number of frauds by bankers, brokers, and S&L officials was uncovered last month. The press coverage alone was staggering. Consider the following examples:
  - Gerald Klein, formerly of Merritt Commercial S&L in Maryland (it collapsed in 1985), was indicted on 40 counts of various frauds. (*Wall Street Journal,* 3/26/87.)
  - Marvin L. Warner of Home State Savings in Cincinnati was sentenced to serve three and a half years in prison and to pay $22 million in restitution for his involvement in the collapse of Home State Savings in 1985 and its related company in Florida, ESM Government Securities. (*Wall Street Journal,* 3/31/87.)
  - Home State's ex-president, Burton Bongard, was treated even more harshly. He received a 10-year prison sentence for his involvement. (*Wall Street Journal,* 4/1/87.)
  - A former director of the Federal Reserve Bank of New York is under investigation for leaking information on the bank's dis-

count rate in advance of its public disclosure. (*Wall Street Journal*, 4/10/87.)

- A young branch manager of a Tampa, Florida, bank took off with $124,000 in cash and $37,000 in money orders. He vanished last month, leaving behind his wife and an infant child. He also left a thoughtful reminder of his genius: a memo to himself in which he sized up the risks and rewards of his theft in very methodical terms, concluded the rewards outweighed the risks, and formulated a strategy to accomplish his goal—"Order extra cash from the main office." (*Detroit Free Press*, 4/12/87.)
- A Paine Webber salesman in New York who earned $2.4 million in one recent year was indicted for laundering $700,000 in currency for his customers "with the approval and participation of conspirators who were supervisors" at Paine Webber. (*Wall Street Journal*, 3/13/87.)
- A superstar salesman at E.F. Hutton's West Palm Beach office was sentenced to serve 15 years in prison for manipulating the trading accounts of his great uncle. He incurred millions of dollars in trading losses for his relative and earned thousands of dollars in commissions for himself. (*Wall Street Journal*, 3/31/87.)
- Dennis Levine, whose arrest sparked the current Wall Street insider trading scandal (by implicating Ivan Boesky), was sentenced to serve two years in prison. He will be eligible for parole after serving one-third of that time. (*Wall Street Journal*, 4/7/87.)
- Arbitrage traders Robert M. Freeman of Goldman Sachs and Richard B. Wigton and Timothy L. Tabor of Kidder, Peabody & Co. were indicted on insider trading charges. (*Wall Street Journal*, 4/10/87.)
- Anheuser-Busch led the parade of embarrassed companies last month when five executives left or were terminated. The problem was one of executive ethics at a minimum and possibly of illegality. Accepting gifts from suppliers is frowned on at Anheuser-Busch and violates company policy. However, it became at least an occasional practice in some departments. "It was part of the corporate culture," said one terminated official. (*Wall Street Journal*, 3/30/87, 3/31/87, 4/2/87, 4/3/87, 4/6/87.)
- Volkswagen AG is still attempting to untangle the confusion in its currency trading unit. As reported last month in *Computer Security Digest*, the VW case may go down in the annals of corporate fraud as the largest to date: $259 million. It surpasses Equity Funding, which involved $200 million in overstated corporate revenue. (*Wall Street Journal*, 3/13/87, 3/16/87, 3/17/87, 3/18/87, 3/23/87, 3/26/87, 4/8/87.)

- The former president of Empire of Carolina, a toy manufacturer, was sentenced to a year and a day in prison for taking a leading role in a kickback scheme in which he received $400,000 from sales reps who did business with his company. (*Wall Street Journal*, 3/12/87.)
- A group of New York tax shelter promoters who accommodated taxpayers (unwittingly) by providing $350 million in fictitious deductions was indicted by a federal grand jury in New York. A number of Hollywood stars and corporate executives were participants in the phony tax shelters but were unaware of the scam. (*Wall Street Journal*, 3/26/87.)
- Robert B. Anderson, former secretary of the treasury under Eisenhower, was indicted and pleaded guilty to tax evasion last month. Despite Anderson's age—he is 76—the U.S. Attorney in New York intends to urge the trial judge to impose a prison sentence. (*Wall Street Journal*, 3/27/87.)

May 1987

- A high-level broker with Shearson Lehman Bros. was accused of embezzling $19 million of the firm's funds during the past year. (*Detroit News*, 4/26/87.)
- Certain employees of GAF Corp. and a computer paper supplier were allegedly involved in a fraudulent scheme that cost GAF about $1 million. Bogus invoices were submitted by the supplier and approved by the GAF employees. (*Wall Street Journal*, 4/20/87.)
- In an insider trading case, 13 employees of NCR Corp. were discharged for allegedly trading in their company's stock on the basis of confidential information acquired on the job. The principals were alleged to be middle managers in financial planning and analysis functions. (*MIS Week*, 5/11/87.)
- Delco Wire and Cable Co. was indicted by a Philadelphia federal grand jury for fraud, bribery, and tax evasion in connection with a Defense Department contract. The government claims that it received wire inferior to that specified in its bid and accordingly was overcharged by about $20 million. (*Wall Street Journal*, 5/11/87.)
- Wickes Co. of Santa Monica, California, reports that a recently acquired subsidiary may have defrauded purchasers of carpeting by supplying phony samples to a carpet testing lab. The samples met fire code specifications, but the actual carpeting sold allegedly did not. In all, about $360 million of this carpeting was sold to commercial and institutional customers, including the federal government. The liability could become a legal nightmare.
- A stiff prison sentence of seven and a half years was meted out to

David L. Miller, a former financial executive who was charged with embezzling $1.3 million from a recent employer. His indictment last fall for tax evasion was his first criminal charge, but he admitted to a *Wall Street Journal* reporter that he had embezzled funds from five previous employers since 1966, none of whom elected to prosecute him after he agreed to pay back the embezzled funds. A psychiatrist testifying in his behalf said that he had a "compulsory need to buy love or friendship." (*Wall Street Journal,* 4/29/87.)

June 1987

- Price-fixing and bid-rigging in the waste disposal business is the subject of inquiry by federal grand juries in 11 jurisdictions. (*Wall Street Journal,* 6/4/87.)
- Intelstat is trying to recover $50 million in damages from its former director general, charging that he bilked the company in an elaborate kickback scheme. Certain funds were allegedly funneled to the director general through Panamanian Shell Corporations and Swiss bank accounts. (*Wall Street Journal,* 5/21/87.)
- Saudi Arabia's educational attaché in the U.S. and his assistant were indicted by a federal grand jury in Houston, Texas, for allegedly bilking $35 million from a Saudi educational assistance program designed to aid citizens of that country who are studying in the U.S. The two men double-billed the Saudi government for aid grants and used the proceeds to acquire real estate in Texas. (*Wall Street Journal,* 6/4/87.)
- Wespercorp of Santa Ana, California, a maker of computer peripheral devices, has been charged by the SEC with misstating financial results by prematurely recognizing revenue from certain contracts. (*Wall Street Journal,* 5/19/87.)

July 1987

- July is a great month for parades, but one parade that few people expected was the parade of alleged white-collar criminals who appeared in courts for trial or sentencing. The following are but a few:
  - Former treasury secretary Robert B. Anderson was sentenced to a month in prison for tax evasion. (*Wall Street Journal,* 6/26/87.)
  - An E.F. Hutton vice-president was indicted for conspiring to launder $450,000 in drug trafficking money. (*Wall Street Journal,* 6/19/87.)
  - Another E.F. Hutton vice-president was accused of alerting

drug traffickers in the so-called Pizza Connection case that they were under federal scrutiny. Although not charged in a criminal case, the vice-president was placed on leave pending a management review of the circumstances. (*Wall Street Journal*, 6/29/87.)

- A former vice-president of Shearson Lehman Bros. pleaded guilty to misappropriating the firm's funds in a check-kiting scheme that involved about $19 million. (*Wall Street Journal*, 6/19/87.)

- A former vice-president of Morgan Guaranty Trust Co. was indicted in a kickback scheme with another former vice-president of Morgan. The latter had allegedly stolen approximately $4.3 million of his customer's funds. The kickbacks involved the billing of inflated consulting services to Morgan. (*Wall Street Journal*, 6/12/87.)

- A former director of Capitol Bankcorp of Boston was indicted for using his position to facilitate a loan shark operation. He and 10 other men made $2.5 million in loans at rates as high as 7% per week. (*Wall Street Journal*, 6/17/87.)

- A unit of Occidental Petroleum Co. sued its former president who allegedly engaged in a scheme to secure kickbacks on natural gas sales made at less than market value. (*Wall Street Journal*, 6/10/87.)

- The former head of public relations of Revlon, Inc., pleaded guilty to tax evasion charges in connection with an inflated invoice scheme that cost Revlon $1.1 million over a four-year period. (*Wall Street Journal*, 6/8/87.)

- Two pension fund advisors of the Teamsters and Sheet Metal Union locals in New York were indicted for racketeering, kickbacks, and embezzlement in a scheme that allegedly netted them $22 million in illegal profits. (*Wall Street Journal*, 6/17/87.)

- A former financial officer of the University of Illinois was found to have embezzled $660,000 from 1977 to 1981, which he used to buy sexual favors from several strippers at a nightclub. He failed to report the embezzled funds to the IRS. When challenged by the IRS, he claimed that he had been mentally ill, had been "controlled" by the dancers and the nightclub manager, and had not even enjoyed his fling. A tax court judge was not impressed by his plea and ordered him to pay $347,000 in taxes and $173,000 in penalties. (*Wall Street Journal*, 7/1/87.)

- Marvin L. Warner, former owner of Cincinnati's Home State Savings Bank, was found not guilty of federal charges that he conspired to defraud the bank's depositors. (*Wall Street Journal*, 6/22/87.)

October 1987

- The Bowery Savings Bank of New York claims to be the victim of a $750,000 embezzlement by one of its vice-presidents. The embezzlement scheme allegedly involved setting up a dummy corporation and approving payments to it. The vice-president pleaded not guilty at his arraignment. (*Wall Street Journal,* 9/14/87.)
- The former president of Bevil, Bresler and Schulman, Inc., was sentenced to serve eight years in prison for tax fraud and conspiracy in relation to the collapse of the government securities firm. (*Wall Street Journal,* 9/10/87.)
- John Galanis, a tax shelter promoter awaiting trial on fraud charges, was indicted again for fraudulently taking over three mutual funds in California and a thrift in Connecticut. (*Wall Street Journal,* 9/16/87.)
- A subsidiary of Waste Management, Inc., was charged with conspiring to violate federal antitrust laws by dividing up customers in Dade and Broward Counties, Florida, with competitors. The alleged conspiracy ran from 1980 to 1985. (*Wall Street Journal,* 9/25/87.)
- Bid-rigging was alleged against major pipe suppliers and fabricators in a suit filed by the Justice Department in San Diego. The piping went into nuclear energy plants and industrial plants across the country. (*Wall Street Journal,* 8/31/87.)
- The Justice Department, in the first survey of its kind on federal white-collar crime, reports that there were 18% more convictions for white-collar crimes in 1985 than in 1980. There were 10,733 convictions in 1985: 55% for fraud, 19% for forgery, 16% for embezzlement, 5% for counterfeiting, and 5% for regulatory offenses. The average white-collar criminal was given a prison sentence of 29 months. The average sentence for other offenders was 50 months. (*Detroit Free Press,* 9/28/87.)
- TRW, Inc., pleaded guilty to making false statements to the DOD and agreed to pay $17 million in restitution. The case involved TRW units that overcharged the Pentagon. TRW discovered the overcharges itself through an internal audit and brought the matter to the attention of the DOD. High-level managers instructed lower-level employees to shift nondefense labor costs to government contracts. (*Wall Street Journal,* 9/4/87.)
- Raymark Industries, Inc., brought suit against two lawyers and three doctors whom it claims conspired to produce false or misleading reports of employee asbestosis. The conspirators allegedly attempted to lure Raymark into paying $5 million in fake medical claims to about 2000 workers employed in Raymark's Ohio tire manufacturing plants. (*Wall Street Journal,* 9/18/87.)

- The fraud phenomenon is certainly not unique to the United States and Canada. Deception seems to be a global problem today, as shown by the following news stories from around the world:
  - *Argentina.* The Argentine Central Bank recently closed six banks because of "the serious deterioration of their solvency and liquidity and fraudulent administration." (*Wall Street Journal,* 9/25/87.)
  - *West Germany.* Volkswagen continues to unravel the mystery of its losses in currency transactions. VW's former chief currency trader has confessed to complicity in the fraud that caused VW trading losses of $260 million. Burkhard Junger, the VW trader, confessed that he and fugitive foreign exchange broker, Joachim Schmidt, falsified currency contracts in the name of the National Bank of Hungary. (*Wall Street Journal,* 9/14/87.)
  - *West Germany.* A West German unit of Tektronix, Inc., suffered a $3.4 million loss from "improprieties and possible fraud." The unit made an unauthorized loan to a West German leasing company that later went bankrupt. (*Wall Street Journal,* 9/14/87.)
  - *Great Britain.* The *Financial Times* found itself with a problem that the *Wall Street Journal* faced a few years ago: insider trading by reportorial staff members. The *Financial Times* plans to fire two statistical clerks who allegedly used advanced knowledge to gain personal profits. The British government is investigating 21 other cases of alleged insider trading. (*Wall Street Journal,* 9/14/87.)
  - *Japan.* Insider trading has become a problem in Japan as well. The Tokyo Stock Exchange investigates about eight hundred allegations of insider trading each year, but its regulatory machinery usually metes out warnings and suspensions rather than criminal prosecutions. Only five criminal actions have been brought during the past 39 years. However, the United States is pressuring Japan to take more vigorous action. Thus far, Japan has not taken that message to heart. Insider trading may be illegal in Japan, but it is not considered taboo. The prevailing view is that, in an information society, no one can define insider trading or advance knowledge. (*Wall Street Journal,* 9/14/87.)
  - *Sweden.* The big news in Sweden is the allegation that a Swedish arms maker paid bribes to win a $1 billion contract from the government of India. The allegations include charges that $47 million were secretly deposited into Swiss bank accounts for the bribe recipients—whoever they are. (*Wall Street Journal,* 9/18/87.)
  - *Yugoslavia.* The former financial manager of a state-owned agricultural company was arrested and charged with issuing $290 to

$500 million in promissory notes that lacked adequate financial backing. The scandal resulted in the expulsion of 42 members of the Yugoslavian Communist Party and the country's vice-president. The bank that provided the endorsement on the noncollateralized notes has gone bankrupt. (*Wall Street Journal*, 8/31/87, 9/24/87.)

- John G. Heimann, a former U.S. comptroller of the currency, said, "The new global financial-service marketplace, while full of opportunities, brings new types of risks and greater damage potential from old types of risk." Heimann added that much of the capital market's business by securities dealers "slips through the regulatory cracks." Heimann feels that more international cooperation, regulation, and policing are needed. (*Barron's*, 9/18/87.)

December 1987

- An inventory variance of $50 million is a serious problem. This is the fate of Crazy Eddie, Inc., an Edison, New Jersey, consumer electronics chain. What happened? No one seems to know how almost half of the company's inventory disappeared. Bookkeeping errors were alleged by one manager, but that is a colossal amount of error. Employee theft was presumably not the problem. The company was very conscious of security. Employees were scanned with metal detectors when they left work, and even the garbage was checked before being taken out. (*Wall Street Journal*, 11/20/87.)
- Health-care providers will be scrutinized more closely by insurers who have armed themselves with a computerized weapon. A centralized data base will now allow insurers to exchange information on fraudulent providers. (*Detroit News*, 11/15/87.)
- The FSLIC filed a $279 million civil suit against the former top management of First South, a failed Pine Bluff, Arkansas, S&L. The suit alleges that the former CEO of First South approved more than $300 million in loans to a Dallas realty partnership whose principals were major owners of First South. The loans were made without requiring board approval, personal guarantees, audits, or appraisals. About $93 million of these loans are outstanding. (*Wall Street Journal*, 11/12/87.)
- Norway's biggest bank, Den Norske Creditbank, reported that it may have incurred a $94.2 million loss from the unauthorized trades of one of its securities dealers. He exceeded internal trading limits. (*Wall Street Journal*, 11/9/87.)
- In Sweden, Goetabanken, a large commercial bank, claimed that improper options trading by one of its brokers caused losses of

$41.2 million. Internal trading rules were violated and so possibly were securities laws. (*Wall Street Journal*, 11/9/87.)

February 1988

- Barry Minkow, ZZZZ Best's 21-year-old founder and CEO, was charged with racketeering, money laundering, and fraud by a Los Angeles federal court. (*Wall Street Journal*, 1/18/88.)
- Gucci American, Inc., pleaded guilty to tax law violations and agreed to repay $20.5 million for back taxes, penalties, and interest. The fraud, perpetrated by a former president of the firm, ran for about 10 years before it was uncovered. (*Wall Street Journal*, 1/22/88.)
- The U.S. Department of Justice (Bureau of Justice Statistics) reported that between 1980 and 1985, wire fraud convictions increased 36% and lending/credit fraud convictions rose 33%. During that same period, the white-collar crime conviction rate was 85% (vs. 78% for other crimes), and the average white-collar prison sentence in 1985 was 20% longer than in 1980. (*Security*, January 1988.)
- Murder for insurance combines both white-collar and blue-collar crime, and it seems to be on the increase, says *Wall Street Journal* reporter Stanley Penn. One such technique is to buy a large key-man insurance policy on the life of an executive with the proceeds going to the corporation, then have him killed. Another technique is to borrow money for a sick friend or relative, buy debtor-life insurance coverage on the loan, and then wait or have the insured borrower killed off. The smaller amount of such policies can be compensated for by taking out several loans in the name of the intended victim. (*Wall Street Journal*, 1/14/88.)

March 1988

- Several former principals of ZZZZ Best have entered guilty pleas to reduced charges in return for their cooperation. (*Wall Street Journal*, 2/18/88.)
- A former employee of GE's credit subsidiary was charged with taking bribes to arrange loans. Phony invoices and bills of sale were allegedly used to fraudulently convince GE that the loans were collaterized. (*Wall Street Journal*, 2/11/88.)
- Two executives of Professional Care, Inc., pleaded guilty to charges in what has been labeled the nation's largest Medicaid fraud in the home health-care industry. Involved are $11 million in fraudulent overpayments. (*Wall Street Journal*, 2/24/88.)
- The record industry is being investigated again for "payola" prac-

tices. Indictments of disk jockeys and record promoters are due to be announced soon. (*Wall Street Journal,* 2/26/88.)

- A Disneyland warehouse manager found embezzlement more rewarding than work. He was accused of masterminding an embezzlement scheme in which he allowed toys, souvenirs, and clothing to leave the premises without being properly billed. The merchandise was then sold to retailers, but some of it began to show up at flea markets and garage sales at "distress" prices for new and freshly packaged goods. One curious person called a friend in the security department at Disneyland, and the $500,000 alleged embezzlement was discovered. (*Distribution Magazine,* January 1988.)

June 1988

- Late spring usually brings with it a rash of criminal allegations, indictments, and convictions for white-collar crimes. This year was no exception:
  - New York's largest owners of posh buildings, Harry and Leona Helmsley, were indicted for failing to report as income more than $4 million in personal expenses charged to their various businesses. They deny the charge and counter with the fact that they have already paid $250 million in income taxes in the past five years. (*Wall Street Journal,* 4/15/88.)
  - Two former high-ranking officials of Anheuser-Busch were indicted for accepting kickbacks from suppliers. (*Wall Street Journal,* 4/18/88.)
  - Six people were indicted in Los Angeles for defrauding 15 financial institutions of $23 million by borrowing funds on phony leases for recording and audio equipment. (*Wall Street Journal,* 5/12/88.)
  - A former middleman for MCA's record division was convicted of tax evasion in a "payola"-related case. (*Wall Street Journal,* 4/11/88.)
  - In another tax evasion case, a New Jersey garment maker was convicted of concealing wage payments to illegal immigrants who worked in his Passaic, New Jersey, plant. He withheld income and social security taxes from their pay, but neither reported them as employees nor turned over the taxes he withheld. (*Wall Street Journal,* 5/24/88.)
  - The founder of a defunct Virginia Beach, Virginia, second-mortgage lender was indicted for inflating appraisals and improper transfers of funds to affiliates. This scheme allegedly victimized about 40 thrift institutions, three of which later failed. (*Wall Street Journal,* 4/22/88.)
  - The brother of former South Korean president Chun Doo Hwan

admitted to embezzling $9.3 million from a government-sponsored organization. (*Wall Street Journal,* 3/31/88.)

- In Brazil, an alleged fraud at an IBM subsidiary has caused it to lose $2.8 million. Three scams were in operation at the subsidiary: (1) a diversion of corporate funds to a private bank account that earned interest for the culprits (three employees of IBM's foreign exchange department), (2) falsified payroll claims made by employees in the payroll department, and (3) falsified invoices from construction contractors approved by a senior officer in charge of internal controls. (*Wall Street Journal,* 4/25/88.)
- West Germany seems to be experiencing more than its share of frauds, what with the VW scandal and now the Krupp-Stahl case, in which its former chairman stands accused of awarding inflated service contracts to friends. As if that were not enough, last January two managers of West Germany's Nukem nuclear services group were suspended on allegations of bribery. In February, the PR chief of Nixdorf Computer was accused of defrauding the company of millions of marks.

  The West German Ministry of Justice reports that economic crime has soared from 1982, when 96,000 charges were filed, to 1985, when 505,000 charges were filed. Karlhans Liebl, a criminologist at the Max Planck Institute, says that business and professional people in West Germany are looking at the unethical activities of others and thinking, "Why don't we do the same?" He adds another concern. Doctors in one West German state, North Rhine-Westphalia, are being investigated for billing insurers for the treatment of deceased patients. (*Wall Street Journal,* 4/26/88.)
- Doctors in the United States allegedly have their own scams going. In the Philadelphia area, about four hundred doctors are accused of taking kickbacks from medical labs for steering patients their way. (*Wall Street Journal,* 5/20/88.)
- It is not just the medical profession that is under scrutiny in the United States. New York State has undertaken a major investigation of Wall Street brokers and their employees, whom it claims are derelict in state income tax filings and payments. (*Wall Street Journal,* 4/13/88.)
- In Cleveland, Ohio, former TRW, Inc., employees of a defense-related subsidiary were indicted for making false statements and padding expenses on DOD contracts. They had previously sued TRW, Inc., on behalf of the U.S. government, alleging that the company cheated on DOD contracts for engine blades. Indeed, one former TRW employee in that defense-related subsidiary won a $700,000 judgment against the company for wrongful dis-

charge. TRW is appealing that judgment. (*Wall Street Journal*, 4/8/88.)

- Sundstrand Corp., another major defense supplier, has agreed in principle to plead guilty to a criminal charge of overbilling on military work. It also agreed to repay $12.5 million. (*Wall Street Journal*, 3/29/88.)
- Northrup Corp., primary contractor for the Stealth bomber, finds itself in a potential legal battle brought on by an attorney who seeks out employees of defense contractors who have information about overcharges. Using an old Civil War law that grants to complainants in actions for false and inflated contract claims a share of the recovered amount, this attorney has successfully sued other defense contractors. He now seeks to recover about $400 million from Northrup, which he claims is the amount of the overcharge on the Stealth bomber. For his services he receives the usual contingent fee that lawyers seek in negligence cases: about one-third of the amount recovered by the complaining employees. (*Wall Street Journal*, 5/12/88.)

September 1988

- Insurance giant American International Group, a major underwriter of fidelity bonds, believes itself to be the victim of one of its own executive's infidelities. A former vice-president of a subsidiary allegedly embezzled $1.7 million by submitting false disbursement vouchers and bogus invoices for services that were never provided. (*Wall Street Journal*, 8/22/88.)
- In another phony invoice scheme, Coca Cola was the alleged victim of a $5 million fraud by two former employees of its Baltimore, Maryland, syrup plant (*Wall Street Journal*, 8/26/88.)

October 1988

- In a case said to involve the largest defense fraud settlement ever, Sundstrand Corp. will pay $100 million to the federal government for overbilling on contracts for aircraft parts. (*Business Week*, 9/26/88.)
- A former employee of Goodyear Tire stands accused by the U.S. government of paying about $1 million in bribes to two Iraqi officials to win tire business. Goodyear itself discovered the matter and reported it to the U.S. Department of Justice. (*Wall Street Journal*, 9/7/88.)
- International Medical Centers of Miami was once the nation's largest Medicare-approved HMO. Now defunct, the company and

some of its former officials have been accused of bilking Medicare out of $355,000. The funds were allegedly misapplied for the criminal defense bill of one of the officials. (*Wall Street Journal*, 9/6/88.)

- The former deputy director-general of Intelstat pleaded guilty to participating in a kickback scheme in which contractors for Intelstat's new corporate headquarters building inflated costs and paid back the excess to some of Intelstat's top officials. (*Wall Street Journal*, 9/19/88.)

November 1988

- The big news in banking last month was the indictment of Luxembourg-based Bank of Credit & Commerce International Holdings, S.A. (BCCI), for conspiring to launder more than $32 million of profits from cocaine traffickers in Panama and Colombia. Included among the customers for whom BCCI allegedly laundered secret profits from cocaine trafficking was General Manual Noriega of Panama. The alleged laundering scheme involved the purchase of CDs with drug-related profits and the loan of funds using the CDs as collateral. If the loans were not paid, the CDs were subject to foreclosure. In Noriega's case, it was alleged that he used some of his funds from drug trafficking to lead a lavish lifestyle and to funnel money to Panamanian politicians. BCCI's shareholders include members of royal families in the Persian Gulf. (*Wall Street Journal*, 10/11/88, 10/12/88, 10/13/88, 10/14/88, 10/31/88; *Business Week*, 10/24/88.)
- Two former Anheuser-Busch officials were convicted of tax fraud for failing to report income derived as kickbacks from vendors (cash and gifts). The defense claimed that the acceptance of gifts from vendors was a common practice even among senior management people, including the CEO and his second in command. (*Wall Street Journal*, 10/4/88, 11/1/88.)
- The SEC charged two former officials of American Biomaterials with creating a dummy executive-recruiting firm and then causing their company to pay $400,000 to the dummy firm. (*Wall Street Journal*, 9/30/88.)
- Recognition Equipment, Inc., and two of its top officials were indicted on charges related to a fraudulent postal contract award. (*Wall Street Journal*, 10/7/88.)
- A 26-year-veteran government clerk, who disbursed travel expense checks to employees of the Agency for International Development, was charged with stealing $1.2 million in agency funds. He allegedly tapped into the unspent travel funds by ordering disbursements from those funds to a fictitious employee and then

approving the disbursements himself. (*Detroit Free Press*, 10/16/88.)

- John Peter Galanis will be long remembered because he drew the longest jail sentence in history (27 years) for selling bogus tax shelters. (*Wall Street Journal*, 9/29/88.)
- A federal grand jury in New York City is looking into allegations that Wall Street underwriters who handle state and municipal bond issues may have illegally contributed money to the election campaigns of state and municipal officials whose bond business they sought. (*Wall Street Journal*, 9/7/88.)
- Sundstrand Corp. pleaded guilty in a defense-procurement fraud case said to involve about $115 million in overpayments. In separate legal actions, Sundstrand may have to pay an additional amount that could exhaust its reserves. (*Wall Street Journal*, 10/13/88, 10/24/88.)
- ITT Corp. pleaded guilty to a charge that involved a defense-related subsidiary's practice of providing sports tickets, liquor, meals, and golf outings to government procurement people in exchange for proprietary information that other bidders had submitted. (*Wall Street Journal*, 10/25/88.)
- Aetna Life and Casualty wants its medical insurance clients to help it reduce frauds perpetrated by physicians and surgeons. Patients should be wary of doctors who give them blank claim forms to sign "for future use." An Aetna spokesman says that such frauds add $50 billion to the U.S. health-care bill. (*Wall Street Journal*, 10/27/88.)
- Equitable Life has another sort of fraud problem: life insurance salespeople who write policies on nonexistent people, collect their commissions, and then skip off to warmer climates. (*Wall Street Journal*, 10/18/88.)
- KPMG Peat Marwick warns employers to be wary of dramatic changes in employee lifestyle. A new luxury car can be an indicator of white-collar crime in progress. (*Wall Street Journal*, 10/17/88.)
- The Bureau of National Affairs, a D.C. publisher, just issued a report called "Thieves at Work," which concludes that people may steal on the job because they do not view it as being illegal but rather a "well-deserved perk." (*Wall Street Journal*, 10/18/88.)
- Is this generation really more litigious than previous generations? No, says Mark Galanter, a law professor at the University of Wisconsin. He says that what appears to be an increase in litigation is more a result of contract actions between businesses than it is tort suits by consumers against manufacturers. Galanter says that contract actions were up 258% between 1960 and 1986, and tort actions rose only 114%. (*Wall Street Journal*, 10/17/88.)

- West Germany was hit by another currency/commodity trading scandal. This one involves Kloeckner & Co.'s oil trading staff, all of whom were replaced after a loss of $382 million from unauthorized speculation in forward oil contracts (futures) was discovered. (*Wall Street Journal,* 10/14/88.)

February 1989

- In a new twist on ending inventory plugs to bolster profits, the SEC charged Rocky Mount Undergarment Co. with falsifying its financial statements and enlisting the aid of a vendor to deceive its auditors on the matter. The vendor allegedly supplied Arthur Andersen & Co. with a written confirmation of inventory that was false. Employees of Rocky Mount were also allegedly directed to overstate inventory on the pretense that if profits were reduced, their jobs would be jeopardized. (*Wall Street Journal,* 1/10/89.)

March 1989

- The former CEO and the former CFO of vacuum cleaner maker Regina Co. pleaded guilty to mail fraud. They admitted to falsifying financial records to ward off investor fears that the company was in trouble. Sales and earnings were inflated by such schemes as rigging the company's computers so that returned sales would not be recorded. (*Wall Street Journal,* 2/9/89.)
- In New York, a grand jury indicted two promoters in a scheme that generated $38 billion in fraudulent government securities and transactions in order to create $511 million in fake tax deductions. (*Wall Street Journal,* 2/9/89.)
- The Royal Canadian Mounted Police charged five former executives of National Business Systems, Inc., with theft and fraud. The latter charge included false sale and earnings figures in the company's annual report. (*Wall Street Journal,* 2/16/89.)
- In France, five people, including a close friend of President François Mitterand, were indicted for insider trading in the stock of Triangle Industries, Inc., at a time when Triangle was about to be acquired by France's state-owned Pechiney, S.A. (*Wall Street Journal,* 2/17/89.)
- The Anti-Drug Abuse Act of 1988 provides new tools against money laundering by the underworld, which is estimated to involve $60 to $100 billion a year. The new provision, although directed at foreign financial institutions, also serves notice on the U.S. business community that it should keep its skirts clean too. The law lowers the reportable amount of cash exchange or transfer from $10,000 to $3000 and requires proof of identification from

anyone who buys a monetary instrument of $3000 or more, for example, money orders and traveler's checks. It also gives federal law enforcement officials more power to get bank records and even allows them to waive the Right to Financial Privacy Act of 1978 if there is reason to believe that anyone is violating laws that relate to crimes against financial institutions. (*Wall Street Journal*, 1/5/89.)

April 1989

- After a lengthy investigation and lots of media hype on the activities of junk bond guru Michael R. Milken, a federal grand jury in Manhattan returned a 98-count indictment against him. The charges involve the "parking" of stock for Ivan F. Boesky and racketeering. Under the federal Racketeer Influenced Criminal Organization (RICO) statute, the government may claim all of the proceeds earned from such a crime. In Milken's case, that could amount to $1.2 billion—a U.S. record in RICO forfeitures. (*Wall Street Journal*, 3/30/89.)
- The federal government joined a citizen's lawsuit brought under the False Claims Act against the Singer Co. for overcharging by $77 million labor costs on a contract to manufacture flight simulation equipment. Since 1986, about 140 similar lawsuits have been brought against defense contractors, but few have been tried or settled yet. (*Wall Street Journal*, 3/15/89.)
- Three former officials of Sundstrand Corp. were indicted by a federal grand jury in Chicago for "concealing through cost accounting practices" Sundstrand's overbillings to the Defense Department. (*Wall Street Journal*, 3/17/89.)
- Teledyne, Inc., agreed to plead guilty to charges that it conspired to defraud the government and filed false statements with the Pentagon. (*Wall Street Journal*, 3/23/89.)
- After some years of an increasing number of malpractice lawsuits against other professionals, lawyers themselves are getting a taste of their own medicine. For example, as more thrifts have gone broke, regulators are moving against anyone with deep pockets and any causal connection to the insolvencies. Accountants were their first choice, and now law firms are being sued too. FSLIC claims that the law firms provided poor legal advice. Last year, FSLIC recovered $105 million in judgments and settlements with people linked to failed S&Ls. Of that sum, $10 million came from lawyers. One law firm in Philadelphia is currently negotiating a settlement for $29 million in an FSLIC action against it. (*Wall Street Journal*, 3/16/89.)
- New York State claims that many lawyers are delinquent in filing

state income tax returns. A state tax official complains that while law firm employees (nonlawyers) have one of the best compliance rates, their bosses have one of the worst. (*Wall Street Journal,* 3/23/89.)

- Barry Minkow, who took his ZZZZ Best Co. public and then took the public itself for $70 million, was sentenced to 25 years in prison and ordered to make restitution of $26 million. The long sentence (a rarity in cases of white-collar crime) was justified by the trial judge as a warning to discourage other white-collar criminals. (*Wall Street Journal,* 3/31/89.)

May 1989

- Laundering drug money is said to be an enterprise worth $100 billion a year. A Colombian bank, Banco de Occidente, was indicted last month for its role in laundering funds from cocaine trafficking. Because the bank's Colombian funds are hard to reach through the judicial process, the U.S. Department of Justice found a novel way to get at the funds. It attached account balances owed the Banco de Occidente by American banks doing business in Colombia, including Chase, Citibank, Bank of America, Marine Midland, and Barclay's of Miami. (*Business World,* 4/17/89.)
- Sahlen & Associates, a private detective agency in Florida, uncovered accounting discrepancies in its own books and records. Receivables and revenue were too high, and therefore, earnings may have been overstated. (*Wall Street Journal,* 4/14/89.)
- Medicare discovered that it was paying health-care costs for people who were already covered by private health insurers. Medicare claims that these private insurers owe Medicare about $10 billion for these overpayments. (*Wall Street Journal,* 4/7/89.)
- The Transit Casualty collapse is the largest insurance company failure ever—around $2 billion. It was caused by internal fraud, said regulators and receivers appearing at a congressional committee hearing in Washington, D.C. (*Wall Street Journal,* 4/6/89.)
- A multistate raid on "boiler rooms" led to 10 felony arrests. More than 10,000 victims have lost $50 million in an assortment of telemarketing scams involving oil and gas partnerships and gold mines. (*Wall Street Journal,* 4/21/89.)
- Jane Bryant Quinn, writing in the *Detroit Free Press,* offers this list of new telemarketing scams: prize offers, penny stocks, magazines, credit file enhancement, gold, oil, coins, gems, free travel, art and antiques, and business ventures. If you are called, she advises you to hang up or get the caller's name, address, and phone number and then call your attorney general. (*Detroit Free Press,* 4/16/89.)

- Meanwhile, Florida securities regulators hustled for two years to get $1.5 million for defrauded investors in Wynwood Mercantile Corp., who were due to lose $30 million in the venture—but to no avail. The IRS grabbed the funds for unpaid employer taxes. Now Florida is suing the IRS, claiming that the seizure of funds was "illegal, illogical, unfair and just plain mean spirited." (*Wall Street Journal*, 3/2/89.)

June 1989

- Alaskan oil has brought more than income to the state: the recent oil spill and political corruption. Two North Slope Borough contractors were convicted of charges of bribery, kickbacks, and racketeering in the biggest white-collar crime in Alaskan history. (*Wall Street Journal*, 5/24/89.)
- A Miami, Florida, financial planner received a 30-year sentence for defrauding his clients and was ordered to make restitution of $12.5 million. (*Wall Street Journal*, 5/11/89.)
- A former Johnson Matthey executive was charged with embezzling $9.2 million by writing checks to himself and a business he owned. (*Wall Street Journal*, 5/19/89.)
- The former CEO of a software firm was indicted in Philadelphia for filing false financial reports with the SEC. He allegedly inflated company earnings by $1.7 million to boost the value of its stock. (*Wall Street Journal*, 5/4/89.)
- A former credit union CEO was indicted in Omaha for embezzling $12 million over a four-year period. The credit union itself failed in 1988 in the second largest credit union failure in history ($40 million). (*Wall Street Journal*, 5/22/89.)
- Three men who allegedly caused Bank of America a loss of $95 million in 1984 in a mortgage-backed securities fraud were indicted in Los Angeles. (*Wall Street Journal*, 5/11/89.)
- A former Housing and Urban Development (HUD) official in Washington, D.C., was indicted for bribery in the award of a $400,000 HUD urban development contract. (*Wall Street Journal*, 5/11/89.)

July 1989

- Another major investigation of corruption in contract awards is brewing in Washington. Housing and Urban Development is looking into large fees paid to consultants for the construction and renovation of low-income housing. The developers of these projects allegedly engaged the services of high-level former government officials to win these contracts. (*Wall Street Journal*, 6/8/89.)

- HUD is also investigating whether escrow agents handling foreclosure sales embezzled any government funds. (*Wall Street Journal*, 6/12/89.)
- A former Irving Trust Co. employee and two associates were charged in a civil suit with embezzling $5.5 million. Criminal charges may be filed later. The three defendants allegedly spent the money on homes and lavish gifts for friends. (*Wall Street Journal*, 6/12/89.)
- The IRS says that it will not allow money paid to make restitution for embezzlement to be deducted as a business expense even though the gross embezzled amount is treated as income. (*Wall Street Journal*, 6/4/89.)
- The IRS is investigating a company that promoted tax shelters in Irvine, California, which it alleges created $1 billion in "fraudulent deductions" for its investors. (*Wall Street Journal*, 6/9/89.)
- Garbage haulers on Long Island who were dominated by organized crime were charged in a civil RICO suit of corrupt activities, that is, eliminating competition and bribing local officials. The suit is the largest ever brought under the civil RICO law. (*Wall Street Journal*, 6/8/89.)
- In an article on black marketing and corruption in the USSR, *Business Week* reports that "84% of the Soviet population gets the goods they need on the black market," and "illegal trade is worth some 150 billion rubles a year." (*Business Week*, 6/5/89, p. 66.)
- Are employees today less loyal, less satisfied, and more stressed than they were formerly? An *Industry Week* poll came up with some surprising answers:
  - Employees are more loyal today to their employers, according to 46% of those polled.
  - Employees feel more satisfied today.
  - Most respondents (71%) felt a greater sense of success.
  - Job security has diminished slightly, however.
  - Jobs are more demanding; 63% said they are working harder, 57% said they are working longer hours, and 46% found work more stressful today. (*Industry Week*, 6/5/89.)
- In cases of internal fraud or corruption, particularly those that involve middle- or upper-level managers, many firms seek outside counsel to conduct the investigation. This strategy provides a measure of protection via the lawyer-client privilege; evidence can be safeguarded from government subpoena or media inquiry. (*Wall Street Journal*, 6/14/89.)
- The billing practices of a large New York law firm are being reviewed by U.S. postal inspectors for the possibility of fraud. One of the firm's clients was allegedly overbilled by about $2 million. The law firm denies that charge and counters that the client is in

arrears by about $3 million for past services. (*Wall Street Journal,* 6/5/89.)

- New York insurance broker Frank B. Hall & Co. settled a charge of fraud brought by the State Superintendent of Insurance for $48 million. The fraud was alleged to have involved the insolvency of one of Hall's subsidiary companies. The Hall Co. said that it agreed to settle to avoid costly and lengthy litigation. (*Wall Street Journal,* 6/5/89.)
- Both Sahlen & Associates and Crazy Eddie, Inc., under scrutiny for possible securities frauds, sought or will seek protection from creditors under Chapter 11 of the Bankruptcy Act. (*Wall Street Journal,* 5/31/89, 6/1/89.)

August 1989

- Criminal charges were brought by the U.S. Department of Justice against the National Mortgage Bank of Greece in connection with an alleged money laundering scheme worth $700 million. The bank allegedly helped Greek-Americans to evade federal income tax by funneling their money into secret bank accounts in Greece. (*Wall Street Journal,* 6/22/89.)
- A former director of the Federal Reserve Bank pleaded guilty in New York to leaking inside information on the federal rediscount rate to Wall Street traders Bevil, Bresler & Schulman (now defunct). (*Wall Street Journal,* 6/22/89.)
- Two former officers of Home Insurance Co. pleaded guilty to defrauding the insurer of $5.5 million by submitting false claims (*Wall Street Journal,* 6/16/89.)
- A former Shearson broker was indicted for conspiracy to commit mail and wire fraud and illegal entry. After severing his employment with First National Bank of Chicago, he allegedly continued to enter the premises at night to gather information on impending mergers and then traded in the securities of the companies. (*Wall Street Journal,* 6/16/89.)
- Operation Ill Wind, the grand jury investigation of defense contractor frauds, caught a retired Navy engineer taking a $75,000 bribe from Honeywell in exchange for providing inside information about a large computer contract. (*Wall Street Journal,* 7/17/89.)
- A recent survey indicates that purchasing agents are now more willing to accept gifts from vendors than they were in a previous survey. Only 3% of the purchasing agents interviewed said they would *not* accept favors, a decrease from 17% in 1975. Of the companies surveyed, 72% have an ethics policy against accepting favors, a decrease from 78%. More significantly, management

guidance on such matters has also diminished. (*Wall Street Journal*, 6/26/89.)

- *Forbes* reports on a survey of business ethics that found that only 39% of workers polled believed that their managers are honest, upright, and ethical. Lou Harris, who conducted the survey, concludes that such mistrust may be caused by the spate of mergers, aquisitions, and restructuring. (*Forbes*, 7/17/89, p. 27.)
- An *Industry Week* survey also suggests that takeovers have a negative impact on employees. When asked who benefited most from takeovers, 85% of the managers responded that shareholders and top managers did. Only 15% felt that employees derived any significant benefits. (*Industry Week*, 7/17/89.)
- An article called "Earnings Helper" in *Forbes* describes the accounting games used to deceive shareholders, including depreciation, lease-held improvement, and inventory valuation rules. (*Forbes*, 6/12/89.)
- A *Forbes* report examines the debacle of Sahlen & Associates, the Florida security guard and investigative firm that is now in Chapter 11 proceedings. It appears that the company's books had some $45 million in fake accounts receivable, the result of faked revenues in prior periods. (*Forbes*, 6/29/89.)

September 1989

- A $5 million fine was levied against the Panamanian subsidiary of Banco de Occident for laundering $411 million in cash from cocaine sales. The fine is the largest ever imposed against a foreign bank for laundering cash. The scam involved drug dealers who took their cash to bogus jewelry businesses who, in turn, transferred the funds to other bogus jewelers in New York. The New York jewelers would then have their banks wire transfer funds to banks in Europe, Central America, and South America. The bogus jewelers took a 7% cut of the proceeds for expediting the laundering process. Part of the scam also involved the exchange of gold-painted lead bars among the jewelers to generate phony gold bullion transactions and thereby conceal the cocaine profits. (*Detroit Free Press*, 8/11/89, 8/15/89.)
- How large is the underworld trafficking in funds from ill-gotten gains? Each year, the nations of the world export $100 billion more in capital than they receive. (*Last Days of the Sicilians* by Ralph Blumenthal, New York: Pocket Books, 1988, p. 117.)
- Bank fraud and embezzlement investigations by the FBI soared in 1988 (17,053 investigations in 1988 versus 11,807 in 1987—an increase of 44%). The increase may be a result of bank and S&L failures. (*Security Letter*, 7/17/89.)

- Commodities brokers were big news last month; the media were filled with charges of trading irregularities in the grain and other pits in Chicago. Both the Mercantile Exchange and the U.S. Attorney brought charges. The U.S. Attorney indicted 46 traders for a number of felony counts. (*Wall Street Journal,* 8/1/89, 8/3/89, 8/4/89.)
- The founder of a high-tech company (Endotronics, Inc., Coon Rapids, Minnesota) that failed has been charged with wire fraud. He allegedly used $645,000 of company funds to pay off a personal bank loan. (*Wall Street Journal,* 7/26/89.)
- Embezzlement of more than $1 million was alleged against a former branch manager at Society for Savings Bancorp in Hartford, Connecticut. The embezzlement was discovered during a routine internal audit. The FBI is investigating the matter, but formal criminal charges have not yet been brought. (*Wall Street Journal,* 8/11/89.)
- An Argentine banker and movie producer, Jacobo Finkielstain, pleaded guilty to charges of defrauding the now defunct Central National Bank of New York of $38 million. (*Wall Street Journal,* 8/18/89.)
- Counterfeiting $17 million in U.S. currency and $4.6 million in traveler's checks were among the charges brought against five Soviet émigrés in New York City. (*Wall Street Journal,* 8/18/89.)
- Home Insurance Co. was a victim of a $5.5 million fraud by two of its former vice-presidents. They submitted false claims to Home's reinsurance subsidiary. Both were sentenced by a Manhattan federal judge to serve two-year prison sentences and make restitution. (*Wall Street Journal,* 8/18/89.)
- Even the sacred privilege between psychiatrist and patient is being compromised today. A New York psychiatrist was charged with insider trading when a patient made a confidential aside that Bank of America might soon have a new CEO who would infuse new capital into the corporation. The shrink allegedly told his broker to buy Bank of America stock ($171,130 worth) which he sold later at a profit of $27,475 when news of the attempted takeover was announced. The doctor now stands indicted. (*Wall Street Journal,* 7/27/89.)
- The *Wall Street Journal* reports that embezzlements cost businesses $70 to $100 billion a year. Although these numbers may be at least a little too high, embezzlement losses are substantial and are growing rapidly in number of incidents and in dollars. (*Wall Street Journal,* 7/27/89.)

Embezzlement is a far more serious threat for small companies that it is for large firms who can afford security and audit safeguards. In today's small businesses, the accounting staff consists of one person, and the accounting system consists of a personal computer. No internal or external auditor checks the system or the operator-bookkeeper-analyst-programmer, and because the one-person accounting staff is usually not trained very well in accounting, there are no clear audit trails. Documentation may not even exist for programs and modifications. Who can say whether the company bookkeeper is a crook? Worse yet, who can *prove* that the company bookkeeper is a crook?

- Boeing, which had not been mentioned often in any of the DOD-related contracting inquiries, came into its own last month. The Air Force claimed that a Boeing unit overcharged $5.9 million on various computer projects. The overcharge allegedly consisted of improper overhead allocation. Boeing denies the charges. (*Wall Street Journal,* 8/16/89.)

October 1989

- This seems to be the time to convict, fine, sentence, indict, or file civil charges against white-collar offenders. Consider the following:
  - A Unisys vice-president received a sentence of 32 months for his role in the Pentagon procurement scandal. (*Wall Street Journal,* 9/18/89.)
  - The former chairman of Singer Co. got four years in prison and a $1.5 million fine for his role in securities frauds. This is the toughest sentence yet in the Wall Street crackdown. (*Wall Street Journal,* 9/28/89.)
  - Leona Helmsley was found guilty of tax evasion. (*Wall Street Journal,* 8/31/89.)
  - A First Jersey Securities broker pleaded guilty to money laundering charges. (*Wall Street Journal,* 9/6/89.)
  - A former president of Vernon S&L in Dallas was convicted of defrauding the S&L. (*Wall Street Journal,* 9/6/89.)
  - A former chairman of Ashland Oil pleaded guilty to selling confidential company documents to Iran. (*Wall Street Journal,* 9/15/89.)
  - A Wall Street speculator pleaded guilty to manipulating the stock of Fireman's Fund to help American Express sell part of its stake at a better price. (*Wall Street Journal,* 8/31/89.)
  - A former HUD accountant was indicted for allegedly embezzling $1 million from a federal program intended to help the poor acquire housing. (*Wall Street Journal,* 8/30/89.)
  - A unit of ITT settled a consumer fraud charge and may have to repay $100 million to those it defrauded. (*Wall Street Journal,* 9/22/89.)

- A Whittaker Corp. subsidiary pleaded guilty to bribing a Marine Corps acquisitions official. (*Wall Street Journal*, 9/27/89.)
- The SEC charged the "Crazy Eddie" founder and others with defrauding stockholders by overstating earnings. (*Wall Street Journal*, 9/7/89.)
- Italy's Banco Nazionale del Lavoro claimed that its U.S. branch in Atlanta was involved in manipulating letters of credit on exports to Iran. (*Wall Street Journal*, 8/30/89, 9/6/89, 9/9/89.)
- Computerland Corp. reported a drop in earnings due to fraud in its Hong Kong office. (*Wall Street Journal*, 9/20/89.)
- The SEC suspended a current partner and former partner of Coopers & Lybrand from practice before the Commission for approving misleading financial statements of the Savin Corp. (*Wall Street Journal*, 9/13/89.)
- A committee that investigated Miniscribe Corp., a maker of disk drives, reported, "It appears Miniscribe's senior management perpetrated a massive fraud on the company, its directors, outside auditors, and the investing public." (*Computerworld*, 9/18/89; *Wall Street Journal*, 9/12/89.)
- Convictions this year for fraud against the Small Business Administration (SBA) nearly doubled last year's total, which was itself a record. (*Wall Street Journal*, 9/11/89.)
- Some East Coast colleges are under investigation for the possible price-fixing of tuition rates. (*Wall Street Journal*, 9/12/89.)
- The IRS is looking into the role of the nation's largest commodities trader in an offshore scam in which trading losses were fabricated so that U.S. taxpayers could offset the losses against income. (*Business Week*, 10/2/89.)
- Fraud is booming at banks. Tony Adamski, the FBI's chief of financial crimes, says that before 1982, most bank losses were from teller embezzlements. Now it occurs in the upper echelons. Bank, S&L, and credit union fraud and embezzlement losses rose from $382.3 million in 1983 to $2.19 billion in 1988. (*Detroit Free Press*, 9/15/89.)

November 1989

- The Federal Trade Commission charged a number of title insurance companies with price-fixing on their search and examination services. (*Wall Street Journal*, 10/20/89.)
- Miniscribe Corp. admitted publicly a few months ago that it was the victim of an internal fraud in which sales and profits were substantially overstated. The maker of disk drives now says that it may have to file for protection under the federal bankruptcy law. Miniscribe claims a negative net worth of $88 million as of July 2,

1989. The internal fraud allegedly consisted of inventory overstatements and fictitious sales. (*Wall Street Journal,* 11/1/89.)

- Federal prosecutors, pursuing an overcharge case against GE on a defense contract, allege that company managers and lawyers withheld information about certain questionable billing practices. GE contends that the billing practices did not involve criminal activity, but rather technical disputes, and that prosecutors are engaging in "reckless and baseless mudslinging." (*Wall Street Journal,* 10/25/89.)

- A federal grand jury indicted PR agency Young & Rubicam and two senior executives for bribing Jamaican tourist board officials to win their advertising account in 1981. (*Wall Street Journal,* 10/9/89.)

- *U.*, the national college newspaper, reports on a survey conducted by the American Council of Education that found that the number of first-year college students who cheat frequently or occasionally increased 6.2% in 1988. The survey also indicated that 36.6% of the students surveyed admitted to cheating, and 57.1% admitted that they copied the work of other students. One expert cited claims that cheating cuts across class ranks; that is, good students engage in it as well as poor students, and it is not just a phenomenon among first-year students. It involves even graduate students. (*U.*, October 1989.)

- In another article in the same issue, a UCLA assistant dean says that some students buy term papers, theses, and even dissertations. A judge in Los Angeles recently issued a preliminary injunction against a woman who advertised such services in a flyer distributed to students. (*U.*, October 1989.)

December 1989

- The Lincoln S&L debacle may be in the news for many years to come. As it continues to unravel, evidence of fraud and influence-peddling continues to mount. The latest news is that about half of Lincoln's reported profits, after its acquisition by Charles Keating, were derived from "sham" transactions that were allegedly approved by its outside auditors, Arthur Young & Co. Indeed, Richard Breeden, the SEC chairman, said that Arthur Young's auditors were "very unhelpful, very unforthcoming and very uncooperative" during an SEC investigation of Lincoln. (*Wall Street Journal,* 11/15/89.)

- A guilty plea was entered by a former Ford Motor Company buyer who accepted $2.5 million in kickbacks from suppliers. (*Detroit Free Press,* 11/3/89.)

- An independent record promoter was indicted by a Los Angeles federal grand jury for providing "payola" in the form of cash and cocaine to disc jockeys in exchange for air time for his music. (*Wall Street Journal,* 12/1/89.)

- British defense contractor Ferranti International Signal PLC claims that one of its units in the United States was the victim of a $157 million theft by insiders. Fictitious contracts were allegedly entered into the books to compensate for the transfer of funds to Swiss and Panamanian enterprises, which have since been liquidated. (*Wall Street Journal,* 11/29/89.)
- *Business Week* magazine continues to be a victim of leaks of its buy-sell advice column called "Inside Wall Street." Last year, an employee of a printing firm that prints the magazine was convicted of using information from the column to buy and sell securities before that information was generally available to the public. This time, the SEC says an employee of a typesetting firm did the same thing. Thus far, the SEC has brought one criminal action and four civil suits against employees of *Business Week* contractors for insider trading. (*Wall Street Journal,* 12/1/89.)
- Charles A. Intriago, a Miami attorney, has begun to publish a newsletter on money laundering. He launched *Money Laundering Alert* recently and sells subscriptions at $245 per year. (*Wall Street Journal,* 11/8/89.)
- White-collar defendants cannot trust the tender mercies of federal judges in sentencing if the judges believe that they committed perjury at their trials. Federal judges have recently added extra jail time to the sentence when they believed that defendants compounded their felonies by perjuring themselves. (*Wall Street Journal,* 11/17/89.)
- *Forbes* magazine describes a new variety of white-collar crime. Modern computer graphics can provide a cheap and convenient way to duplicate the payroll and payables checks of Fortune 500 companies. The fabrications are made by duplicating blank checks on desktop computers with laser printers. The forged checks look so real that an inattentive bank teller could easily be deceived. (This development may hasten the adoption of Electronic Data Interchange and the electronic deposit of payroll checks.) (*Forbes,* 11/27/89.)
- Waste, fraud, and abuse in past federal spending may cost taxpayers more than $300 billion during the next few years, according to the General Accounting Office (GAO). (With the scandals in HUD, the S&Ls, the DOD, defaults in student loans and farm credit, and mismanagement in Medicare, $300 billion sounds conservative.) (*Detroit Free Press,* 11/30/89.)
- A Honeywell Corp. employee alleged that he accepted secret Pentagon budget data from a Boeing Corp. employee because Honey-

well's Management by Objectives (MBO) system forced him to use illegal means to meet company goals. One of his objectives was to "establish meaningful contacts with the Air Force," which he construed to mean "getting classified documents." (*Detroit Free Press,* 12/7/89.)

- The testimony of this Honeywell employee led to the conviction of a Boeing employee for trafficking in confidential Defense Department bidding and budget documents. (*Wall Street Journal,* 12/8/89.)
- Crazy Eddie's founder squirreled away $60 million in foreign banks, according to the SEC. (*Wall Street Journal,* 12/13/89.)
- Two oil traders formerly employed by Enron Corp. were charged with defrauding the company of $1.4 million through a series of sham oil-trading contracts. (*Wall Street Journal,* 12/21/89.)
- A former vice-president of Kaneb Services, Inc., was awarded $32.4 million by a Houston, Texas, jury in a wrongful discharge suit. He contended that his dismissal was related to his refusal to certify allegedly fraudulent tax returns and to approve personal expenditures of senior management as corporate expenses. The award is thought to be the largest ever in a wrongful discharge suit. (*Wall Street Journal,* 12/5/89.)
- Stock price manipulations in penny stocks are commonplace. In one case, securities had been pumped up by $400 million when the plug was pulled. The October 1987 crash was blamed for the downturn. In fact, it was an opportune time for the manipulators to cash in and find a convenient scapegoat. (*Wall Street Journal,* 12/11/89.)

February 1990

- Bank of Credit and Commerce International (BCCI) of Luxembourg pleaded guilty to laundering drug money. It agreed to forfeit $14.8 million to the U.S. government, the largest such forfeiture in history. BCCI may also supply information at the trial of Manual Noriega. One of the bank's former officials served as Noriega's personal banker. (*Wall Street Journal,* 1/17/90.)
- Operation Ill Wind, the government's long investigation into improprieties in defense contract awards, is drawing to a close. It is rumored in Washington that one major contractor may have to pay restitution for $175 million in ill-gotten profits. Thus far, 33 convictions have been brought. (*Wall Street Journal,* 1/8/90.)
- A summary of Operation Ill Wind is contained in a front-page article in the *Wall Street Journal.* The story is a sad commentary on the extent to which some defense contractors went to get "inside information" for bidding. (*Wall Street Journal,* 1/15/90.)

- Another government agency (the SEC) is setting its sights on corruption in another area: Wall Street. William McLucas, the newly appointed director of enforcement, says that he will focus on the profile of firms most often cited by the SEC:
  - start-up companies
  - troubled companies
  - industries undergoing rapid technological change

  These firms most often fabricate revenue, he said. Banks and S&Ls will come under scrutiny too. McLucas also warned public accountants that they would be watched carefully for any weakness in fraud prevention. (*Wall Street Journal,* 1/10/90.)
- Nynex created a purchasing subsidiary to buy in volume and purportedly pass on the savings to its customers, but it did not turn out that way. Because it escaped regulation on profit, the subsidiary charged Nynex units more for parts, supplies, and equipment than they were worth. These units then used their inflated costs to justify higher phone service rates, and the purchasing subsidiary's profits dropped nearly to the bottom line. A federal audit showed that the subsidiary overcharged other units by about $120 million over the years. (*Wall Street Journal,* 1/9/90.)
- Eddie Antar, founder of Crazy Eddie's appliance stores, was ordered to repatriate the $52 million that he transferred to Israel in 1987. The money came from a sale of his stock before his company foundered. It was alleged, however, that during his tenure as CEO, profits were greatly overstated, and that is why his stock was sold at such a high value. The company is in Chapter 11. (*Wall Street Journal,* 1/24/90.)
- Two Columbia University business professors conducted a survey of the business ethics experiences of 1070 graduates from the classes of 1953 through 1987. About 40% reported that they had been rewarded by their employers for taking actions they considered ethically questionable. Only 20% were rewarded for refusing to do something ethically wrong. (*Wall Street Journal,* 1/25/90.)
- A veteran employee of the City of Ann Arbor, Michigan, stands accused of embezzling $92,000. The employee, a clerk in the transportation department, allegedly submitted phony invoices for road patch material, salt, sand, gravel, and hot asphalt, using the pretense that the goods were supplied by a subcontractor of a firm with whom the city had a legitimate contract. When the first check was issued, the clerk allegedly attempted to cash it at a nearby bank, but without an assumed name on file, the bank would not honor the check. According to the indictment, the clerk then filed an assumed name and opened a new account at the bank, and the bank honored her checks. She was caught when another clerk, in

reconciling canceled checks, noticed that the transportation clerk's name appeared on a check as the second endorser. (*Ann Arbor News,* 2/27/90.)

- In another Michigan embezzlement, the city clerk of Imlay City skimmed $226,000 from residents' tax and utility bills. She knew the system's internal control weaknesses because she had supervised the installation of a new computer billing application. She was the only employee who understood the system. (*Detroit Free Press,* 2/7/90.)

- The Money Laundering Control Act of 1986 continues to be applied at the federal level. Although used mainly in drug trafficking cases, it is also applied in cases involving any transaction where cash is used and known to have come from illegal activities, including securities fraud, gambling, and prostitution. (*Wall Street Journal,* 2/6/90.)

- The March 1, 1990, issue of the *Wall Street Journal* has a front-page story by John Fialka on how cocaine traffickers converted their currency into gold and then used wire transfers to further disguise the illegal source of the funds. (*Wall Street Journal,* 3/1/90.)

- The FCC ruled that Nynex units overcharged users by about $120 million by purchasing equipment and services from an unregulated Nynex unit at inflated prices. A fine of $1.4 million was imposed, and refunds were ordered. (*Network World,* 2/12/90.)

April 1990

- A suit, by a number of insurance carriers against a group of attorneys called *the Alliance,* alleges that the attorneys conspired to fatten their fees by raising useless motions, taking unnecessary depositions, billing junior time at senior or partner rates, and inflating travel and other expenses. (*Wall Street Journal,* 3/29/90.)

- William Galvin, a defense industry consultant, pleaded guilty to bribing DOD officials. He also agreed to cooperate with the government in its continuing investigation of DOD bidding irregularities and bribery. (*Wall Street Journal,* 3/29/90.)

May 1990

April 1990 may go down in legal history as a record month for prosecutions of white-collar crimes. Not only did Michael Milken fall, but so did a slew of others:

- Kimball Dean Richards, a California concert promoter, was sentenced to 15 years in prison for a phony leasing scheme that defrauded banks and S&Ls of $23 million. (*Wall Street Journal*, 5/1/90.)

- Gordon Weaver and Steve Ross, former executives of Paramount Pictures, were indicted for taking kickbacks from suppliers. (*Wall Street Journal*, 4/30/90.)
- Fourteen California lawyers were indicted for scheming to defraud insurance carriers of some $50 million. (*Wall Street Journal*, 4/25/90.)
- Woody Lemons, former CEO of the defunct Vernon S&L, was given a 30-year prison sentence for bank fraud and taking a kickback on a loan. This sentence is the harshest meted out in S&L cases to date. (*Wall Street Journal*, 4/6/90.)
- In tears, Michael Milken faced a judge who may send him to prison for five years. Will this end the decade of greed? No one conviction will do that. Milken's likely sentence, fines, restitution, and bad publicity may or may not discourage other yuppies from following in his tracks. (*Wall Street Journal*, 4/25/90.)
- The IRS has been harassed by tax protesters who have submitted phony Form 1099s in the names of prominent political leaders for income that was never earned. This action provokes needless audits of the targeted individuals. In Albuquerque, New Mexico, the U.S. Attorney received a phony Form 1099 showing payment to him of some $32 million. (*Wall Street Journal*, 4/16/90.)
- In Fargo, North Dakota, a federal grand jury indicted a tax protester who is believed to have developed the scheme of submitting phony 1099s. To date, the IRS has uncovered more than 2600 phony 1099s, filed by 193 people in 27 states, that report income payments of more than $11 billion. (*Wall Street Journal*, 4/25/90.)

June 1990

- A former Citibank vice-president who was in charge of the safekeeping of bank assets was convicted of embezzling $25 million in bearer securities. He stole the securities while inspecting a vault to "improve" security procedures. (*Wall Street Journal*, 5/4/90.)
- A former official of Bear Stearns was indicted by a federal grand jury for allegedly obstructing a money laundering investigation. (*Wall Street Journal*, 5/8/90.)
- A former Grumman Corp. middle manager pleaded guilty to conspiracy to defraud the government in a defense procurement scam. (*Wall Street Journal*, 5/9/90.)
- In Los Angeles, Robert Fine, Jr., was sentenced to four years in prison for fraudulently assuming the identity of property owners and then using their property as collateral for loans. (*Wall Street Journal*, 5/9/90.)

- A former broker and senior vice-president with Prudential-Bache Securities, Inc., was indicted by a federal grand jury in Brooklyn, New York, for laundering $400,000 for clients. (*Wall Street Journal*, 5/25/90.)
- The SEC alleged the overstatement of revenue and earnings by some $8 million in 1986 in a case involving four former officials of Thortec International, Inc. (*Wall Street Journal*, 5/25/90.)
- McDonnell Douglas fired about 150 employees that it alleged borrowed up to $4000 interest-free to buy personal computers when in fact the funds were used for other purposes. Phony bills of sale were allegedly used to support the loan applications. (*Wall Street Journal*, 5/29/90.)
- The Central Bank of Yugoslavia has sued Drexel Burnham Lambert claiming that it was duped into investing $70 million in loans to Drexel's parent company when it thought it was investing in high-grade securities. (*Wall Street Journal*, 5/15/90.)
- The U.S. government is investigating the billing practices of a New York law firm. Allegations include the overbilling of legal charges to Shearson Lehman and the United Food and Commercial Workers' Union to the tune of $2 million and $550,000, respectively. (*Wall Street Journal*, 5/17/90.)

July 1990

- A federal court jury in Los Angeles convicted a Palos Verdes resident of defrauding financial institutions, including Bank of America, of about $144 million in a scheme to sell them worthless mortgage loans. It was said to be one of the largest single frauds ever perpetrated against S&Ls—except for those involving insiders. (*Wall Street Journal*, 6/11/90.)
- Three California travel agents allegedly found a way to create 50 fake frequent flyer accounts in American Airlines' reservation system. They accumulated credits in those accounts when they booked flights for nonmembers of American's frequent flyer club. When enough credits were accumulated, they issued tickets for themselves and sold them for cash. (*Wall Street Journal*, 6/6/90.)
- California's largest minority-owned car dealership went under in 1988. Now eight of its employees stand charged in a federal prosecution with defrauding numerous lenders, including GE Capital Corp. and First Los Angeles Bank. The alleged fraudulent techniques involved the deletion of negative information in credit reports, the submission of the same loan papers to three different lenders, and the failure to disclose that customer loan defaults had occurred. (*Wall Street Journal*, 6/14/90.)
- The head of Florida Federal Savings Bank's student loan division

in Tampa was indicted for his role in defrauding the U.S. Department of Education on student loans. The thrift itself came under scrutiny in 1988 for allegedly filing 17,000 fraudulent insurance claims on $35 million in student loans. (*Wall Street Journal*, 6/7/90.)

- In Los Angeles, a defense subcontractor who supplied inferior nuts and bolts for aircraft engines in the B-1 bomber and the F-18, F-16, and F-14 fighters is due to be sentenced after pleading guilty to falsifying test results. Federal prosecutors want him to serve a substantial period in prison. (*Wall Street Journal*, 6/18/90.)

August 1990

- In New Jersey, an attorney was ordered to pay the opposition's costs for a lawsuit brought on frivolous grounds. (*Wall Street Journal*, 7/16/90.)
- In June, the U.S. Supreme Court upheld a $21,000 fine against a Washington, D.C., law firm that brought an antitrust suit on the basis of what turned out to be groundless allegations. What constitutes a frivolous lawsuit has not been judicially defined. Lawyers therefore fret about using "imaginative advocacy." What is frivolous today may become precedent tomorrow, said one judge. (*Wall Street Journal*, 7/20/90.)
- An article in *Business Week* reports that liability claims against accounting firms have risen fourfold in the 80s. The FDIC has some 500 liability claims pending against legal and accounting firms. (*Business Week*, 7/23/90.)
- In New York State, the Fund for Client Protection, which oversees cases of attorneys who defraud clients, is almost broke. One lawyer's clients were awarded a total of $2.3 million recently. The annual contribution of members of the bar to the fund has tripled over the past few years. (*Wall Street Journal*, 7/17/90.)

September 1990

- Lamar Savings Association of Austin, Texas, was in the news again last month. Its former owner and three ex-officers were indicted on charges of conspiring to conceal from regulators the financially precarious condition of the S&L. One technique they allegedly used was to force potential borrowers into sham loans, for example, to purchase repossessed real estate. This technique enabled the S&L to record the immediate gain on the new loan and "dispose" of the troubled loan. (*Wall Street Journal*, 8/8/90.)
- A number of reasons have been advanced for S&L failures. They include poor management, poor lending practices, poor accounting

practices, poor internal controls, overvalued real estate, high interest paid to depositors, junk bond investments, and finally, fraud, theft, and embezzlement. According to some authorities, fraud was involved in 25 to 75% of the S&L failures, but S&L consultant Bert Ely says fraud will account for only 3% of S&L losses. (*Wall Street Journal*, 7/20/90.)

- Sundstrand Corp. settled a shareholder class action suit for $15 million. The suit was brought against Sundstrand officers and directors in response to a guilty plea Sundstrand had entered in a fraud case brought by the Defense Department. Sundstrand has already paid the DOD $115 million to settle the procurement fraud case. (*Wall Street Journal*, 8/10/90.)

- The IRS says that foreign companies are not paying their fair share of income tax to the United States. Many use transfer pricing formulas on sales to their U.S. subsidiaries that overstate U.S. costs and understate U.S. income. The industries represented in these schemes include electronics, automobile, and motorcycle manufacturers. Of the 36 companies in these categories, 25 are from Pacific Rim countries and 11 are European. (*Wall Street Journal*, 7/11/90.)

October 1990

- Two more indictments of thrift chairmen led the S&L news last month. Charles Keating, Jr., whose American Continental Corp. stands to become the largest of the S&L failures to date, was indicted on 42 counts of assorted banking and fraud violations. Oliver A. Trigg, former chairman of Family S&L of California, was indicted on fraud charges too. (*Wall Street Journal*, 9/14/90, 9/18/90, 9/19/90.)

- Stanford University may have submitted false and fraudulent claims on U.S. government research projects. The university is now investigating these allegations. Allocations of cost for library resources, use of facilities, maintenance, and utility expenses are being scrutinized by a university internal audit team. (*Wall Street Journal*, 9/13/90.)

- Martin-Marietta paid $2.5 million to settle charges that one of its divisions overcharged the U.S. government for use of computer facilities. (*Wall Street Journal*, 9/4/90.)

- In another mischarge allegation, three Sundstrand executives will face criminal trial on allegations that they misstated how company books were kept. The defense will argue that government regulations were so confusing that the contractor did not know how to account properly for overhead and other expenses. (*Wall Street Journal*, 9/12/90.)

- In a wrongful discharge suit, three former auditors of Lockheed accuse the company of firing them because they challenged the structural integrity of the C-5B cargo plane. The company says that they were fired for "unprofessional conduct" and for circumventing policies and audit procedures. (*Wall Street Journal*, 9/26/90.)

November 1990

- The Federal Bureau of Investigation recently released its annual report on bank crime, which covers violations at federally insured financial institutions. The report disclosed the following statistics for 1989:

	Robbery, Burglary, and Larceny	Fraud and Embezzlement
Total Investigations	7106	13,486
Total Gross Losses	$49,958,194	$1,284,101,771
Average per violation	$7030	$95,217

- First Fidelity Bankcorp filed a civil lawsuit charging a former senior IS executive with defrauding the bank of $6.2 million. The suit, which asks for triple the amount of actual damages to the bank, alleges that over a period of eleven years the executive filed false invoices for office supplies and equipment for the IS department from two dummy companies. The bank also took legal action to freeze his assets, which include a $1.85 million home in Warren, New Jersey, and a 1989 Jaguar. (*Information Week*, 10/15/90.)
- In Jakarta, Indonesia, P.T. Bank Duta reported that its losses in foreign exchange trading since 1988 amount to $419 million but gave few details of how the losses were incurred. A former deputy president of the bank has been detained by police since September. (*Wall Street Journal*, 10/5/90.)
- The union of East and West Germany created a golden opportunity for traders who converted East German rubles into West German marks. The cost of the currency scam against the Bonn government stands at about $325 million but may go higher. Thus far, four suspects have been arrested. (*Wall Street Journal*, 10/17/90.)
- In Japan, Sumitomo Bank's chairman resigned to take responsibility for the bank's role in illegally inducing clients to lend $175 million to stock market speculators. Sumitomo, the world's third largest bank with assets of $370 billion, is not the only bank facing a financial scandal in Japan. Bank of Tokyo was assessed $7 million for hiding $15 million in income in sham transactions. Two

securities brokers, Daiwa and Yamaichi, were fined for paying $123 million to favored clients to compensate them for losses in the stock market. (*Business Week,* 10/22/90.)

December 1990

- Nynex is still sorting through charges of bribery, kickbacks, and bid-rigging in its building maintenance contracts. Thus far, 28 employees have been fired or have quit, and 28 more have been disciplined. The 28 who left allegedly took $50,000 from contractors. (*Wall Street Journal,* 11/16/90.)
- In another bribery case, two former postal workers were charged with accepting money from a catalog company and two direct mailers to reduce their mailing costs by $7.5 million. (*DM News,* 12/3/90.)

Fraud in the 1980s

The 1980s were noted for many things. In business circles, the 80s represented the best of times and the worst of times. After the recession of 1981 to 1982, the U.S. economy took off on a steady course of sustained growth. Unfortunately, good times often make people less discerning in their investment decisions. As a consequence, growth in the 80s brought with it an increase in business frauds.

The most notable business frauds of the '80s involved stock trading by insiders in corporate takeovers and leveraged buyouts and the lending, promotional, and investment practices of savings and loan institutions. The two are somewhat related by "junk bonds," which are high-risk, high-yield instruments of corporate indebtedness used to buy stock in cases of acquisition and merger. (This indebtedness helped the United States out of the recession of the early '80s.) Indebtedness is also referred to as *leverage,* as in *leveraged buyouts* and *leveraged corporate takeovers* (hostile or friendly).

In simple terms, the availability of funds for high-risk ventures like corporate takeovers and leveraged buyouts depends on the rate of interest to be paid by the borrowers, the likelihood that they will repay the principal and interest, and the break-up value of corporate assets of the firm to be acquired. The break-up value differs from the book value of the assets. Takeovers and leveraged buyouts are predicated on the assumption that assets are worth more by the piece than they are as a whole. After a takeover or buyout, certain selected assets are spun off (sold)—at a profit, it is hoped, that is, for more than book value. The profit goes to pay interest and reduce the principal amount of the debt.

Inherent in this scheme is the assumption that investors from the general public do not know the true value of the about-to-be acquired firm. When the acquiring group makes its tender offer, it offers more than the current market price for the company's stock as an inducement to current stockholders to sell their shares. The tender offer price is below what the acquiring group believes to be the real value of the assets, but the stockholders do not complain because they stand to do at least a little better than the current market price.

The ethic of the tender offer in takeovers and buyouts is predicated on the notion that there is a little greed in everyone. Appealing to the little greed of the little investor makes possible a lot of greed for big investors. Everyone gets some return from their greed. From a utilitarian perspective, it might be argued that in takeovers and buyouts, the greatest good is done for the greatest number and that the economic benefits outweigh the social costs. This seems to be the line of reasoning taken by those who would dismiss the excesses of Michael Milken, Ivan Boesky, Dennis Levine, Charles Keating, and others.

If the '80s brought the United States prosperity, they did so at a terrible price. Greed was practiced on a wholesale level by some members of the financial community. Their insatiable greed led to their downfall. The tab for their greed will now be settled by many innocent people—people who elected to take no risk or who could ill-afford to take a risk. Despite their innocence and poverty, they will be forced to pay for a share of the greed of others in the form of new taxes.

Is the level of greed experienced in the United States in the '80s something new? Not really. It was preceded by the Panics of 1857, 1873, and 1929; the Teapot Dome Scandal; Credit Mobilier; and the Black Friday Panic of 1869, when Jay Gould and Jim Fiske tried to corner the gold market.

The Industrial Revolution brought many good things, but along with it, a new class evolved: a class of men and women who traded on the self-interest, gullibility, and greed of others. Sometimes called snake oil peddlers, confidence men, or bunco artists, these people preyed on the innocent with blandishment, promises of instant riches, and valuable secrets. The promised return on investment seemed too good to be true, and indeed it often was.

These small-time swindlers soon discovered that their ploys worked just as well against the rich as they did against the poor. They discovered that men and women of wealth were even more greedy than the poor. Schemes that worked on the poor worked even better on the newly wealthy as long as the swindlers assumed a higher social class than their prey. Con artists who assumed a lower social class than their marks had to appeal to their innate sense of justice or charity, and this technique brought small returns. No less an authority on abnormal psychology and American letters than Herman Melville exposed the character of the swindler in *The Confidence Man,* which was published in 1857. In his critique of Melville's book, John W. Schroeder writes that Melville's confidence man is "a practical shape-shifter; his existence but a succession of pious disguises."[1]

The "pious disguise" is still assumed by con artists today. Those recently convicted in the S&L and Wall Street scandals had that characteristic in common. They claimed to be men of great charity, devoted family men, and religious men. They were thought to be brilliant. They were relatively young, and they worked long hours. They were creative professionals who were respected by their professional colleagues. They also made a lot of money at the expense of others.

One pundit argued in a business publication that these modern confidence men killed no one, robbed no one, raped no one, and hurt no one. That last comment cannot be supported. Many people were hurt, but they do not know it yet.

The High Cost of Greed

American history is replete with incidents of political corruption and greed. One historical period is even referred to as the Era of the Robber Barons. These men learned that they could make more money building railroads than operating them—just as many of today's land developers have learned that they can make more money constructing office buildings, hotels, and shopping centers than operating them. Corporate raiders have discovered that there is more money in breaking up companies than in building or operating them.

The glue that binds the Robber Barons to their modern counterparts is an excessive desire to accumulate wealth or power—in other words, greed. Greed has become a part of American tradition and culture. Greed is more than mere economic survival. Coupled with envy, greed becomes avarice, an obsession with the accumulation of money and other things of value. When greed becomes an end in itself, rather than a means, it corrupts. Evidence of this phenomenon can be seen in today's financial scandals: insider trading, S&L failures, overbilling by defense contractors, defrauding of stockholders by top managers of public companies, commercial bribery, political corruption, and money laundering.

A little greed may be tolerable in a capitalist society—indeed, it helps provide an economic incentive for growth and development—but excessive greed and gross self-interest are destructive. To work best, the capitalist system requires a measure of balance between economic self-interest and public interest. Fairness is a requirement. The masses will not play the economic game if fairness cannot be guaranteed.

Some people claim that the 10-year sentence of Michael Milken is excessive and does not befit the crime. If Milken is not an illustration of excessive greed, unfairness, and fraud on a broad scale, what is dishonesty? A more serious question is how such men came to such ends. They were well-educated. Many had outstanding academic records and advanced degrees from well-respected colleges which supposedly teach their students something about ethics. Where did society go wrong?

Note

1. John W. Schroeder, "Sources and Symbols for Melville's *Confidence-Man,*" *Publications of the Modern Language Association,* 66 (June, 1951), 363–380.

CHAPTER 13

State and Federal Fraud Statutes

State Criminal Fraud Statutes

At common law, *larceny* was generally defined as the wrongful taking and carrying away of the personal property of another with intent to convert it or to deprive the owner of its use and possession. If the taking was by stealth, the crime committed was larceny. If the taking was by guile or deception, by false representation, or by concealment of that which should have been disclosed, the crime committed was fraud. Fraud, then was any kind of artifice employed by one person to deceive another.

Because of its generic use and applications, the word *fraud* now means behavior that may be either criminal or civil. In a contractual sense, fraud may be found in the inducement of a contract or in the execution of a contract.

Embezzlement, at common law, was generally defined as the fraudulent appropriation of property by a person to whom it had been entrusted, or to whose hands it had lawfully come. It implied a breach of trust or fiduciary responsibility.

The major distinction between common law larceny and embezzlement lay in the issue of the legality of custody of the article stolen. In larceny, the thief did not have "legal" custody. He or she "feloniously" took the article from the owner. In embezzlement, the thief is legally authorized by the owner to take or receive the article and to possess it for a time. The thief may formulate intent to steal the article after taking possession of it or concurrently with initial possession. If initial possession and intent to steal occurred simultaneously, the crime was larceny. If intent to steal occurred after initial possession, the crime was embezzlement.

Samples of typical state statutes on larceny, embezzlement, false pretenses, and forgery follow:

Larceny: Any person who shall commit the offense of larceny by stealing, of the property of another, any money, goods or chattels, or any bank note, bank bill, bond, promissory note, due bill, bill of exchange or other bill, draft, order, or certificate, or any book of account for or concerning money or goods due or to become due, or to be delivered, or any deed or writing containing a conveyance of land, or any other valuable contract in force, or any receipt, release or defeasance, or any writ, process or public record, if the property stolen exceeds the value of $100 shall be guilty of a felony. If the property shall be of the value of $100 or less, such person shall be guilty of a misdemeanor.

According to this statute, then, the six elements of misdemeanor larceny are as follows: (1) The defendant actually or constructively took (2) carried away (3) the property of another (4) without the owner's consent and against the owner's will (5) with intent to permanently deprive the owner of the property, (6) which is valued at $100 or less.

The crimes of embezzlement, larceny by conversion, and larceny by false personation, as described in the following extracts, are felonies if the value of the stolen property exceeds $100.

Embezzlement: Any person who as the agent, servant, or employee of another, or as the trustee, bailee, or custodian of the property of another or of any partnership, voluntary association, public or private corporation, or of this State, or of any county, city, village, township or school district within this State, shall fraudulently dispose of or convert to his own use without the consent of his principal, any money or other personal property of his principal, which shall have come to his possession or shall be under his charge or control by virtue of his being such agent, servant (etc.) shall be guilty of the crime of embezzlement.

Larceny by Conversion: Any person to whom any money, goods or other property which may be the subject of larceny shall have been delivered, who shall embezzle or fraudulently convert to his own use, or shall secrete with the intent to embezzle, or fraudulently use such goods, money or other property, or any part thereof, shall be deemed by so doing to have committed the crime of larceny.

Larceny by conversion has two important elements: (1) the delivery of property and (2) fraudulent conversion or concealment.

Larceny by False Personation: Any person who shall falsely personate or represent another, and in such assumed character shall receive any money, or other property whatever, intended to be delivered to the party so impersonated, with intent to convert the same to his own use, shall be deemed by so doing, guilty of the crime of larceny.

False Pretenses with Intent to Defraud (obtaining money or goods under false pretenses): Any person who, with intent to defraud or cheat, shall designedly, by color of any false token or writing or by any false or bogus check or other written, printed or engraved instrument, by spurious coin or metal in the similitude of coin, or by any other false pretense cause any person to grant, convey, assign, demise, lease or mortgage any land or interest in land, or obtain the signature of any person to any written instrument the making where-of would be punishable as forgery, or obtain from any person any money or personal property or the use of any instrument, facility or article or other valuable thing or service, or by means of any false weights or measures obtain a larger amount or quantity or property than was bargained for, if such land or interest in land, money, personal property, use of such instrument, facility or article, valuable thing, service, larger amount obtained or less amount disposed of, shall be of the value of $100 or less shall be guilty of a misdemeanor; and if such land, interest in land, money, personal property (etc.) be of the value of more than $100, such person shall be guilty of a felony, punishable by 10 years or $5,000.

Forgery of Record and Other Instruments: Any person who shall falsely make, alter, forge or counterfeit any public record, or any certificate, return or attestation or any clerk of a court, public registrar, notary public, justice of the peace, township clerk, or any other public officer in relation to any matter wherein such certificate, return or attestation may be received as legal proof, or any charter, deed, will, testament, bond or writing obligatory, letter of attorney, policy of insurance, bill of lading, bill of exchange, or other property, or any waiver, release claim or demand, or any acceptance of a bill of exchange, or endorsement, or assignment of a bill of exchange or promissory note for the payment of money, or any accountable receipt for money, goods or other property, with intent to injure or defraud any person, shall be guilty of a felony.

Federal Criminal Fraud Statutes

Under U.S. law, the prosecution of most common-law, white-collar crimes—such as embezzlement, larceny, and false pretenses—is left to the states. The criminal fraud statutes in the U.S. Code require some basis for federal jurisdiction, such as an effect on interstate commerce, the use of the mails, or some other federal nexus. The federal laws are often used to prosecute the larger and more serious crimes, primarily because of the superior resources of federal law enforcement agencies and their nationwide jurisdiction.

All federal criminal laws are the product of statutes, which come in great numbers and variety, from the trivial to the monumental—from a statute barring the unauthorized use of the Smoky the Bear emblem to the criminal provisions of the Antitrust Laws. The most important of the hundreds of federal laws, rules, and regulations prohibiting a wide range of fraudulent conduct are extracted in this chapter.

Mail Fraud (18 U.S.C. 1341)

The mail fraud statute is the workhorse of federal white-collar prosecutions. It has been used against virtually all types of commercial frauds, public corruption, and violations of security law. The statute provides the following:

1341. Frauds and Swindles

Whoever, having devised or intending to devise any scheme or artifice to defraud, or for obtaining money or property by means of false or fraudulent pretenses, representations, or promises, or to sell, dispose of, loan, exchange, alter, give away, distribute, supply or furnish or procure for unlawful use any counterfeit or spurious coin, obligation, security, or other article, or anything represented to be or intimated or held out to be such counterfeit or spurious article, for the purpose of executing such scheme or artifice or attempting so to do, places in any post office or authorized depository for mail matter, any matter or thing whatever to be sent or delivered by the Postal Service, or takes or received therefrom, any such matter or thing, or knowingly causes to be delivered by mail according to the direction thereon, or at the place at which it is directed to be delivered by the person to whom it is addressed, any such matter or thing, shall be fined not more than $1,000 or imprisoned not more than five years, or both.

The heart of the statute is the use of the mails; without it, no matter how large or serious the fraud, there is no federal jurisdiction. The mailing itself need not contain the false and fraudulent representations as long as it is an "integral" part of the scheme. What is integral depends on the facts of each case; generally, any mailing that helps advance the scheme in any significant way is considered sufficient.

"Frauds and swindles" are not defined in this statute or elsewhere in the U.S. Code. Most cases treat any intentional scheme to deceive and deprive another of any tangible property as being within the statute.

Mail fraud counts have often been included in official corruption prosecutions under the theory that the payment or receipt of bribes deprived the public of their right to the honest and unbiased services of their public servants. The Supreme Court's 1987 ruling in *McNally v. U.S.*[1] that the statute's language indicated that it was not intended to reach such "intangible" rights, but rather was limited to the protection of pecuniary interests, seemed to end this use of the statute.

In 1988, however, in response to the *McNally* decision, Congress passed a new law[2] that provides a clear definition: "For the purpose of this chapter, the term 'scheme or artifice to defraud' includes a scheme or artifice to deprive another of the intangible right of honest services." Section 1346 eliminated the grounds on which the Supreme Court based its decision, and it permits the continued use of the mail fraud statute as an effective prosecution tool in bribery cases.

It is not necessary that the fraudulent scheme succeed or that the victim actually suffer a loss for the statute to apply. It is also not necessary that the predicate mailing travel in interstate commerce; any use of the U.S. Postal Service provides sufficient grounds for federal jurisdiction.

Wire Fraud (18 U.S.C. 1343)

The wire fraud statute provides the following:

1343. Fraud by Wire, Radio, or Television
Whoever, having devised or intending to devise any scheme or artifice to defraud, or for obtaining money or property through false or fraudulent pretenses, representations, or promises by means of, transmits or causes to be transmitted by means of wire, radio, or television communication in interstate or foreign commerce, any writings, signs, signals, pictures, or sounds for the purpose of executing such scheme or artifice, shall be fined not more than $1,000 or imprisoned not more than five years, or both.

The wire fraud statute is often used in tandem with mail fraud counts in federal fraud prosecutions. Unlike mail fraud, however, the wire fraud statute requires that an interstate or foreign communication occur if the statute is to apply.

Interstate Transportation of Stolen Property (18 U.S.C. 2314)

The pertinent part of this statute provides the following:

2314. Transportation of Stolen Goods, Securities, Moneys, Fraudulent State Tax Stamps, or Articles Used in Counterfeiting
Whoever transports in interstate or foreign commerce any goods, wares, merchandise, securities or money, of the value of $5,000 or more, knowing the same to have been stolen, converted or taken by fraud; or
Whoever, having devised or intending to devise any scheme or artifice to defraud, or for obtaining money or property by means of false or fraudulent pretenses, representations, or promises transports or causes to be transported, or induces any person to travel in, or to be transported in interstate commerce in the execution or concealment of a scheme or artifice to defraud that person of money or property having a value of $5,000 or more; . . .
Shall be fined not more than $10,000 or imprisoned not more than ten years, or both.

Section 2314, popularly known as *ITSP,* is often used in fraud prosecutions in conjunction with mail or wire fraud counts or to provide federal jurisdiction in their absence when proceeds valued at $5000 or more and obtained by fraud are transported across state lines. The statute is also violated if a defendant induces the victim to travel by interstate commerce as part of the scheme to defraud. The individual transportation of money or other items valued at less than $5000 as part of the same scheme may be aggregated to meet the $5000 requirement.

Racketeer Influenced and Corrupt Organizations (18 U.S.C. 1961 et seq.)

The Racketeer Influenced and Corrupt Organizations statute (RICO) is probably the most well-known and controversial federal statute in use today. It was originally enacted in 1970, ostensibly to fight organized crime's infiltration of legitimate business. Its powerful criminal and civil provisions have been used in a wide range of common fraud cases. As applied in these cases, the statute prohibits, in general, the investment of ill-gotten gains in another business enterprise, the acquisition of an interest in an enterprise through certain illegal acts, and the conduct of the affairs of an enterprise through such acts. Criminal penalties include stiff fines and jail terms and the forfeiture of all illegal proceeds or interests acquired. Civil remedies include treble damages, attorney fees, dissolution of the offending enterprise, and other measures. The complex statute provides, in part, the following:

1962. Prohibited Activities

(a) It shall be unlawful for any person who has received any income derived, directly or indirectly, from a pattern of racketeering activity or through collection of an unlawful debt in which such person has participated as a principal within the meaning of Section 2, Title 18, United States Code, to use or invest, directly or indirectly, any part of such income, or the proceeds of such income, in acquisition of any interest in, or the establishment or operation of, any enterprise which is engaged in, or the activities of which affect, interstate or foreign commerce. A purchase of securities on the open market for purposes of investment, and without the intention of controlling or participating in the control of the issuer, or of assisting another to do so, shall not be unlawful under this subsection if the securities of the issuer held by the purchaser, the members of his immediate family, and his or their accomplices in any pattern or racketeering activity or the collection of an unlawful debt after such purchase do not amount in aggregate to one percent of the outstanding securities of any one class, and do not confer, either in law or in fact, the power to elect one or more directors of the issuer.

(b) It shall be unlawful for any person through a pattern of racketeering activity or through collection of an unlawful debt to acquire or maintain, directly or indirectly, any interest in or control of any enterprise which is engaged in, or the activities of which affect, interstate or foreign commerce.

(c) It shall be unlawful for any person employed by or associated with any enterprise engaged in, or the activities of which affect, interstate or foreign commerce, to conduct or participate, directly or indirectly, in the conduct of such enterprise's affairs through a pattern of racketeering activity or collection of unlawful debt.

(d) It shall be unlawful for any person to conspire to violate any of the provisions of subsection (a), (b), or (c) of this section.

1963. Criminal Penalties

(a) Whoever violates any provision of section 1962 of this chapter shall be fined not more than $25,000 or imprisoned not more than twenty years, or both, and shall forfeit to the United States, irrespective of any provision of State law—

  (1) any interest the person has acquired or maintained in violation of section 1962.

1964. Civil Remedies

(a) The district courts of the United States shall have jurisdiction to prevent and restrain violations of section 1962 of this chapter by issuing appropriate orders, including, but not limited to: ordering any person to divest himself of any interest, direct or indirect, in any enterprise; imposing reasonable restrictions on the future activities or investments of any person, including, but not limited to, prohibiting any person from engaging in the same type of endeavor as the enterprise engaged in, the activities of which affect interstate or foreign commerce; or ordering dissolution or reorganization of any enterprise, making due provision for the rights of innocent persons.

(b) The Attorney General may institute proceedings under this section. Pending final determination thereof, the court may at any time enter such restraining orders or prohibitions, or take such other actions, including the acceptance of satisfactory performance bonds, as it shall deem proper.

(c) Any person injured in his business or property by reason of a violation of section 1962 of this chapter may sue therefor in any appropriate United States district court and shall recover threefold the damages he sustains and the cost of the suit, including a reasonable attorney's fee.

(d) A final judgment or decree rendered in favor of the United States in any criminal proceeding brought by the United States under this chapter shall estop the defendant from denying the essential allegations of the criminal offense in any subsequent civil proceeding brought by the United States.

Probably the most commonly used segment of the statute is section 1962(c). The elements of a subsection (c) offense are the following:

1. The defendant was associated with an "enterprise," as defined in the statute, which may be a business, a union, a group of individuals "associated in fact," or even a single individual.
2. The enterprise was engaged in or affected interstate commerce.
3. The defendant conducted the affairs of the enterprise through a "pattern of racketeering activity," that is, two or more illegal acts, enumerated in the statute as predicate violations, such as mail fraud, wire fraud, and ITSP violations.

RICO's complexity is due in part to efforts by the drafters to avoid constitutional problems like those that voided attempted antiracketeering legisl. uon in the 1930s. Those provisions were found to be unconstitutional because they punished the mere "status" of being a gangster, rather than any particular wrongful conduct. The authors of RICO avoid this impediment by basing the definition of *racketeering* and the enhanced penalties on patterns of conduct defined in the statute.

The most controversial aspect of RICO is its civil provisions. Civil actions may be brought by the government or any private party injured in his business or property. Critics complain that private-party suits have been used to reach "deep-pocket" defendants who cannot be characterized as racketeers, such as accounting firms, and to coerce unwarranted settlements from blameless defendants fearful of possible treble-damage judgments. Supporters contend that plaintiffs cannot recover unless they prove fraud or other criminal acts, whoever the defendant may be, justifying the stigma of being alleged a racketeer and the award of treble damages. Several bills to repeal or amend RICO, particularly its civil provisions, have been introduced in Congress in recent years, and some amendment is expected.

Federal Securities Laws

Numerous federal statutes prohibit false statements and other fraudulent activity in connection with security transactions. The most commonly used are Section 17(a) of the Securities Act of 1933 and Rule 10(b)5, promulgated under the Securities Exchange Act of 1934. Both contain civil and administrative remedies (such as the power to initiate actions to enjoin further violations) enforced by the Securities and Exchange Commission as well as criminal sanctions enforced by the Department of Justice. Whether a particular violation is prosecuted civilly or criminally depends in large measure on the degree of willfulness that can be proved.

Section 17(a) of the 1933 act makes it unlawful to employ fraudulent devices or misrepresentations in connection with the offer or sale of securities through jurisdictional facilities (for example, the U.S. mails). Rule 10(b)5 of the 1934 act prohibits the same conduct in connection with the purchase or sale of any security by any person. Because Rule 10(b)5 has the broadest reach—including insider trading—it is used most often. The rule (17 C.F.R. 240.10(b)5) specifically provides the following:

240.10(b)5. Employment of Manipulative and Deceptive Devices

It shall be unlawful for any person, directly or indirectly, by the use of any means or instrumentality of interstate commerce, or of the mails or of any facility of any national securities exchange,

(a) To employ any device, scheme, or artifice to defraud,
(b) To make any untrue statement of a material fact or to omit to state a material fact necessary in order to make the statements made, in the light of the circumstances under which they were made, not misleading, or
(c) To engage in any act, practice, or course of business which operates or would operate as a fraud or deceit upon any person, in connection with the purchase or sale of any security.

Specific intent to defraud is an essential element of the violation of Section 17(a) and Rule 10(b)5; however, *intent to defraud* is defined more broadly in securities regulation than in other areas of common-law fraud. It includes reckless statements as well as the knowing circulation of half-truths and false opinions or predictions, which elsewhere may be considered nonactionable puffery.

Good faith is always a defense to a Section 17(a) or Rule 10(b)5 fraud action. Intent, however, may be (and usually is) proved by circumstantial evidence, as in any fraud case. Violations of other indirect antifraud provisions of the federal securities laws, such as certain registrations and disclosure requirements, do not require a showing of fraudulent intent.

To be actionable, a false statement must be material. The test for materiality is whether there is a substantial likelihood, under all of the circumstances, that a reasonable investor would have considered the misstated or omitted facts significant in deciding whether to invest. Materiality is most often expressed in terms of its effect on financial statements, but it may also relate to serious questions of management's integrity, regardless of the dollar amounts involved.

SEC civil actions are often settled by consent decrees, in which the party agrees to stop the offending practice without admitting to or denying having engaged in it. Violations of such decrees may be punishable as contempt and may carry jail terms or fines.

The Foreign Corrupt Practices Act of 1977 (15 U.S.C. 78m(b)2)

The Foreign Corrupt Practices Act (FCPA) amended the 1934 act to prohibit certain security issuers (publicly held companies) from making corrupt payments to foreign officials or political organizations. Other amendments to the act, incorporated in Title 18 of the U.S. Code, make it illegal for any U.S. citizen to make such payments. The statute was the result of disclosures from the Watergate investigations of corporate "grease" payments to foreign officials to obtain business overseas. Of more current interest are the separate "books and records" provisions of the FCPA (Section 13(b)2), which require certain issuers to

(a) make and keep books, records, and accounts, which, in reasonable detail, accurately and fairly reflect the transactions and dispositions of the assets of the issuer; and

(b) devise and maintain a system of internal accounting controls sufficient to provide reasonable assurance that—

   (i) transactions are executed in accordance with management's general or specific authorization;

   (ii) transactions are recorded as necessary (1) to permit preparation of financial statements in conformity with generally accepted accounting principles or any other criteria applicable to such statements, and (2) to maintain accountability for assets;

   (iii) access to assets is permitted only in accordance with management's general or specific authorization; and

   (iv) the recorded accountability for assets is compared with the existing assets at reasonable intervals and appropriate action is taken with respect to any differences.

SEC regulations enforcing these provisions specifically require the following:

Rule 13(b)(2)-1.

No person shall, directly or indirectly, falsify or cause to be falsified, any book, record or account subject to Section 13(b)(2)(A) of the Securities Exchange Act.

Rule 13(b)(2)-2.

(a) No director or officer of an issuer shall, directly or indirectly, make or cause to be made a materially false or misleading statement, or

(b) omit to state, or cause another person to omit to state, any material fact necessary in order to make statements made, in light of the circumstances under which such statements were made, not misleading to an accountant in connection with (1) any audit or examination of the financial statements of the issuer required to be made pursuant to this subpart or (2) the preparation of filing of any document or report required to be filed with the Commission pursuant to this subpart or otherwise.

The statute and regulations thereunder effectively give the SEC supervisory authority over the financial management and reporting functions of publicly held corporations. The SEC has interpreted their powers under the FCPA broadly, announcing that "it is important that issuers . . . review their accounting procedures, systems of internal accounting controls, and business practices in order that they may take any actions necessary to comply with the requirements (of) the Act."[3]

Violations of the statute may be punished by a corporate fine of up to

$1 million and an individual fine of up to $10,000, a jail term of up to five years, or both. Administrative and civil relief is also available.

Conspiracy (18 U.S.C. 371)

The principal federal conspiracy statute provides the following:

371. Conspiracy to Commit Offense or to Defraud United States

If two or more persons conspire either to commit any offense against the United States, or any agency thereof, in any manner or for any purpose, and one or more of such persons do any act to effect the object of the conspiracy, each shall be fined not more than $10,000 or imprisoned not more than five years, or both.

If, however, the offense, the commission of which is the object of the conspiracy, is a misdemeanor only, the punishment for such conspiracy shall not exceed the maximum punishment provided for such misdemeanor.

The essential elements of this deceptively simple but extremely important statute are (1) that the conspiracy was willfully formed, (2) that the accused willfully became a member of it, and (3) that at least one of the conspirators knowingly committed at least one overt act in furtherance of the conspiracy. The gist of the offense is a combination or agreement of two or more persons to accomplish an unlawful purpose by lawful means or a lawful purpose by unlawful means. The purpose of the conspiracy need not be accomplished for the statute to be violated; however, at least one of the conspirators must have carried out at least one "overt act" in furtherance of the conspiracy. The overt act need not be criminal in itself, and it may be as innocuous as making a phone call or writing a letter.

Conspiracy counts are favored by the prosecution because they provide certain evidential and pleading advantages. If a conspiracy is shown, the acts and statements of one conspirator may be admitted into evidence against all, and each conspirator may be convicted for the underlying substantive offense (for example, destroying government property) committed by any one of its members.

A corporation cannot conspire with one of its own employees to commit an offense because the employee and the employer are legally viewed as one. A corporation may, however, conspire with other business entities or third parties in violation of the statute.

Aiding and Abetting (18 U.S.C. 2)

The aiding and abetting statute defines *principal* as follows:

2. Principals

(a) Whoever commits an offense against the United States or aids, abets, counsels, commands, induces or procures its commission, is punishable as a principal.

(b) Whoever willfully causes an act to be done, which if directly performed by him or another, would be an offense against the United States, is punishable as a principal.

Under this fundamental tenet of criminal law, anyone who induces another to commit an offense or who aids in its commission may be charged and convicted of the underlying offense and subject to its penalties. This statute differs from the conspiracy statute in that to be guilty of aiding and abetting, the underlying offense must actually be committed by someone.

Obstruction of Justice (18 U.S.C. 1503 et seq.) and Perjury (18 U.S.C. 1621, 1623)

The obstruction of justice and perjury statutes punish efforts to impede or obstruct the investigation or trial of other substantive offenses. Prosecutors are pleased to discover such violations because they add a more sinister flavor to what may be common white-collar charges, and they help to prove underlying criminal intent. In many instances, these charges eclipse the underlying offenses and draw the stiffest penalties.

Several obstruction statutes in the federal code punish, among other things, the attempted or actual destruction of evidence and the tampering with or threatening of witnesses, jurors, or other court personnel. Perjury, of course, is an intentional false statement on a material point that is given under oath. Under a related federal statute (18 U.S.C. 1623), the government may allege and prove perjury if the defendant makes two irreconcilable, contradictory statements; the government need not prove which is true and which is false. False and fraudulent oral or written statements made to a government agency on a material matter may also be punished as a felony under a variety of statutes. The statement need not be given under oath.

Tax Evasion, False Returns, and Failure to File (26 U.S.C. 7201, 7203, 7206(1), et seq.)

Fraud and corruption prosecutions may include counts of tax evasion, filing false returns, or failure to file if, as is often the case, the recipient of illegal payments has not reported them as income or if the payer has attempted to conceal and deduct them as a legitimate business expense. Surprisingly, a company may be able to deduct lawfully commercial bribes and kickbacks as "ordinary and necessary" business expenses if the state has no commercial bribery law or if the statute is generally not enforced.

Bankruptcy Fraud (18 U.S.C. 151 et seq.)

Two related but somewhat different types of criminal conduct fall under the general heading of bankruptcy fraud. The first is the "planned bankruptcy" or "bust out" scheme, in which the wrongdoer sells off inventory obtained on credit (often through false or inflated financial statements) for cash, usually below cost, and absconds with the proceeds. Formal bankruptcy proceedings are often not initiated, and the crime may be prosecuted under general fraud statutes, such as mail or wire fraud.

The second type of bankruptcy offense involves misconduct by a person or entity that is actually involved or contemplates becoming involved in a formal bankruptcy proceeding. The federal criminal laws that regulate bankruptcy proceedings are set out in the following:

151. Definition

As usual in this chapter, the term "debtor" means a debtor concerning whom a bankruptcy petition has been filed under title 11 of the United States Code.

152. Concealment of Assets; False Oaths and Claims: Bribery

Whoever knowingly and fraudulently conceals from a custodian, trustee, marshal, or other officer of the court charged with the control or custody of property, or from creditors in any case under title 11, any property belonging to the estate of a debtor; or

Whoever knowingly and fraudulently makes a false oath or account in or in relation to any case under title 11; or

Whoever knowingly and fraudulently makes a false declaration, certificate, verification, or statement under penalty or perjury as permitted under section 1746 of title 28, United States Code, in or in relation to any case under title 11; or

Whoever knowingly and fraudulently presents any false claim for proof against the estate of a debtor, or uses any such claim in any case under title 11, personally, or by agent, proxy, or attorney, or as agent, proxy, or attorney; or

Whoever knowingly and fraudulently receives any material amount of property from a debtor after the filing of a case under title 11, with intent to defeat the provisions of title 11; or

Whoever, knowingly and fraudulently gives, offers, receives or attempts to obtain any money or property, remuneration, compensation, reward, advantage, or promise thereof, for acting or forbearing to act in any case under title 11; or

Whoever, after the filing of a case under title 11 or in contemplation thereof, knowingly and fraudulently conceals, destroys, mutilates, falsifies, or makes a false entry in any document affecting or relating to the property or affairs of a debtor; or

Whoever, after the filing of a case under title 11, knowingly and fraudulently withholds from a custodian, trustee, marshal, or other officer of the court entitled to its possession, any recorded information, including books, documents, records, and papers, relating to the property or financial affairs of a debtor—

Shall be fined not more than $5,000 or imprisoned not more than five years, or both.

153. Embezzlement by Trustee or Officer

Whoever knowingly and fraudulently appropriates to his own use, embezzles, spends, or transfers any property or secretes or destroys any document belonging to the estate of a debtor which came into his charge as trustee, custodian, marshal, or other officer of the court—

Shall be fined not more than $5,000 or imprisoned not more than five years, or both.

154. Adverse Interest and Conduct of Officers

Whoever, being a custodian, trustee, marshal, or other officer of the court, knowingly purchases, directly or indirectly, any property of the estate of which he is such officer in a case under title 11; or

Whoever being such officer, knowingly refuses to permit a reasonable opportunity for the inspection of the documents and accounts relating to the affairs of estates in his charge by parties in interest when directed by the court to do so—Shall be fined not more than $500, and shall forfeit his office, which shall thereupon become vacant.

155. Fee Arrangements in Cases under Title 11 and Receiverships

Whoever, being a party in interest, whether as a debtor, creditor, receiver, trustee or representative of any of them, or attorney for any such party in interest, in any receivership or case under title 11 in any United States court or under its supervision, knowingly and fraudulently enters into any agreement, express or implied, with another such party in interest or attorney for another such party in interest, for the purpose of fixing the fees or other compensation to be paid to any party in interest or to any attorney for any party in interest for services rendered in connection therewith, from the assets of the state, shall be fined not more than $5,000 or imprisoned not more than one year, or both.

The most commonly used of these statutes is Section 152, which prohibits, among other things, the concealment of assets and false claims in a bankruptcy proceeding. The elements of a typical section 152 offense are (1) that the defendant contemplated a bankruptcy proceeding; (2) that in contemplation of such a proceeding, the defendant transferred or concealed assets that belonged to the bankrupt estate; and (3) that the defendant acted, knowingly and willfully, with intent to defeat the bankruptcy law.

Federal Corruption Statutes (18 U.S.C. 201 et seq.)

Chapter 11 of Title 18 of the U.S. Code has separate criminal provisions that define and prohibit a wide variety of conflicts of interest and other corrupt and unethical conduct involving public officials. The statutes of particular interest to fraud examiners follow:

201. Bribery of Public Officials and Witnesses

(a) For the purpose of this section—

    (1) The term "public official" means Member of Congress, Delegate, or Resident Commissioner, either before or after such official has qualified, or an officer of any department, agency, or branch of Government thereof, including the District of Columbia, in any official function, under or by authority of any such department, agency, or branch of Government, or a juror;

    (2) the term "person who has been selected to be a public official" means any person who has been nominated or appointed to be a public official, or has been officially informed that such person will be soon nominated or appointed; and

    (3) the term "official act" means any decision or action on any question, matter, cause, suit, proceeding or controversy, which may at any time be pending, or which may by law be brought before any public official, in such official's official capacity or in such official's place of trust or profit.

(b) Whoever—

    (1) directly or indirectly, corruptly gives, offers or promises anything of value to any public official or person who has been selected to be a public official, or offers or promises any public official, or any person who has been selected to be a public official to give anything of value to any person or entity, with intent . . .

       (A) to influence any official act; or

       (B) to influence such public official or person who has been selected to be a public official to commit or aid in committing, or collude in, or allow, any fraud, or make opportunity for the commission of any fraud on the United States; or

       (C) to induce such public official or such person who has been selected to be a public official to do or omit to do any act in violation of the lawful duty of such official or person;

    (2) being a public official or person selected to be a public official, directly or indirectly, corruptly demands, seeks, receives, accepts, or agrees to receive or accept anything of value personally or for any other person or entity, in return for:

       (A) being influenced in the performance of any official act;

       (B) being influenced to commit or aid in committing, or to collude in, or allow, any fraud, or make opportunity for the commission of any fraud, on the United States; or

       (C) being induced to do or omit to do any act in violation of the official duty of such official or person;

(3) directly or indirectly, corruptly gives, offers, or promises anything of value to any person, or offers or promises such person to give anything of value to any other person or entity, with intent to influence the testimony under oath or affirmation of such first-mentioned person as a witness upon a trial, hearing, or other proceeding, before any court, any committee of either House or both Houses of Congress, or any agency, commission, or officer authorized by the laws of the United States to hear evidence or take testimony, or with intent to influence such person to absent himself therefrom;

(4) directly or indirectly, corruptly demands, seeks, receives, accepts or agrees to receive or accept anything of value personally or for any other person or entity in return for being influenced in testimony under oath or affirmation as a witness upon any such trial, hearing, or other proceeding, or in return for absenting himself therefrom—

   Shall be fined no more than three times the monetary equivalent of the thing of value, or imprisoned for not more than fifteen years or both, and may be disqualified from holding any office of honor, trust, or profit under the United States.

(c) Whoever—

(1) otherwise than as provided by law for the proper discharge of official duty—

   (A) directly or indirectly gives, offers or promises anything of value to any public official, former public official, or person selected to be a public official, for or because of any official act performed or to be performed by such public official, former public official, or person selected to be a public official; or

   (B) being a public official, former public official, or person selected to be a public official, otherwise than as provided by law for the proper discharge of official duty, directly or indirectly demands, seeks, receives, accepts, or because of any official act performed or to be performed by such official or person;

(2) directly or indirectly gives, offers, or promises anything of value to any person, for or because of the testimony under oath or affirmation given or to be given by such person as a witness upon a trial, hearing, or other proceeding, before any court, any committee of either House or both Houses of Congress, or any agency, commission, or officer authorized by the laws of the United States to hear evidence or take testimony or for or because of such person's absence therefrom;

(3) directly or indirectly, demands, seeks, receives, accepts, or agrees to receive or accept anything of value personally for or because of the testimony under oath or affirmation given or to be given by such person as a witness upon any such trial, hearing, or other proceeding, or for or because of such person's absence therefrom;

Shall be fined under this title or imprisoned for not more than two years, or both.

(d) Paragraphs (3) and (4) of subsection (b) and paragraphs (2) and (3) of subsection (c) shall not be construed to prohibit the payment or receipt of witness fees provided by law, or the payment by the party upon whose behalf a witness is called and receipt by a witness of the reasonable cost of travel and subsistence incurred and the reasonable value of time lost in attendance at any such trial, hearing, or proceeding, or in the case of expert witnesses, a reasonable fee for time spent in the preparation of such opinion, and in appearing and testifying.

(e) The offenses and penalties prescribed in this section are separate from and in addition to those prescribed in sections 1503, 1504, and 1505 of this title.

212. Offer of Loan or Gratuity to Bank Examiner

Whoever, being an officer, director, or employee of a bank which is a member of the Federal Reserve System or the deposits of which are insured by the Federal Deposit Insurance Corporation, or of any National Agricultural Credit Corporation, or any land bank, Federal Land Bank Association or other institution subject to examination by a farm credit examiner, or of any small business investment company, makes or grants any loan or gratuity, to any examiner or assistant examiner who examines or has authority to examine such bank, corporation, or institution, shall be fined not more than $5,000 or imprisoned not more than one year, or both; and may be fined a further sum equal to the money so loaned or gratuity given.

The provisions of this section and section 213 of this title shall apply to all public examiners and assistant examiners who examine member banks of the Federal Reserve System or insured banks, or National Agricultural Credit Corporations, whether appointed by the Comptroller of the Currency, by the Board of Governors of the Federal Reserve System, by a Federal Reserve Agent, by a Federal Reserve bank, or by the Federal Deposit Insurance Corporation, or appointed or elected under the laws of any state; but shall not apply to private examiners or assistant examiners employed only by a clearing-house association or by the directors of a bank.

213. Acceptance of Loan or Gratuity by Bank Examiner

Whoever, being an examiner or assistant examiner of member banks of the Federal Reserve System or banks the deposits of which are insured by the Federal Deposit Insurance Corporation, or a farm credit examiner or examiner of National Agricultural Credit Corporations, or an examiner of small business investment companies, accepts a loan or gratuity from any bank, corporation, association or organization examined by him or from any person connected herewith, shall be fined not more than $5,000 or imprisoned not more than one year, or both; and may be fined a further sum equal to the money so loaned or gratuity given, and shall be disqualified from holding office as such examiner.

215. Receipt of Commissions or Gifts for Procuring Loans

(a) Whoever—
   (1) corruptly gives, offers, or promises anything of value to any person, with intent to influence or reward an officer, director, employee, agent, or attorney of a financial institution in connection with any business or transaction of such institution; or
   (2) as an officer, director, employee, agent, or attorney of a financial institution, corruptly solicits or demands for the benefit of any person, or corruptly accepts or agrees to accept, anything of value from any person, intending to be influenced or rewarded in connection with any business or transaction of such institution—

   Shall be fined not more than $5,000 or three times the value of the thing given, offered, promised, solicited, demanded, accepted, or agreed to be accepted, whichever is greater, or imprisoned not more than five years, or both, but if the value of the thing given, offered, promised, solicited, demanded, accepted, or agreed to be accepted does not exceed $100, shall be fined not more than $1,000 or imprisoned not more than one year, or both.

(b) As used in this section, the term "financial institution" means—
   (1) a bank with deposits insured by the Federal Deposit Insurance Corporation;
   (2) an institution with accounts insured by the Federal Savings and Loan Insurance Corporation;
   (3) a credit union with accounts insured by the National Credit Union Share Insurance Fund;
   (4) a Federal home loan bank or a member, as defined in section 2 of the Federal Home Loan Bank Act (12 U.S.C. 1422), of the Federal Home Loan Bank system;
   (5) a Federal land bank, Federal intermediate credit bank, bank for cooperatives, production credit association, and Federal Land Bank Association;
   (6) a small business investment company, as defined in section 103 of the Small Business Investment Act of 1958 (15 U.S.C. 662);
   (7) a bank holding company as defined in section 2 of the Bank Holding Company Act of 1956 (12 U.S.C. 1841); or
   (8) a savings and loan holding company as defined in section 408 of the National Housing Act (12 U.S.C. 1730a).

(c) This section shall not apply to bona fide salary, wages, fees, or other compensation paid, or expenses paid or reimbursed, in the usual course of business.

(d) Federal agencies with responsibility for regulating a financial institution shall jointly establish such guidelines as are appropriate to assist an officer, director, employee, agent, or attorney of a financial institution to comply with this section. Such agencies shall make such guidelines available to the public.

Section 201, the principal federal anticorruption statute, applies to virtually any U.S. official, juror, or witness. The section actually contains two separate offenses. Section 201(b), "Bribery," prohibits giving or receiving anything of value with the *intent to influence* an official act. Section 201(c), "Illegal Gratuity," outlaws giving or receiving anything of value *for or because of* an official act.

The illegal gratuity statute is a lesser included offense of bribery. A *bribe* is a payment made with the purpose of influencing (changing) official conduct; a *gratuity* is a payment made to reward or compensate an official for performing duties he is already lawfully required to perform. Note that bribery is punishable by up to 15 years imprisonment, fine, and disqualification from holding public office and that an illegal gratuity carries only a maximum two-year term, a fine, or both.

Sections 212 and 213 forbid the giving of any loan or gratuity to a bank examiner. Intent to influence or be influenced does not appear to be an element of the offense; the only reported case construing these statutes held that the prosecution need not prove that the loan or gratuity was given or received with any corrupt or wrongful intent. This strict interpretation of the statute is justified by the public's need for disinterested bank examiners.

Section 215 bars the corrupt giving or receiving of anything of value to influence the actions of any employee or agent of a federally connected financial institution. The statute is aimed primarily at reducing corrupt influences in making loans. Unlike Sections 212 and 213, a specific intent to influence or be influenced through the illegal payment must be proved to obtain a conviction. Payments made after the loan has been approved and disbursed may be in violation of the law if made as part of a prearranged plan or agreement.

Embezzlement and Misapplication of Bank Funds (18 U.S.C. 656 et seq.)

Sections 656 and 657 are the principal federal embezzlement statutes. The statutes provide the following:

656. Theft, Embezzlement, or Misapplication by Bank Officer or Employee

Whoever, being an officer, director, agent or employee of, or connected in any capacity with any Federal Reserve Bank, member bank, national bank or insured bank, or a receiver of a national bank, or any agent or employee of the receiver, or a Federal Reserve Agent, or an agent or employee of a Federal Reserve Agent or of the Board of Governors of the Federal Reserve System, embezzles, abstracts, purloins, or willfully misapplies any of the moneys, funds or credits of such bank or any moneys, funds, assets or securities intrusted to the custody or care of such bank, or to the custody or care of any such agent, officer, director, employee or receiver, shall be fined not more than $5,000 or imprisoned not more than five years, or both; but if the amount embezzled, abstracted, purloined, or misapplied does not exceed $100, he shall be fined not more than $1,000 or imprisoned not more than one year, or both.

As used in this section, the term "national bank" is synonymous with "National Banking Association"; "member bank" means and includes any national bank, state bank, or bank and trust company which has become a member of one of the Federal Reserve Banks; and "insured bank" includes any bank, banking association, trust company, savings bank, or other banking institution, the deposits of which are insured by the Federal Deposit Insurance Corporation.

657. Lending, Credit and Insurance Institutions

Whoever, being an officer, agent or employee of or connected in any capacity with the Reconstruction Finance Corporation, Federal Deposit Insurance Corporation, National Credit Union Administration, Home Owners' Loan Corporation, Farm Credit Administration, Department of Housing and Urban Development, Federal Crop Insurance Corporation, Farmers' Home Corporation, the Secretary of Agriculture acting through the Farmers' Home Administration, or any land bank, intermediate credit bank, bank for cooperatives or any lending, mortgage, insurance, credit or savings and loan corporation or association authorized or acting under the laws of the United States or any institution the accounts of which are insured by the Federal Savings and Loan Insurance Corporation, or by the Administrator of the National Credit Union Administration or any small business investment company, and whoever, being a receiver of any such institution, or agent or employee of the receiver, embezzles, abstracts, purloins or willfully misapplies any money, funds, credits, securities, or other things of value belonging to such institution, or pledged or otherwise intrusted to its care, shall be fined not more than $5,000 or imprisoned not more than five years, or both; but if the amount or value embezzled, abstracted, purloined or misapplied does not exceed $100, he shall be fined not more than $1,000 or imprisoned not more than one year, or both.

Embezzlement is generally defined as the wrongful taking or conversion of the property of another by one who lawfully acquired possession of it by virtue of office, employment, or position of trust. The five essential elements of a typical Section 656 violation are these: (1) The defendant was an officer, director, agent, or employee of (2) a federally insured bank (3) who willfully (4) embezzled (as just defined) funds of the bank (5) with the intent to injure or defraud the bank.

The terms *abstract, purloin,* and *misapply,* as used in the statutes, are largely redundant, and in normal usage, they simply mean to take or convert bank funds for one's own use or for the use of a third party, for improper purposes, without the bank's knowledge or consent.

Section 657 prohibits the embezzlement of funds from designated federally connected lending, credit, and insurance organizations. The basic elements of a violation are the same as for Section 656.

False Statements and Entries (18 U.S.C. 1001 et seq.)

Chapter 47 of Title 18 of the U.S. Code contains a number of related provisions that provide punishment for false or fraudulent oral or written statements made to various federal agencies and departments. The principal statute is Section 1001, which prohibits such statements in general and overlaps many of the more specific laws, such as Section 1014, which applies to false statements made on certain loan and credit applications.

Section 1001 is most often used to prosecute false statements to law enforcement or regulatory officials, not made under oath, in the course of an official investigation or on applications for federal employment, credit, visas, and so on. The felony statute may also be used in lieu of the misdemeanor provisions of the IRS Code for filing false documents with tax returns. The false statement statutes of greatest importance to the fraud examiner follow:

1001. Statements or Entries Generally

Whoever, in any manner within the jurisdiction of any department or agency of the United States knowingly and willfully falsifies, conceals or covers up by any trick, scheme, or device a material fact, or makes any false, fictitious or fraudulent statements or representations, or makes or uses any false writing or document knowing the same to contain any false, fictitious or fraudulent statement or entry, shall be fined not more than $10,000 or imprisoned not more than five years, or both.

1005. Bank Entries, Reports and Transactions

Whoever, being an officer, director, agent, or employee of any Federal Reserve Bank, member bank, national bank or insured bank, without authority from the directors of such bank, issues or puts in circulation any notes of such bank; or

Whoever, without such authority, makes, draws, issues, puts forth, or assigns any certificate of deposit, draft, order, bill of exchange, acceptance, note, debenture, bond, or other obligation, or mortgage, judgment or decree; or

Whoever makes any false entry in any book, report or statement of such bank with intent to injure or defraud such bank, or any other company, body politic or corporate, or any individual person, or to deceive any officer of such bank, or the Comptroller of the Currency, or the Federal Deposit Insurance Corporation, or any agent or examiner appointed to examine the affairs of such bank, or the Board of Governors of the Federal Reserve System—

Shall be fined not more than $5,000 or imprisoned not more than five years, or both.

1014. Loan and Credit Applications Generally; Renewals and Discounts; Crop Insurance

Whoever knowingly makes any false statement or report or willfully overvalues any land, property or security, for the purpose of influencing in any way the action of the Reconstruction Finance Corporation, Farm Credit Administration, Federal Crop Insurance Corporation, Farmers' Home Corporation, the Secretary of Agriculture acting through the Farmers' Home Administration, any Federal intermediate credit bank, or any division, officer, or employee thereof, or of any corporation organized under section 1131-1134m of Title 12, or of any regional agricultural credit corporation established pursuant to law, or of the National Agricultural Credit Corporation, a Federal Home Loan Bank, the Federal Home Loan Bank Board, the Home Owners' Loan Corporation, a Federal Savings and Loan Association, a Federal Land Bank, a Federal Land Bank association, a Federal Reserve Bank, a small business investment company, a Federal credit union, an insured State-chartered credit union, any institution the accounts of which are insured by the Federal Savings and Loan Insurance Corporation, any bank the deposits of which are insured by the Federal Deposit Insurance Corporation, any member of the Federal Home Loan Bank system, the Federal Deposit Insurance Corporation, the Federal Savings and Loan Insurance Corporation, or the Administrator of the National Credit Union Association, upon any application, advance, discount, purchase, purchase agreement, repurchase agreement, commitment, or loan, or any change or extension of any of the same, by renewal, deferment of action or otherwise, or the acceptance, release, or substitution of security therefor, shall be fined not more than $5,000 or imprisoned not more than two years, or both.

A statement is "false" for the purposes of Section 1001 if it were known to be untrue when made, and it is "fraudulent" if it were known to be untrue and was made with the intent to deceive a government agency. For a violation to occur, the agency need not actually be deceived, nor must the agency rely on the false statement. However, the statement must be "material," that is, capable of influencing the agency involved.

The five elements of a typical Section 1001 violation are these: (1) The defendant made a false statement (or used a false document), (2) which was material, (3) regarding a matter within the jurisdiction of any agency of the

United States (4) with knowledge of its falsity and (5) knowingly and willfully (or with reckless disregard for truth or falsity).

Among other things, Section 1005 makes it unlawful for any officer, director, agent, or employee of a federally insured or chartered bank to make any false entries on the books of the institution with the intent to injure or defraud the bank or third parties or to deceive any bank officer, examiner, or government agency. Section 1014 prohibits false statements or reports on any credit application or related comment submitted to a federally insured bank or credit institution for the purpose of influencing the organization's actions in any way. As with Section 1001, the false statements must be willful but need not be relied on and need not actually deceive the agency involved for a violation to occur.

Bank Fraud (18 U.S.C. 1344 et seq.)

A relatively new federal statute makes it a crime to defraud or attempt to defraud a federally chartered or insured bank. Such offenses were previously prosecuted under the more generic fraud statutes, such as mail or wire fraud. The bank fraud statute and related Section 1345, which provides for civil actions by the government to enjoin fraudulent activity, are set out in the following:

1344. Bank Fraud

(a) Whoever knowingly executes, or attempts to execute, a scheme or artifice—

    (1) to defraud a federally chartered or insured financial institution; or

    (2) to obtain any of the moneys, funds, credits, assets, securities, or other property owned by or under the custody or control of a federally chartered or insured financial institution by means of false or fraudulent pretenses, representations, or promises, shall be fined not more than $10,000, or imprisoned not more than five years, or both.

(b) As used in this section, the term "federally chartered" or "insured financial institution" means

    (1) a bank with deposits insured by the Federal Deposit Insurance Corporation;

    (2) an institution with accounts insured by the Federal Savings and Loan Insurance Corporation;

    (3) a credit union with accounts insured by the National Credit Union Administration Board;

    (4) a Federal home loan bank or a member, as defined in section 2 of the Federal Home Loan Bank Act (12 U.S.C. 1422), of the Federal Home Loan Bank System; or

    (5) a bank, banking association, land bank, intermediate credit bank, bank for cooperatives, production credit association, land bank association, mortgage association, trust company, savings bank, or other banking or financial institution organized or operating under the laws of the United States.

1345. Injunctions against Fraud

Whenever it shall appear that any person is engaged or is about
to engage in any act which constitutes or will constitute a violation
of this chapter, the Attorney General may initiate a civil proceeding
in a district court of the United States to enjoin such violation. The
court shall proceed as soon as practicable to the hearing and determination of such an action, and may, at any time before final determination, enter such a restraining order or prohibition, or take such
other action, as is warranted to prevent a continuing and substantial
injury to the United States or to any person or class of persons for
whose protection this action is brought. A proceeding under this section is governed by the Federal Rules of Civil Procedure, except
that, if an indictment has been returned against the respondent, discovery is governed by the Federal Rules of Criminal Procedure.

As in the mail and wire fraud statutes, the terms *scheme* and *artifice
to defraud* include any misrepresentations or other conduct intended to
deceive others to obtain something of value. The prosecution must prove
only an attempt to execute the scheme and need not show that actual loss
occurred, that the victim institution was actually deceived, or that the
defendant personally benefited from the scheme.

Fraud in Connection with Federal Interest Computers (18 U.S.C. 1030)

Computer crime is a new and somewhat amorphous term, referring
both to cases in which a computer is the instrument of a crime and those in
which it is the object. As the instrument, for example, a computer may be
used to direct calls in an otherwise routine fraud scheme to sell shares in a
nonexistent gold mine, or it may be used to steal funds from a bank account;
as the object of a crime, the information contained in a computer may be
stolen or destroyed.

Most computer crimes of both types are prosecuted under traditional
fraud, theft, and embezzlement statutes. A statute enacted in 1984 (18
U.S.C. 1030) makes certain computer-related activity a specific federal
offense. The lengthy statute provides the following:

1030. Fraud and Related Activity in Connection with Computers
  (a) Whoever—
    (1) knowingly accesses a computer without authorization or exceeds
        authorized access, and by means of such conduct obtains
        information that has been determined by the United States
        Government pursuant to an Executive order or statute to require
        protection against unauthorized disclosure for reasons of national
        defense or foreign relations, or any restricted data, as defined in
        paragraph r of section 11 of the Atomic Energy Act of 1954, with
        the intent or reason to believe that such information so obtained

is to be used to the injury of the United States, or to the advantage of any foreign nation;

(2) intentionally accesses a computer without authorization or exceeds authorized access, and thereby obtains information contained in a financial record of a financial institution or of a card issuer as defined in section 1602(n) of title 15, or contained in a file of a consumer reporting agency on a consumer, as such terms are defined in the Fair Credit Reporting Act (15 U.S.C. 1681 et seq.);

(3) intentionally, without authorization to access any computer of a department or agency of the United States, accesses such a computer of that department or agency that is exclusively for the use of the Government of the United States or, in the case of a computer not exclusively for such use, is used by or for the Government of the United States and such conduct affects the use of the Government's operation of such computer;

(4) knowingly and with intent to defraud, accesses a Federal interest computer without authorization, or exceeds authorized access, and by means of such conduct furthers the intended fraud and obtains anything of value, unless the object of the fraud and the thing obtained consists only of the use of the computer;

Shall be punished as provided in subsection (c) of this section.

(5) intentionally accesses a Federal interest computer without authorization, and by means of one or more instances of such conduct alters, damages or destroys information in any such Federal interest computer, or prevents authorized use of any such computer or information, and thereby—

(A) causes loss to one or more others of a value aggregating $1,000 or more during any one year period; or

(B) modifies or impairs, or potentially modifies or impairs, the medical examination, medical diagnosis, medical treatment, or medical care of one or more individuals; or

(6) knowingly and with intent to defraud traffics (as defined in section 1029) in any password or similar information through which a computer may be accessed without authorization, if—

(A) such trafficking affects interstate or foreign commerce; or

(B) such computer is used by or for the Government of the United States;

(b) Whoever attempts to commit an offense under subsection (a) of this section shall be punished as provided in subsection (c) of this section.

(c) The punishment for an offense under subsection (a) or (b) of this section is—

(1) (A) a fine under this title or imprisonment for not more than ten years, or both, in the case of an offense under subsection (a)(1) of this section which does not occur after a conviction for another offense under such subsection, or an attempt to commit an offense punishable under this subparagraph; and

    (B) a fine under this title or imprisonment for not more than twenty years, or both, in the case of an offense under subsection (a)(1) of this section which occurs after a conviction for another offense under such subsection, or an attempt to commit an offense punishable under this subparagraph; and

  (2) (A) a fine under this title or imprisonment for not more than one year, or both, in the case of an offense under subsection (a)(2), (a)(3) or (a)(6) of this section which does not occur after a conviction for another offense under such subsection, or an attempt to commit an offense punishable under this subparagraph; and

    (B) a fine under this title or imprisonment for not more than ten years, or both, in the case of an offense under subsection (a)(2), (a)(3) or (a)(6) of this section which occurs after a conviction for another offense under such subsection, or an attempt to commit an offense punishable under this subparagraph; and

  (3) (A) a fine under this title or imprisonment for not more than five years, or both, in the case of an offense under subsection (a)(4) or (a)(5) of this section which does not occur after a conviction for another offense under such subsection, or an attempt to commit an offense punishable under this subparagraph; and

    (B) a fine under this title or imprisonment for not more than ten years, or both, in the case of an offense under subsection (a)(4) or (a)(5) of this section which occurs after a conviction for another offense under such subsection, or an attempt to commit an offense punishable under this subparagraph.

(d) The United States Secret Service shall, in addition to any other agency having such authority, have the authority to investigate offenses under this section. Such authority of the United States Secret Service shall be exercised in accordance with an agreement which shall be entered into by the Secretary of the Treasury and the Attorney General.

(e) As used in this section—

  (1) the term "computer" means an electronic, magnetic, optical, electrochemical, or other high-speed data-processing device performing logical, arithmetic, or storage functions, and includes any data storage facility or communications facility directly related to or operating in conjunction with such device, but such term does not include an automated typewriter or typesetter, a portable hand-held calculator, or other similar device;

  (2) the term "federal interest computer" means a computer—

    (A) exclusively for the use of a financial institution or the United States Government, or, in the case of a computer not exclusively for such use, used by or for a financial institution or the United States Government and the conduct constituting the offense affects the use of the financial institution's operation or the Government's operation of such computer; or

(B) which is one of two or more computers used in committing the offense, not all of which are located in the same State;

(3) the term "State" includes the District of Columbia, the Commonwealth of Puerto Rico, and any other possession or territory of the United States;

(4) the term "financial institution" means—

(A) a bank with deposits insured by the Federal Deposit Insurance Corporation;

(B) the Federal Reserve or a member of the Federal Reserve including any Federal Reserve Bank;

(C) an institution with accounts insured by the Federal Savings and Loan Insurance Corporation;

(D) a credit union with accounts insured by the National Credit Union Administration;

(E) a member of the Federal Home Loan Bank System and any home loan bank;

(F) any institution of the Farm Credit System under the Farm Credit Act of 1971;

(G) a broker-dealer registered with the Securities and Exchange Commission pursuant to section 15 of the Securities Exchange Act of 1934; and

(H) the Securities Investor Protection Corporation;

(5) the term "financial record" means information derived from any record held by a financial institution pertaining to a customer's relationship with the financial institution;

(6) the term "exceeds authorized access" means to access a computer with authorization and to use such access to obtain or alter information in the computer that the accesser is not entitled so to obtain or alter; and

(7) the term "department of the United States" means the legislative or judicial branch of the Government or one of the executive departments enumerated in section 101 of title 5.

(f) This section does not prohibit any lawfully authorized investigative, protective, or intelligence activity of a law enforcement agency of the United States, a State, or a political subdivision of a State, or of an intelligence agency of the United States.

In brief, Section 1030 punishes any intentional, unauthorized access to "federal interest" computers for these purposes:

1. obtaining restricted data regarding national security
2. obtaining confidential financial information
3. using a computer that is intended for use by the United States government
4. committing a fraud
5. damaging or destroying information contained in the computer

The Electronic Funds Transfer Act (15 U.S.C. 1693n)

The Electronic Funds Transfer Act provides, in part, that whoever

1) knowingly, in a transaction affecting interstate or foreign commerce, uses or attempts or conspires to use any counterfeit, fictitious, altered, forged, lost, stolen, or fraudulently obtained debit instrument to obtain money, goods, services, or anything else of value, which within any one-year period has a value aggregating $1,000 or more; or
2) with unlawful or fraudulent intent, transports or attempts or conspires to transport in interstate or foreign commerce a counterfeit, fictitious, altered, forged, lost, stolen, or fraudulently obtained debit instrument knowing the same to be counterfeit, fictitious, altered, forged, lost, stolen or fraudulently obtained, or
3) with unlawful or fraudulent intent, uses any instrumentality of interstate or foreign commerce to sell or transport a counterfeit, fictitious, altered, forged, lost, stolen, or fraudulently obtained debit instrument knowing the same to be counterfeit, fictitious, altered, forged, lost, stolen, or fraudulently obtained; or
4) knowingly receives, conceals, uses or transports money, goods, services, or anything else of value (except tickets for interstate or foreign transportation) which (A) within any one-year period has a value aggregating $1,000 or more, (B) has moved in or is part of, or which constitutes interstate or foreign commerce, and (C) has been obtained with a counterfeit, fictitious, altered, forged, lost, stolen, or fraudulently obtained debit instrument; or
5) in a transaction affecting interstate or foreign commerce, furnishes money, property, services, or anything else of value, which within any one-year period has a value aggregating $1,000 or more, through the use of any counterfeit, fictitious, altered, forged, lost, stolen or fraudulently obtained debit instrument knowing the same to be counterfeit, fictitious, altered, forged, lost, stolen, or fraudulently obtained . . . shall be fined no more than $10,000 or imprisoned not more than ten years, or both.

As used in this section, the term *debit instrument* means a card, code, or other device, other than a check, draft, or similar paper instrument, with which a person may initiate an electronic funds transfer.

Prosecuting Computer-Related Frauds

Federal and state legislatures have moved very quickly to make criminal all manner of computer frauds and abuses, including the theft and destruction of hardware, the misappropriation of software, and the unauthorized accessing of computers and data communications facilities to steal data or money or to cause mischief.

The basic federal law on computer crime (18 U.S.C. 1030(a)(4) makes it illegal when one accesses a Federal interest computer without authorization, or exceeds authorized access.

A *federal interest computer,* under that code, means (1) a computer owned or used by the federal government, (2) one owned or used by a financial institution, or (3) one of two or more computers located in more than one state that were used in committing an offense. The elements of the crime include (1) unauthorized access (or exceeding one's authority), (2) an intent to defraud, and (3) obtaining anything of value. Software, as a thing of value, seems to be included; money is certainly included.

Section 1030(1)(5) provides that anyone who accesses a federal interest computer without authorization, alters or destroys information, and causes an aggregate loss of $1000 or more in one year commits a felony. The penalty for violations of Sections 1030(a)(4) and 1030(a)(5) is up to five years of imprisonment and substantial fines for repeat offenders.

The Federal Computer Fraud and Abuse Act of 1984 (as amended in 1986) does not cover the full body of computer abuses. Its language, for example, does not make it a criminal offense to copy software or misappropriate computer data. Furthermore, it does not cover the unauthorized accessing of computers owned by private businesses or by state governments. However, most states have now enacted laws that make the unauthorized access of computers a crime. The statutes of some states—for example, New York—forbid unauthorized duplication and possession of computer data.

At the state level, statutes that may be of use in prosecuting computer crimes include the penal code violations of larceny (in its many forms), false pretenses, forgery, fraud, embezzlement, vandalism, property destruction, malicious mischief, proprietary information, theft, commercial bribery, and extortion. In addition, most states now expressly provide penalties for crimes perpetrated with computers or perpetrated against computers.

Fraud Laws with Forfeiture Provisions

Money-Laundering Offenses (18 U.S.C. 981)

Title 18, Section 981, of the U.S. Code, as added to by Section 1366(a) of the Anti-Drug Abuse Act of 1986 (Pub. L. 99-570), authorizes civil forfeiture relating to money laundering. Subsection 981(a)(1), which describes three types of property forfeitable to the United States, provides the following:

981. Civil Forfeiture

(a) (1) Except as provided in paragraph (2), the following property is subject to forfeiture to the United States:

(A) Any property, real or personal, which represents the gross receipts a person obtains, directly or indirectly, as a result of a violation of section 1956 or 1957 of this title, or which is traceable to such gross receipts.

(B) Any property within the jurisdiction of the United States, which represents the proceeds of an offense against a foreign nation involving the manufacture, importation, sale, or distribution of a controlled substance (as such term is defined for the purposes of the Controlled Substances Act), within whose jurisdiction such offense or activity would be punishable by death or imprisonment for a term exceeding one year and which would be punishable by imprisonment for a term exceeding one year if such act or activity had occurred within the jurisdiction of the United States.

(C) Any coin and currency (or other monetary instrument as the Secretary of the Treasury may prescribe) or any interest in other property, including any deposit in a financial institution, traceable to such coin or currency involved in a transaction or attempted transaction in violation of section 5313(a) or 5324 of title 31 may be seized and forfeited to the United States Government. No property or interest in property shall be seized or forfeited if the violation is by a domestic financial institution examined by a Federal bank supervisory agency or a financial institution examined by a Federal bank supervisory agency or a financial institution regulated by the Securities and Exchange Commission or a partner, director, officer, or employee thereof.

Bribe Money (18 U.S.C. 3612)

Section 3612 requires that moneys that have been "paid to or received by any official as a bribe" and "received or tendered in evidence in any United States court, or before any office thereof," must be deposited in the court's registry for disposal in accordance with court order. The statute states that the deposit shall be made "after the final disposition of the case, proceeding or investigation" and that the moneys are "to be subject . . . to the provisions of Section 2042 of Title 28."

Section 2042 provides that where a right to money deposited in court has been adjudicated or is not in dispute and the money has remained on deposit with the court unclaimed by the person entitled to it for at least five years, "such court shall cause such money to be deposited in the Treasury in the name and to the credit of the United States." A claimant entitled to "any such money" may obtain a court order directing payment to him or her "on petition to the court and upon notice to the United States Attorney and full proof of the right thereto."

Section 3612 is clearly not an *in rem* forfeiture statute. However, it has been interpreted to authorize the courts to order the forfeiture of money used to bribe federal or state officials. Underlying these decisions is the equitable principle that a wrongdoer should not be able to call on the power of a court to obtain the return of money tendered to a public official in violation of the law.

One court has emphasized that neither Section 3612 nor Section 2042 contains a provision making it discretionary with the court whether to order the return of bribe money. The court has no discretion to return bribe money where there was no evidence that the defendant had paid the money as a result of fraud or oppression.

Other Seizure Provisions

The following federal statutes and regulations contain provisions for seizure:

Statute	Description
15 C.F.R. 30	Foreign trade statistics
15 C.F.R. 30.7	Information required on SED
15 C.F.R. 370.3	Prohibited exports
15 C.F.R. 371	General licenses
15 C.F.R. 372	Validated licenses
15 C.F.R. 379.5	Validated license applications
15 C.F.R. 386	Export clearance
15 C.F.R. 386.1	Shipper's export declarations
15 C.F.R. 386.9	Recall of merchandise
19 C.F.R. 10.31	Temporary importation bonds
19 C.F.R. 10.37	Extension of time for temporary importation
19 C.F.R. 10.39	Temporary importation of articles
19 C.F.R. 18.2	Receipt by carrier; manifest
19 C.F.R. 18.7	Lading for exportation
19 C.F.R. 18.8	Shortages; irregular delivery; nondelivery
19 C.F.R. 18.11	Immediate transportation without appraisement
19 C.F.R. 113.41	Entry made prior to production of documents
19 C.F.R. 113.42	Time period for production of documents
19 C.F.R. 113.43	Extension of time period for production of documents
19 C.F.R. 113.45	Charge against continuous bond
19 C.F.R. 133	Copyright regulations
19 C.F.R. 141.61	Completion of entry and entry summary documentation
19 C.F.R. 141.113	Demand for redelivery; EPA; DOT; recall of merchandise released from customs custody
19 C.F.R. 142.12	Time for filing entry summary
19 C.F.R. 142.13	When entry summary must be filed
19 C.F.R. 142.15	Failure to file entry summary promptly
19 C.F.R. 148.12	Oral declaration of merchandise
19 C.F.R. 148.16	Amendment of declaration
19 C.F.R. 148.18	Declaration of merchandise
19 C.F.R. 161.5	Offers in compromise

Statute	Description
19 C.F.R. 162.31	Content of seizure notices
19 C.F.R. 162.44	Release upon payment of appraised value; authority to accept
19 C.F.R. 162.45	Publication and posting of intent to summarily forfeit
19 C.F.R. 162.48	Summary sale
19 C.F.R. 162.76	Prepenalty notices; vessel repairs
19 C.F.R. 171.5	Extensions of time to file petition
19 C.F.R. 171.11	Petition for relief
19 C.F.R. 171.31	Cancellation of case by district director
19 C.F.R. 172.21	Liquidated damages: petitions acted on by district director
19 C.F.R. 172.22	Liquidated damages: special cases acted on by district director
22 C.F.R. 121.1	U.S. munitions list
22 C.F.R. 123.1	Export license
22 C.F.R. 123.3	In-transit license
22 C.F.R. 123.4	Temporary export license
22 C.F.R. 123.25	Filing licenses and SEDs
22 C.F.R. 123.27	Temporary exports
22 C.F.R. 125.2	Export of unclassified technical data
22 C.F.R. 127.05	Recall of cargo
22 C.F.R. 127.2	Misrepresentation and omission of facts
31 C.F.R. 103.11	Definition of monetary instruments
17 U.S.C. 601	Manufacturing clause
17 U.S.C. 602	Parallel imports
18 U.S.C. 545	Smuggling; nonconforming vehicles
18 U.S.C. 1001	Criminal liability; monetary instruments
19 U.S.C. 1337	Patents
19 U.S.C. 1433	Report of arrival of aircraft and vessels
19 U.S.C. 1434	Entry of U.S. aircraft and vessels
19 U.S.C. 1435	Entry of foreign aircraft and vessels
19 U.S.C. 1436	Penalties; failure to enter aircraft and vessels
19 U.S.C. 1439	Failure to deliver manifest
19 U.S.C. 1440	Failure to correct manifest
19 U.S.C. 1448	Retaining merchandise for entry and delivery permit; permits to unlade
19 U.S.C. 1453	Unlading merchandise without permit
19 U.S.C. 1454	Unlading passengers without permit
19 U.S.C. 1459, 1460	Seizure of undeclared merchandise; nonconforming vehicles
19 U.S.C. 1466	Equipment and repair of vessels
19 U.S.C. 1497	Seizure of undeclared merchandise; nonconforming vehicles

Statute	*Description*
19 U.S.C. 1499	Delivery without inspection, examination, or appraisal
19 U.S.C. 1526	Trademarks
19 U.S.C. 1552	Entry for immediate transportation
19 U.S.C. 1553	Entry for transportation and exportation
19 U.S.C. 1584	Manifests
19 U.S.C. 1592	Commercial fraud and negligence
19 U.S.C. 1594	Common carrier exception to seizure and forfeiture
19 U.S.C. 1595a(a)	Conveyance seizures and forfeitures
19 U.S.C. 1595a(b)	Illegal importations
19 U.S.C. 1602, 1603	Seizure; report to U.S. Attorney
19 U.S.C. 1604	U.S. Attorney; prosecute or decline
19 U.S.C. 1606	Appraisal of seized property
19 U.S.C. 1607	Notice of intent to forfeit and sell
19 U.S.C. 1612	Immediate sale of seized property
19 U.S.C. 1613	Disposition of proceeds of forfeited property; claim for proceeds of sale
19 U.S.C. 1614	Substitution of collateral
19 U.S.C. 1617	Offers in compromise
19 U.S.C. 1619	Award of compensation to informers
19 U.S.C. 1621	Statute of limitations for forfeitures under customs laws and navigation laws
19 U.S.C. 1623	Customs bonds
19 U.S.C. 1627	Importation and exportation of vehicles
19 U.S.C. 1644	Application of customs laws to aircraft
19 U.S.C. 1703	Conveyances outfitted for smuggling
21 U.S.C. 881	Conveyance seizures; common carrier exemption
22 U.S.C. 401	Seizure and forfeiture for illegal exportation
22 U.S.C. 2778	Export and import of defense articles
28 U.S.C. 2415	Statute of limitations for bond violations
31 U.S.C. 5316	Monetary instrument reporting
31 U.S.C. 5317	Seizure of unreported monetary instruments
31 U.S.C. 5322	Criminal liability for unreported monetary instruments
31 U.S.C. 5323	Awards of compensation to informers
46 U.S.C. 91	Departure of vessels and aircraft
46 U.S.C. 289	Coastwise transportation: passengers
46 U.S.C. 883	Coastwise transportation: merchandise
49 U.S.C. 781, 782	Conveyance seizures and forfeitures

Statute	*Description*
49 U.S.C. 1474	Violations of 49 U.S.C. 1509
49 U.S.C. 1509	Entry and clearance of aircraft

Notes

1. McNally v. U.S., 107 S.Ct. 2875 (1987).
2. 18 U.S.C. 1346.
3. 15 U.S.C. 78m(b)2.

CHAPTER 14

Chronology of Computer-Related Crime: 1985 to 1990

A large number of corporate frauds today involve the falsification of accounting and other data that are processed by computer. These manipulations of data are generally committed by corporate insiders in an effort to deceive outsiders such as stockholders, bank lenders, and government regulators. There is also a growing trend of outsiders, sometimes called computer *hackers,* attempting to manipulate corporate computer systems and data bases for their own illegal purposes. The range of such illegal acts includes toll-call fraud (charging long-distance calls to someone else), theft of trade secrets, theft of computer time, destruction of data, and virus implanting. A review of some of the more celebrated incidents, as reported in the *Computer Security Digest,* may provide some insight on the nature and scope of the problem. (The *Computer Security Digest* is a monthly newsletter published by Computer Protection Systems, Inc., Plymouth, Michigan, and is edited by Jack Bologna.)

News Summaries

January 1985

• An investigation of an American neo-Nazi group called the White American Bastion or Bruder Schweigen (German Silent Brotherhood) uncovered microcomputers and data bases allegedly used to carry out terrorist activities. Group members used a computer network to keep in contact with each other and to maintain a list of their enemies. According to the *Detroit Free Press,* "The network, created by an electronics engineer who belongs to the group, allows members to call phone numbers in Idaho and Texas and to call up an 'Aryan Database' on the home micros. The network has seven levels of access, each reached by typing in code words; and it includes hit lists of Jewish groups and individuals."

The group, which has an estimated 150 members, allegedly finances itself in part by robbing armored cars and by counterfeiting. One large weapons and munitions cache has been uncovered. The neo-Nazi group allegedly used an award system for candidates for membership: To become an "Aryan warrior," applicants had to accumulate a total of one point. Fractions of a point were awarded for such things as murdering a federal judge, an FBI agent, and other federal officials and employees and murdering Jewish people, blacks, and others. This group is suspected in the machine-gun execution of a Denver radio personality who spoke out against anti-Semites and white supremacists. (*Detroit Free Press*, 12/30/84.)

• Albert Collins, 25, a clerk in the U.S. Customs Service's financial management division, has been arrested and charged with accessing a government computer and modifying data without proper authorization. Between August and October 1984, Collins allegedly wrote more than 40 U.S. Treasury Department checks for Patrick A. Bell, Lonzie W. Hunt, and Bernie Nelson. The checks, which had been cashed, amounted to almost $160,000. Bell, Hunt, and Nelson have been charged with attempting to file a false claim with the U.S. government, defrauding the government, and embezzling. The possible penalty is up to 25 years in prison and a $30,000 fine. Collins faces the same charges in addition to the illegal access and modification charge. His possible penalty is up to 26 years in prison and a $36,000 fine. (*Computerworld*, 12/3/84.)

• Scott Robinson, a trustee-inmate at the Santa Clara County Jail, California, allegedly signed onto a terminal and changed his release date from December 31 to December 5. He wanted to be home for Christmas with his two children. Robinson, who is serving time for stealing video games, was apparently able to gain access to a terminal while working in the misdemeanor booking area of the sheriff's department. Robinson's Christmas wish was spoiled when a deputy who heard him mention his release date became suspicious and checked written records. He had apparently learned how to use the terminal and its access code by looking over the shoulder of the terminal operator. It is unknown if other prisoner release dates were changed or how he managed to use the terminal in an area supposedly staffed by at least two deputies. (*Detroit Free Press*, 12/25/84.)

• A computer club in Hamburg has allegedly broken the secret video text network code of the Bundespost, the West German postal and telephone authority. The breaking of the code by the Chaos Computer Club allowed members to use a bank's phone account to make 13,000 calls over a 13-hour period. Because of the calls, Hamburger Sparkasse, the large savings bank group, was charged the equivalent of $45,000 in communication usage fees. (*Security Letter*, 12/17/84.)

• A 19-year-old hacker allegedly used a microcomputer to access a British telecommunications data base in which he changed the rate for converting pounds to dollars in a London Stock Exchange account. He was also able to access a personal message from Prince Philip to Princess Diana. (*Security Letter*, 12/17/84.)

• A two-week investigation led to the apprehension of a 15-year-old in Clayton, Missouri, for theft and fraudulent use of a credit card. St. Louis County police arrested the boy, who allegedly used credit card numbers taken from discarded charge receipts to buy more than $3000 in merchandise, including a $1000 microcomputer. He allegedly had approximately 250 carbon receipts that he had taken from trash containers in various stores in a local mall. Police say that the youth used his computer to gain access to the computer network of the Credit Information Bureau in Florida and that he checked the credit limits on the accounts from the carbon receipts and ordered merchandise by phone, using the valid account numbers. The merchandise was sent to a vacant house, where he allegedly retrieved it. The investigation is continuing because other students may have been involved. (*Detroit Free Press*, 12/21/84.)

• Recent research describes the possibility of using computer program "viruses" to destroy a computer's processing capabilities. A computer virus is a small program that "infects" other programs, usually by inserting devastating instructions into them. Security specialists in both the private and public sectors are quite concerned about the potential for damage from the virus-like programs. Some believe the concept to be so sensitive that it should not be a topic for public discussion. However, computer games that resemble a controlled "viral" attack have already been devised. (*Detroit News*, 12/6/84; *Discovery Magazine*, November 1984.)

• Two reporters, Mike Wendland of WDIV-TV in Detroit and Richard Sandza of *Newsweek*, claim to be the victims of retaliation for their reports exposing hacker antics and the underground bulletin boards that hackers run. The retaliation by the hackers against Sandza allegedly included the following:

- hundreds of calls, some threatening to blow up his home, disconnect his telephone, or turn off his power
- the accessing of his credit records on the TRW data base
- the posting of his credit card number on Pirate 80, an electronic bulletin board in Charleston, West Virginia.

USA Today reported that when Sandza unplugged his phone to avoid harassing phone calls, one sympathetic hacker sent him a bouquet of flowers that had been charged to a stolen credit card number. (*Detroit Free Press*, 12/5/84 to 12/8/84; *MIS*, 12/12/84; *USA Today*, 12/13/84.)

February 1985

• Robert J. Hoxie, 24, a self-employed programmer, has been charged with the theft of $100,000 in what Harris County, Texas, authorities said was a high-tech fraud involving the illegal accessing of the Greater Houston Credit Bureau's computerized records. Hoxie allegedly accessed the credit history of 38 affluent local residents, used the names and credit information to acquire 76 Mastercard and VISA credit cards from the First City Bank in Dallas, and used the cards to obtain at least $100,000 from a number of automated teller machines (ATMs). Investigators have not yet found any computer equipment that Hoxie may have used to access the credit bureau's data base. The credit cards were mailed to addresses and post office boxes that differed from the home addresses of the residents.

While using the ATMs, Hoxie allegedly wore a wig and sunglasses to elude photographic surveillance cameras. An investigation into a delinquent credit card account led to the investigation of Hoxie. The case is still under investigation by Houston authorities. (*Computerworld*, 1/14/85.)

• Minneapolis police asked hacker Peter Leppik, 15, to help them break a security system that prevented them from reading a 37-year-old programmer's accounts of sex with young boys. The stories were stored on floppy disks. Leppik needed only 45 minutes to break the security system that had confounded police for almost a month. (Leppik was involved in an investigation about a year ago when he allegedly accessed a bank's computer.) The computer programmer was arrested last year for allegedly paying a 13-year-old boy for sex. Police searched the suspect's apartment and confiscated the computer disks. Leppik used the computer vendor's documentation manuals and a "convert" command to break the coding scheme used to protect the disks, which allegedly contained graphic narrative about sexual involvement with juvenile boys. It is currently unknown whether the accounts are fact or fantasy. The investigation is continuing. (*Detroit Free Press*, 1/15/85.)

• A bomb planted in a baby carriage in a Stuttgart, West Germany, industrial center exploded, causing about $1 million in damages to a computer center. The bomb went off prematurely, killing a convicted terrorist and injuring a woman suspected of being his accomplice. The bomb may have been intended for a government research site or a state police building, both 150 yards away from the site of the blast. Authorities said that the bombing appeared to be the latest in a series of bombings in support of a hunger strike by imprisoned members of the extreme leftist Red Army Faction, originally known as the Baader-Meinhof gang. (*Detroit Free Press*, 1/22/85.)

March 1985

• A computer programmer, Philip Gonzales Fadriquela, 26, has been indicted by a federal grand jury on seven counts for illegally accessing the U.S. Department of Agriculture's computer and the Forest Service's computer in Colorado. Fadriquela allegedly used the GTE Telenet and Tymnet, Inc., communications networks to access the computers and made unauthorized use of a special password to enter the Telenet network. Fadriquela allegedly inserted fraudulent user codes and passwords into the computer programs and printed out information from the computer fields. GTE personnel noticed unusual communications traffic, leading to the investigation now being conducted by the U.S. Attorney's office in Denver and the FBI.

The indictment contains seven charges:

- four misdemeanor charges brought under the new federal Computer Fraud and Abuse Act of 1984,
- two charges of felony wire fraud,
- one charge of making false statements to a federal agency.

The charges cover a period from December 22 to January 26. (*Computerworld*, 2/11/85.)

- The January 28 issue of *Computerworld* reports on recent terrorist activities in West Germany:

  - During the first quarter of 1984, there were 17 bombings and 45 fires.
  - At least 24 bombings were directed at computer centers in 1984.
  - Since December 4, 1984, there have been more than 40 terrorist attacks against computer centers.

The Red Army Faction has claimed responsibility for many of the attacks in protest against American business and military installations in West Germany. (*Computerworld*, 1/28/85.)

April 1985

- A government report entitled "Electronic Funds Transfer Fraud," released by the U.S. Department of Justice, indicates that the fraudulent use of ATMs costs banks and their customers $70 to $100 million in 1983. Among the report's findings are these:

  - Approximately 2.7 billion ATM transactions involving $262 billion were processed in 1983. About 43,800 ATMs are installed in the United States.
  - A sample study of 2707 "problem incidents" indicated that 45% were potentially fraudulent, involving unauthorized use of lost or stolen cards, overdrafts, and bad deposits.
  - Of the cases involving stolen cards, 72% involved users who had kept their personal identification numbers near their cards (in their purses or wallets or written on the cards themselves).
  - The findings were based on information supplied by 16 large banks, all but one with deposits in excess of $1 billion.
  - The 16 participating banks reported 139 "problem" electronic funds transfer (EFT) transactions involving an average of more than $800,000 each. About 56% of these incidents resulted in an actual loss to the bank.
  - A report by the Bureau of Justice Statistics indicates that as much as $10,000 has been stolen through a single cash card, despite safeguards built into the system.
  - Federal Regulation E of the Electronic Funds Transfer Act of 1978 limits account holder liability to $50 if an ATM card is reported

missing within two days of discovery or $500 if the card is reported later. The rest of the loss is absorbed by the bank.

- Some losses are attributed to bank employees who take newly issued cards from the mailing room or take cards that have been returned because of an incorrect mailing address.
- A number of losses to customers were attributed to ATM technical failure or human error.
- The Bureau of Justice Statistics arrived at the estimated loss of $70 to $100 million by comparing the ratio of fraud losses in the banks surveyed to the volume of their ATM transactions and then extrapolating that ratio to U.S. banks generally.

- BPI Systems of Austin, Texas, has filed suit against KWIK-KOPY Corp. of Houston for illegally copying and distributing BPI software. BPI's suit alleges that since 1981, KWIK-KOPY has required an estimated nine hundred franchises to buy from the corporation the pirated versions of BPI general ledger and accounts receivable software for the Apple II Plus. KWIK-KOPY allegedly tried to disguise the software by deleting BPI's copyright notice from the software itself and from the user's manual. Several program instructions that instructed the computer to check for the presence of BPI's copy protection device were also supposedly deleted. The alleged copying scam was uncovered when a BPI salesman visited a KWIK-KOPY franchise and was given a demo that the salesman recognized was identical to BPI's package. (*Computerworld*, 3/18/85; *MIS*, 3/20/85.)

May 1985

- Eight people were arraigned in Boston on charges of illegal gambling, conspiracy, money laundering, and evasion of state taxes. The charges were the result of an investigation into a multimillion dollar computerized bookmaking operation known as the National Sports Betting Syndicate. The high-tech operation included the use of personal computers, telephone call diverters, and communication scramblers.

One computer security specialist indicated that the syndicate probably used a system such as those used by some banks and retail businesses. Touch-Tone phones were used to gain access to a computer. After an account number was entered, a computer-based voice-response system gave instructions for entering the required information (racetrack ID, race number, and horse ID). Telephone call diverting equipment was allegedly used to transfer calls to a Boston computer to avoid the calls being traced. (*Computerworld*, 4/15/85.)

- The Los Angeles Police Department's computer fraud unit is currently investigating a programmed "logic bomb" that halted operations on the Department of Water and Power's IBM 3081 computer. It is thought that an insider is responsible for placing the logic bomb, which caused the system to crash every time it was used. A Department of Water and Power spokesperson said that it took 20 people almost a week to track down the problem and bring the system back up to stay. While the system was crashing, DWP personnel were unable to enter orders for new water and electricity connections. (*Computerworld,* 4/15/85.)

• The U.S. Secret Service has arrested six high-school students in Milwaukee for allegedly taking part in a nationwide caper by computer hackers to obtain computer goods and services valued at thousands of dollars. Among the case highlights are the following (*Milwaukee Journal,* 4/30/85):

> • More than three dozen computer hobbyists are thought to be involved, and most are juveniles. More arrests are anticipated in Detroit, Seattle, Los Angeles, Chicago, and Memphis.
>
> • The students allegedly used the hacking scheme to buy computers and related equipment with stolen credit card numbers. The equipment was sent to a mailbox rental service in Waukesha. The Secret Service installed a surveillance camera at the site in March to monitor pickups from the mailbox.
>
> • Operational procedures on how to perpetrate the scam were posted on an electronic bulletin board, The World of Cryton, which was operated out of Milwaukee and also contained a list of stolen credit card numbers. The procedures were written by someone known as Iceman, Leader of the Black Triangle.
>
> • The stolen credit card numbers were allegedly obtained from computer data bases that the hackers had illegally accessed and by foraging for discarded carbon receipts of credit card purchases.
>
> • Stolen credit card numbers were used to establish accounts with CompuServe and the Source. These accounts allow users to exchange electronic messages and to buy goods and services from their home or office.

June 1985

• Detroit-area hackers have been arrested and charged in the recent crackdown by federal, state, and local law enforcement agencies. Interesting case information is contained in the news accounts that sheds some light on the various methods used by hackers. Prudent computer security personnel should be aware of the hackers' techniques and methods so that they can take adequate security measures. The following are summaries of two incidents involving the Detroit-area hackers:

> • Andrew John Dennis, 17, a senior at Grosse Pointe North High School, was arrested after picking up a package delivered to a vacant Grosse Pointe Farms, Michigan, home. It is alleged that Dennis collected more than $5000 in consumer goods by obtaining credit card numbers from discarded charge slips that he found in

the trash behind local businesses and charging mail-order goods to the account numbers. Dennis allegedly used an underground electronic bulletin board to learn how to order goods by phone. Because he cooperated with investigating authorities, he was charged with a misdemeanor rather than a felony. He could face up to 90 days in jail, a $500 fine, or both, if convicted.

A search of Dennis's computer uncovered restricted telephone numbers for the White House and the Secret Service. He allegedly gained access to a teleconferencing network that allowed him to make free phone calls to all over the world. Investigators from several agencies were involved: United Parcel Service, Michigan National Bank, Michigan State Police, Grosse Pointe Farms Police, the FBI, and the U.S. Secret Service. The investigation was initiated after a credit card customer found several charges from mail-order firms that he had not made.

- Another young hacker known as Time Lord, Ruler of Cosmos, ruled his electronic kingdom from his bedroom in West Bloomfield, Michigan. The 16-year-old hacker, whose name has not been released by authorities, is a sophomore at Birmingham Groves High School. The youth allegedly masterminded one of the most notorious electronic bulletin boards in the United States and ran the equivalent of a street gang with an Apple II computer. The hacker gang allegedly traded information on how to make bombs and smuggle drugs. The youth said that only the "elite" among computer hackers frequented his board, which took the name Cosmos from Michigan Bell Telephone Co.'s computer system. A Farmington Hills police officer said that the bulletin board served as a model for others. There were eight levels of access, and hackers could buy their way up with credit card numbers and other information. The 16-year-old said that he had intended to quit the hacking business once he became 18 because he knew that the penalty of getting caught and being charged as an adult would be much greater than that of being charged as a minor. (*Detroit Free Press*, 5/1/85; 5/19/85.)

- *Computerworld* reported that hackers gained access to the U.S. Geological Survey's computer system on five occasions. No harm was reportedly done, and most hackers were traced and caught. The latest hacking incident was allegedly done by a 10-year-old child. (*Computerworld*, 5/20/85.)
- The American military is making illicit copies of microcomputer software, according to *Datamation*. Attorneys are investigating evidence that four thousand personal computer users at one military base are using copied software. Vendors report that users of pirated software at military bases are adding insult to injury by calling the software help lines for assistance. Their calls led to the investigation. (*Datamation*, 5/1/85.)

August 1985

• Two data-entry operators from Consumer Retail Services, Inc., in Denver have agreed to plead guilty to charges of computer crime and credit card fraud. The two women were participants in a crime ring that created about 40 fraudulent credit cards and accumulated charges of $50,000. The operators allegedly assigned new account numbers to themselves and their associates and issued new credit cards. The cards were used to purchase merchandise up to the credit limit, and the computer records were then altered so that bills would be sent to fictitious addresses. (*Computerworld,* 7/15/85.)

October 1985

• Charles Kevin Smith, 22, has been charged under federal wire fraud laws for using his personal computer to access a GM computer near Flint, Michigan. Four others were allegedly involved in the unauthorized access, but because they were minors, they could not be charged under federal law. FBI officials stated that there was no theft or tampering with GM's computer files, but the group's alleged use of the computer deprived GM of the computer time it needed to service its dealer orders. It is not known how much processing time the company lost. (*Detroit Free Press,* 9/12/85.)

November 1985

• A tip has apparently sparked what is believed to be the first formal federal investigation of a software piracy case. A $3 million lawsuit filed by lawyers for Pagetec, Inc., alleges that the Institute of Scientific Information, a publisher, provided Ralph Garner Associates, a New York typesetting firm, with an unauthorized copy of a $4800 data base program licensed by Pagetec. FBI agents also uncovered other allegedly pirated software, including Micropro International's Wordstar programs. The FBI is continuing the investigation of the Institute and Garner Associates for violation of federal copyright statutes and for interstate transportation of stolen property. (*Computerworld,* 10/14/85.)

December 1985

It appears that organizations have not yet learned to secure their computer systems. FBI agents have seized 25 microcomputer systems from San Diego area teens who allegedly accessed Interactive Data Corp.'s computer. Interactive Data, a subsidiary of Chase Manhattan Corp., located in Waltham, Massachusetts, maintains Chase's financial records. Among the case highlights are these (*Computerworld,* 10/28/85):

  • Allegedly involved in the unauthorized access were 23 teenagers, ages 13 to 17, some of whom know each other.

- Apparently, no money was taken or transferred from accounts.
- The youths changed a number of passwords that prevented authorized access to accounts.
- One fictitious account was created and files were destroyed or modified.
- The hackers allegedly threatened to destroy records unless they were given free access to the system.
- The investigation began when Interactive Data found that several unsuccessful attempts were made to enter Chase's records via a toll-free number used by qualified system users. The FBI traced the unauthorized phone calls to the computer.
- The teens could be charged under the Federal Computer Fraud and Abuse Act of 1984.

March 1986

- An Atlanta, Georgia, consultant was arrested by police in Madison Heights, Michigan, and charged with larceny for stealing a computerized list of 11,000 customers from McIntyre's Mini Computer Sales Group, which is based in Troy, Michigan. The consultant has been charged with using a computer to commit larceny of more than $100. McIntyre's is a seven-year-old company that buys, sells, trades, and services minicomputers. President Michael McIntyre charges that the consultant copied the company's list of Data General users and sold the information to competition around the country. (*Crain's Detroit Business,* 2/10/86.)
- Michael P. Wilkerson, 18, of Kirkland, Washington, admitted to accessing the computers of four Seattle-area companies, including Microsoft Corp. Wilkerson was apparently able to issue payroll checks at one company and to establish new accounts and passwords, locking out system operators, at others. He also allegedly copied files. Police seized several computers and more than three hundred disks from Wilkerson's home. They also confiscated a list of credit card numbers with names and expiration dates; printouts of information from Microsoft; and directions and access codes to dial up the credit reporting agency, TRW. Wilkerson admitted to checking some 50,000 telephone numbers for modem tones. (*Computerworld,* 2/17/86.)
- Thomas Taylor, 68, of Taylor Systems in Lafayette, California, was found guilty on five counts of federal copyright infringement. Taylor reproduced and distributed at least two copies of Cimarron 4.03, a court reporting software package developed by Stenograph Corp. of Skokie, Illinois. The software package normally sells for $30,000. Taylor duplicated the software protect board as well as the software itself, and he sold it for about $15,000. Taylor faces a maximum of four years in prison and a $50,000 fine. (*MIS Week,* 2/10/86; *Computerworld,* 2/10/86.)
- Alvin Frost, a Washington, D.C., city accountant, created a password that prevented others from accessing files containing background statistics and

administrative information. His reason for the action was to bring to light the city's financial management system, which he claims "is rife with incompetence, mismanagement, negligence, political favoritism, intimidation [and] indifference." Frost said he used language from the Declaration of Independence to formulate the seven-character password. He said that reading the Declaration would provide clues, adding that he could not remember the exact password himself, only the clues. He claimed to have put clues in the classified section of the *Washington Post* and promised free trips to the Washington Monument for children who wrote him with the correct answer. Frost resigned from his job, but a letter informing him of his dismissal was waiting for him at the office. (*Detroit Free Press,* 2/14/86.)

May 1986

• A high-tech "sting" operation by police authorities in the Silicon Valley disclosed that area teenage hackers had penetrated a dozen corporate, government, and university mainframes. The police agency created its own bulletin board and assumed the identity of a hacker. It then "baited" its board with some valid system passwords and account numbers and waited to see who would take the bait. (*Computerworld,* 3/17/86.)

• A veteran FBI specialist in Soviet counterintelligence is under investigation for selling government secrets he acquired in the FBI's computer center in Washington, D.C. He is said to have needed the money to pay gambling debts. (*Detroit Free Press,* 4/28/86.)

• Even the Congress is not immune to computer security problems. Two House members claim that outsiders accessed their office computer systems and destroyed letters and mailing addresses. However, the Office Automation (OA) equipment supplier disputes this contention, suggesting that it would take a password, two security codes, and a Ph.D. in math or computer science to breach the system as alleged. (*Computerworld,* 4/14/86.)

The City of Detroit finds itself with a problem. A department head in the city's income tax processing section has been arrested for allegedly engineering a scheme in which he caused phony income tax refund checks amounting to over $100,000 to be issued. The indictment charges that the refund checks were made payable to several of his friends, who cashed the checks and divided the proceeds 60/40 with him. The department head had been assigned to a project team that designed the income tax processing system for the city, which allegedly made him knowledgeable about the system's control weaknesses. (*Detroit Free Press,* 6/5/86.)

July 1986

• A strange case of homicide, not by a computer but because of a computer, took place in Southfield, Michigan, in June. Giuseppe Paletta, 42, was shot by his wife while on an elevator to visit their stockholder's office to confirm their account balance. His wife claimed that she had been beaten by Paletta before and feared for her life. She had lost money trading in the commodities market with a computer program he had designed for her. She lost their entire savings of about $1.5 million, but she had told her husband that they were ahead by about $30 million. (*Detroit Free Press*, 6/20/86.)

• Captain Midnight, who amazed the nighttime world of cable television viewers, was unmasked after a three-month search by the Federal Communications Commission (FCC). Captain Midnight turned out to be a satellite dish retailer from Ocala, Florida, who had a grudge against cable broadcaster HBO. HBO's decision to scramble its transmissions cut into the retailer's sales of satellite dishes. In retaliation, he overrode HBO's signal in April. He now faces a $5000 fine and revocation of his radio license. (*Computerworld*, 7/28/86.)

• A 15-year-old part-time custodial employee of the C&P Telephone Company is alleged to have set a fire at C&P's data support center in Silver Spring, Maryland. There was no data loss, and phone service was not interrupted. However, two hundred IBM terminals and personal computers were reduced to rubble, and peripheral equipment will need extensive repair. The loss may cost C&P up to $5 million. The alleged arsonist was said to be suffering from "personal problems." (*MIS Week*, 7/28/86.)

• The Swedish Crime Prevention Council underwrote a research effort on computer crime in Sweden. A summary of the findings has been published by the U.S. Department of Justice (National Institute of Justice/NCJRS, NCJ 99853). The report presents some interesting data:

   • Sixty percent of computer-related crimes (embezzlements) were committed over a period of one to nine years before detection.
   • The overwhelming majority of cases involved manipulation of input data.
   • Most EDP-related embezzlers tended to be younger than other embezzlers.
   • Most offenders had no prior criminal records, and they had manifested no previous problem behavior on the job. (U.S. Department of Justice: National Institute of Justice/NCJRS, NCJ 99853).

September 1986

• Computer hackers were the subject of a lot of news attention in August. A 17-year-old Rocky River, Ohio, boy was charged with using his home computer—a Commodore 64—to break into school computers in Ohio, Texas, and Wisconsin. He allegedly also accessed a computer system of the U.S. Congress in Washington, D.C. (*Computerworld*, 8/11/86.)

• In California, a former USC student was convicted of using a university computer to change his grades. (*Computerworld*, 9/1/86.)

• Five North Carolina men, ages 23 to 40, were indicted on charges of

computer fraud. They are alleged to have exchanged information about long-distance telephone access codes by way of their home computers. (*Computerworld,* 9/1/86.)
• In New Zealand, a school boy outsmarted a bank ATM by using a piece of cardboard from a lollipop packet to transfer $1 million (NZ) into his own account. The headmaster at his school did not consider the boy to be one of the brighter students—"until now." (*USA Today,* 8/15/86.)

October 1986

• Printed circuit boards and peripherals made by Digital Equipment Corp. (DEC) are in great demand in the underground market. In September, the Ohio State University College of Engineering was burglarized. The university lost about $450,000 in equipment, including 22 VAX 8500 printed circuit boards. Similar VAX thefts have been reported from DEC-user sites in other states too. Last spring, a Slumberger subsidiary in Westerville, Ohio, lost 50 VAX-11-780 printed circuit boards worth about $200,000. DEC's own facility in Tacoma, Washington, was also hit for about $200,000 in circuit boards. The loot is most likely going to Iron Curtain countries. The FBI announced the arrest of a computer technician suspected in the Ohio theft. (*Computerworld,* 9/29/86, 10/6/86; *Detroit Free Press,* 10/10/86.)
• *Telecomputist,* a hacker newsletter, ran copies of the Bloom County comic strip recently—without the permission of the strip's creator, Berke Breathed, or its syndicator, the Washington Post Writer's Group. *Telecomputist* was told to cease and desist from any further copyright infringements. (*Detroit News,* 9/23/86.)

March 1987

• The computerized financial records of Prescott Valley, Arizona, were erased recently. No one knows how much money has been spent this year or on what account, and no one knows how much cash is left. Each account shows a zero balance. A town clerk says it was a deliberate attack by one person, who has not been identified yet. The records can be manually reconstructed, but it will take much time and effort. Police have undertaken an investigation. (*New York Times,* 2/15/87.)
• Two top executives of Intelstat were accused of diverting $5 million in funds from the international satellite consortium. The case surfaced when Intelstat's outside auditors, Peat Marwick Mitchell & Co., discovered an unauthorized payment of $1.35 million to loan brokers who were refinancing the company's headquarters building in a Washington D.C., suburb. (*Network World,* 2/3/87.)
• A former senior vice-president of Mitsubishi Bank of California was charged with embezzling $44 million from the bank and its Tokyo-based parent company. He allegedly created 135 fraudulent loans and loan renewals

to conceal his embezzlement and used the proceeds to pay off personal gambling debts and invest in the stock market. The bank executive returned to Tokyo after the alleged defalcation was discovered. The L.A. District Attorney is now seeking his extradition to the United States to stand trial. (*Wall Street Journal*, 2/20/87.)

August 1987

• A former employee of Eastman-Kodak was convicted of computer tampering. He shut down Eastman-Kodak's telephone lines by tapping into the company's local area network (LAN) from his home computer. It took repair technicians two hours to restore service at the facility. A script file, which monitors system activity, was used to track down the suspect. The printed logs and the culprit's home phone bills were used in evidence against him. (*Computerworld*, 7/27/87.)

October 1987

• Computer hobbyists in West Germany allegedly planted a Trojan horse in a NASA data base that granted them easy access to nonclassified information for about three months. Their activities were discovered by a system manager for a user organization. The incident apparently caused more embarrassment than financial damage for NASA. Although all incidents of unauthorized access carry the danger of data destruction or alteration, it does not appear that the hacker intrusions resulted in any such damage. A spokesman for the hackers said that such behavior would have violated "hacker ethics." The NASA system uses a VAX computer that has been upgraded for security in the United States, but the European network did not have the new facility. (*New York Times*, 9/16/87.)

• A Chicago teenager allegedly accessed Bell System computers and copied certain nonsensitive programs. He also shared his experience on a Texas electronic bulletin board for computer enthusiasts who seek to penetrate public-sector computer systems. Secret Service agents confiscated the boy's home computer equipment and the bootlegged software. In analyzing his telephone toll calls, they found that he was also attempting to gain access to other systems, such as the *Washington Post*'s accounts payable program. (*Detroit News*, 9/18/87.)

November 1987

• A recent news story details a case in which detected discrepancies were used to uncover a computer crime. A branch manager of the Family Bank of Ogden, Utah, in attempting to cover up a sour loan he had made to a gambler, "borrowed" more money from the bank for the gambler, who assured him that he would parlay the money into a large enough sum to pay everything back. The branch manager's scheme involved fabricating $4 million in loan accounts using the bank's computer. The scheme was discovered by the bank's president, who accidentally picked up a sheaf of computer records and found therein a usually dormant account with about $800,000 in it. It made him curious, but not soon enough to save the bank. It collapsed in 1986. (*Wall Street Journal*, 10/2/87.)

January 1988

• IBM's E-mail network played host to a holiday message of cheer that reverberated worldwide last month. The network is not used exclusively by IBM; it can be accessed by outside customers and suppliers. One outside customer or supplier apparently employs a programmer with a distorted sense of humor or a big heart for holiday cheer. The holiday message to other IBM network users also contained a program that searched the files of individual users for automatic distribution lists. The holiday message was then sent to those people, and *their* files were combed for distribution lists. The geometric progression of holiday messages soon overtaxed the network. IBM tracked down the problem after a few hours and feels confident that it can prevent such messages from clogging its system again. (*Wall Street Journal*, 12/17/87; *Computerworld*, 12/21/87.)
• Two teenage brothers who live in the Detroit area allegedly ran up $15,000 in phone calls charged to the J.L. Hudson Co. executive phone system. The boys allegedly used a home computer to carry on their masquerade. The caper was discovered when a telecommunications service provider used a software package to monitor unusual patterns of use by subscribers. It was the boys' second arrest in four months. A probate court will look into the possibility of lodging charges of educational neglect against the parents because the younger brother, 14, allegedly missed 120 days of school during the 1986-87 school year. (*Detroit Free Press*, 1/14/88.)

June 1988

• The attempted $70 million funds transfer scam allegedly engineered by several employees of First National Bank of Chicago (with outside help) may become the event that gets bankers to better funds transfer security. What is so scary about First National's problem is that the attempt got as far as it did before anyone was the wiser. The bank did not discover it. Its customers, whose accounts were rifled, gave first notice. The scam itself was rather simple: hit the accounts of customers with the largest overdraft protection. That way, the loss would go undetected. However, finance people at the targeted accounts balked when they were notified of or discovered the overdrafts. When bank auditors began to investigate the discrepancies, the scam was uncovered. (*Chicago Tribune*, 5/22/88.)

August 1988

• NASA's Jet Propulsion Lab (JPL) has asked the FBI to investigate a hacker intrusion into one of its nonsensitive data bases, which is accessible through Arpanet. The suspect allegedly gained access to the JPL's computer by using his own name as the password. His name is the same as that of a JPL employee. (*Computerworld*, 6/20/88.)
• Another foiled EFT scam surfaced last month in London. About $54 million was transferred to a Swiss bank. The funds have been frozen by Swiss authorities pending completion of an investigation. (*Wall Street Journal*, 7/5/88.)

September 1988

• The Chicago District Attorney (DA) brought charges against a teenager who allegedly used a home computer to steal $1 million in software from AT&T and the government. The DA's vigorous prosecution of the case as a felony signals the start of a tougher policy toward computer crimes. (*Detroit Free Press*, 8/10/88.)
• Marcus Hess, the West German hacker who is believed to have hounded scientific data bases of universities, defense contractors, and the U.S. Defense Department for a year or two, was stalked by Clifford Stoll, a computer science researcher at the Lawrence Berkeley Laboratory. Hess allegedly intruded into these systems by giving himself system manager privileges and then covered up his audit trail. Stoll traced Hess's calls through a web of phone lines and packet-switching networks, then set a trap. He created fake directories that would attract Hess long enough to trace him back to his own computer and phone. West German authorities refused to prosecute Hess, and they have even returned his computer without examining its data. (*Computerworld*, 8/8/88.)
• The insurance industry is looking deeply into the computer virus problem and finding ways to absolve itself from liability for past and current viruses and avoid risk completely in the future. A Lloyds of London spokesman remarked at a bankers' convention that the number of outstanding claims related to computer crime would devastate the insurance industry if they all had to be paid. (*Computerworld*, 8/15/88.)

October 1988

• The voice-messaging system of a wholesale grocer in Los Angeles was commandeered by a small band of hackers who used the system to run a prostitution ring and disseminate data about drugs. Some months ago, legitimate voice-mail users began to complain that they were denied access to their voice mailboxes because their passwords had been invalidated. An investigation disclosed that the hackers overrode security features and appropriated two hundred voice mailboxes to their own use.

This case is not exceptional. The security of voice-messaging systems must be improved. The best ideas for now are to monitor unusual activity, use the manufacturer's recommended password code structure, make passwords more complex (longer and alphanumerical), and change them often. Also, separate the company's toll-free number used by the general public from the number used by voice-mail subscribers. (*Network World,* 9/12/88.)

• In Forth Worth, Texas, a computer security officer erased 168,000 payroll records on an IBM System/38 and then planted a time bomb to erase more of the records every month. The erasure and time bomb were discovered shortly thereafter. The downtime and other damage cost the firm at least $12,000. The importance of the case as a precedent is twofold: (1) It involved a time bomb, not a virus implant, and (2) the defendant was prosecuted and convicted of a felony. The second point made the case one of "first impression," as lawyers often say. The Fort Worth DA was brave enough to take a complex high-tech criminal case and present it to a jury, which fortunately contained several people with systems backgrounds. (*Computerworld,* 9/26/88.)

February 1989

• Kevin David Mitnick, 25, who was convicted in 1981 and 1983 of stealing technical information from Pacific Bell and accessing computers at University of Southern California, stands charged with a new offense: defrauding DEC and MCI and transporting proprietary software across state lines. Other charges may also be added. The proprietary software involved in the case is an unauthorized copy of DEC's Security Software System, which allegedly made it possible for Mitnick to intrude into DEC's computer system, causing DEC $4 million in damage. After his arrest, Mitnick was held in a high-security area of a Los Angeles jail because the judge felt he was a risk and danger to the public. The judge also refused to allow him access to a telephone for fear he might have programmed a computer to trigger programs by phone. (*Computerworld,* 1/9/89.)

March 1989

• Headline news was made this month over three West German hackers who invaded U.S. military computer networks in behalf of the Soviet Union. The KGB was said to have paid the hackers several hundred thousand Deutsche marks for passwords that could be used to gain entry to the networks. The hackers were discovered when an improper 75¢ charge was made to the account of one network user who scrupulously audited his own account. In ferreting out the improper charge, he realized that hackers had accessed the system. (*Wall Street Journal,* 3/3/89, 3/6/89; *Detroit Free Press,* 3/4/89; *Computerworld,* 3/6/89.)

• In one of the first cases where a hacker was sent to jail, 18-year-old

Herbert D. Zinn, Jr., of Chicago was given a nine-month sentence with no parole. The case was the first conviction under the Computer Fraud and Abuse Act of 1986. Zinn was found guilty of copying $1.2 million worth of AT&T programs; destroying files valued at $174,000; and publishing passwords, telephone numbers, and directions on how to breach AT&T's computer security system. (*Computerworld,* 2/20/89.)

• In another first, a Florida television newsreporter was arrested for allegedly breaking into a competitor's computer system and stealing confidential information. (*Computerworld,* 2/13/89.)

June 1989

• European hackers allegedly penetrated the European Economic Community's computers in Brussels but were quickly discovered. Last October, a hacker penetrated the Belgian government's computer system and for several months read the electronic mail of the prime minister and 10 of his cabinet ministers. The hacker said that he discovered other "burglars" in the system. (*Wall Street Journal,* 5/15/89.)

• In Richmond, Virginia, teenage hackers held a company's voice-mail system hostage. They wrested control of four mailboxes and left obscene and threatening messages for about 120 subscribers. (*Network World,* 5/1/89.)

• Chaos, the infamous West German hacker's club, claims that it has found a gaping hole in the PC Secure encryption program. The Chaos hackers claim to have discovered the master key by using a file comparison program. The encryption program was not designed for sensitive documents, however. (*Business Week,* 5/29/89, p. 1020.)

• The National Research Council has formed an expert panel to study computer crime. The chair is David D. Clark of the Massachusetts Institute of Technology. Its report is due in late 1990 and will focus on solutions to the problem of computer crime. (*Computerworld,* 5/8/89.)

July 1989

• About 50 teenage hackers throughout the United States are suspected of involvement in a voice-mail computer scam in which they allegedly exchanged credit and long-distance calling card numbers, invaded voice-mail systems, and stole telephone and computer services. U.S. Secret Service agents arrested juveniles in Georgia, Illinois, Massachusetts, Michigan, Ohio, and California. The alleged ringleader, 36, was arrested in Chicago. Police authorities estimate the total cost of the frauds to be over $1 million. (*Computerworld,* 5/29/89, 6/5/89.)

• The Cornell University graduate student who caused the stir over viruses last year was suspended by the university for breaching its code of academic integrity. There is still no word on his prosecution, however. (*Computerworld,* 5/29/89.)

October 1989

• The U.S. Secret Service office in Detroit made its third arrest in a year of a local "phone phreak" and hacker who is suspected of accessing the systems of certain credit card and phone companies and defrauding them of $100,000 in goods and services. Special Agent in Charge James Huse said that his agency will continue to pursue these cases with vigor because he feels that hacking is a growing menace. FBI agents today are better trained and more oriented toward computer crimes than ever before. (The U.S. Secret Service shares jurisdiction over computer crime with the FBI, but the FBI's case load—the agency also investigates bank frauds, stock frauds, and drug trafficking—does not leave much room for investigating computer capers. It appears that the Secret Service will focus more of its time and attention on computer crime.) (*Detroit Free Press,* 9/9/89.)
• A raid by Ashton-Tate and Lotus representatives of Montedison in Milan, Italy, disclosed that about 90% of the company's software on site had been illegally copied. Software piracy is a serious problem in Europe—perhaps worse than in Asia. Americans buy an average of 1.5 applications per PC. In Europe, the average is far less: 1.31 in the United Kingdom, 0.64 in West Germany, 0.38 in Italy, and 0.34 in Spain. (*PC/Computing,* September 1989.)

November 1989

• In a *Computerworld* interview, Steven Levy, author of *Hackers,* talks about the current crop of hackers. He notes that hackers today are remarkably similar in personality to those of a few years ago, but today's hackers are more isolated and feel less cultural constraint on their actions. As a consequence, they now do things that cause real—though perhaps unintentional—damage. (*Computerworld,* 10/23/89.)
• The hacker represents an outside threat to systems security. The inside threat—that is, authorized users—are a greater security concern. Consider, for example, the recent case of a contract programmer working at GTE who allegedly breached system security and stole the account information and personal IDs of 7500 Bank of America customers. When arrested, he and four confederates were making 7500 cardboard ATM cards with encoded magnetic stripes. Their scheme could have netted $14 million. (*BAI Bank Security Bulletin,* August 1989; *Computerworld,* 10/23/89.)
• Magnetic cards for access to ATMs are certainly marketable in the underworld, but so are computer chips. Indeed, chips are being stolen by armed robbers in the Silicon Valley in $500,000 increments. (*Business Week,* 10/30/89.)

• The theft of proprietary information and competitive intelligence is also becoming a major security concern. How is it done? The compromising of insiders is one way, but a growing trend involves intercepting communications systems, such as satellite transmissions. To do this, a thief needs (1) a microwave receiver, (2) an amplifier, and (3) a VCR recorder. The thief directs the receiver against a nearby satellite dish. One possible safeguard is to encrypt proprietary information and competitive intelligence. (*Wall Street Journal,* 10/20/89.)

• An insidious threat of electronic eavesdropping may lie with such new hits in EDP technology as LANS and EDI. Here you "invite" others, i.e., customers, suppliers and network members, to access your system for a limited purpose. But once on, what else can they access? (*Computerworld,* 10/23/89, 10/16/89.)

• Well, Friday, the 13th came and went with few incidents of virus problems despite the wide coverage of the subject by the media. Practically every daily in the nation and most weekly magazines did a story on the Datacrime and Friday, the 13th viruses. (The media is beginning to show the same inclination toward Fridays, the 13th that they show at Thanksgiving time. That is, they run the same story of the turkey farmer near town. He gets an annual spread because it has become a newspaper tradition. Viruses are becoming topical and traditional too. Yet this year, on October 13th, what we had was not so much a failure of computing systems as a failure of the stock market system.)

December 1989

• The trial of Robert Morris, Jr., began last week. Morris allegedly infected the Internet network. Every data security administrator in the country will no doubt study the case for whatever lessons might be learned. Hackers will study the case, too, but from a different perspective. If Morris is convicted and given a prison sentence, it may deter hackers and virus implanters. (*Business Week,* 12/4/89.)

• Current intelligence suggests that hackers are turning their skills in the direction of industrial espionage. They are supposedly selling their talent to competitors who will pay for the interception of unencrypted data communications signals from satellites. The work is said to be "cleaner" than breaking into systems just to harass the owners or to damage the data. For their espionage, the hackers get paid, and their clients are not likely to turn them in to police authorities.

• Sprint reports that it has been so successful in thwarting hackers who were trying to steal its long-distance authorization codes that the hackers have now shifted their attention to invading and charging their phone calls to private- and public-sector phone branch exchange (PBXs). (*Computerworld,* 10/30/89.)

January 1990

• Editorial: Many legal scholars oppose the idea of more criminal laws to combat computer abuses. They reason that common law precedents and the statutory codifications thereof are adequate for prosecuting computer crimes. Indeed, these statutes and their case precedents give prosecutors enough leverage to do an effective job. New laws, on the other hand, invite legal challenge because they have not been tested for constitutionality.

According to this logic, embezzlement by computer is not a separate and distinct crime from statutory embezzlement. The means do not count as much as the ends. Using that rationale, electronic intrusion is the same as breaking and entering or common-law burglary. In the computer era, however, some new state criminal statutes require that a computer system be physically secured and that passwords be protected before a prosecution for unauthorized access can be brought. That is the height of folly. If applied to burglary, these statutes would require that a home be locked and barred shut and then broken into before a successful prosecution could be had. That clearly is not the general law. Even if the front door and the windows are open, a physical penetration and intent are required. If a thief finds that a car door is open, the keys are in the ignition, and the motor is running, is it any less a theft if he or she drives the car away?

This mad rush to get new laws passed is part of an American mindset that suggests that all vices can be disposed of by passing more and tougher laws. Once the law has been passed, citizens and legislators can feel secure because the police authorities have the burden of eliminating the vice. However, passing laws alone does not make a country law-abiding. Dictators pass laws all day long, but their subjects are unlikely to follow them with any amount of zeal.

February 1990

• The Morris defense that a computer security experiment went awry and that he had no intention of causing loss or damage did not impress the jury or the judge. "The worm caused no permanent damage and was not designed to cause permanent damage," defense attorney Thomas Guidoboni argued in his opening remarks. The jury saw it differently, however. Mark Rasch, the government's trial attorney, told the jurors that Robert Morris, Jr., devoted a "lot of time, energy and research" in planning the assault. The worm was designed to penetrate as many computers as possible and was programmed to "hide itself to frustrate victims of the attack," Rasch said. (*Computerworld*, 1/15/89.)
• The U.S. Secret Service office in Detroit and the Michigan State Police have formed a Computer Crime Task Force. "Computer crimes in Michigan are becoming significant enough to justify a concerted effort," said Captain Richard Maloche of the state police. In their first joint project, the state

police and the U.S. Secret Service arrested two teenage boys for allegedly incurring $410,000 in telephone toll calls and charging them against the accounts of the U.S. Treasury Department, MCI, ITT, and electronic data systems (EDS). One of the boys is a college student majoring in computer science. The two boys allegedly used a "demons dialer" to facilitate their charade. (*Detroit Free Press*, 1/23/90.)

• NASA also has hacker intrusion problems, says the GAO. In a recent audit, the GAO found 67 hacker break-ins from January 1988 to March 1989. The incidents of unauthorized access were facilitated by the fact that some NASA users either had no password protection for their accounts or used easy-to-guess passwords. (*Computerworld*, 1/22/90.)

• Some Tennessee State Prison inmates have been granted access to computers to learn an honest way to make a living. They are trained as data-entry clerks, and when training is completed, they provide data-entry services to the prison. They are paid at the rate of 10¢ per 1000 keystrokes. They also generate the data on their production and then input it. Needless to say, several inmates fudged their production numbers to earn bonuses of $20 to $500 each. The system itself flagged the abnormal transactions, and now the inmates have to pay the money back. The data-entry training continues, but inmates can no longer access the payroll system. (*Computerworld*, 1/15/90.)

• Three former SRI employees were indicted for allegedly conspiring to break into government and Pacific Bell computers, stealing access codes and equipment, and wiretapping conversations. It was also alleged that one suspect had a classified document in his possession. How he got it, no one will say. (*Computerworld*, 1/22/90.)

March 1990

• BellSouth was the victim of an attack by a "phrackers" group on its 911 services in nine states. The suspected group calls itself the Legion of Doom. One principal of the group is alleged to have stolen a BellSouth program that controls its 911 services and then uploaded it to an electronic bulletin board.

How vulnerable are telephone systems to hacker attacks? A recently published report to Congress by the Office of Technology Assessment suggests that the communications infrastructure of the United States is at greater risk to hacker attacks than ever before. Business and government reliance on communications and information-based systems has increased, thus much more is at stake when those systems fail, the report stated. (*Computerworld*, 2/12/90; *Wall Street Journal*, 2/7/90.)

• The GAO found security weaknesses at several major networks, including the Fedwire network run by the Federal Reserve System. Fedwire transfers about $253 trillion per year among the federal reserve banks, depository institutions, and government agencies. (*Computerworld*, 2/26/90.)

- "The introduction of distributed systems and use of networks and communications facilities for carrying data have increased the need for network security measures to protect data during its transmission," William Stalling writes in *Computerworld*. (*Computerworld*, 1/29/90.)
- Speakers at a conference called "Threats to Computer Networks: Piracy, Terrorism and Espionage" warned that increasing network security may make systems more difficult to use and could limit free communication among users. "One problem that may arise is that users will find a network too user-unfriendly and just not use it," said Anne Wells Branscomb, keynote speaker and a research associate at the Harvard Program on Information Resources Policy. (*Network World*, 2/5/90.)
- An editorial in *Network World* argues that "it's time the courts made it crystal clear that hacking and network intrusion are not amusing pastimes for the technologically literate. Networks are the lifeblood of many businesses today. They're not a proving ground for hackers seeking to show off their skills or demonstrate their computer prowess." (*Network World*, 2/5/90.)

April 1990

- The current reinvasion of Internet allegedly by an Australian hacker is the third time in recent years that a major break-in has occurred. In each break-in, super user privileges were assumed, audit trails were buried, identities were faked, passwords were stolen and decrypted (by dictionary or guessing), and sensitive files were accessed. While direct damage did not occur, many hours were wasted in vain efforts to safeguard the system. The worm implanted by Robert Morris, Jr., caused considerable damage by way of lost processing capabilities and time lost in decontaminating the system.

  Improving the access controls of networks is a long way from finished. Some networks have not changed anything yet. They assume what they have is enough, but what they have in defensive security is 10 years behind what hackers have in offensive technology. (*New York Times*, 3/19/90, 4/4/90; *Information Week*, 3/26/90; *Network World*, 3/26/90.)
- Two hackers, members of the Legion of Doom, claim to have made $66,000 each by entering Citicorp's Decnet and effecting electronic transfers of funds to a Swiss bank account. (*Computerworld*, 3/5/90.)
- Frost and Sullivan, Inc., says that European companies lost about $10 billion in 1987 because of poor computer security practices that led to system failures, data corruption, and fraud. The use of networks "will only compound the problem," the company says. (*Computerworld*, 4/2/90.)
- European companies are not the only ones to lose to computer frauds. BellSouth reports that it spent more than $1 million in less than a year to thwart the efforts of a group of determined phreaks. (*Computerworld*, 2/19/90.)

May 1990

• The most recent report about computer hackers involves a 12-year-old. His mother said that he spent four to five hours a night during the week and up to 14 hours a day on weekends "playing" with his Apple computer. She was stunned when the Michigan State Police and U.S. Secret Service agents showed up to arrest him. The youngster allegedly accessed TRW's credit data base, secured from such files the credit card numbers of several people, and then posted them on bulletin boards around the country. He also allegedly ordered some merchandise for himself. How did he get the TRW access number and log-in? Social engineering—not hacking. (Social engineering means masquerading as an authorized user who needs a little help to perform some computer-user function.)

• The most recent suspected Internet hackers—"Dave" and several cohorts in Australia—were arrested by Australian authorities following a complaint made by the FBI. (*Computerworld,* 4/9/90.)

• An unidentified hacker posted a decryption utility on an electronic bulletin board that enabled users to decode and read the E-mail messages of others. This forced the supplier of the E-mail program to introduce a new version with enhanced security features. The supplier also notified its customers of the problem and set up a toll-free hotline. About 400,000 E-mail users at 7000 to 10,000 firms were affected. The decryption utility allowed users to break the encryption scheme in less than 10 minutes. (*Computerworld,* 4/6/90.)

• A computer programmer in Waukesha, Wisconsin, allegedly tried to buy a measure of security for his programming talent by planting a time bomb in a program he had contracted to develop and then pulled the pin when the client refused to pay. It is the first case brought under Wisconsin's computer-crime law. The programmer argues that he merely repossessed his own property, but the judge disagreed. The programmer will stand trial. (*Computerworld,* 4/23/90.)

June 1990

• The sentencing of Robert T. Morris, Jr., last month was widely reported in the media. (*Wall Street Journal,* 5/7/90; *Computerworld,* 5/7/90, 5/14/90; *Information Week,* 5/7/90; *PC/Computing,* June 1990; *Network World,* 5/14/90.) Morris was sentenced to three years of probation, a $10,000 fine, and four hundred hours of community service. The consensus is that the sentence was light, but justice did prevail. The case was one of the first prosecutions under the recent Computer and Fraud Abuse Act, and no one could foretell how the judge might construe the law.

• The operator of a Chicago day-care center, with 150 conspirators, fraudulently obtained 481 telephone credit cards and published them in voice-mail systems accessible by other hackers. This led to a loss of $600,000 to

telecommunications carriers. She pleaded guilty and will soon be sentenced. (*Wall Street Journal,* 5/2/90; *Computerworld,* 5/7/90.)
• The U.S. Secret Service and state law enforcement officers executed 28 search warrants in six states to break up a ring of hackers alleged to have caused $50 million in loss and damage to credit cardholders and telecommunications carriers (long-distance phone services and voice-mail operators). A sting in the form of a hacker bulletin board was created to trap the alleged conspirators. (*Computerworld,* 5/14/90.)
• A "Galactic Hacker Party," held in August 1989 in Amsterdam, attracted several hundred "techno-anarchists" who discussed ways to break into networks and infect them with viruses and worms. In Australia, *Cyberpunk* magazine has a "hack of the month" column listing tempting targets for hackers. (*Detroit Free Press,* 5/15/90.)
• Crime detection techniques are not always as scientific or state-of-the-art as James Bonds fans are led to believe. Indeed, Interpol is just moving out of the manual era and into the twentieth century. Its one million dossiers had been kept in their original condition for 70 years. Members of Interpol can now get records, fingerprints, and *modus operandi* files in about two hours. In 1986, a similar search took 14 days. (*Information Week,* 5/7/90.)
• The U.S. Treasury Department has created a Financial Crimes Enforcement Network, an expert system data base that hunts down money-laundering suspects. (*Communications Week,* 4/30/90.)

July 1990

• Mitch Kapor, founder of Lotus Development Corp., says that he will create a legal defense fund for hackers. Kapor told the *Washington Post,* "I'm concerned that hackers' civil liberties are being violated. I'm concerned these kids, which is mostly what hackers are, aren't getting a fair shake in the legal system. They don't have access to legal counsel that would let them adequately defend their rights." (*Computerworld,* 6/4/90.)
• What do you make of the CIA's offer to provide secret intelligence to high-tech manufacturers in the United States on the state of technology in other countries of both the East Bloc and the West? Is this the peace dividend we have been expecting? (*Detroit Free Press,* 6/21/90.)
• The DOD wants to research the possibility of using computer viruses as electronic countermeasures against military communications systems. The DOD also wants to know if viruses can be injected into an enemy's computer system by radio transmissions. (*Computerworld,* 6/18/90.)
• The National Security Agency wants to shift its "listening" resource capabilities away from the Soviet military threat and use them to spy on world trade and financial transactions. (*Ann Arbor News,* 6/18/90.)
• The IRS wants to shift some of its resources to foreign banks doing business in the United States. Foreign banks now control 22.6% of U.S. banking assets and make 28.5% of U.S. business loans. Foreign banks are not giving

the IRS a fair accounting of their income, however. In audits of 10 foreign banks last year, the IRS found a total tax deficiency of $100 million. (*Ann Arbor News,* 6/18/90.)
• In Kuala Lumpur, Malaysia, a young bank officer allegedly compromised the computer's security system and stole $1.5 million. He drew attention to himself when he bought a Lamborghini, three Porsches, and a Mercedes. (*Ann Arbor News,* 6/18/90.)
• Two travel agents found a way to deceive American Airlines' reservation system into setting up fake frequent flier accounts. They issued themselves free tickets for travel, which they sold for cash. (*Computerworld,* 6/11/90.)

August 1990

• U.S. Secret Service agents raided the homes of 28 hackers in 14 cities this spring in the culmination of the two-year Operation Sundevil investigation. The agents seized computers, disks, and other equipment related to the alleged electronic theft and publication of BellSouth Corp.'s documentation for an enhanced 911 emergency telephone system. A number of the hackers involved in the case called themselves the Legion of Doom.
The U.S. Attorney in Atlanta, Georgia, where three of the hackers were charged, said that the group disrupted telecommunications, monitored private telephone lines, modified credit information, fraudulently obtained property, and disseminated access information so other hackers could then enter the BellSouth computer system. The Atlanta hackers allegedly obtained the access code information from a BellSouth trash bin.
Mitch Kapor, founder of Lotus Development Corp., and Steve Wozniak, cofounder of Apple Computer, came to the financial rescue of several of the principals in the case, whose rights under the First and Fourth Amendments of the U.S. Constitution had, they felt, been violated. Kapor believes that hacking, a venerated tradition among early systems enthusiasts, is not done by responsible systems people to harass or destroy, but to test security strengths and weaknesses. "If responsible hacking is outlawed, creativity is stifled," Kapor said. Law enforcement professions do not see it that way. Making distinctions between responsible and reckless hacking is hard to do, they say. One clear legal standard is better than an ambiguous double standard.
Kapor and Wozniak's main concern is that among those arrested was a student at the University of Missouri who ran an electronic bulletin board that published BellSouth's 911 documentation. The bulletin board was closed down, and Kapor argues that its closure constitutes a "prior restraint" and a violation of the First Amendment free speech and free press provisions. Kapor, Wozniak, and others have created a foundation to provide legal and financial assistance to the bulletin board's publisher. The fund, says Kapor, is not a legal defense fund for hackers. It is intended to safeguard the constitutional rights of electronic publishers that are in some doubt, vis-à-

vis the print, radio, and television news media. People who intentionally alter, damage, or destroy the information resources of others, deny them service, or gain unauthorized access will not be assisted by the fund. The bottom line, Kapor says, is that digital media should be afforded the same constitutional protections as traditional media. (*Information Week,* 7/16/90; *Wall Street Journal,* 7/11/90; *Computerworld,* 6/25/90.)

Meanwhile, the three Atlanta-area hackers pleaded guilty, and the bulletin board publisher went to trial in Chicago. (*Computerworld,* 6/16/90.)

September 1990

• The recent acquittal of Craig Neidorf, the 20-year-old University of Missouri student and coeditor of *Phrack,* a hacker newsletter, received little media attention. Neidorf was accused of publishing some documentation of BellSouth's 911 emergency phone system in his electronic newsletter. This, BellSouth charged, constituted a number of federal crimes. Perhaps because it was a confusing set of circumstances or a confusing set of federal laws, the U.S. government accepted the case for prosecution without probing deeply enough into BellSouth's allegations. The BellSouth allegations gave rise to a major deployment of agent personnel by the U.S. Secret Service.

One story circulating in law enforcement circles is that the Secret Service and the FBI share investigative jurisdiction over computer crime cases. The Bureau concentrates on EFT frauds and bank-related computer frauds, and the Secret Service handles credit card frauds. However, when a well-publicized case comes along, both may jockey for position. In the Sun Devil Case, the Secret Service won out because the case fell within its avenue of investigative expertise. Had the case been handled by professionals who were more knowledgeable about information technology and were more experienced, the case against Neidorf may never have been brought. The case was evidentially tenuous and presented a constitutional issue of major proportions. The combination of these factors made prosecution difficult.

The real hitch in the government's case was that the BellSouth 911 documentation had previously been offered for public sale (the "proprietary information" designation on the documentation notwithstanding). Neidorf's lawyer is now considering a suit against BellSouth. (*Computerworld,* 8/6/90.)

• The Air Force was the victim of hacker intrusions for several months this year. The accessed system was unclassified. With the aid of several police organizations, 13 people were arrested for the break-ins: five adults and eight juveniles. (*Computerworld,* 8/20/90.)

October 1990

• Leslie Lyn Doucette was sentenced to 27 months in prison for her role in a nationwide hacking operation that shortchanged Ma Bell of some $600,000.

Her sentence is said to be the longest ever imposed for hacking. (*Computerworld*, 8/27/90.)
- West Germany's Chaos Computer Club is recruiting hackers in the U.S., a reliable source says. (*Computerworld*, 9/3/90.)
- Robert T. Morris, Jr., found guilty of infecting the Internet network with a worm, is appealing his conviction. (*Computerworld*, 9/3/90.)
- Politicians are becoming hackers too. In New Jersey, a Republican official admitted to knowing that the computer of the Democrat members of the New Jersey legislature had been improperly accessed by a GOP staffer who has since been fired. (*Computerworld*, 9/17/90.)

December 1990

- The combination of desktop publishing and color copier technologies are giving rise to an outbreak of forgery and counterfeiting cases. The fabrication of cashier's checks and money orders is being practiced as a fine art these days. In one recent case in Michigan, a college student and his friend were charged with making fake ID cards and cashier's checks and reaping about $40,000 in illegal income. The two were arrested by U.S. Secret Service agents. They allegedly used college computing resources to carry out their illegal scheme at first, and with increased income, they bought their own PC and laser printer. They allegedly used a laser scanner to create a computer image of cashier's checks and other documents. Their fake ID files included yacht club memberships, educational degrees, and birth certificates. (*Detroit Free Press*, 10/22/90.)
- Although the theft of long-distance services from the telephone companies is declining—90% lower, according to Gale Thackeray, an Assistant D.A. in Arizona—such abuse is now moving to private systems: corporate PBXs. Private networks are not as well secured as AT&T, Sprint, and MCI. (*Information Week*, 10/15/90.)
- The New Jersey Legislature is still reeling from the discovery that the files of Democratic legislators were improperly accessed by one or more Republican staff members. On the other hand, certain Democratic legislators used a data base for political purposes, which is contrary to New Jersey law. (*Computerworld*, 10/1/90.)
- Hackers are gathering for a Christmas conference in Houston, Texas, in December. (*Computerworld*, 10/22/90.)
- New York City has become a popular place for PBX fraud, according to Jim Snyder, an attorney for MCI. He estimates that 70 to 80% of fraudulent calls originate there and are directed to the 809 area code (Puerto Rico, Dominican Republic, and Virgin Islands). The loss to unsuspecting PBX owners can go as high as $25,000 on a weekend. The possibilities for preventing PBX fraud include programming the PBX to impose service restrictions on outbound dialing, and limiting the number of users making overseas calls. (*Network World*, 10/29/90.)

- Two teenage voice-mail hackers allegedly got into the computer of International Data Group (*Computerworld*'s parent) and caused more than $2 million in damage before they were apprehended. (*Information Week*, 11/12/90; *Network World*, 11/12/90.)
- In the United Kingdom, two MIS employees of British Aerospace were charged with computer fraud for attempting a money-transfer scheme. (*Computerworld*, 10/29/90.)
- In the United States, three Atlanta hackers, members of the Legion of Doom, were sentenced to serve a year or more in prison and to make restitution of $223,000 each to BellSouth. (*Computerworld*, 11/26/90.)
- The Software Publishers' Association (SPA) has launched an educational program at Comdex called "Don't Copy That Floppy." The program is designed to discourage software piracy. Since 1988, the SPA has taken the following actions in its campaign against illegal copying (*Computerworld*, 11/12/90):

  - sent more than three hundred cease-and-desist letters
  - conducted more than 50 audits (the program was begun in 1989)
  - collected more than $1 million in penalties
  - generated $5 to $10 million in additional sales from court cases
  - distributed 10,000 copies of a self-auditing kit
  - filed 60 suits
  - received an average of 20 calls per day on its toll-free line

- Investigations led by Microsoft and Everex Systems have uncovered an alleged software counterfeiting ring. According to a report in the *Financial Times*, the manufacturers uncovered a U.S.-based counterfeit ring that allegedly produced more than 30,000 illegal copies of MS-DOS. Microsoft and Everex Systems, a California PC manufacturer, have filed lawsuits against 10 individuals and six firms in New Jersey and northern California. (*Internal Auditor*, December 1990.)
- First Fidelity Bancorp. filed a civil lawsuit charging a former senior IS executive with defrauding the bank of $6.2 million. The suit alleges that the executive filed false invoices for office supplies and equipment for the IS department from two dummy companies over a period of 11 years. (*Information Week*, 10/15/90.)

Note

1. National Criminal Justice Reference Service, Box 6000, Rockville, MD 20850.

CHAPTER 15

Landmark Cases in Criminal Law

A criminal law is not only what a legislature says it is in a statute but what courts subsequently interpret it to mean. In that sense, government and police investigators must become familiar with the particular criminal laws they enforce, with the judicial interpretations of those laws, and with their constitutionality. A review of some of the major cases in the criminal law field with fraud implications may therefore be of interest to the reader.

False Pretenses: *State v. Mills*[1]

LOCKWOOD, VICE CHIEF JUSTICE: Defendants appeal from a conviction on two counts of obtaining money by false pretenses in violation of A.R.S. 13-661.A.3 and 13-633.A.1.

The material facts, viewed " . . . in the light most favorable to sustaining the conviction," State v. Evans, 88 Ariz. 364, 366, 356, P.2d 1106, 1107 (1960) are as follows: Defendant William Mills was a builder and owned approximately 150 homes in Tucson in December 1960. Mills conducted his business in his home. In 1960 defendant Winifred Mills, his wife, participated in the business generally by answering the telephone, typing, and receiving clients who came to the office.

In December 1960, Mills showed the complainant, Nathan Pivowar, a house at 1155 Knox Drive and another at 1210 Easy Street, and asked Pivowar if he would loan money on the Knox Drive house. Pivowar did not indicate at that time whether he would agree to such a transaction. Later in the same month, Nathan Pivowar told the defendants that he and his brother, Joe Pivowar, would loan $5,000 and $4,000 on the two houses. Three or four days later Mrs. Mills, at Pivowar's request, showed him these homes again.

Mills had prepared two typed mortgages for Pivowar. Pivowar objected to the wording, so in Mills' office, Mrs. Mills retyped the mortgages under Pivowar's dictation. After the mortgages had been recorded on December 31, 1960, Pivowar gave Mills a bank check for $5,791.87, some cash, and a second mortgage formerly obtained from Mills in the approximate sum of

$3,000. In exchange Mills gave Pivowar two personal notes in the sums of $5,250 and $4,200 and the two mortgages as security for the loan.

Although the due date for Mills' personal notes passed without payment being made, the complainant did not present the notes for payment, did not demand that they be paid, and did not sue upon them. In 1962, the complainant learned that the mortgages, which he had taken as security in the transaction, were not first mortgages on the Knox Drive and Easy Street properties. These mortgages actually covered two vacant lots on which there were outstanding senior mortgages. On learning this, Pivowar signed a complaint charging the defendants with the crime of theft by false pretenses.

On appeal, defendants contend that the trial court erred in denying their motion to dismiss the information. They urge that a permanent taking of property must be proved in order to establish the crime of theft by false pretenses. Since the complainant had the right to sue on the defendants' notes, the defendants assert that complainant cannot be said to have been deprived of his property permanently.

Defendants misconceive the elements of the crime of theft by false pretenses. Stated in a different form, their argument is that although the complainant has parted with his cash, a bank check, and a second mortgage, the defendants intend to repay the loan.

Defendants admit that the proposition of law which they assert is a novel one in this jurisdiction. Respectable authority in other states persuades us that their contention is without merit. *A creditor has a right to determine for himself whether he wishes to be a secured or an unsecured creditor. In the former case, he has a right to know about the security. If he extends credit in reliance upon that which is falsely represented to be adequate, he has been defrauded even if the debtor intends to repay the debt. His position is now that of an unsecured creditor; at the very least, an unreasonable risk of loss has been forced upon him by reason of deceit.* This risk, which he did not intend to assume, has been imposed upon him by the intentional act of the debtor, and such action constitutes an intent to defraud. . . .

The cases cited by defendants in support of their contention are distinguishable from the instant case in that they involved theft by larceny. Since *the crime of larceny is designed to protect a person's possessory interest in property whereas the crime of false pretenses protects one's title interest, the requirements of a permanent deprivation is appropriate to the former. Accordingly, we hold that an intent to repay a loan obtained on the basis of a false representation of the security for the loan is no defense.* Affirmed in part, reversed in party, and remanded for resentencing.

Conspiracy: *United States v. Falcone*[2]

L. HAND, CIRCUIT JUDGE: These appeals are from convictions for a conspiracy to operate illicit stills. . . .

The case against Joseph Falcone was that during the year 1937 he sold sugar to a number of grocers in Utica, who in turn sold to the distillers. He was a jobber in Utica, and bought his supply from a New York firm of sugar brokers. Between March 1 and September 14, 1938, he bought 8,600 bags of sugar of 100 pounds each, which he disposed of to three customers: Frank Bonomo & Company, Pauline Aiello, and Alberico and Funicello, all wholesale grocers in Utica. Some of the bags in which this was delivered were later found at the stills when these were raided by the officials; and Falcone was seen on one occasion assisting in delivering the sugar at Bonomo's warehouse when a truckload arrived. His business in sugar was far greater while the stills were active than either before they were set up or after they were seized, and we shall assume that the evidence was enough to charge him with notice that his customers were supplying the distillers. . . .

In the light of all this, it is apparent that the first question is whether the seller of goods, in themselves innocent, becomes a conspirator with . . . or, what is in substance the same thing, an abettor of . . . the buyer because he knows that the buyer means to use the goods to commit a crime. That came up a number of times in circuit courts of appeal while the Eighteenth Amendment was in force, and the answer was not entirely uniform. . . .

We are ourselves committed to the view of the Fifth Circuit, United States v. Peoni, 2 Cir., 100 F.2d 401. In that case we tried to trace down the doctrine as to abetting and conspiracy, as it exists in our criminal law, and concluded that the seller's knowledge was not alone enough. Civilly, a man's liability extends to any injuries which he should have apprehended to be likely to follow from his acts. If they do, he must excuse his conduct by showing that the interest which he was promoting outweighed the dangers which its protection imposed upon others; but in civil cases there has been a loss, and the only question is whether the law shall transfer it from the sufferer to another. There are indeed instances of criminal liability of the same kind, where the law imposes punishment merely because the accused did not forbear to do that from which the wrong was likely to follow; but in prosecutions or conspiracy or abetting, his attitude towards the forbidden undertaking must be more positive. It is not enough that he does not forego a normally lawful activity of the fruits of which he knows that others will make an unlawful use; he must in some sense promote their venture himself, make it his own, have a stake in its outcome. The distinction is especially important today when so many prosecutors seek to sweep within the dragnet of conspiracy all those who have been associated in any degree whatever with the main offenders. That there are opportunities of great oppression in such a doctrine is very plain, and it is only by circumscribing the scope of such all comprehensive indictments that they can be avoided. We may agree that morally the defendants at bar should have refused to sell to illicit distillers; but, both morally and legally, to do so was totally different from joining with them in running the stills.

For these reasons the prosecution did not make out a case against either of the Falcones, Alberico, or John Nole; and this is especially true of Salvatore Falcone. As to do business as the "Acme Yeast Company," he hid behind the name of cousin, whom he caused to swear falsely that the affiant was to do the business. Yet it seems to us that this was as likely to have come from a belief that it was a crime to sell the yeast and the cans to distillers as from being, in fact, any further involved in their business. It showed a desire to escape detection, and that was evidence of a guilt, but the consciousness may have as well arisen from a mistake of law as from a purpose to do what the law, in fact, forbade. We think, therefore, that even as to him no case was made out.

(Convictions Reversed)

Intent: *Morissette v. United States*[3]

MR. JUSTICE JACKSON delivered the opinion of the Court. . . .

On a large tract of uninhabited and untilled land in a wooded and sparsely populated area of Michigan, the Government established a practice bombing range over which the Air Force dropped simulated bombs at ground targets. These bombs consisted of a metal cylinder about forty inches long and eight inches across, filled with sand and enough black powder to cause a smoke puff by which the stroke could be located. At various places about the range, signs read "Danger—Keep Out—Bombing Range." Nevertheless, the range was known as good deer country and was extensively hunted.

Spent bomb casings were cleared from the targets and thrown into piles "so that they will be out of the way." They were not stacked or piled in any order but were dumped in heaps, some of which had been accumulating for four years or upwards, were exposed to the weather and rusting away.

Morissette, in December of 1948, went hunting in this area but did not get a deer. He thought he could meet expenses of the trip by salvaging some of these casings. He loaded three tons of them on his truck and took them to a nearby farm, where they were flattened by driving a tractor over them. After expending this labor and trucking them to market in Flint, he realized $84. . . .

The loading, crushing and transporting of these casings were all in broad daylight, in full view of passersby, without the slightest effort of concealment. When an investigation was started, Morissette voluntarily, promptly and candidly told the whole story to the authorities, saying that he had no intention of stealing but thought the property was abandoned, unwanted, and considered of no value to the Government. He was indicted, however, on the charge that he "did unlawfully, willfully and knowingly steal and convert" property of the United States of the value of $84, in violation of 18 U.S.C. 641, which provides that "whoever embezzles, steals, purloins, or knowingly converts" government property is punishable by fine and imprisonment. Morissette was convicted and sentenced to imprisonment for two months or to pay a fine of $200. The Court of Appeals affirmed, one judge dissenting.

On his trial, Morissette, as he had at all times told investigating officers, testified that from appearances he believed the casings were cast off and abandoned, that he did not intend to steal the property, and took it with no wrongful or criminal intent. The trial court, however, was unimpressed, and ruled: " . . . I don't think anybody can have the defense they thought the property was abandoned on another man's piece of property. . . ." The court refused to submit or allow counsel to argue to the jury whether Morissette acted with innocent intention. . . .

The contention that an injury can amount to a crime only when inflicted by intention is no provincial or transient notion. It is as universal and persistent in mature systems of law as belief in freedom of the human will and a consequent ability and duty of the normal individual to choose between good and evil. A relation between some mental element and punishment for a harmful act is almost as instinctive as the child's familiar exculpatory, "but I didn't mean to," and has afforded the rational basis for a tardy and unfinished substitution of deterrence and reformation, in place of retaliation and vengeance, as the motivation for public prosecution. Unqualified acceptance of this doctrine by English common law in the eighteenth century was indicated by Blackstone's sweeping statement that to constitute any crime there must first be a "vicious will." Common-law commentators of the nineteenth century early pronounced the same principle, although a few exceptions not relevant to our present problem came to be recognized.

Crime, as a compound concept, generally constituted only from concurrence of an evil-meaning mind with an evil-doing hand, was congenial to an intense individualism and took deep and early roots in American soil. As the States codified the common law of crimes, even if their enactments were silent on the subject, their courts assumed that the omission did not signify disapproval of the principle, but merely recognized that intent was so inherent in the idea of the offense that it required no statutory affirmation. Courts, with little hesitation or division, found an implication of the requirement as to offenses that were taken over from the common law. The unanimity with which they have adhered to the central thought that wrongdoing must be conscious to be criminal is emphasized by the variety, disparity and confusion of their definitions of the requisite but elusive mental element. However, courts of various jurisdictions, and for the purposes of different offenses, have devised working formulae, if not scientific ones, for the instruction of juries around such terms as "felonious intent," "criminal intent," "malice aforethought," "guilty knowledge," "fraudulent intent," "willfulness," "scienter," to denote guilty knowledge, or "mens rea," to signify an evil purpose or mental culpability. By use or combination of these various tokens, they have sought to protect those who were not blameworthy in mind from conviction of infamous common-law crimes.

However, [certain other] offenses belong to a category of another character, with very different antecedents and origins. The crimes there involved depend on no mental element but consist only of forbidden acts or omissions. This, while not expressed by the Court, is made clear from examination of a century-old but accelerating tendency, discernible both here and in England, to call into existence new duties and crimes which disregard any ingredient of intent. The industrial revolution multiplied the number of workmen exposed to injury from increasingly powerful and complex mechanisms, driven by freshly discovered sources of energy, requiring higher precautions by employers. Traffic velocities, volumes, and varieties unheard of came to subject the wayfarer to intolerable casualty risks if owners and drivers were not to observe new cares and uniformities of conduct. Congestion of cities and crowding of quarters called for health and welfare regulations undreamed of in simpler times. Wide distribution of goods became an instrument of wide distribution of harm when those who dispersed food, drink, drugs, and even securities did not comply with reasonable standards of quality, integrity, disclosure, and care. Such dangers have engendered increasingly numerous and detailed regulations which heighten the duties of those in control of particular industries, trades, properties, or activities that affect public health, safety, or welfare.

While many of these duties are sanctioned by a more strict civil liability, lawmakers, whether wisely or not, have sought to make such regulations more effective by invoking criminal sanctions to be applied by the familiar technique of criminal prosecution and convictions. This has confronted the courts with a multitude of prosecutions, based on statutes or administrative regulations, for what have been aptly called "public welfare offenses." These cases do not fit neatly into any of such accepted classifications of common-law defenses, such as those against the State, the person, property, or public morals. Many of these offenses are not in the nature of positive aggressions or invasions, with which the common law so often dealt, but are in the nature of neglect where the law requires care, or inaction where it imposes a duty. Many violations of such regulations result in no direct or immediate injury to person or property but merely create the danger or probability of it, which the law seeks to minimize. While such offenses do not threaten the security of the State in the manner of treason, they may be regarded as offenses against its authority, for their occurrence impairs the efficiency of controls deemed essential to the social order as presently constituted. In this respect, whatever the intent of the violator, the injury is the same; and the consequences are injurious or not according to fortuity. Hence, legislation applicable to such offenses, as a matter of policy, does not specify intent as a necessary element. The accused, if he does not will the violation, usually is in a position to prevent it with no more care than society might reasonably exact from one who assumed his responsibilities. Also, penalties commonly are relatively small, and conviction does no grave damage to an offender's reputation. Under such considerations, courts have turned to construing statutes and regulations which make no mention of intent as dispensing with it and holding that the guilty act alone makes out the crime. This has not, however, been without expressions of misgiving. . . .

Neither this Court nor, so far as we are aware, any other has undertaken to delineate a precise line or set forth comprehensive criteria for distinguishing between crimes that require a mental element and crimes that do not. We attempt no closed definition, for the law on the subject is neither settled nor static. . . .

Stealing, larceny, and its variants and equivalents were among the earliest offenses known to the law that existed before legislation. They are invasions of rights of property which stir a sense of insecurity in the whole community and arouse public demand for retribution. The penalty is high; and when a sufficient amount is involved, the infamy is that of a felony, which, says Maitland, is " . . . as bad a work as you can give to man or thing." State courts of last resort, on whom fall the heaviest burden of interpreting criminal law in this country, have consistently retained the requirement of intent in larceny-type offenses. If any State has deviated, the exception has neither been called to our attention nor disclosed by our research. . . .

The Government asks us by a feat of construction radically to change the weights and balances in the scales of justice. The purpose and obvious effect of doing away with the requirement of a guilty intent is to ease the prosecution's path to conviction, to strip the defendant of such benefit as he derived at common law from innocence of evil purpose, and to circumscribe the freedom heretofore allowed juries. Such a manifest impairment of the immunities of the individual should not be expanded to common-law crimes on judicial initiative.

The spirit of the doctrine, which denies to the Federal judiciary power to create crimes forthrightly, admonishes that we should not enlarge the reach of enacted crimes by constituting them from anything less than the incriminating components contemplated by the words used in the statute. And where Congress borrows terms of art in which are accumulated the legal tradition and meaning of centuries of practice, it presumably knows and adopts the cluster of ideas that were attached to each borrowed word in the body of learning from which it was taken and the meaning its use will convey to the judicial mind unless otherwise instructed. In such case, absence of contrary direction may be taken as satisfaction with widely accepted definitions, not as a departure from them.

We hold that mere omission from 641 of any mention of intent will not be construed as eliminating that element from the crimes denounced.

Congress, by the language of this section, has been at pains to incriminate only "knowing" conversions. But, at common-law, there are unwitting acts which constitute conversions. In the civil tort, except for recovery of exemplary damages, the defendant's knowledge, intent, motive, mistake, and good faith are generally irrelevant. If one takes property which turns out to belong to another, his innocent intent will not shield him from making restitution or indemnity, for his well-meaning may not be allowed to deprive another of his own.

Had the statute applied to conversions without qualification, it would have made crimes of all unwitting, inadvertent, and unintended conversions. Knowledge, of course, is not identical with intent and may not have been the most apt words of limitation. But knowing conversion requires more than knowledge that defendant was taking the property into his possession. He must have had knowledge of the facts, though not necessarily the law, that made the taking a conversion. In the case before us, whether the mental element that Congress required be spoken of as knowledge or as intent, would not seem to alter its bearing on guilt. For it is not apparent how Morissette could have knowingly or intentionally converted property that he did not know could be converted, as would be the case if it was, in fact, abandoned or if he truly believed it to be abandoned and unwanted property. . . .

Of course, the jury, considering Morissette's awareness that these casings were on government property, his failure to seek any permission for their removal and his self-interest as a witness, might have disbelieved his profession of innocent intent and concluded that his assertion of a belief that the casings were abandoned was an afterthought. Had the jury convicted on proper instructions, it would be the end of the matter. But juries are not bound by what seems inescapable logic to judges. They might have concluded that the heaps of spent casings left in the hinterland to rust away presented an appearance of unwanted and abandoned junk, and that lack of any conscious deprivation of property or intentional injury was indicated by Morissette's good character, the openness of the taking, crushing, and transporting of the casings, and the candor with which it was all admitted. They might have refused to brand Morissette as a thief. Had they done so, that too would have been the end of the matter.

Reversed.

Intent: *United States v. Park*[4]

MR. CHIEF JUSTICE BURGER delivered the opinion of the Court.

We granted certiorari to consider whether the jury instructions in the prosecution of a corporate officer under 301(k) were appropriate under United States v. Dotterweich, 320 U.S. 277 (1943).

Acme Markets, Inc., is a national retail food chain with approximately 36,000 employees, 874 retail outlets, 12 general warehouses, and 4 special warehouses. Its headquarters, including the office of the president, respondent Park, who is Chief Executive Officer of the corporation, are located in Philadelphia, Pennsylvania. In a five-count information filed in the United States District Court of Maryland, the Government charged Acme and respondent with violations of the Federal Food, Drug, and Cosmetic Act. Each count of the information alleged that the defendants had received food that had been shipped in interstate commerce and that, while the food was being held for sale in Acme's Baltimore warehouse following shipment in interstate commerce, they caused it to be held in a building accessible to rodents and to be exposed to contamination by rodents. These acts were alleged to have resulted in the food's being adulterated within the meaning of 21 U.S.C. 342(a) (3) and (4), in violation of 21 U.S.C. 331(k).

Acme pleaded guilty to each count of the information. Respondent pleaded not guilty. The evidence at trial demonstrated that in April 1970 the Food and Drug Administration (FDA) advised respondent by letter of unsanitary conditions in Acme's Philadelphia warehouse. An FDA consumer safety officer testified concerning evidence of rodent infestation and other unsanitary conditions discovered during a 12-day inspection of the Baltimore warehouse in November and December 1971. He also related that a second inspection of the warehouse had been conducted in March 1972. On that occasion the inspectors found that there had been improvement in the sanitary conditions, but that "there was still evidence of rodent activity in the building and in the warehouses and we found some rodent-contamination in lots of food items."

The Government also presented testimony to the Chief of Compliance of the FDA's Baltimore office, who informed respondent by letter of the conditions at the Baltimore warehouse after the first inspection. There was testimony by Acme's Baltimore division vice president, who had responded to the letter on behalf of Acme and respondent, and who described the steps taken to remedy the unsanitary conditions discovered by both inspections. The Government's final witness, Acme's vice president for legal affairs and assistant secretary, identified respondent as the president and chief executive officer of the company and read a bylaw prescribing the duties of the chief executive officer. He testified that respondent functioned by delegating "normal operating duties," including sanitation, but that he retained "certain things, which are the big, broad principles of the operation of the company," and had the "responsibility of seeing that they all work together."

At the close of the Government's case in chief, respondent moved for a judgment of acquittal on the ground that the "evidence in chief has shown that Mr. Park is not personally concerned in this Food and Drug violation." The trial judge denied the motion, stating that the United States v. Dotterweich, 320 U.S. 277 (1943), was controlling.

Respondent was the only defense witness. He testified that, although all of Acme's employees were in a sense under his general direction, the company had an "organizational structure for responsibilities for certain functions" according to which different phases of its operation were "assigned to individuals who, in turn, have staff and departments under them." He identified those individuals responsible for sanitation and related that upon receipt of the January 1971 FDA letter, he had conferred with the vice president for legal affairs, who informed him that the Baltimore division vice president "was investigating the situation immediately and would be taking corrective action to reply to the letter." Respondent stated that he did not "believe there was anything (he) could have done more constructively than what (he) found was being done."

On cross-examination, respondent conceded that providing sanitary conditions for food offered for sale to the public was something that he was "responsible for in the entire operation of the company," and he stated that it was one of many phases of the company that he assigned to "dependable subordinates." Respondent was asked about, and over the objections of his counsel, admitted receiving the April 1970 letter addressed to him from the FDA regarding unsanitary conditions at Acme's Philadelphia warehouse. He acknowledged that, with the exception of the division vice president, the same individuals had responsibility for sanitation in both Baltimore and Philadelphia. Finally, in response to questions concerning the Philadelphia and Baltimore incidents, respondent admitted that the Baltimore problem indicated the system for handling sanitation "wasn't working perfectly," and as Acme's Chief Executive Officer, he was responsible for "any result which occurs in our company."

At the close of the evidence, respondent's renewed motion for a judgment of acquittal was denied. The relevant portion of the trial judge's instructions to the jury challenged by respondent is set out in the margin. Respondent's counsel objected to the instructions on the ground that they failed to reflect fairly our decision in United States v. Dotterweich, supra, and to define "responsible relationship." The trial judge overruled the objection. The jury found respondent guilty on all counts of the information, and he was subsequently sentenced to pay a fine of $50 on each count.

The Court of Appeals reversed the conviction and remanded for a new trial. . . .

The question presented by the Government's petition for certiorari in United States v. Dotterweich, supra, and the focus of this Court's opinion was whether "the manager of a corporation, as well as the corporation itself, may be prosecuted under the Federal Food, Drug and Cosmetic Act of 1938 for the introduction of misbranded and adulterated articles into interstate commerce." In Dotterweich, a jury had disagreed as to the corporation, a jobber purchasing drugs from manufacturers, and shipping them in interstate commerce under its own label, but had convicted Dotterweich, the corporation's president and general manager. The Court of Appeals reversed the conviction on the ground that only the drug dealer, whether corporation or individual, was subject to the criminal provisions of the Act, and that where the dealer was a corporation, an individual connected therewith might be held personally only if he was operating the corporation "as his alter ego."

In reversing the judgment of the Court of Appeals and reinstating Dotterweich's conviction, this Court looked to the purposes of the Act and noted that they "touch phases of the lives and health of people which, in the circumstances of modern industrialism, are largely beyond self-protection." It observed that the Act is of a "now familiar type" which "dispenses with the conventional requirement for criminal conduct—awareness of some wrongdoing. In the interest of the larger good, it puts the burden of acting at hazard upon a person otherwise innocent but standing in responsible relation to a public danger."

Central to the Court's conclusion that individuals other than proprietors are subject to the criminal provisions of the Act was the reality that "the only way in which a corporation can act is through the individuals who act on its behalf."

The Court recognized that, because the Act dispenses with the need to prove "consciousness of wrongdoing," it may result in hardship even as applied to those who share "responsibility in the business process resulting in a violation. . . ."

The rule that corporate employees who have a "responsible share in the furtherance of the transaction which the statute outlaws" are subject to the criminal provisions of the Act was not formulated in a vacuum. See, for example, *Morissette v. United States, 342 U.S. 246, 258 (1952).* Cases under the Federal Food and Drug Act of 1906 reflected the view both that knowledge or intent were not required to be proved in prosecutions under its criminal provisions, and that responsible corporate agents could be subjected to the liability thereby imposed. . . .

The rationale of the interpretation given the Act in Dotterweich, as holding criminally accountable the persons whose failure to exercise the authority and supervisory responsibility reposed in them by the business organization resulted in the violation complained of, has been confirmed in our subsequent cases. Thus, the Court has reaffirmed the proposition that "the public interest in the purity of its food is so great as to warrant the imposition of the highest standard of care on distributors."

Thus Dotterweich, and the cases which have followed, reveal that in providing sanctions which reach and touch the individuals who execute the corporate mission—and this is by no means necessarily confined to a single corporate agent or employee—the Act imposes not only a positive duty to seek out and remedy violations when they occur but also, and primarily, a duty to implement measures that will insure that violations will not occur. The requirements of foresight and vigilance imposed on responsible corporate agents are, beyond question, demanding and perhaps onerous; but they are no more stringent than the public has a right to expect of those who voluntarily assume positions of authority in business enterprises whose services and products affect the health and well-being of the public that supports them. . . .

Reading the entire charge satisfies us that the jury's attention was adequately focused on the issue of respondent's authority with respect to the conditions that formed the basis of the alleged violations. Viewed as a whole, the charge did not permit the jury to find guilt solely on the basis of respondent's position in the corporation; rather, it fairly advised the jury that to find guilt it must find respondent "had a responsible relation to the situation," and "by virtue of his position . . . had . . . authority and responsibility" to deal with the situation. The situation referred to could only be "food . . . held in unsanitary conditions in a warehouse with the result that it consisted, in part, of filth or . . . may have been contaminated with filth. . . ."

Our conclusion that the Court of Appeals erred in its reading of the jury charge suggests as well our disagreement with that court concerning the admissibility of evidence demonstrating that respondent was advised by the FDA in 1970 of unsanitary conditions in Acme's Philadelphia warehouse. We are satisfied that the Act imposes the highest standard of care and permits conviction of responsible corporate officials who, in light of this standard of care, have the power to prevent or correct violations of its provisions. . . .

Reversed.

Invasion of Privacy: *Nader v. General Motors Corp.*[5]

CHIEF JUDGE FULD: On this appeal, taken by permission of the Appellate Division on a certified question, we are called upon to determine the reach of the tort of invasion of privacy as it exists under the law of the District of Columbia.

The complaint, in this action by Ralph Nader, pleads four causes of action against the appellant, General Motors Corporation and three other defendants allegedly acting as its agents. The first two causes of action charge an invasion of privacy. . . . This appeal concerns only the legal sufficiency of the first two causes of action which were upheld in the courts below as against the appellant's motion to dismiss.

The plaintiff, an author and lecturer on automotive safety, has, for some years, been an articulate and severe critic of General Motors' products from the standpoint of safety and design. According to the complaint— which, for present purposes we must assume to be true—the appellant, having learned of the imminent publication of the plaintiff's book, *Unsafe at Any Speed,* decided to conduct a campaign of intimidation against him in order to "suppress plaintiff's criticism of and prevent his disclosure of information" about its products. To that end, the appellant authorized and directed the other defendants to engage in a series of activities which, the plaintiff claims in his first two causes of action, violated his right to privacy.

Specifically, the plaintiff alleges that the appellant's agents: (1) conducted a series of interviews with acquaintances of the plaintiff, "questioning them about, and casting aspersions upon (his) political, social . . . racial and religious views, . . . his integrity, his sexual proclivities and inclinations, and his personal habits; (2) kept him under surveillance in public places for an unreasonable length of time; (3) caused him to be accosted by girls for the purpose of entrapping him into illicit relationships; (4) made threatening, harassing and obnoxious telephone calls to him; (5) tapped his telephone and eavesdropped, by means of mechanical and electronic equipment, on his private conversations with others; and (6) conducted a "continuing" and harassing investigation of him. . . ."

The threshold choice of law question requires no extended discussion. In point of fact, the parties have agreed—at least for purposes of this motion—that the sufficiency of these allegations is to be determined under the law of the District of Columbia. . . .

Turning then to the law of the District of Columbia, it appears that its courts have not only recognized a common-law action for invasion of privacy, but have broadened the scope of that tort beyond its traditional limits. Thus, in the most recent of its cases on the subject, *Pearson v. Dodd* (410 F.2d 701), the Federal Court of Appeals for the District of Columbia declared (p. 704):

> We approve the extension of the tort of invasion of privacy to in-
> stances of intrusion, whether by physical trespass or not, into spheres
> from which an ordinary man in a plaintiff's position could reasonably
> expect that the particular defendant should be excluded. . . .

Quite obviously, some intrusions into one's private sphere are inevitable concomitants of life in an industrial and densely populated society, which the law does not seek to proscribe even if it were possible to do so. "The law does not provide a remedy for every annoyance that occurs in everyday life. . . ."

It should be emphasized that the mere gathering of information about a particular individual does not give rise to a cause of action under this theory. Privacy is invaded only if the information sought is of a confidential nature and the defendant's conduct was unreasonably intrusive. . . . In order to sustain a cause of action for invasion of privacy, therefore, the plaintiff must show that the appellant's conduct was truly "intrusive" and that it was designed to elicit information which would not be available through normal inquiry or observation. . . .

Turning then to the particular acts charged in the complaint, we cannot find any basis for a claim of invasion of privacy, under District of Columbia law, in the allegations that the appellant, through its agents or employees, interviewed many persons who knew the plaintiff, asking questions about him and casting aspersions on his character. Although those inquiries may have uncovered information of a personal nature, it is difficult to see how they may be said to have invaded the plaintiff's privacy. Information about the plaintiff, which was already known to others, could hardly be regarded as private to the plaintiff. Presumably, the plaintiff had previously revealed the information to such other persons, and he would necessarily assume the risk that a friend or acquaintance in whom he had confided might breach the confidence. If, as alleged, the questions tended to disparage the plaintiff's character, his remedy would seem to be by way of an action for defamation, not for breach of his right to privacy.

Nor can we find any actionable invasion of privacy in the allegations that the appellant caused the plaintiff to be accosted by girls with illicit proposals, or that it was responsible for the making of a large number of threatening and harassing telephone calls to the plaintiff's home at odd hours. Neither of these activities, howsoever offensive and disturbing, involved intrusion for the purpose of gathering information of a private and confidential nature.

As already indicated, it is manifestly neither practical nor desirable for the law to provide a remedy against any and all activity which an individual might find annoying. On the other hand, where severe mental pain or anguish is inflicted through a deliberate and malicious campaign of harassment or intimidation, a remedy is available in the form of an action for the intentional infliction of emotional distress—the theory underlying the plaintiff's third cause of action. . . .

Apart, however, from the foregoing allegations which we find inadequate to spell out a cause of action for invasion of privacy under District of Columbia law, the complaint contains allegations concerning other activities by the appellant or its agents which do satisfy the requirements for such a cause of action. The one which most clearly meets those requirements is the charge that the appellant and its co-defendants engaged in unauthorized wiretapping and eavesdropping by mechanical and electronic means. The Court of Appeals in the *Pearson* case expressly recognized that such conduct constitutes a tortious intrusion and other jurisdictions have reached a similar conclusion. In point of fact, the appellant does not dispute this, acknowledging that, to the extent the two challenged counts charge it with wiretapping and eavesdropping, an actionable invasion of privacy has been stated.

There are additional allegations that the appellant hired people to shadow the plaintiff and keep him under surveillance. In particular, he claims that on one occasion one of his agents followed him into a bank, getting sufficiently close to him to see the denomination of the bills he was withdrawing from his account. From what we have already said, it is manifest that the mere observation of the plaintiff in a public place does not amount to an invasion of his privacy. But under certain circumstances, surveillance may be so "overzealous" as to render it actionable. Whether or not the surveillance in the present case falls into this latter category will depend on the nature of the proof. A person does not automatically make public everything he does merely by being in a public place, and the mere fact that Nader was in a bank did not give anyone the right to try to discover the amount of money he was withdrawing. On the other hand, if the plaintiff acted in such a way as to reveal that fact to any casual observer, then it may not be said that the appellant intruded into his private sphere. In any event though, it is enough for present purposes to say that the surveillance allegation is not insufficient as a matter of law.

Since, then, the first two causes of action do contain allegations which are adequate to state a cause of action for invasion of privacy under District of Columbia law, the courts below properly denied the appellant's motion to dismiss those causes of action.

False Imprisonment: *Lester v. Albers Super Markets*[6]

MATTHEWS, JUDGE: As we viewed the record, it raises the fundamental questions of what is imprisonment. Before any need for a determination of illegality arises there must be proof of imprisonment.

In 35 C.J.S., False Imprisonment, 11, pages 512, 513, it is said: "Submission to the mere verbal direction of another, unaccompanied by force or by threats of any character, cannot constitute a false imprisonment; and there is no false imprisonment where an employer interviewing an employee declines to terminate the interview if no force or threat of force is used and false imprisonment may not be predicated on a person's unfounded belief that he was restrained."

Many cases are cited in support of the text. . . .

In Fenn v. Kroger Grocery & Baking Co., Mo. Sup., 209 S.W. 885, 887, the Court said:

> A case was not made out for false arrest. The plaintiff said she was intercepted as she started to leave the store; that Mr. Krause stood where she could not pass him in going out. She does not say that he made any attempt to intercept her. She says he escorted her back to the desk, that he asked her to let him see the change.
>
> . . . She does not say that she went unwillingly. . . . Evidence is wholly lacking to show that she was detained by force or threats. It was probably a disagreeable experience, a humiliating one to her, but she came out victorious and was allowed to go when she desired with the assurance of Mr. Krause that it was all right. The demurrer to the evidence on both counts was properly sustained.

The result of the cases is epitomized in 22AM.Jr.368, as follows:

> A customer or patron who apparently has not paid for what he has received may be detained for a reasonable time to investigate the circumstances; but upon payment of the demand, he has the unqualified right to leave the premises without restraint, so far as the proprietor is concerned, and it is false imprisonment for a private individual to detain one for an unreasonable time, or under unreasonable circumstances, for the purpose of investigating a dispute

over the payment of a bill alleged to be owed by the person detained for cash services. . . .

For those reasons, the judgment is reversed and final judgment entered for the defendant-appellant.

Intentional Infliction of Emotional Distress: Eckenrode v. Life of America Insurance Co.[7]

KILEY, CIRCUIT JUDGE: Plaintiff, a resident of Pennsylvania, filed this three-count diversity complaint to recover damages for severe emotional injury suffered as a result of the deliberate refusal of Life of America Insurance Company (Insurer), of Chicago, to pay her the proceeds of Insurer's policy covering the life of her husband. The District Court dismissed the suit. Plaintiff has appealed. We reverse. . . .

Taking the allegations, properly pleaded in Counts II and III, as true, the following facts are stated: Defendant's life insurance policy covering plaintiff's husband issued September 22, 1967. Under the policy, Insurer agreed to pay plaintiff $5,000 immediately upon due proof of death from "accidental causes." On December 17, 1967, insured was an accidental victim of homicide. Plaintiff met all conditions of the policy and repeatedly demanded payment, but Insurer refused to pay. Decedent left plaintiff with several children, but no property of value. She had no money, none even for the funeral expenses. Denied payment by Insurer, she was required to borrow money to support her family, while her financial condition worsened. The family was required to live with and accept charity from relatives.

Further . . . Insurer, knowing full well that plaintiff needed the proceeds of the policy to provide necessaries for her children, applied "economic coercion" in refusing to make payment on the policy, and in "inviting" plaintiff to "compromise" her claim by implying it (Insurer) had a valid defense to the claim.

The issue before us with respect to Counts II and III is whether plaintiff—beneficiary of her husband's life insurance policy—may on the foregoing "facts" recover damages for severe mental distress allegedly suffered as a result of Insurer's conduct. Illinois law controls our decision, and, in anticipation that the Illinois Supreme Court would hold as we do, we decide the issue in favor of plaintiff.

We have no doubt, in view of Knierim v. Izzo, 22 Ill. 2d 73, 174 N.E. 2d 157 (1961), that the Illinois Supreme Court would sustain plaintiff's complaint against Insurer's motion to dismiss.

In *Knierim,* plaintiff filed a wrongful death action alleging, inter alia, that defendant Izzo threatened her with the murder of her husband, carried out the threat, and thereby proximately caused her severe emotional distress. The trial court dismissed her complaint, but the Illinois Supreme Court reversed and held that plaintiff had stated a cause of action for an intentional causing of severe emotional distress by Izzo's "outrageous conduct."

The court recognized the "new tort" of intentional infliction of severe emotional distress, following similar recognition by an "increasing number of courts," and cited several state decisions. The Court rejected reasons given by other courts not recognizing the "new tort." As to the reason that mental disturbance is incapable of financial measurement, the Court pointed out that "pain and suffering" and "mental suffering" are elements of damage, respectively, in personal injury and malicious prosecution cases.

As to the reason that mental consequences are too evanescent for the law to deal with, the Court noted that psychosomatic medicine had learned much in the past "thirty years" about the bodily effects of man's emotions, and that symptoms produced by "stronger emotions" are now visible to the professional eye. As to the reason that recognizing the "new tort" would lead to frivolous claims, the Court observed that triers of fact from their own experiences would be able to draw a line between "slight hurts" and "outrageous conduct" . . .

In *Knierim* the Court, inter alia, relied upon State Rubbish Collectors Association v. Siliznoff, 38 Cal, 2d 330, 240 P.2d 282 (1952), and Restatement, Torts S 46 (1948 Supp.). In *Siliznoff,* the California Supreme Court, in an opinion by Justice Roger Traynor, recognized the "new tort" for the first time and held that Siliznoff could recover from the cross-defendant Rubbish Collectors Association for mental distress caused by the Association's severe threats to beat him up, destroy his truck, and put him out of business unless Siliznoff offered to pay over certain proceeds to the Association. . . .

We think that the California court in Fletcher, supra, set out correctly the elements of a prima facie case for the tort of "intentional infliction of severe emotional distress"

(1) Outrageous conduct by the defendant;
(2) The defendant's intention of causing or reckless disregard of the probability of causing emotional distress;
(3) The plaintiff's suffering severe or extreme emotional distress; and
(4) Actual and proximate causation of the emotional distress by the defendant's outrageous conduct. . . .

Here Insurer's alleged bad faith refusal to make payment on the policy, coupled with its deliberate use of "economic coercion," i.e., by delaying and refusing payment it increased plaintiff's financial distress, thereby coercing her to compromise and to force a settlement, clearly rises to the level of "outrageous conduct" to a person of "ordinary sensibilities."

Furthermore, it is common knowledge that one of the most frequent considerations in procuring life insurance is to ensure the continued economic and mental welfare of the beneficiaries upon the death of the insured. The very risks insured against presuppose that upon the death of the insured, the beneficiary might be in difficult circumstances and thus particularly susceptible and vulnerable to high pressure tactics by an economically powerful entity. In the case before us, Insurer's alleged high pressure methods (economic coercion) were aimed at the very thing insured against, and we think that the insurance company was on notice that plaintiff would be particularly vulnerable to mental distress by reason of her financial plight. . . .

Reversed.

Liability of Principals for Criminal Act of Their Agents: *Gross v. State*[8]

HADLEY, J.: Appellant was found guilty of selling oleo margarine for dairy butter, in violation of the pure food law of 1907 (Acts 1907, p. 153, c. 104). The overruling of his motion for a new trial, because the finding by the court was contrary to law and the evidence, is the only error assigned. The question for decision is: Can a principal be held criminally liable for this sale, by a clerk or agent of adulterated food, the sale being made in the absence of the principal, and in violation of his instructions?

The general rule is that criminal statutes must be strictly construed, to avoid the creation of penalties by construction; but such reasonable view must be taken of a statute as will effectuate the manifest intent and purpose of the lawmakers. It is too obvious for discussion that the pure food statute, before us, was enacted as a means of protecting the people against the fraud and imposition of manufacturers and vendors of inferior and unwholesome food and medicinal products. The statute is of great public interest, and such interpretation should be given it—if possible, within sound canons of construction—as will secure to the people the benefits intended by the General Assembly. In the first place, the offense created by the statute belongs to that class in which knowledge or guilty intent is immaterial, and need not be shown in order to justify a conviction. It falls under the general rule (of) statutes which declare the doing of a certain thing shall constitute an offense against the public, without reference to whether done without notice or with guilty knowledge. In such cases it is in the act itself, not the intent, that determines the guilt; the actual harm to the public being the same in one case as in the other. The distribution of impure or adulterated food for consumption is an act perilous to human life and health; hence a dangerous act, and cannot be made innocent and harmless by the want of knowledge or the good faith of the (vendor).

The offense under consideration is thus defined: "It shall be unlawful for any person to manufacture for sale within this State, offer for sale therein, or sell within this State, any drug, or article of food which is adulterated, or misbranded. . . . For the purpose of this act, an article shall be deemed as adulterated . . . if any substance has been substituted wholly, or in part, for the article." Guilty intent is not an ingredient in the crime, as we have seen; hence the fuel that governs in that large class of offenses, which rest upon criminal intent, has no application here. Cases like this are founded largely upon the principle that he who voluntarily deals in perilous articles must be cautious how he deals. The sale of oleo margarine in an adulterated form, or as a substitute for butter, is a crime against the public health. Whoever, therefore, engages in its sale, or in the sale of any article interdicted by the law, does so at his peril, and impliedly undertakes to conduct the business himself, or by clerks or agents; but, if he chooses the latter, the duty is imposed upon him to see to it that those selected by him to sell the article to the public obey the law in the matter of selling; otherwise he, as the principal and the responsible proprietor of the business, is liable for the penalty imposed by the statute.

We do not believe it was the legislative intent that such proprietor should escape by showing that an unlawful sale made by his clerk was unauthorized. We must take a practical, common sense view of the whole statute to give effect to the legislative purpose. To hold that the proprietor should be held liable only when the sale was made in his presence, or with his knowledge or consent, would be to prepare a way of easy escape. When we take into consideration the community of interest of the proprietor and clerk in a case like this, and that private instructions to a clerk may be given in such a way that there may be more meaning in the manner than in the words spoken, and adding thereto the fact that the modern method of ordering supplies by wire renders the identification of the seller generally impossible we are led to the conclusion that to sustain appellant's contention would operate as a virtual overthrow of the statute. Upon the same subject it was said by a learned judge in the State of Ohio:

> To hold that by private instructions to a clerk a person in the oleo margarine business might escape prosecution or punishment would go a long way, it seems to us, toward destroying the beneficial effects and purposes of this law. In many cases, such goods are ordered by telephone and the clerk is not seen. There is no way of identifying him. . . . Where the article is sold by his authority, it is not like a case where a party has prohibited his clerks from selling the article at all, or where the clerk, without any authority, has sold the article, or where someone has come into his store without authority and sold the article. But here is a case where the party is engaged in the business of selling where he intends to sell it, and where his clerks are authorized and employed to sell it. . . .

The evidence discloses the following facts:

Appellant is the proprietor of a stall in the Indianapolis market house. Among many other food products, he keeps for sale oleo margarine and creamery butter, but not dairy butter. In April 1907, one Bruner, an inspector in the employ of the State Board of Health, presented himself at appellant's stall and applied for the purchase of one pound of dairy butter. Appellant was not present. The stall was in sole charge of a young lady, a clerk and employee of appellant, who answered Bruner's application by moving a short distance, and then by stooping, took from under the counter a package, which she wrapped and handed to Bruner, and for which she charged and received 25¢. The package was wrapped in a paper that had stamped upon it in large letters the word "Oleomargarine," but which word was not observed by Mr. Bruner until the day of the trial of this cause. Appellant had previously given instructions to the young lady clerk to sell everything in the stall for just what it was, and to sell nothing as a substitute for something else. These facts show that the sale was made by a clerk who was employed by appellant to sell oleo margarine from the particular stall, along with butter and other things. The sale was made in the regular course of business, in the exercise of the usual duties of her employment made for appellant, upon his apparent authority, and for his benefit; and it seems clear that he should be answerable if he had failed to apply the necessary precautions in the selection, counseling, and oversight of his agent, or, in other words, held responsible for what he had done by another. . . .

Judgment affirmed.

Insider Trading: *Dirks v. Securities Exchange Commission*[9]

JUSTICE POWELL delivered the opinion of the court. Petitioner Raymond Dirks received material nonpublic information from "insiders" of a corporation with which he had no connection. He disclosed this information to investors who relied on it in trading in the shares of the corporation. The question is whether Dirks violated the antifraud provisions of the Federal securities laws by this disclosure.

I.

In 1973, Dirks was an officer of a New York broker-dealer firm who specialized in providing investment analysis of insurance company securities to institutional investors. On March 6, Dirks received information from Ronald Secrist, a former officer of Equity Funding of America. Secrist alleged that the assets of Equity Funding, a diversified corporation primarily engaged in selling life insurance and mutual funds, were vastly overstated as the result of fraudulent corporate practices. Secrist also stated that various agencies had failed to act on similar charges made by Equity Funding employees. He urged Dirks to verify the fraud and disclose it publicly.

Dirks decided to investigate the allegations. He visited Equity Funding's headquarters in Los Angeles and interviewed several officers and employees of the corporation. The senior management denied any wrongdoing, but certain corporation employees corroborated the fraud charges.

Neither Dirks nor his firm owned or traded any Equity Funding stock, but throughout his investigation, he openly discussed the information he had obtained with a number of clients and investors. Some of these persons sold their holdings of Equity Funding securities, including five investment advisers who liquidated holdings of more than $16 million.

While Dirks was in Los Angeles, he was in touch regularly with William Blundell, the *Wall Street Journal*'s Los Angeles bureau chief. Dirks urged Blundell to write a story on the fraud allegations. Blundell did not believe, however, that such a massive fraud could go undetected and declined to write the story. He feared that publishing such damaging hearsay might be libelous.

During the two-week period in which Dirks pursued his investigation and spread word of Secrist's charges, the price of Equity Funding stock fell from $26 per share to less than $15 per share. This led the New York Stock Exchange to halt trading on March 27. Shortly thereafter, California insurance authorities impounded Equity Funding's records and uncovered evidence of the fraud. Only then did the Securities and Exchange commission (SEC) file a complaint against Equity Funding and only then, on April 2, did the *Wall Street Journal* publish a front-page story based largely on information assembled by Dirks. Equity Funding immediately went into receivership.

The SEC began an investigation into Dirk's role in the exposure of the fraud. The SEC concluded: "Where 'tippees'—regardless of their motivation or occupation—come into possession of material 'information that they know is confidential and know or should know came from a corporate insider,' they must either publicly disclose that information or refrain from trading," 21 S.E.C. Docket 1401, 1407 (1981) [footnote omitted] (quoting *Chiarella v. United States*, 445 U.S. 222, 230 n. 12 (1980)). Recognizing, however, that Dirks "played an important role in bringing (Equity Funding's) massive fraud to light," 21 S.E.C. Docket, at 1412, the SEC only censured him.

Dirks sought review in the Court of Appeals for the District of Columbia Circuit. The court entered judgment against Dirks "for the reasons stated by the Commission in its opinion." . . .

In view of the importance to the SEC and to the securities industry of the question presented by this case, we granted a writ of certiorari. U. S. (1982). We now reverse.

II.

In the seminal case of in re *Cady, Roberts & Co.*, 40 S.E.C. 907 (1961), the SEC recognized that the common law in some jurisdictions imposes on "corporate 'insiders,' particularly officers, directors, or controlling stockholders" an "affirmative duty of disclosure . . . when dealing in securities." The SEC found that not only did breach of this common law duty also establish the elements of a Rule 10b-5 violation, but that individuals other than corporate insiders could be obligated either to disclose material nonpublic information before trading or to abstain from trading altogether. In *Chiarella,* we accepted the two elements set out in *Cady, Roberts* for establishing a Rule 10b-5 violation: "(i) the existence of a relationship affording access to inside information intended to be available only for a corporate purpose and (ii) the unfairness of allowing a corporate insider to take advantage of that information by trading without disclosure." In examining whether Chiarella had an obligation to disclose or abstain, the Court found that there is not a general duty to disclose before trading on material nonpublic information, and held that "a duty to disclose under Section 10(b) does not arise from the mere possession of nonpublic market information." Such a duty arises rather from the existence of a fiduciary relationship.

Not "all breaches of fiduciary duty in connection with a securities transaction," however, come within the ambit of Rule 10b-5. There must also be "manipulation or deception." In an insider-trading case, this fraud derives from the "inherent unfairness involved where one takes advantage" of "information intended to be available only for a corporate purpose and not for the personal benefit of anyone." In re *Merrill Lynch, Pierce, Fenner & Smith, Inc.,* 43 S.E.C. 933, 936 (1968). Thus, an insider will be liable under Rule 10b-5 for inside trading only where he fails to disclose material nonpublic information before trading on it and thus makes "secret profits." *Cady, Roberts,* 40 S.E.C., at 916, n.31.

III.

We were explicit in *Chiarella* in saying that there can be no duty to disclose where the person who has traded on inside information "was not [the corporation's] agent . . . was not a fiduciary [or] was not a person in whom the sellers [of securities] had placed their trust and confidence." Not to require such a fiduciary relationship, we recognized, would "depar[t] radically from the established doctrine that duty arises from a specific relationship between two parties" and would amount to "recognizing a general duty between all participants in market transactions to forego actions based on material, nonpublic information." This requirement of a specific relationship between the shareholders and the individual trading on inside information has created analytical difficulties for the SEC and courts in policing tippees who trade on inside information. Unlike insiders who have independent fiduciary duties to both the corporation and its shareholders, the typical tippee has no such relationships. In view of this absence, it has been unclear how a tippee acquires the *Cady, Roberts* duty to refrain from trading on inside information. . . .

In determining whether a tippee is under an obligation to disclose or abstain, it thus is necessary to determine whether the insider's "tip" constituted a breach of the insider's fiduciary duty. All disclosures of confidential corporate information are not inconsistent with the duty insiders owe to shareholders. In contrast to the extraordinary facts of this case, the more typical situation in which there will be a question whether disclosure violates the insider's *Cady, Roberts* duty is when insiders disclose information to analysts. In some situations, the insider will act consistently with his fiduciary duty to shareholders, and yet release of the information may affect the market. For example, it may not be clear—either to the corporate insider or to the recipient analyst—whether the information will be viewed as material nonpublic information. Corporate officials may mistakenly think the information already has been disclosed or that it is not material enough to affect the market. Whether disclosure is a breach of duty, therefore, depends in large part on the purpose of the disclosure. This standard was identified by the SEC itself in *Cady, Roberts:* a purpose of the securities laws was to eliminate "use of inside information for personal advantage." Thus, the test is whether the inside personally will benefit, directly or indirectly, from his disclosure. Absent some personal gain, there has been no breach of duty to stockholders. And absent a breach by the insider, there is no derivative breach. . . .

Determining whether an insider personally benefits from a particular disclosure, a question of fact, will not always be easy for courts. But it is essential, we think, to have a guiding principle for those whose daily activities must be limited and instructed by the SEC's inside-trading rules; and we believe that there must be a breach of the insider's fiduciary duty before the tippee inherits the duty to disclose or abstain. In contrast, the rule adopted by the SEC in this case would have no limiting principle.

IV.

Under the inside-trading and tipping rules set forth above, we find that there was no actionable violation by Dirks. It is undisputed that Dirks himself was a stranger to Equity Funding, with no pre-existing fiduciary duty to its shareholders. He took no action, directly or indirectly, that induced the shareholders or officers of Equity Funding to repose trust or confidence in him. There was no expectation by Dirk's sources that he would keep their information in confidence. Nor did Dirks misappropriate or illegally obtain the information about Equity Funding. Unless the insiders breached their *Cady, Roberts* duty to shareholders in disclosing the nonpublic information to Dirks, he breached no duty when he passed it on to investors as well as to the *Wall Street Journal.*

It is clear that neither Secrist nor the other Equity Funding employees violated their *Cady, Roberts* duty to the corporation's shareholders by providing information to Dirks. The tippers received no monetary or personal benefit for revealing Equity Funding's secrets, nor was their purpose to make a gift of valuable information to Dirks. As the facts of this case clearly indicate, the tippers were motivated by a desire to expose the fraud. In the absence of a breach of duty to shareholders by the insiders, there was no derivative breach by Dirks. Dirks, therefore, could not have been a "participant after the fact in [an] insider's breach of a fiduciary duty." *Chiarella*, 445 U.S., at 230, n.12.

We conclude that Dirks, in the circumstances of this case, had no duty to abstain from use of the insider information that he obtained. The judgment of the Court of Appeals therefore is reversed.

Net Worth Method of Reconstructing Income: *Holland v. United States*[10]

THE SUPREME COURT states:

"To protect the revenue from those who do not render true accounts, the Government must be free to use all legal evidence available to it in determining whether the story told by the taxpayer's books accurately reflect his financial history."

The formula for computing funds from unknown or illegal sources using the net worth method is:

	Assets
Less:	*Liabilities*
Equals:	Net Worth
Less:	*Prior Years' Net Worth*
Equals:	Net Worth Increase (Decrease)
Plus:	*Living Expenses*
Equals:	Income (or Expenditures)
Less:	*Funds from Known Sources*
Equals:	Funds from Unknown/Illegal Sources

The net worth method is often used when several of the subject's assets and/or liabilities have changed during the period under investigation if the following conditions exist:

1. The subject maintains no books and records
2. The subject's books and records are not available
3. The subject's books and records are inadequate
4. The subject withholds his or her books and records

Notes

1. State v. Mills, 96 Ariz. 377, 396, P.2d 5 (1964).
2. United States v. Falcone, 109 F.2d 579 (2d Cir. 1940).
3. Morissette v. United States, 342 U.S. 246 (1952).
4. United States v. Park, 421 U.S. 658 (1975).
5. Nader v. General Motors Corp., 25 N.Y. 2d 560, 255 N.E. 2d 765 (1970).

6. Lester v. Albers Super Markets, ncl 94 Ohio App. 313, 114 N.E. 2d 529 (1952).

7. Eckenrode v. Life of America Insurance Co., 470 F.2d 1 (7th Cir. 1972).

8. Gross v. State, 171 Ind. 547, 85 N.E. 769 (1908).

9. Dirks v. Securities Exchange Commission, 103 S.Ct. 3255, 77 L.Ed. 2d 911 (1983).

10. *Holland v. United States,* 348 U.S. 121 (1954).

Selected Bibliography on White-Collar Crime: 1980 to 1991

Key to Abstract Interpretation

ACCN	National Institute of Justice/NCJRS Accession Number
TITL	English Title
JCIT	Journal Citation
PAUT	Personal Author
CORP	Corporate Author
SPON	Sponsoring Agency
SALE	Sales Agency
PDTE	Date of Publication
PAGE	Number of Pages
ORIG	Country of Origin
LANG	Language
PNUM	Publication Number
CNUM	Contract Number
GNUM	Grant Number
NOTE	Supplemental Note
ANNO	Annotation
SUBJ	Index Terms
CDTE	Date Item Entered the Data Base

The following bibliographic entries were taken from the *Topical Bibliography on White Collar Crime,* issued by the National Institute of Justice in 1991.

Investigation of White-Collar Crime

ACCN: 038592
TITL: Massachusetts Curriculum Development Assistance for Training
        Programs to Combat Organized and White Collar Crime—Police
        Technical Assistance Report
PAUT: Dunman, WH
CORP: Westinghouse Justice Institute, Arlington, VA 22202;
SPON: US Department of Justice Law Enforcement Assistance Administration;
SALE: National Institute of Justice/ National Criminal Justice Reference
        Service Microfiche Program, Box 6000, Department F, Rockville, MD
        20850; MF Microfiche.
PDTE: 1976   PAGE: 124 p
ORIG: United States   LANG: English
GNUM: J-LEAA-003-76
PNUM: 76-163(A); R-76-209
TYPE: Materials
ANNO: November 1976 Report on efforts to develop training programs in the
        areas of organized crime investigation and intelligence.

ACCN: 039865
TITL: Seventh Basic Investigative Technique—Analyzing Financial
        Transactions in the Investigation of Organized Crime and White Collar
        Crime Targets
PAUT: Nossen, RA
CORP: National Conference on Organized Crime;
SPON: US Department of Justice Law Enforcement Assistance Administration;
SALE: National Institute of Justice/National Criminal Justice Reference Service
        Microfiche Program, Box 6000, Department F, Rockville, MD 20850;
        MF Microfiche.
PDTE: 1975   PAGE: 56 p
ORIG: United States   LANG: English
ANNO: The handbook presents investigative accounting techniques to be used
        by criminal investigators who are reluctant to investigate financial
        crimes and transactions.

ACCN: 040553
TITL: Investigation of White Collar Crime—A Manual for Law Enforcement
        Agencies
PAUT: Stotland, E; Walsh, M; Weinberg, M
CORP: Battelle Human Affairs Research Centers, Seattle, WA 98105;
SPON: US Department of Justice Law Enforcement Assistance Administration;
SALE: Superintendent of Documents GPO, Washington, DC 20402; DO
        Document. National Institute of Justice/National Criminal Justice
        Reference Service Microfiche Program, Box 6000, Department F,
        Rockville, MD 20850; MF Microfiche.
PDTE: 1977   PAGE: 393 p
ORIG: United States   LANG: English
GNUM: 76-TA-99-0011
TYPE: Training handbooks/manuals
ANNO: This manual was developed for the use of those who investigate white-
        collar crime and related abuses and to assist those who supervise and
        must interact with investigators in this field.

ACCN: 045789
TITL: White Collar Crime Conference—Investigative Training and Patience
JCIT: Security Management, V 22, N 3 (March 1978), P 38–40, 42
PAUT: Weber, W; Graziano, JB; Henehan, J
CORP: American Society for Industrial Security, Arlington, VA 22209;
PDTE: 1978   PAGE: 4 p   CLSS: Article
ORIG: United States   LANG: English
ANNO: Three basic problems in the investigation of white-collar crime are
        identified: what constitutes such a crime, level of skill of investigative
        personnel, and prosecution and punishment.

ACCN: 051996
TITL: Investigative Planning—Operational Guide to White Collar Crime
        Enforcement—A Report of the National Center on White-Collar Crime
PAUT: O'Neill, R
CORP: Battelle Human Affairs Research Centers, Law and Justice Study
        Center, Seattle, WA 98105;
SPON: US Department of Justice Law Enforcement Assistance Administration;
SALE: National Institute of Justice/National Criminal Justice Reference Service
        Microfiche Program, Box 6000, Department F, Rockville, MD 20850;
        MF Microfiche.
PDTE: 1977   PAGE: 23 p
ORIG: United States   LANG: English
GNUM: 77-TA-99-0008
ANNO: This step-by-step manual is written to help the police agency unfamiliar
        with the complexity of white-collar crime to plan and carry out
        investigations. Techniques, warnings, and hints are provided.

ACCN: 061075
TITL: Police and White-Collar Crime
JCIT: Policy Studies Journal, V 7, Special Issue (1978), P 431–436
PAUT: Brintnall, MA
CORP: Policy Studies Organization, Urbana, IL 61801;
PDTE: 1978   PAGE: 6 p   CLSS: Article
ORIG: United States   LANG: English
ANNO: The actual and potential roles of police in investigating white collar crime are considered.

ACCN: 079781
TITL: Model Curriculum and Trainer's Guide for Programs to Combat White-Collar Crime
PAUT: KarchmerEdelhertz, CL,H
CORP: Battelle Human Affairs Research Centers National Center on White-Collar Crime, Seattle, WA 98105;
SPON: US Department of Justice Law Enforcement Assistance Administration;
SALE: National Institute of Justice/National Criminal Justice Reference Service Microfiche Program, Box 6000, Department F, Rockville, MD 20850; MF Microfiche.
PDTE: 1980   PAGE: 42 p
ORIG: United States   LANG: English
GNUM: 77-TA-99-0008; 78-TA-AX-0050
NOTE: When ordering from GPO, please note that the title reads 'Model Curriculum and Teachers' Guide for Programs to Combat White Collar Crime.'
TYPE: Materials
ANNO: This manual contains suggestions for setting up seminars and recruiting instructors and a 14-unit course outline covering the detection and investigation of white-collar crime.

ACCN: 088960
TITL: Detection, Investigation and Prosecution of Financial Crimes (White Collar, Political Corruption and Racketeering)
PAUT: Nossen, RA
SALE: Richard A Nossen and Associates, 11410 Edenberry Drive, Richmond, VA 23236; PB Paperback.
PDTE: 1982   PAGE: 132 p
ORIG: United States   LANG: English
ANNO: Law enforcement personnel and prosecutors should be aware of a powerful new tool in investigating and prosecuting financial crimes—the net worth and expenditures investigation. This report sets out the steps and formulas involved in conducting the net worth investigation, and describes rules of evidence regarding financial documents and investigative report writing rules.

ACCN: 096426
TITL: Problems in the Investigation of White Collar Crime—A Case Study
JCIT: International Journal of Comparative and Applied Criminal Justice,
        V 8, N 1–2 (Spring/Winter 1984), P 21–42
PAUT: Holland, RC
PDTE: 1984   PAGE: 21 p   CLSS: Article
ORIG: United States   LANG: English
NOTE: Paper prepared for presentation at the 1982 Annual Meeting of the
        Southwestern Sociological Association held March 17–20 in San
        Antonio, Texas.
ANNO: This paper describes an instance of white-collar crime and outlines some
        of the problems encountered by the investigator when attempting to
        reconstruct the offense and bring the offenders to justice.

ACCN: 098135
TITL: Advanced Investigative Techniques for Private Financial Records
PAUT: Nossen, RA
SALE: Paladin Press, PO Box 1307, Boulder, CO 80302; DO Document.
PDTE: 1983   PAGE: 82 p
ORIG: United States   LANG: English
ANNO: The purpose of this guide is to familiarize state and local investigators
        with some basic techniques used to trace financial transactions of white-
        collar crime violators.

ACCN: 112874
TITL: Team Approach to Curtailing White-Collar Crime
JCIT: Police Chief, V 55, N 8 (August 1988), P 60–68
PAUT: Gosseaux, JS; Curran, DJ
SALE: National Institute of Justice/National Criminal Justice Reference Service
        Microfiche Program, Box 6000, Department F, Rockville, MD 20850;
        MF Microfiche.
PDTE: 1988   PAGE: 8 p
ORIG: United States   LANG: English
ANNO: This article discusses the challenge white-collar crime presents to law
        enforcement officials and describes the "proactive" investigative
        approach of the Federal Bureau of Investigation (FBI).

ACCN: 117092
TITL: National Institute on Economic Crime Investigative Techniques in
        Complex Financial Crimes
PAUT: Kramer, WM
PDTE: 1988   PAGE: 215 p   CLSS: Document
ORIG: United States   LANG: English
TYPE: Overview texts
ANNO: This text examines the investigation of complex financial crimes in the
        areas of interview, interrogation, and impeachment; proving illicit
        financial transactions, and case strategies and tactics.

Prosecution of White-Collar Crime

ACCN: 050659
TITL: Prosecuting Computer Criminals
JCIT: Security World, V 15, N 8 (August 1978), P 62–66
PAUT: Hemphill, CF; Hemphill, RD
CORP: Security World Publishing Company, Inc., Los Angeles, CA 90034;
PDTE: 1978   PAGE: 5 p   CLSS: Article
ORIG: United States   LANG: English
ANNO: White-collar crime that stems from the abuse of computers is explored
        in terms of the investigation and prosecution of perpetrators.

ACCN: 060985
TITL: White Collar Crimes 1978
PAUT: Anonymous
CORP: Practicing Law Institute, New York, NY 10019;
SALE: Practicing Law Institute, 810 Seventh Avenue, New York, NY 10019;
        PB Paperback.
PDTE: 1978   PAGE: 176 p
ORIG: United States   LANG: English
PNUM: 100
NOTE: Litigation and Administrative Practice Series—Criminal Law and Urban
        Problems—Course Handbook Series
TYPE: Materials
ANNO: This course handbook, which can be used as a reference manual by
        attorneys and related professionals, examines seven aspects of the
        prosecution of white-collar crimes that have been affected by court
        decisions.

ACCN: 090534
TITL: Principal White Collar Crimes (From Business Crimes—A Guide for
        Corporate and Defense Counsel, P 1–63, 1982, Jeffrey Glekel, ed.—
        See NCJ-90533)
PAUT: Beckler, RW; Epner, MS
SALE: Practicing Law Institute, 810 Seventh Avenue, New York, NY 10019;
        DO Document.
PDTE: 1982   PAGE: 63 p
ORIG: United States   LANG: English
ANNO: This discussion of principal white-collar crimes covers mail and wire
        fraud, false statements, perjury, securities law violations, violations of
        the Hobbs and Travel acts as well as the Racketeer Influenced and
        Corrupt Organizations Act (RICO), conspiracy, aiding and abetting,
        and obstruction of justice.

ACCN: 090574
TITL: White Collar Crime—A Legal Overview
JCIT: University of Cincinnati Law Review, V 52, N 2 (1983), P 378–384
PAUT: Marcus, P
SALE: National Institute of Justice/National Criminal Justice Reference Service
Microfiche Program, Box 6000, Department F, Rockville, MD 20850;
MF Microfiche. National Institute of Justice/National Criminal Justice
Reference Service Paper Reproduction Sales, Box 6000, Department F,
Rockville, MD 20850; AR Article.
PDTE: 1983   PAGE: 7 p
ORIG: United States   LANG: English
ANNO: Legal issues bearing on the prosecution of white-collar crime include the
application of the concept of "group danger," the use of the remedy of
mandatory forfeiture to the government (under the Racketeer
Influenced and Corrupt Organizations Act) of ill-gotten gains, and the
relationship of the conspiracy doctrine to the corporate defendant.

ACCN: 099920
TITL: Road Not Taken—The Elusive Path to Criminal Prosecution for White-
Collar Offenders
JCIT: Law and Society Review, V 19, N 2 (1985), P 179–217
PAUT: Shapiro, SP
SPON: US Department of Justice National Institute of Justice, Washington, DC
20531;
PDTE: 1985   PAGE: 39 p   CLSS: Article
ORIG: United States   LANG: English
GNUM: 78-NI-AX-0017
NOTE: An earlier version of this paper was presented at the 1984 annual
meeting of the American Society of Criminology.
ANNO: In the control of stock fraud, criminal prosecution is the road not
taken: only six of every hundred parties investigated by the Securities
and Exchange Commission ultimately stand in judgment before a
criminal court.

White-Collar Crime Bibliographies

ACCN: 051994
TITL: Compendium of Operational and Planning Guides to White-Collar Crime Enforcement.
PAUT: Karchmer, C; Randall, D
CORP: Battelle Human Affairs Research Centers Law and Justice Study Center, Seattle, WA 98105;
SPON: US Department of Justice Law Enforcement Assistance Administration;
SALE: Superintendent of Documents GPO, Washington, DC 20402; DO Document. National Institute of Justice/National Criminal Justice Reference Service Microfiche Program, Box 6000, Department F, Rockville, MD 20850; MF Microfiche.
PDTE: 1979   PAGE: 79 p
ORIG: United States   LANG: English
GNUM: 77-TA-99-0008
NOTE: A Report of the National Center on White-Collar Crime
TYPE: Bibliographies
ANNO: This annotated bibliography cites studies, books, monographs, and articles relating to the investigation and prosecution of white-collar crime, organized crime, and corruption cases.

ACCN: 069331
TITL: White Collar Crime—A Selected Bibliography
CORP: National Institute of Justice/National Criminal Justice Reference Service, Rockville, MD 20850;
SPON: US Department of Justice National Institute of Justice, Washington, DC 20531;
SALE: Superintendent of Documents GPO, Washington, DC 20402; DO Document. National Institute of Justice/National Criminal Justice Reference Service Microfiche Program, Box 6000, Department F, Rockville, MD 20850; MF Microfiche.
PDTE: 1980   PAGE: 89 p
ORIG: United States   LANG: English
GNUM: J-LEAA-023-77
TYPE: Bibliographies
ANNO: The bibliography highlights the literature on white-collar crime; 250 annotated citations treat such topics as official corruption, abuse of government programs, marketplace crime, and computer abuse.

ACCN: 093937
TITL: White Collar Crime—A Bibliography
PAUT: Vance, M
SALE: Vance Bibliographies, PO Box 229, Monticello, IL 61856; DO Document.
PDTE: 1983   PAGE: 18 p
ORIG: United States   LANG: English
PNUM: P-1232
NOTE: Public Administration Series—Bibliography
TYPE: Bibliographies
ANNO: These 210 citations on white-collar crime include magazine and journal articles, books, monographs, proceedings of meetings, bibliographies, and federal government publications.

White-Collar Crime and Public Policy

ACCN: 050060
TITL: White Collar Crime—The Problem and the Federal Response
PAUT: Saxon, M
CORP: Library of Congress Congressional Research Service, Washington, DC 20540
SALE: National Institute of Justice/National Criminal Justice Reference Service Microfiche Program, Box 6000, Department F, Rockville, MD 20850; MF Microfiche.
PDTE: 1978   PAGE: 77 p
ORIG: United States   LANG: English
PNUM: 78-72 EPW
NOTE: Committee Print No 16 of the Subcommittee on Crime, Committee on the Judiciary, House of Representatives, 95th Congress, 2nd Session
ANNO: This report was prepared for the House Committee on the Judiciary's Subcommittee on Crime to define the nature and scope of white-collar crime and federal efforts to control such crime.

ACCN: 052523
TITL: White Collar Crime—We Cannot Afford It!
JCIT: Government Accountants Journal (Spring 1978), P 53–57
PAUT: Agro, DT
CORP: Association of Government Accountants, Arlington, VA 22202;
PDTE: 1978   PAGE: 5 p   CLSS: Article
ORIG: United States   LANG: English
ANNO: The scope of white-collar crime is examined in relation to cost, the criminal, the environment, and possible solutions.

ACCN: 063724
TITL: Social Response to White Collar (From Critical Issues in Criminal
         Justice, 1979, by RG Iacovetta and Dae H Chang—See NCJ-63717)
PAUT: Endres, ME
CORP: Carolina Academic Press, Durham, NC 27707;
PDTE: 1979   PAGE: 15 p   CLSS: Document
ORIG: United States   LANG: English
ANNO: This article examines society's perception of white-collar crime as
         opposed to ordinary crime and presents various responses that address
         the injustices of the present dual system.

ACCN: 070875
TITL: National Priorities for the Investigation and Prosecution of White Collar
         Crime
CORP: US Attorney General, Washington, DC 20530;
SALE: National Institute of Justice/National Criminal Justice Reference Service
         Microfiche Program, Box 6000, Department F, Rockville, MD 20850;
         MF Microfiche.
PDTE: 1980   PAGE: 81 p
ORIG: United States   LANG: English
ANNO: Based on analysis conducted by the Justice Department from October
         1979 through June 1980, this report presents the Attorney General's
         national law enforcement priorities for white-collar crime.

ACCN: 071090
TITL: Thinking about White Collar Crime—Matters of Conceptualization and
         Research
PAUT: Shapiro, S
CORP: Yale University Law School, New Haven, CT 06520;
SPON: US Department of Justice National Institute of Justice, Washington, DC
         20531
SALE: National Institute of Justice/National Criminal Justice Reference Service
         Microfiche Program, Box 6000, Department F, Rockville, MD 20850;
         MF Microfiche.
PDTE: 1980   PAGE: 90 p
ORIG: United States   LANG: English
GNUM: 78-NI-AX-0017
ANNO: This two-part paper critically reviews conceptual themes in white-collar
         crime literature, proposes additional definition distinctions, and suggests
         a research agenda.

ACCN: 072805
TITL: Notes toward a National Strategy to Deal with White-Collar Crimes
(From National Strategy for Containing White-Collar Crime, P 21–46,
1980, Herbert Edelhertz and Charles H Rogovin, eds.—See NCJ-72804)
PAUT: Moore, MH
SALE: DC Heath and Company, 125 Spring Street, Lexington, MA 02173; DO
Document
PDTE: 1980 PAGE: 26 p
ORIG: United States LANG: English
ANNO: This contribution to a symposium on white-collar crime containment
strategies categorizes the component phenomena of white-collar crime
and proposes several principles of approach toward the development of
a national strategy of containment.

ACCN: 072806
TITL: White-Collar Crime and the Criminal-Justice System—Problems and
Challenges (From National Strategy for Containing White-Collar Crime,
P 57–75, 1980, Herbert Edelhertz and Charles H Rogovin, eds.—See
NCJ-72804)
PAUT: Skoler, DL
SALE: DC Heath and Company, 125 Spring Street, Lexington, MA 02173; DO
Document.
PDTE: 1980 PAGE: 19 p
ORIG: United States LANG: English
ANNO: The ability of the components of the criminal justice system (police,
prosecution, courts, corrections, criminal defense) to control white-
collar crime on the federal, state, and local levels is analyzed, and
improvements, including a greater federal role, are suggested.

ACCN: 072808
TITL: Developing a Strategy to Contain White-Collar Crime (From National
Strategy for Containing White-Collar Crime, P 85–94, 1980, Herbert
Edelhertz and Charles H Rogovin, eds.—See NCJ-72804)
PAUT: Morrill, WA
SALE: DC Heath and Company, 125 Spring Street, Lexington, MA 02173; DO
Document.
PDTE: 1980 PAGE: 10 p
ORIG: United States LANG: English
ANNO: Common elements needed for a general strategy of societal action to
combat social problems are proposed, and their application to white-
collar crime containment strategy specified in terms of prevention,
detection, prosecution, and penalties.

ACCN: 072810
TITL: Implementing a National Strategy (From National Strategy for
        Containing White-Collar Crime, P 103–111, 1980, Herbert Edelhertz
        and Charles H Rogovin, eds.—See NCJ-72804)
PAUT: Edelhertz, H; Rogovin, CH
SALE: DC Heath and Company, 125 Spring Street, Lexington, MA 02173; DO
        Dccument.
PDTE: 1980   PAGE: 9 p
ORIG: United States   LANG: English
ANNO: Efforts to coordinate the white-collar crime containment activities of
        several agencies and to develop a national strategy are described with
        emphasis on the seminal role of the National District Attorneys
        Association (NDAA) symposium of July 1978.

ACCN: 072811
TITL: White-Collar Crime—Appendix B (From National Strategy for
        Containing White-Collar Crime, P 119–131, 1980, Herbert Edelhertz
        and Charles H Rogovin, eds.—See NCJ-72804)
PAUT: Edelhertz, H
SALE: DC Heath and Company, 125 Spring Street, Lexington, MA 02173; DO
        Document.
PDTE: 1980   PAGE: 13 p
ORIG: United States   LANG: English
NOTE: Statement presented at the Hearings of the House Subcommittee on
        Crime to Examine the Subject of White-Collar Crime
ANNO: The nature of white-collar crime, past and present efforts to control it,
        and recommendations for developing a national strategy of containment
        are presented in this statement of the Director of the Battelle Law and
        Justice Study Center before the House Subcommittee on Crime.

ACCN: 077882
TITL: Eight Factor Theory of White Collar Crime
JCIT: Assets Protection, V 6, N 2 (March/April 1981), p 22–25
PAUT: Bologna, J
PDTE: 1981   PAGE: 4 p   CLSS: Article
ORIG: United States
ANNO: Eight theories of white-collar crime are presented with respect to their
        advocate groups, putative causes, and recommended solutions.

ACCN: 086252
TITL: Concept of White-Collar Crime (From Ethics, Public Policy, and
        Criminal Justice, P 59–77, 1982, Frederick Elliston and Norman Bowie,
        eds.—See NCJ-86248)
PAUT: Reck, AJ
SALE: Oelgeschlager, Gunn and Hain, Publishers, Inc, 131 Clarendon Street,
        Boston, MA 02116; DO Document.
PDTE: 1982   PAGE: 14 p
ORIG: United States   LANG: English
ANNO: This essay sketches the components of a general explanation of crime
        and designates the main areas for application, particularly with
        reference to white-collar crime.

White-Collar Crime Victims

ACCN: 040335
TITL: Victimization Patterns in White-Collar Crime (From Victimology—A
        New Focus, V 5 Exploiters and Exploited, 1975, by I Drapkin and E
        Viano—See NJC-17231)
PAUT: Geis, G
CORP: DC Heath and Company, Lexington, MA 02173;
PDTE: 1975   PAGE: 17 p   CLSS: Document
ORIG: United States   LANG: English
ANNO: This paper focuses on white-collar crimes incidental to and in
        furtherance of business operations, but not the central purposes of the
        business, and takes most of its examples from the general area of
        consumer fraud.

ACCN: 086208
TITL: Victims of White Collar Crimes (From Victim in International
        Perspective, P 257–273, 1982, Hans Joachim Schneider, ed.—See NCJ-
        86192)
PAUT: Delord-Raynal, Y
SALE: Walter de Gruyter & Company, Genthiner Str 13, 1 Berlin 30, West
        Germany; DO Document.
PDTE: 1982   PAGE: 17 p
ORIG: West Germany   LANG: English
NOTE: Translated from French by Raimund Hermes and Adriane Rinsche.
ANNO: This essay examines the dynamics of the interaction of offender and
        victim in white-collar crime and suggests steps to prevent such
        victimization.

ACCN: 086209
TITL: Victims of White-Collar Crimes (From Victim in International
        Perspective, P 274–278, 1982, Hans Joachim Schneider, ed.—See NCJ-
        86192)
PAUT: Tomlin, JW
SALE: Walter de Gruyter & Company, Genthiner Str 13, 1 Berlin 30, West
        Germany; DO Document.
PDTE: 1982   PAGE: 5 p
ORIG: West Germany   LANG: English
ANNO: The proposed typology of the victims of white-collar crime covers the
        individual as victim, corporate enterprises as victims, government
        institutions as victims, the international order as victim, and society as
        victim.

Investigation of Specific White-Collar Crimes

ACCN: 040206
TITL: Conspiracy, the Business Enterprise, White Collar Crime and Federal
        Prosecution—A Primer for Practice
JCIT: Creighton Law Review, V 9, N 4 (June 1976) P 647–676
PAUT: Hermann, DH
CORP: Creighton University School of Law, Omaha, NE 68178;
PDTE: 1976   PAGE: 30 p   CLSS: Article
ORIG: United States   LANG: English
ANNO: Review of the substantive law of criminal conspiracy as it applies to the
        business enterprise, as well as specific statutory provisions that make
        particular agreements illegal.

ACCN: 066083
TITL: Investigation of Computer Crime—An Operational Guide to White
        Collar Crime Enforcement
PAUT: Beckeredelhertz, J J, H
CORP: Battelle Human Affairs Research Centers, National Center on White-
        Collar Crime, Seattle, WA 98105;
SPON: US Department of Justice Law Enforcement Assistance Administration;
SALE: Superintendent of Documents GPO, Washington, DC 20402; DO
        Document. National Institute of Justice/National Criminal Justice
        Reference Service Microfiche Program, Box 6000, Department F,
        Rockville, MD 20850; MF Microfiche.
PDTE: 1980   PAGE: 77 p
ORIG: United States   LANG: English
GNUM: 77-TA-99-0008
ANNO: For investigators of computer-assisted crime, this operational guide
        discusses various approaches to the investigation, evidence collection,
        and possible legal problems impeding the investigation.

ACCN: 076451
TITL: Corporate Criminal Liability
JCIT: Practical Lawyer, V 26, N 6 (September 1980), P 23–36
PAUT: Brosnahan, JJ; Miller, SR; Foy, RE
PDTE: 1980   PAGE: 14 p   CLSS: Article
ORIG: United States   LANG: English
NOTE: Article based on a chapter in White Collar Crimes
ANNO: The article sketches the expanding imposition of criminal liability upon
         existing and dissolved corporations as a result of the criminal acts,
         knowledge, and admissions of agents and employees.

ACCN: 078914
TITL: Antitrust Violation as a Crime (From White Collar Crimes, P 1–31,
         1980, Gary P Naftalis, ed.—See NCJ-78913)
PAUT: Klingsberg, D
SALE: American Law Institute—American Bar Association Committee on
         Continuing Professional Education, 4025 Chestnut Street, Philadelphia,
         PA 19104; DO Document.
PDTE: 1980   PAGE: 31 p
ORIG: United States   LANG: English
ANNO: This paper explains the nature of criminal antitrust offenses and
         presents guidelines for use by criminal defense attorneys in handling
         each step in such a case.

ACCN: 078915
TITL: Defending Charges of Conspiracy (From White Collar Crimes, P 33–
         104, 1980, Gary P Naftalis, ed.—See NCJ-78913)
PAUT: Obermaier, OG
SALE: American Law Institute—American Bar Association Committee on
         Continuing Professional Education, 4025 Chestnut Street, Philadelphia,
         PA 19104; DO Document.
PDTE: 1980   PAGE: 71 p
ORIG: United States   LANG: English
ANNO: This paper describes the major principles of federal law related to
         conspiracy in economic regulatory offenses and presents techniques for
         use by defense attorneys in both pretrial procedures and trials.

ACCN: 078916
TITL: Income Tax Evasion—A Dynamic Discussion (From White Collar
         Crimes, P 145–170, 1980, Gary P Naftalis, ed.—See NCJ-78913)
PAUT: Hochman, BI
SALE: American Law Institute—American Bar Association Committee on
         Continuing Professional Education, 4025 Chestnut Street, Philadelphia,
         PA 19104; DO Document.
PDTE: 1980   PAGE: 25 p
ORIG: United States   LANG: English
ANNO: Typical problems that confront attorneys in the defense of income tax
         evasion cases are described, and potential solutions are suggested.

ACCN: 078917
TITL: Extortion (From White Collar Crimes, P 171–185, 1980, Gary P
          Naftalis, ed.—See NCJ-78913)
PAUT: Collins, GB
SALE: American Law Institute—American Bar Association Committee on
          Continuing Professional Education, 4025 Chestnut Street, Philadelphia,
          PA 19104; DO Document.
PDTE: 1980   PAGE: 15 p
ORIG: United States   LANG: English
ANNO: The application of the Hobbs Act, the federal law on extortion, to
          labor-related crimes, political crimes, and ordinary business cases is
          discussed, and several approaches defense attorneys may use regarding
          extortion charges are outlined.

ACCN: 078918
TITL: Corporate Criminal Liability and Procedure (From White Collar
          Crimes, P 187–205, 1980, Gary P Naftalis, ed.—See NCJ-78913)
PAUT: Brosnahan, JJ; Miller, SR; Foy, RE
SALE: American Law Institute—American Bar Association Committee on
          Continuing Professional Education, 4025 Chestnut Street, Philadelphia,
          PA 19104; DO Document.
PDTE: 1980   PAGE: 19 p
ORIG: United States   LANG: English
ANNO: Federal court decisions regarding corporate criminal liability and
          procedure are reviewed, with emphasis on the issues of the acts of
          agents, double jeopardy, criminal liability of dissolved corporations, and
          corporate rights under the fourth and fifth amendments.

ACCN: 081483
TITL: Elite Deviance
PAUT: Simon, DR; Eitzen, DS
SAVE: Allyn and Bacon, Inc, 470 Atlantic Avenue, Boston, MA 02210; PB
          Paperback.
PDTE: 1982   PAGE: 282 p
ORIG: United States   LANG: English
ANNO: This book describes wrongdoing—criminal, moral, ethical—by wealthy
          and powerful individuals in corporate and governmental organizations.
          It expresses concern for a lack of social scientific knowledge of high-
          level deviance and suggests social and economic solutions.

ACCN: 082943
TITL: Organizational Offenders—Why Solutions Fail to Political, Corporate, and Organized Crime
PAUT: Albanese, JS
SALE: Apocalypse Publishing Co, PO Box 1, Niagara Falls, NY 14305; PB Paperback. National Institute of Justice/National Criminal Justice Reference Service Microfiche Program, Box 6000, Department F, Rockville, MD 20850; MF Microfiche.
PDTE: 1982   PAGE: 169 p
ORIG: United States   LANG: English
ANNO: This analysis of organizational crime focuses on the cases of Lockheed Corporation's payments to Japanese officials to sell aircraft, the Valachi hearings on La Cosa Nostra, and the financing of Watergate to demonstrate how new laws against bribery of government officials fail to address the causes of these white-collar crimes.

ACCN: 090573
TITL: White Collar Crime—Symposium
JCIT: University of Cincinnati Law Review, V 52, N 2 (1983), P 378–463
PAUT: Marcus, P; Holderman, JF; Webb, DK; Turow, SF; Brickey, KF; Nagel, IH; Plager, SJ
SAVE: National Institute of Justice/National Criminal Justice Reference Service Microfiche Program, Box 6000, Department F, Rockville, MD 20850; MF Microfiche. National Institute of Justice/National Criminal Justice Reference Service Paper Reproduction Sales, Box 6000, Department F, Rockville, MD 20850; AR Article.
PDTE: 1983   PAGE: 86 p
ORIG: United States   LANG: English
ANNO: Symposium papers analyze the Racketeer Influenced and Corrupt Organizations Act (RICO) to determine whether it transcends traditional notions of substantive criminal responsibility, evaluate the use of forfeiture under RICO, and consider the application of traditional criminal law principles to the corporate defendant.

ACCN: 094173
TITL: Investigation and Prosecution of Illegal Money Laundering—A Guide to the Bank Secrecy Act
CORP: US Department of Justice Criminal Division, Washington, DC 20530;
SALE: National Institute of Justice/National Criminal Justice Reference Service Microfiche Program, Box 6000, Department F, Rockville, MD 20850; MF Microfiche. National Institute of Justice/National Criminal Justice Reference Service Paper Reproduction Sales, Box 6000, Department F, Rockville, MD 20850; DO Document.
PDTE: 1983 PAGE: 273 p
ORIG: United States LANG: English
NOTE: Narcotic and Dangerous Drug Section Monograph
ANNO: This monograph analyzes the Bank Secrecy Act and the developing case law pertaining to it so that investigators may be assisted in the investigation of groups dealing in substantial sums of illegal money, whether the underlying criminal conduct involves narcotics, organized crime, or white-collar crime.

ACCN: 097951
TITL: RICO (Racketeer Influenced and Corrupt Organizations)—Business Disputes and the 'Racketeering' Laws—Federal and State
CORP: Commerce Clearinghouse, Inc., Chicago, IL 60646;
SALE: Commerce Clearinghouse, Inc., 4025 West Peterson Avenue, Chicago, IL 60646, PB Paperback.
PDTE: 1984 PAGE: 192 p
ORIG: United States LANG: English
ANNO: This volume explains the Federal Racketeer Influenced and Corrupt Organizations (RICO) law, discusses state RICO laws, and provides texts of both. Court decisions are noted in both the federal law explanation and the discussion of state laws.

ACCN: 099346
TITL: Racketeer Influenced and Corrupt Organizations (RICO)—A Manual for Federal Prosecutors
PAUT: White, AS; Joseph, LM; Watson, D; Yenouskas, J
CORP: US Department of Justice Criminal Division Organized Crime and Racketeering Section, Washington, DC 20530;
SALE: National Institute of Justice/National Criminal Justice Reference Service Microfiche Program, Box 6000, Department F, Rockville, MD 20850; MF Microfiche. National Institute of Justice/National Criminal Justice Reference Service Paper Reproduction Sales, Box 6000, Department F, Rockville, MD 20850; DO Document.
PDTE: 1985 PAGE: 128 p
ORIG: United States LANG: English
ANNO: In providing informal guidance for federal prosecutors on the criminal aspect of the Racketeer Influenced and Corrupt Organizations Act (RICO), this manual discusses important legal issues and advises prosecutors on preparing legally sufficient indictments that conform to the approval guidelines of the U.S. Justice Department's Criminal Division.

ACCN: 109132
TITL: Address of Arnold I Burns before the 1988 Winter Conference of New
          York State District Attorneys Association, January 21, 1988
PAUT: Burns, AI
SALE: National Institute of Justice/National Criminal Justice Reference Service
          Microfiche Program, Box 6000, Department F, Rockville, MD 20850;
          MF Microfiche. National Institute of Justice/National Criminal Justice
          Reference Service Paper Reproduction Sales, Box 6000, Department F,
          Rockville, MD 20850; DO Document.
PDTE: 1988   PAGE: 15 p
ORIG: United States   LANG: English
TYPE: Speeches
ANNO: The problem of abuse of the public trust by public officials and public
          employees can be found at every level of government.

ACCN: 110055
TITL: Remarks of William F Weld before the Morning Newsmaker, The
          National Press Club, Washington, DC, March 8, 1988
PAUT: Weld, W
SALE: National Institute of Justice/National Criminal Justice Reference Service
          Microfiche Program, Box 6000, Department F, Rockville, MD 20850;
          MF Microfiche. National Institute of Justice/National Criminal Justice
          Reference Service Paper Reproduction Sales, Box 6000, Department F,
          Rockville, MD 20850; DO Document.
PDTE: 1988   PAGE: 13 p
ORIG: United States   LANG: English
TYPE: Speeches
ANNO: This speech focuses on public corruption as a problem for states as well
          as for the federal government (executive and legislative branches).

ACCN: 112738
TITL: RICO (Racketeer Influenced and Corrupt Organizations) and
          Enterprise Criminality: A Response to Gerard E Lynch
JCIT: Columbia Law Review, V 88, N 4 (May 1988), P 774–801
PAUT: Goldsmith, M
PDTE: 1988   PAGE: 28 p   CLSS: Article
ORIG: United States   LANG: English
TYPE: Legislation/policy analysis
ANNO: In his 1987 article, Gerard E. Lynch asserts that the broad scope of the
          Racketeer Influenced and Corrupt Organizations (RICO) law was a
          historical accident and that Congress never anticipated the major uses
          for which RICO has been employed.

ACCN: 113423
TITL: RICO Forfeitures of Business: The Scope of Forfeiture Should Fit the Crime
JCIT: Trial, V 24, N 9 (September 1988), P 52–55
PAUT: Tarlow, B
PDTE: 1988   PAGE: 4 p   CLSS: Article
ORIG: United States   LANG: English
TYPE: Legislation/policy analysis
ANNO: Criminal forfeiture provisions under the Racketeer Influenced and Corrupt Organizations Act (RICO) have been litigated for 10 years, but it is not yet clear how those provisions should apply to businesses.

ACCN: 114258
TITL: White-Collar Crime: The Threat from Within (From Criminal Justice 88/89, P 44–49, 1988, John J Sullivan and Joseph L Victor, eds.—See NCJ-114256)
PAUT: Willis, R
SALE: Dushkin Publishing Group, Inc., Sluice Dock, Guilford, CT 06437; DO Document.
PDTE: 1988   PAGE: 6 p
ORIG: United States   LANG: English
TYPE: Issue overviews
ANNO: White-collar crime takes many forms and should be addressed through efforts to create a corporate culture that values integrity and enforces security.

ACCN: 115076
TITL: Insider Trading Symposium
JCIT: American Criminal Law Review, V 26, N 1 (Summer 1988), complete issue
PDTE: 1988   PAGE: 314 p   CLSS: Article
ORIG: United States   LANG: English
TYPE: Conference/meeting materials
ANNO: These eight papers examine the nature of insider trading in securities and laws, judicial decisions, and legislative proposals for addressing the problem.

ACCN: 115077
TITL: Revised Insider Trading Proscriptions Act of 1988: A Legislative
         Remedy for a Problem that Persists
JCIT: American Criminal Law Review, V 26, N 1 (Summer 1988), P 7–119
PAUT: Pitt, HL; Shapiro, KL
PDTE: 1988   PAGE: 113 p   CLSS: Article
ORIG: United States   LANG: English
TYPE: Legislation/policy analysis
ANNO: The enactment of the Insider Trading Proscriptions Act of 1988 would
         represent a significant step toward the goal of providing a precise and
         clear set of rules to put the public on notice as to what conduct will
         lead to the appropriately harsh criminal sanctions against insider trading
         or securities fraud.

ACCN: 115390
TITL: Keeping the Secret in Trade Secrets
JCIT: Security Management, V 33, N 1 (January, 1989), P 38–42
PAUT: Maxwell, DA
PDTE: 1989   PAGE: 5 p   CLSS: Article
ORIG: United States   LANG: English
TYPE: Issue overviews
ANNO: Security managers are responsible for safeguarding a corporation's
         proprietary information and should consider some of the methods
         currently being used that are protecting trade secret information and
         have been recognized as being legally valid.

ACCN: 115465
TITL: Look Who's Using RICO (Racketeer Influenced and Corrupt
         Organizations Act)
JCIT: ABA (American Bar Association) Journal, (February 1989), P 56–59
PAUT: Harrison, TF
PDTE: 1989   PAGE: 4 p   CLSS: Article
ORIG: United States   LANG: English
TYPE: Legislation/policy analysis
ANNO: The range of legal realms in which the Racketeer Influenced and
         Corrupt Organizations Act (RICO) has been used in recent years
         suggests that far more questions remain to be answered about this
         controversial statute.

ACCN: 116355
TITL: Insider Trading Under Rule 10b-5: The Theoretical Bases for Liability
JCIT: Business Lawyer, V 44, N 1 (November 1988), P 13–41
PAUT: Hagen, WW
PDTE: 1988   PAGE: 29 p   CLSS: Article
ORIG: United States   LANG: English

TYPE: Legislation/policy analysis
ANNO: This article reviews the law regarding the trading of securities on the
        basis of inside information with emphasis on rule 10b-5 of the Securities
        and Exchange Commission (SEC), the fiduciary duty theory, the notion
        of the temporary insider, and the misappropriation theory.

ACCN: 116407
TITL: Insider Trading and the Infringement of Property Rights
JCIT: Corporate Practice Commentator, V 30, N 3 (Fall 1988), P 417–456
PAUT: Morgan, RJ
PDTE: 1988   PAGE: 40 p   CLSS: Article
ORIG: United States   LANG: English
NOTE: Published originally in 48 Ohio State Law Journal 79 (1987)
TYPE: Legislation/policy analysis
ANNO: After briefly reviewing the development of insider trading restrictions
        under Rule 10b-5 of the Securities Exchange Act of 1934, this article
        proposes an analysis of insider trading restrictions that utilize a property
        rights approach, thus resolving certain analytical problems existing in
        the present doctrine.

ACCN: 116839
TITL: Discussion Paper: A Study of Trade Secrets Theft in High-Technology
PAUT: Mock, LF; Rosenbaum, D
SPON: US Department of Justice National Institute of Justice, Washington, DC
        20531;
SALE: National Institute of Justice/National Criminal Justice Reference Service
        Microfiche Program, Box 6000, Department F, Rockville, MD 20850;
        MF Microfiche. National Institute of Justice/National Criminal Justice
        Reference Service Paper Reproduction Sales, Box 6000, Department F,
        Rockville, MD 20850; DO Document.
PDTE: 1988   PAGE: 44 p
ORIG: United States   LANG: English
CNUM: OJP-87-M235
TYPE: Issue overviews
ANNO: This study examines the issue of industrial espionage—the theft of
        proprietary information or trade secrets from U.S. industries—and
        reports the results of a survey of high-technology companies on the
        degree of trade secrets theft.

White-Collar Crime Offenders

ACCN: 070827
TITL: Red-Flagging the White Collar Criminal
JCIT: Management Accounting, (March 1980), P 51–54, 57
PAUT: Romney, MB; Albrecht, WS; Cherrington, DJ
PDTE: 1980   PAGE: 5 p   CLSS: Article
ORIG: United States   LANG: English
ANNO: A profile of the white-collar criminal is presented, and "red flags" that warn of a fraud-conducive environment in a company are reviewed.

ACCN: 112642
TITL: White Collar Crimes and Criminals
JCIT: American Criminal Law Review, V 25, N 3 (Winter 1988), P 331–357
PAUT: Wheeler, S; Weisburd, D; Waring, E; Bode, N
SPON: US Department of Justice National Institute of Justice, Washington, DC 20531;
PDTE: 1988   PAGE: 27 p   CLSS: Article
ORIG: United States   LANG: English
GNUM: 78-NI-AX-0017
TYPE: Studies/research reports
ANNO: To illustrate the nature and salient dimensions of white-collar crime, this study compared fiscal 1976 through 1978 data for two categories of common crime (postal theft and postal forgery) and eight categories of white-collar crime (antitrust offenses, securities fraud, mail fraud, false claims, credit fraud, bribery, tax fraud, and bank embezzlement).

Sentencing White-Collar Offenders

ACCN: 060986
TITL: Sentencing of White Collar Offenders in Federal Court (From White Collar Crimes 1978—See NCJ-60985)
PAUT: Hessenius, RS; Medvene, EM; Shults, RL
CORP: Practicing Law Institute, New York, NY 10019;
PDTE: 1978   PAGE: 24 p   CLSS: Document
ORIG: United States   LANG: English
ANNO: This article examines some of the recommendations suggested by the American Bar Association (ABA, 1968) concerning the role of defense attorneys in the sentencing process of white-collar offenders.

ACCN: 091247
TITL: Punishing White Collar Offenders—An Annotated Bibliography
PAUT: Parks, NE
CORP: US Department of Justice Criminal Division, Washington, DC 20530;
SALE: National Institute of Justice/National Criminal Justice Reference Service
         Microfiche Program, Box 6000, Department F, Rockville, MD 20805;
         MF Microfiche. National Institute of Justice/National Criminal Justice
         Reference Service Paper Reproduction Sales, Box 6000, Department F,
         Rockville, MD 20850; DO Document.
PDTE: 1983   PAGE: 43 p
ORIG: United States   LANG: English
TYPE: Bibliographies
ANNO: The annotated bibliography presents 159 citations covering alternative
         sentencing for white-collar offenders and critiques of white-collar
         sentencing policies and practices.

ACCN: 091789
TITL: White-Collar v Street Crime Sentencing Disparity—How Judges See the
         Problem
JCIT: Judicature, V 67, N 4 (October 1983), P 174–182
PAUT: Pollack, H; Smith, AB
PDTE: 1983   PAGE: 8 p   CLSS: Article
ORIG: United States   LANG: English
ANNO: This survey of New York City judges indicates that while each judge
         has generally defined white-collar crime and resolved the problem of
         sentencing to his or her own satisfaction, there are considerable
         differences among them as to solutions.

ACCN: 097907
TITL: White-Collar and Corporate Crime (From Major Forms of Crime,
         P 137–166, 1983, Robert F Meier, ed.—See NCJ-97901)
PAUT: Geis, G
SALE: Sage Publications, Inc., 2111 West Hillcrest Drive, Newbury Park, CA
         91320, DO Document.
PDTE: 1985   PAGE: 30 p
ORIG: United States   LANG: English
ANNO: This paper reviews studies of white-collar crime pertaining to its
         definition and sentencing.

ACCN: 111065
TITL: Sentencing the White-Collar Offender
JCIT: American Sociological Review, V 53, N 2 (April 1988), P 294–302
PAUT: Benson, ML; Walker, E
SPON: US Department of Justice National Institute of Justice, Washington, DC 20531;
PDTE: 1988   PAGE: 9 p   CLSS: Article
ORIG: United States   LANG: English
TYPE: Applied research
ANNO: With a modified version of the white-collar sentencing model developed by Wheeler, Weisburd, and Bode (1982), sentences for a sample of white-collar offenders adjudicated in one federal court between 1970 and 1980 are analyzed.

Defending White-Collar Criminals

ACCN: 078913
TITL: White Collar Crimes
CORP: American Law Institute—American Bar Association Committee on Continuing Professional Education, Philadelphia, PA 19104;
SALE: American Law Institute—American Bar Association Committee on Continuing Professional Education, 4025 Chestnut Street, Philadelphia, PA 19104; BK Book.
PDTE: 1980   PAGE: 399 p
ORIG: United States   LANG: English
ANNO: Written primarily for criminal defense lawyers, this volume provides detailed information about the main substantive areas of prosecution for white-collar crimes and presents techniques for coping with these areas and with the various types of the white-collar criminal process.

ACCN: 078919
TITL: Representation of Persons in Connection with the Federal Investigation of White Collar Crimes (From White Collar Crimes, P 207–233, 1980, Gary P Naftalis, ed.—See NCJ-78913)
PAUT: Sullivan, TP; Spanner, RA
SALE: American Law Institute—American Bar Association Committee on Continuing Professional Education, 4025 Chestnut Street, Philadelphia, PA 19104; DO Document.
PDTE: 1980   PAGE: 27 p
ORIG: United States   LANG: English
ANNO: This paper presents principles and guidelines for use by defense attorneys in representing persons in connection with the federal investigation of white-collar crimes, with emphasis on the need to develop strategy and tactics tailored to the specifics of each case.

ACCN: 078920
TITL: Pretrial Motions (From White Collar Crimes, P 235–269, 1980, Gary P
        Naftalis, ed.—See NCJ-78913)
PAUT: Stillman, CA
SALE: American Law Institute—American Bar Association Committee on
        Continuing Professional Education, 4025 Chestnut Street, Philadelphia,
        PA 19104; DO Document.
PDTE: 1980   PAGE: 35 p
ORIG: United States   LANG: English
ANNO: The use of two types of pretrial motions—discovery motions and
        substantive motions—by defense attorneys in white-collar criminal cases
        is discussed.

ACCN: 078922
TITL: Sentencing and Postsentencing Remedies (From White Collar Crimes,
        P 299–339, 1980, Gary P Naftalis, ed.—See NCJ-78913)
PAUT: Doyle, JH
SALE: American Law Institute—American Bar Association Committee on
        Continuing Professional Education, 4025 Chestnut Street, Philadelphia,
        PA 19104; DO Document.
PDTE: 1980   PAGE: 41 p
ORIG: United States   LANG: English
ANNO: Intended for defense counsel whose clients have been convicted of
        white-collar crimes, this article presents guidelines for dealing with the
        presentence investigation and the sentencing hearing and discusses
        sentencing law and postsentencing remedies.

ACCN: 090540
TITL: Post-Conviction Proceedings (From Business Crimes—A Guide for
        Corporate and Defense Counsel, P 327–407, 1982, Jeffrey Glekel, ed.—
        See NCJ-90533)
PAUT: Wilson, SV
SALE: Practicing Law Institute, 810 Seventh Avenue, New York, NY 10019;
        DO Document.
PDTE: 1982   PAGE: 81 p
ORIG: United States   LANG: English
TYPE: Studies/research reports
ANNO: By playing an active role in the sentencing process, defense counsel for
        white-collar offenders can favorably impact the sentencing decision, and
        by using the available posttrial motions, notably the motions for new
        trial and reduction or modification of sentence, a more favorable
        disposition may be achieved for the client.

ACCN: 093222
TITL: Post-Conviction Lawyering in White-Collar Cases
CORP: Practicing Law Institute, New York, NY 10019;
SALE: Practicing Law Institute, 810 Seventh Avenue, New York, NY 10019;
         PB Paperback.
PDTE: 1981   PAGE: 301 p
ORIG: United States   LANG: English
NOTE: Litigation and Administration Practice Series, Criminal Law and Urban
         Problems Course Handbook Series, number 120. Prepared for
         distribution at the Post-Conviction Lawyering in White Collar Cases
         Program, January–February 1981.
TYPE: Studies/research reports.
ANNO: This guide for defense counsel in pursuing postconviction client interests
         in white-collar cases focuses on dealing with the probation department,
         dealing with the prosecutor, defense presentation to the court at
         sentencing, and postconviction motions.

ACCN: 096870
TITL: Defending Business and White Collar Crime—Federal and State,
         Volume 1, Second Edition
PAUT: Bailey, FL; Rothblatt, HB
SALE: Lawyers Co-Operative Publishing Company, Aqueduct Building,
         Rochester, NY 14603; BK Book.
PDTE: 1984   PAGE: 575 p
ORIG: United States   LANG: English
NOTE: Volume 1 of a two-volume set
ANNO: This first volume of a two-volume work presents defense attorneys with
         proven methods of handling white-collar criminal cases, from the time
         the attorney is retained through tactics in the trial itself.

ACCN: 096871
TITL: Defending Business and White Collar Crimes—Federal and State,
         Volume 2, Second Edition
PAUT: Bailey, FL; Rothblatt, HB
SALE: Lawyers Co-Operative Publishing Company, Aqueduct Building,
         Rochester, NY 14603; BK Book.
PDTE: 1984   PAGE: 555 p
ORIG: United States   LANG: English
ANNO: This second volume of a two-volume work for defense attorneys
         presents step-by-step guidelines on how to handle 20 specific types of
         white-collar criminal cases.

ACCN: 097288
TITL: Defending White Collar Crime—A Portrait of Attorneys at Work
PAUT: Mann, K
SALE: Yale University Press, 92a Yale Station, New Haven, CT 06520; BK
         Book.
PDTE: 1985   PAGE: 285 p
ORIG: United States   LANG: English
NOTE: Yale Studies on White-Collar Crime
ANNO: An attorney experienced in defending white-collar criminals describes the methods used by white-collar defense lawyers to avoid not only the indictment of their clients but even preliminary investigations that might lead to a criminal charge.

ACCN: 113418
TITL: White-Collar Crime
JCIT: Trial, V 24, N 9 (September 1988), P 22–55
PDTE: 1988   PAGE: 34 p   CLSS: Article
ORIG: United States   LANG: English
TYPE: Legislation/policy descriptions
ANNO: Articles on white-collar crime review serious problems for litigators who take on the defense of alleged white-collar criminals.

ACCN: 113421
TITL: The White-Collar Defendant: High Visibility, High Stakes
JCIT: Trial, V 24, N 9 (September 1988), P 42–48
PAUT: Lawless, JF
PDTE: 1988   PAGE: 7 p   CLSS: Article
ORIG: United States   LANG: English
TYPE: Legislation/policy descriptions
ANNO: Because defending a white-collar criminal is unlike other forms of criminal defense, it is important to adhere to several procedures to avoid pitfalls inherent in white-collar crime prosecutions.

ACCN: 114153
TITL: Representing the White-Collar Defendant: How to Avoid the Trap
JCIT: Trial, V 24, N 10 (October 1988), P 72–78
PAUT: Preiser, SE; Swisher, CC
PDTE: 1988   PAGE: 6 p   CLSS: Article
ORIG: United States   LANG: English
TYPE: Issue overviews
ANNO: It is argued that the criminal justice system is stacked against attorneys defending white-collar offenders and that prosecutorial resources, publicity, and predisposition of jurors to convict makes these cases difficult to defend.

Expert Witnesses

ACCN: 069719
TITL: Role of the Accountant as an Expert Witness
PAUT: Cayson, J
SALE: National Institute of Justice/National Criminal Justice Reference Service
Microfiche Program, Box 6000, Department F, Rockville, MD 20850;
MF Microfiche.
PDTE: 1978   PAGE: 34 p
ORIG: United States   LANG: English
ANNO: The chief accountant for New Jersey's Commission of Investigation
describes the accountant's role in investigating white-collar crime and
appearing as an expert witness for the prosecution.

ACCN: 078921
TITL: Expert Testimony in White Collar Cases (From White Collar Crimes,
P 271–297, 1980, Gary P Naftalis, ed.—See NCJ-78913)
PAUT: Polstein, R
SALE: American Law Institute—American Bar Association Committee on
Continuing Professional Education, 4025 Chestnut Street, Philadelphia,
PA 19104; DO Document.
PDTE: 1980   PAGE: 27 p
ORIG: United States   LANG: English
ANNO: The use of expert testimony in the defense of white-collar prosecutions
is discussed.

White-Collar Crime—Canada

ACCN: 078361
TITL: White Collar Crime—A Bibliography
CORP: Royal Canadian Mounted Police Headquarters Library, Ottawa,
Ontario, Canada K1A OR2;
SALE: National Institute of Justice/National Criminal Justice Reference Service
Microfiche Program, Box 6000, Department F, Rockville, MD 20850;
MF Microfiche.
PDTE: 1980   PAGE: 128 p
ORIG: Canada   LANG: English
TYPE: Bibliographies
ANNO: This bibliography on white-collar crime in Canada presents works on
bankruptcy fraud, corporate crime, tax evasion, and other white-collar
crimes.

ACCN: 096895
TITL: Research on White Collar Crime—Exploring the Issues
PAUT: Varette, SE; Meredith, C; Robinson, RB; Hoffman, D
SPON: Canada Solicitor General Research Division, Ottawa, Ontario, Canada
         K1A OP8;
SALE: Canada Solicitor General Research Division, Ottawa, Ontario, Canada
         K1A OP8; DO Document. National Institute of Justice/National
         Department F, Rockville, MD 20850; MF Microfiche.
PDTE: 1985   PAGE: 123 p
ORIG: Canada   LANG: English
PNUM: 1985-07
NOTE: Programs Branch User Report
ANNO: This text provides an overview of white-collar crime in Canada.

Selected Bibliography on Computer Crime: 1980 to 1990

Key to Abstract Interpretation

ACCN   National Institute of Justice/NCJRS Accession Number
TITL   English Title
JCIT   Journal Citation
PAUT   Personal Author
CORP   Corporate Author
SPON   Sponsoring Agency
SALE   Sales Agency
PDTE   Date of Publication
PAGE   Number of Pages
ORIG   Country of Origin
LANG   Language
PNUM   Publication Number
CNUM   Contract Number
GNUM   Grant Number
NOTE   Supplemental Note
ANNO   Annotation
SUBJ   Index Terms
CDTE   Date Item Entered the Data Base

    The following bibliographic entries were abstracted from the *National Criminal Justice Reference Service*.

Computer Crime—General

ACCN: 079517
TITL: Democratization of White-Collar Crime
JCIT: Computer Security Journal, V 1, N 1 (Spring 1981), P 39–44
PAUT: Courtney, RH
PDTE: 1981   PAGE: 6 p   CLSS: Article
ORIG: United States   LANG: English
ANNO: The selection of cost-effective controls (security measures) for the protection of data and of the means of processing them is dependent on a reasonably accurate problem definition. To the extent that those who attempt the selection and implementation of such controls believe the principal threat to be technically sophisticated intrusions into their systems by highly skilled technical personnel with extensive resources and very high motivation, they will usually fail. Errors and omissions made by people whose loyalty and honesty are unquestioned will always tower over dishonest conduct as a source of loss. In a poor second place are dishonest employees who neither need nor possess significant technical skills but who abuse the resources extended to them for the conduct of their normal jobs. The conversion of manual systems to a computer-based operation provides an opportunity to materially reduce losses previously experienced, but only if the threat is properly defined.

ACCN: 089349
TITL: Fighting Computer Crime
PAUT: Parker, DB
SALE: Charles Scribner's Sons, 597 Fifth Avenue, New York, NY 10017; BK Book.
PDTE: 1983   PAGE: 357 p
ORIG: United States   LANG: English
ANNO: This book considers the nature and extent of computer crime and abuse, computer crime methods, types of computer criminals, ethical conflicts in computing, computer crime in the law, and future vulnerabilities and risk reduction.

ACCN: 092991
TITL: Is Computer Crime Important?
PAUT: Simkim, MG
SALE: National Institute of Justice/National Criminal Justice Reference Service Microfiche Program, Box 6000, Department F, Rockville, MD 20850; MF Microfiche.
PDTE: 1981   PAGE: 18 p
ORIG: United States   LANG: English
NOTE: University of Nevada, Reno, Bureau of Business and Economic Research—Paper Number 81-15
ANNO: The importance of computer crime is considered by examining its growth, average losses, probability of occurrence, and catastrophic nature and how the experts, practitioners, and general public view it.

ACCN: 099853
TITL: Computer Technology and Crime
PAUT: Solarz, A
CORP: National Institute of Justice/National Criminal Justice Reference
           Service, Rockville, MD 20850;
SALE: National Institute of Justice/National Criminal Justice Reference Service
           Microfiche Program, Box 6000, Department F, Rockville, MD 20850;
           MF Microfiche. National Institute of Justice/National Criminal Justice
           Reference Service Paper Reproduction Sales, Box 6000, Department F,
           Rockville, MD 20850; DO Document.
PDTE: 1986   PAGE: 4 p
ORIG: United States   LANG: English
NOTE: International Summaries: a summary of Datorteknik och Brottslighet:
           (NCJ 100521)
TYPE: Studies/research reports
ANNO: This report describes evolving forms of computer crime in Sweden,
           discusses the application of traditional criminological theories to the
           causes and motivation for computer crime, and presents two empirical
           studies of computer crime involving embezzlement and theft.

ACCN: 100111
TITL: Computer Crime and Business Information—A Practical Guide for
           Managers
PAUT: Schweitzer, JA
SALE: Elsevier Science Publishing Co, 52 Vanderbilt Avenue, New York, NY
           10017; BK Book.
PDTE: 1986   PAGE: 199 p
ORIG: United States   LANG: English
ANNO: Viewing computer security as a subset within the issue of information
           resource management (IRM), this book focuses on identifying valuable
           business information; its organization and control; and establishing
           policies, standards, and procedures to manage such information in a
           secure, cost-effective manner.

ACCN: 100243
TITL: Technology Transfer, Industrial Espionage, and Computer
           Crime—the FBI's Activities
JCIT: Computer Security Journal, V 3, N 2 (Winter 1985), P 7–12
PAUT: Webster, WH
PDTE: 1985   PAGE: 6 p   CLSS: Article
ORIG: United States   LANG: English
ANNO: This article illustrates and discusses Federal Bureau of Investigation
           (FBI) efforts to deal with illegal technology transfer, foreign and
           industrial espionage, and computer-related crime.

ACCN: 100729
TITL: Computer Crime
PAUT: Perry, RL
SALE: Franklin Watts, Inc., 387 Park Avenue, S, New York, NY 10016; BK
          Book.
PDTE: 1986   PAGE: 67 p
ORIG: United States   LANG: English
NOTE: Computer-Awareness First Book
ANNO: This book identifies types of computer crime, methods used in their
          commission, and countermeasures.

ACCN: 100790
TITL: Who Is Calling Your Computer Nest? Hacker!
JCIT: Criminal Justice Journal, V 8, N 1 (1985), P 89–114
PAUT: Smith, D
PDTE: 1985   PAGE: 26 p   CLSS: Article
ORIG: United States   LANG: English
ANNO: This note discusses how computers work, the integration of computer
          hardware and software applications, computer system vulnerability to
          criminal abuse, the characteristics of computer crime, computer crime
          legislation, and a proposed strategy for addressing the problem.

ACCN: 100902
TITL: Computer Crime, Computer Security, Computer Ethics—First Annual
          Statistical Report of the National Center for Computer Crime Data
CORP: National Center for Computer Crime Data, Los Angeles, CA 90068
SALE: National Center for Computer Crime Data, 2700 N Cahuenga Blvd.,
          Los Angeles, CA 90068; DO Document.
PDTE: 1986   PAGE: 34 p
ORIG: United States   LANG: English
TYPE: Statistical data
ANNO: Sixty-five graphs and tables, accompanied by narrative commentary,
          portray computer crime victim costs, victim characteristics, defendant
          characteristics, and case dispositions.

ACCN: 101246
TITL: Computer Crime Update
JCIT: Prosecutor, V 19, N 3 (Winter 1986), P 15–28
PAUT: BloomBecker, J
PDTE: 1986   PAGE: 12 p   CLSS: Article
ORIG: United States   LANG: English
NOTE: Reprinted with updating of material from Western New England Law
          Review, V 7, N 3 (1985)
ANNO: This discussion of computer crime committed by computer hobbyists
          focuses on the reactions of defense counsel, law enforcement agencies,
          federal and state legislatures, the business community, the security
          industry, and the courts.

ACCN: 101705
TITL: Computer Security Handbook—Strategies and Techniques for
        Preventing Data Loss or Theft
PAUT: Moulton, RT
SALE: Prentice-Hall, Englewood Cliffs, NJ 07632; BK Book.
PDTE: 1986   PAGE: 248 p
ORIG: United States   LANG: English
TYPE: Overview texts
ANNO: This comprehensive handbook examines the design, implementation,
        and maintenance of computer security controls.

ACCN: 103716
TITL: Fighting Computer Crime
PAUT: Parker, DB
SALE: Charles Scribner's Sons, 597 Fifth Avenue, New York, NY 10017; BK
        Book.
PDTE: 1983   PAGE: 365 p
ORIG: United States   LANG: English
ANNO: This discussion of computer crime and its remedies covers its
        prevalence, computer crime methods, types of computer criminals,
        ethical conflicts in the computer field, computer crime legislation, and
        future vulnerabilities and risk reduction in computer crime.

ACCN: 104816
TITL: Computer Security, Second Edition
PAUT: Carroll, JM
SALE: Butterworth–Heineman (Publishers) Inc., 80 Montvale Avenue,
        Stoneham, MA 02180; BK Book.
PDTE: 1987   PAGE: 478 p
ORIG: United States   LANG: English
TYPE: Overview texts
ANNO: This book discusses computer security threats, security management of
        electronic data processing, computer physical security, communications
        security, systems security, and threat evaluation.

ACCN: 114673
TITL: Computer Crime
JCIT: Information Executive, V 1, N 1 (Fall 1988), P 30–42
PAUT: Hughes, WJ; Vaughn, RL; Johnson, RE; Collins, JE
PDTE: 1988   PAGE: 13 p   CLSS: Article
ORIG: United States   LANG: English
TYPE: Issue overviews
ANNO: These 10 articles discuss the nature and extent of computer crime,
        legislation and other efforts to address the problem, and legislative and
        corporate policy guidelines recommended by the Data Processing
        Management Association (DPMA).

Computer Crime—Prevention

ACCN: 078319
TITL: Short-Circuiting Computer Crime
JCIT: Security Industry and Product News, V 10, N 7 (July 1981), P 18–20
PAUT: Janko, DA; Atkari, FS
PDTE: 1981   PAGE: 3 p   CLSS: Article
ORIG: United States   LANG: English
ANNO: Physical security, segregation of employee duties, internal safeguards,
        signal scrambling, and the auditor's role are discussed as aspects of a
        computer security system.

ACCN: 078390
TITL: Financial Executive's Role in Computer Security
JCIT: Financial Executive, V 49, N 4 (April 1981), P 30–32
PAUT: Vohs, D
PDTE: 1981   PAGE: 3 p   CLSS: Article
ORIG: United States   LANG: English
ANNO: This article examines the growth of computer crime, types of abuse, and
        methods of guarding against computer compromise.

ACCN: 079643
TITL: Spreading Danger of Computer Crime
JCIT: Business Week (April 20, 1981), P 86--92
PAUT: Anonymous
PDTE: 1981   PAGE: 7 p   CLSS: Article
ORIG: United States   LANG: English
ANNO: The growing danger of computer crime and some ways to counter it are
        discussed.

ACCN: 093974
TITL: Computers + Business = Liabilities—A Preventive Guide for
        Management
PAUT: Bequai, A
CORP: Washington Legal Foundation, Washington, DC 20006;
SALE: Washington Legal Foundation, 1612 K Street, NW, Washington, DC
        20006; PB Paperback. National Institute of Justice/National Criminal
        Justice Reference Service Microfiche Program, Box 6000, Department
        F, Rockville, MD 20850; MF Microfiche.
PDTE: 1984   PAGE: 35 p
ORIG: United States   LANG: English
NOTE: One of a series of papers published by Constitutional Institute of
        America, a project of Washington Legal Foundation and Union Mutual
        Foundation.
ANNO: This paper reviews the role business management can play in limiting
        potential legal liabilities that could arise from computer operations.
        Management must understand both the sources of its legal exposure and
        the available remedies.

ACCN: 096939
TITL: Larceny Enters the Electronic Age—The Problem of Detecting and Preventing Computer Crimes
JCIT: Gonzaga Law Review, V 18, N 2 (1982–1983), P 517–538
PAUT: Hyman, WH
PDTE: 1983   PAGE: 22 p   CLSS: Article
ORIG: United States   LANG: English
ANNO: The simple and most effective way to curtail the threat of increasing computer crime is through appropriate internal safeguards by the organizations that use computers.

ACCN: 104860
TITL: Computer Crime Deterrence
JCIT: American Journal of Criminal Law, V 13, N 3 (Summer 1986), P 391–416
PAUT: Roache, JY
PDTE: 1986   PAGE: 26 p   CLSS: Article
ORIG: United States   LANG: English
ANNO: Deterring computer crime will require the public sector to pass improved legislation and the private sector to study, develop, and implement appropriate security measures.

ACCN: 106260
TITL: Computer Underground: Computer Hacking, Crashing, Pirating, and Phreaking
PAUT: Harry, M
SALE: Loompanics Unlimited, PO Box 1197, Port Townsend, WA 98368; PB Paperback.
PDTE: 1985   PAGE: 257 p
ORIG: United States   LANG: English
PNUM: ISBN 0-915179-31-8
ANNO: This book describes various types of computer crime, methods used to implement them, offender profiles, computer security measures, and some methods used to defeat them.

ACCN: 109343
TITL: Safety PINS (Personal Identification Numbers)
JCIT: Security Management, V 32, N 2, (February 1988), P 33–37
PAUT: Keough, H
PDTE: 1988   PAGE: 5 p   CLSS: Article
ORIG: United States   LANG: English
TYPE: Technical reports
ANNO: This article explains access control devices to prevent computer crime, with attention to smart cards that contain personal identification numbers (PINS) and port protection devices (PPD).

ACCN: 110067
TITL: To Catch a Thief
JCIT: Security Management, V 32, N 3 (March 1988), P 72, 74–76, 78
PAUT: Ball, M
PDTE: 1988   PAGE: 5 p   CLSS: Article
ORIG: United States   LANG: English
ANNO: Computer crime incidents are recounted and analyzed for future preventive measures.

Computer Crime—Detection

ACCN: 078297
TITL: MOMM's (Motivations, Opportunities, Methods, Means)—A Taxonomy for Computer Related Employee Theft
JCIT: Assets Protection, V 6, N 3 (May/June 1981), P 33–36
PAUT: Bologna, J
PDTE: 1981   PAGE: 4 p   CLSS: Article
ORIG: United States   LANG: English
ANNO: To effect some uniformity in nomenclature, a classification system for employee computer-related theft is proposed to include motivations, opportunities, means, and methods.

Computer Crime—Investigation

ACCN: 066083
TITL: Investigation of Computer Crime—An Operational Guide to White Collar Crime Enforcement
PAUT: Becker, JJ
CORP: Battelle Human Affairs Research Centers, National Center on White-Collar Crime, Seattle, WA 98105
SPON: US Department of Justice Law Enforcement Assistance Administration;
SALE: Superintendent of Documents GPO, Washington, DC 20402; DO Document. National Institute of Justice/National Criminal Justice Reference Service Microfiche Program, Box 6000, Department F, Rockville, MD 20850; MF Microfiche.
PDTE: 1980   PAGE: 77 p
ORIG: United States   LANG: English
GNUM: 77-TA-99-0008
ANNO: For investigators of computer-assisted crime, this operational guide discusses various approaches to the investigation, evidence collection, and possible legal problems impeding the investigation.

ACCN: 077927
TITL: Computer Crime—Expert Witness Manual
CORP: Koba Associates, Inc., Washington, DC 20009;
SPON: US Department of Justice Bureau of Justice Statistics, Washington, DC 20531;
SALE: National Institute of Justice/National Criminal Justice Reference Service Microfiche Program, Box 6000, Department F, Rockville, MD 20850; MF Microfiche.
PDTE: 1980   PAGE: 155 p
ORIG: United States   LANG: English
CNUM: J-LEAA-007-80
ANNO: This manual is an aid for assessing the need for expert assistance in computer-related crime cases and for identifying, selecting, managing, and using expert witnesses. It is intended for public and private sector personnel involved in the investigation and prosecution of computer-related crime, criminal justice system personnel, and those in government and business.

ACCN: 080042
TITL: Computer-Printed Documents as Part of a Computer Crime Investigation
JCIT: Journal of Forensic Sciences, V 26, N 4 (October 1981), P 730–738
PAUT: Winchester, JM
PDTE: 1981   PAGE: 9 p   CLSS: Article
ORIG: United States   LANG: English
NOTE: Presented at the 33rd Annual Meeting of the American Academy of Forensic Sciences, Los Angeles, California, February 17–20, 1981.
ANNO: General information on computer-related crime and on electronic data processing and computer equipment is provided as orientation material for investigators, and more specific data on computer printout analysis and printouts as evidence in court is given.

ACCN: 084315
TITL: Computers and Crime (From Criminal and Civil Investigation Handbook, P 6-109 to 6-134, 1981, Joseph J Grau and Ben Jacobson, eds.—See NCJ-84274)
PAUT: Hecht, SJ
SALE: McGraw-Hill, 1221 Avenue of the Americas, New York, NY 10020; DO Document.
PDTE: 1981   PAGE: 26 p
ORIG: United States   LANG: English
ANNO: Topics considered are the nature of computer crime, the vulnerability of computer systems, computer security, existing law applicable to computer crimes, and the investigation of computer crimes and abuses.

ACCN: 088603
TITL: Model Training Program in Computer Investigations for Law
           Enforcement Investigations (From Law Enforcement Data Processing
           Symposium Fifth Annual, P 205–218, 1981—See NCJ-88595)
PAUT: Bentley, SW
PDTE: 1981   PAGE: 13 p   CLSS: Document
ORIG: United States   LANG: English
ANNO: Since most computer-related crimes are committed at the less complex
           level, they can be handled by experienced investigators who have
           received basic training in computer operations, computer security, and
           investigative procedures related to computer crime.

ACCN: 090191
TITL: On the Trail of the Binary Bandits—The Computer Explosion Presents
           a Challenge for Police
JCIT: Police Magazine, V 6, N 4 (July 1983), P 44–49
PAUT: Kelly, J
PDTE: 1983   PAGE: 6 p   CLSS: Article
ORIG: United States   LANG: English
ANNO: Although efforts are being made to train police to investigate computer
           crime, the limited reporting of such crimes and the high cost of the
           investigation suggest that the most effective approach is for computer
           users and manufacturers to develop and implement security systems.

ACCN: 101576
TITL: Computer Crime Investigation Manual
PAUT: Schabeck, TA
SALE: Assets Protection, PO Box 2586, San Francisco, CA 94126; DO
           Document.
PDTE: 1980   PAGE: 364 p
ORIG: United States   LANG: English
TYPE: Training materials
ANNO: This manual provides a complete reference handbook to the
           investigation and prosecution of computer crime, with a focus on actual
           investigative processes and procedures.

ACCN: 104469
TITL: Role of Law Enforcement in Computer Crime and Computer Security
           (From Microcomputers in Criminal Justice, P 1–13, 1987, Joseph
           Waldron, et al—See NCJ-104468)
PAUT: Conser, J; Carsone, L
SALE: Anderson Publishing Company, 2035 Reading Road, Cincinnati, OH
           45202; DO Document.
PDTE: 1987   PAGE: 13 p
ORIG: United States   LANG: English
ANNO: The roles and responsibilities of law enforcement agencies in dealing
           with computer crime and computer security are outlined.

ACCN: 109294
TITL: Investigating Computer-Related Crimes Involving Small Computer
       Systems (From Critical Issues in Criminal Investigation, Second Edition,
       P 35–58, 1988, Michael J Palmiotto, ed.—See NCJ-109292)
PAUT: Conser, JA; Carsone, LP; Snyder, R
SALE: Anderson Publishing Company, 2035 Reading Road, Cincinnati, OH
       45202; DO Document.
PDTE: 1988   PAGE: 24 p
ORIG: United States   LANG: English
ANNO: This chapter focuses on criminal investigation associated with small,
       micro-related computer systems.

ACCN: 111025
TITL: Twenty-First Century Impact of Privatization on the Investigation of
       High-Tech Crime
PAUT: Morris, R
CORP: California Commission on Peace Officer Standards and Training,
       Sacramento, CA 95816;
SALE: California Commission on Peace Officer Standards and Training (POST)
       Center for Executive Development, 1601 Alhambra Blvd., Sacramento,
       CA 95816, DO Document. National Institute of Justice/National
       Criminal Justice Reference Service Microfiche Program, Box 6000,
       Department F, Rockville, MD 20850; MF Microfiche.
PDTE: 1987   PAGE: 34 p
ORIG: United States   LANG: English
TYPE: Studies/research reports
ANNO: This paper examines current trends in high-technology crime and
       privatization of investigation and their implications for law enforcement
       agencies.

ACCN: 114505
TITL: Computer Searches and Seizures
JCIT: Law and Order, V 36, N 11 (November 1988), P 68–71
PAUT: Mehnert, G
SALE: National Institute of Justice/National Criminal Justice Reference Service
       Microfiche Program, Box 6000, Department F, Rockville, MD 20850;
       MF Microfiche. National Institute of Justice/National Criminal Justice
       Reference Service Paper Reproduction Sales, Box 6000, Department F,
       Rockville, MD 20850, MD 20850; DO Document.
PDTE: 1988   PAGE: 4 p
ORIG: United States   LANG: English
TYPE: Training materials
ANNO: Investigating computer-related crime and conducting computer search
       and seizures will require some specialized expertise from law
       enforcement personnel.

ACCN: 116547
TITL: Basic Considerations in Investigating and Proving Computer-Related
          Federal Crimes
PAUT: Kondos, GF
CORP: US Department of Justice Management Division, Washington, DC
          20530;
SALE: National Institute of Justice/National Criminal Justice Reference Service
          Microfiche Program, Box 6000, Department F, Rockville, MD 20850;
          MF Microfiche.
PDTE: 1988   PAGE: 131 p
ORIG: United States   LANG: English
TYPE: Technical assistance reports
ANNO: This monograph is intended to help federal prosecutors and
          investigators in cases involving computer-related federal crimes.

ACCN: 118214
TITL: Computer Crime: Criminal Justice Resource Manual
PAUT: Parker, DB; Smith, DC; Turner, GW; Sherizan, S
CORP: SRI International, Menlo Park, CA 94025;
SPON: US Department of Justice National Institute of Justice, Washington, DC
          20531;
SALE: National Institute of Justice/National Criminal Justice Reference Service
          Microfiche Program, Box 6000, Department F, Rockville, MD 20850;
          MF Microfiche.
PDTE: 1989   PAGE: 221 p   CLSS: Document
ORIG: United States   LANG: English
CNUM: OJP-86-C-002
NOTE: Issues and Practices, second edition
TYPE: Policies/procedures handbooks/manuals
ANNO: This extensive training and reference guide for prosecutors and
          investigators of computer crime is useful for both computer technology
          novices and experienced hackers and replaces a previous edition.

ACCN: 118215
TITL: Dedicated Computer Crime Units
PAUT: McEwen, JT; Fester, D; Nugent, H
CORP: Institute for Law and Justice, Inc., Alexandria, VA 22314;
SPON: US Department of Justice National Institute of Justice, Washington, DC
          20531;
SALE: National Institute of Justice/National Criminal Justice Reference Service
          Microfiche Program, Box 6000, Department F, Rockville, MD 20850;
          MF Microfiche.
PDTE: 1988   PAGE: 129 p
ORIG: United States   LANG: English
CNUM: OJP-85-C-006
NOTE: National Institute of Justice Issues and Practices
TYPE: Program/project description/evaluations
ANNO: This report examines special police units established by local
          jurisdictions to investigate computer crime cases.

ACCN: 123759
TITL: Data Diddling, Salami Slicing, Trojan Horses . . . Can Your Agency Handle Computer Crimes?
JCIT: Police Chief, V 57, N 4 (April 1990), P 46, 48–49
PAUT: Manning, WW; White, GH
SALE: National Institute of Justice/National Criminal Justice Reference Service Microfiche Program, Box 6000, Department F, Rockville, MD 20850; MF Microfiche.
PDTE: 1990   PAGE: 3 p   CLSS: Article
ORIG: United States   LANG: English
TYPE: Technical reports
ANNO: The number of crimes involving computers is increasing dramatically; however, most law enforcement agencies currently have little internal training that addresses computer systems and equipment.

Computer Crime—Prosecution

ACCN: 081323
TITL: Trial of a Computer Crime
JCIT: Prosecutor, V 16, N 2 (Winter 1982), P 23–29
PAUT: Becker, J
SALE: National Institute of Justice/National Criminal Justice Reference Service Microfiche Program, Box 6000, Department F, Rockville, MD 20850; MF Microfiche.
PDTE: 1982   PAGE: 7 p
ORIG: United States   LANG: English
ANNO: Guidance for attorneys concerning trials of computer crimes is presented, with attention to the search and seizure issues inherent in computer crimes, the applicability of legislation defining computer crime, the effects of publicity about the case, problems in discovery, and sentencing issues.

ACCN: 097792
TITL: Computer Crime and Punishment—The View from the DA's Office
JCIT: Information Strategy—The Executive's Journal, V 1, N 2 (Winter, 1985) P 11–15, 17
PAUT: Gish, J
PDTE: 1985   PAGE: 6 p   CLSS: Article
ORIG: United States   LANG: English
ANNO: In an interview, Philadelphia District Attorney Edward G. Rendell explains the complex legal issues involved in computer crime and its prosecution.

ACCN: 098194
TITL: Computer-Related Crimes—An Outline
JCIT: Jurimetrics Journal, V 25, N 3 (Spring 1985), P 300–318
PAUT: Thackeray, G
PDTE: 1985   PAGE: 19 p   CLSS: Article
ORIG: United States   LANG: English
ANNO: This article outlines both federal and state statutes that can be used to prosecute information and computer-related crimes, discusses jurisdictional issues, and reviews the advantages and disadvantages of criminal prosecution.

ACCN: 119326
TITL: Prevention and Prosecution of Computer and High Technology Crime
PAUT: Arkin, SS; Bohrer, BA; Cuneo, DL; Donohoe, JP; Kaplan, JM; Kasanof, R; Levander, AJ; Sherizen, S
SALE: Matthew Bender and Company, Inc., 235 East 45th Street, New York, NY 10017; BK Book.
PDTE: 1989   PAGE: 596 p
ORIG: United States   LANG: English
NOTE: 1989 edition with June 1989 supplement
TYPE: Legislation/policy descriptions
ANNO: Written for criminal defense lawyers, prosecutors, corporate counsel, and other attorneys, this volume surveys crucial issues that arise out of the use of computers and other high technology as a tool of crime or civil wrong as well as situations in which the technology itself has been used by people in unauthorized, unlawful ways for their own benefit or to make inappropriate commercial use of it.

Computer Crime—Laws and Legal Precedents

ACCN: 074654
TITL: Computer Crime
JCIT: American Criminal Law Review, V 18, N 2 (Fall 1980), P 370–386
PAUT: Gammer, MA
PDTE: 1980   PAGE: 17 p   CLSS: Article
ORIG: United States   LANG: English
ANNO: This article deals with computer crime—the intentional use of a computer for fraudulent or illegal purposes—and gives concrete examples of possible computer offenses and relevant judicial decisions.

ACCN: 078890
TITL: Computer Crime—Legislative Resource Manual
CORP: Koba Associates, Inc., Washington, DC 20009;
SPON: US Department of Justice, Bureau of Justice Statistics, Washington, DC 20531;
SALE: National Institute of Justice/National Criminal Justice Reference Service Microfiche Program, Box 6000, Department F, Rockville, MD 20850; MF Microfiche.

PDTE: 1980   PAGE: 134 p
ORIG: United States   LANG: English
CNUM: J-LEAA-007-80
ANNO: A background document for investigators and prosecutors involved in computer-related crime cases, this manual discusses existing and proposed state and federal statutes applying to such crime, procedural issues, and privacy and security matters.

ACCN: 098759
TITL: Scuttle the Computer Pirates Software Protection Schemes
PAUT: Baker, RH
SALE: TAB Books, PO Box 40, Blue Ridge Summit, PA 17214; PB Paperback.

PDTE: 1984   PAGE: 208 p
ORIG: United States   LANG: English
ANNO: This book reports on the current legal situation regarding computer software "pirating," examines available options for preventing it, and provides guidance for planning and implementing a preventive strategy.

ACCN: 099404
TITL: Contemporary Legislation Governing Computer Crimes
JCIT: Criminal Law Bulletin, V 21, N 5 (September–October 1985), P 389–412
PAUT: George, BJ
SAE: National Institute of Justice/National Criminal Justice Reference Service Microfiche Program, Box 6000, Department F, Rockville, MD 20850; MF Microfiche. National Institute of Justice/National Criminal Justice Reference Service Paper Reproduction Sales, Box 6000, Department F, Rockville, MD 20850; DO Document.

PDTE: 1985   PAGE: 24 p
ORIG: United States   LANG: English
ANNO: This article describes the nature of contemporary computer crime, discusses the relevance and irrelevance of traditional criminal doctrines to serious computer crimes, and outlines federal and state laws designed to counter specific types of computer crime.

ACCN: 099553
TITL: Federal Computers and Telecommunications—Security and Reliability
        Considerations and Computer Crime Legislative Options
PAUT: Sherizen, S
CORP: Data Security Systems, Inc., Natick, MA 01760;
SPON: US Office of Technology Assessment, Washington, DC 20510;
PDTE: 1985   PAGE: 163 p   CLSS: Document
ORIG: United States   LANG: English
ANNO: Following a consideration of the adequacy of federal computer and
        telecommunications security, trends in computer crime are delineated,
        and limitations to legislative responses to current and future
        technological developments are discussed.

ACCN: 100959
TITL: Challenge of Computer-Crime Legislation—How Should New York
        Respond?
JCIT: Buffalo Law Review, V 33, N 3 (1985), P 777–814
PAUT: Wagner, AM
PDTE: 1985   PAGE: 38 p   CLSS: Article
ORIG: United States   LANG: English
TYPE: Legislation/policy analysis
ANNO: New York's most promising legislative response to computer crime
        would be the modification of related existing legislation and the drafting
        of new provisions to address only the unique aspects of computer crime.

ACCN: 105370
TITL: Computer Abuse—Problems of Instrumental Control
JCIT: Deviant Behavior, V 8, N 2 (1987), P 113–130
PAUT: Pfuhl, EH
PDTE: 1987   PAGE: 18 p   CLSS: Article
ORIG: United States   LANG: English
TYPE: Issue overviews
ANNO: During the seventies and eighties, an overwhelming majority of state
        legislatures acted to protect computer technology by declaring
        unauthorized intrusion into electronic data files and similar offenses
        as crime.

ACCN: 109057
TITL: Recent Amendments to the Canadian Criminal Code Respecting
        Computer Abuse Offenses
JCIT: Santa Clara Computer and High-Technology Law Journal, V 3, N 1
        (January 1987), P 165–187
PAUT: Webber, C
PDTE: 1987   PAGE: 23 p   CLSS: Article
ORIG: United States   LANG: English
NOTE: Portions of this paper were presented as a speech to the Computer Law
        Update Conference, Canadian Bar Association (Ontario Division),
        Toronto, November 1985.
TYPE: Legislation/policy analysis
ANNO: This paper examines the language of the Canadian criminal law
        amendments to the criminal code as they relate to computer abuse
        offenses and compares them to California Penal Code provisions.

ACCN: 110133
TITL: Process of Criminalization: The Case of Computer Crime Laws
JCIT: Criminology, V 26, N 1 (February 1988), P 101–126
PAUT: Hollinger, RC; Lanza-Kaduce, L
SPON: University of Florida Graduate School and Division of Sponsored
        Research, Gainesville, FL 32601;
PDTE: 1988   PAGE: 26 p   CLSS: Article
ORIG: United States   LANG: English
NOTE: An earlier version of this paper was presented at the annual meeting of
        the Academy of Criminal Justice Sciences on March 19, 1986, in
        Orlando, FL.
TYPE: Legislation/policy analysis
ANNO: Scholars are rarely afforded contemporary opportunities to study the
        formation of criminal law. This paper reviews state and federal efforts
        to criminalize various forms of computer abuse.

ACCN: 118437
TITL: Computer Crime Statutes: Are They Bridging the Gap Between Law
        and Technology?
JCIT: Criminal Justice Journal, V 11, N 1 (Fall–Winter 1988), P 203–233
PAUT: McCall, CC
PDTE: 1988   PAGE: 31 p   CLSS: Article
ORIG: United States   LANG: English
TYPE: Legislation/policy analysis
ANNO: This article explores computer crime from both legal and technical
        perspectives.

Computer Crime—Criminals

ACCN: 079169
TITL: Rifkin, A Documentary History
JCIT: Computer/Law Journal, V 2, N 3 (Summer 1980), P 471–720
PAUT: Becker, J
PDTE: 1980   PAGE: 250 p   CLSS: Article
ORIG: United States   LANG: English
TYPE: Studies/research reports
ANNO: Presented for students of computer crime, this article contains a
        summary and selected documents from the United States v. Rifkin case
        in which a computer professional stole $10.2 million from the Security
        Pacific National Bank in Los Angeles by manipulating the wire transfer
        system.

ACCN: 085984
TITL: When Criminals Turn to Computers, Is Anything Safe?
JCIT: Smithsonian, V 13 , N 5 (August 1982), P 116–118 , 120–122 , 124, 126
PAUT: Kolata, G
SALE: National Institute of Justice/National Criminal Justice Reference Service
        Microfiche Program, Box 6000, Department F, Rockville, MD 20850;
        MF Microfiche.
PDTE: 1982   PAGE: 7 p
ORIG: United States   LANG: English
ANNO: Wayward programmers, executives, and even teenagers are participating
        in the computer crime wave that is soaring along with the growth in the
        number of microcomputers and the number of people who know how to
        use them.

ACCN: 099180
TITL: Out of the Inner Circle—A Hacker's Guide to Computer Security
PAUT: Landreth, B
SALE: Microsoft Press, 10700 Northrup Way, Box 97200, Bellevue, 98009; PB
        Paperback, BK Book.
PDTE: 1985   PAGE: 230 p
ORIG: United States   LANG: English
ANNO: This book—written by a former member of an elite group (the "Inner
        Circle") of computer "hackers" committed to penetrating some of the
        nation's most protected computer systems—profiles hackers and their
        goals and methods and suggests steps for defeating their attacks on
        computer security systems.

ACCN: 102926
TITL: Computer Crime—The Who, What, Where, When, Why and How, Part 2
JCIT: Data Processing and Communications Security, V 10, N 2 (Spring 1986), P 25–30
PAUT: Bologna, J
PDTE: 1986   PAGE: 6 p   CLSS: Article
ORIG: United States   LANG: English
ANNO: This article discusses computer crime motivations and outlines organizational and security measures that counter computer crime.

ACCN: 106792
TITL: Computer Crime
PAUT: Francis, DB
SALE: EP Dutton and Company, 2 Park Avenue, New York, NY 10016; BK Book.
PDTE: 1987   PAGE: 120 p
ORIG: United States   LANG: English
PNUM: ISBN 0-525-67192-7
TYPE: Overview texts
ANNO: This text examines computer crime and computer security, with particular focus on offenses committed by youthful computer buffs (hackers).

ACCN: 109094
TITL: Putting Computer-Related Crime in Perspective
JCIT: Journal of Policy Analysis and Management, V 6, N 4 (Summer 1987), P 714–716
PAUT: Molnar, J
PDTE: 1987   PAGE: 3 p   CLSS: Article
ORIG: United States   LANG: English
ANNO: This article points out that most computer crimes are not committed by people skilled in the use of sophisticated computer technology but by clerical, case/claim review, or client services employees.

ACCN: 121472
TITL: Of Mice and Men
JCIT: Security Management, V 33, N 9 (September 1989), P 89–91
PAUT: Reese, LF
PDTE: 1989   PAGE: 3 p   CLSS: Article
ORIG: United States   LANG: English
TYPE: Training materials
ANNO: Security against computer crime by company employees must address offender motivation expressed in the acronym MICE: money, ideology, compromise, and ego.

ACCN: 121536
TITL: Computer Criminal: An Investigative Assessment
PAUT: Coutourie, L
SALE: National Institute of Justice/National Criminal Justice Reference Service Microfiche Program, Box 6000, Department F, Rockville, MD 20850; MF Microfiche.
PDTE: 1989 PAGE: 5 p CLSS: Article
ORIG: United States LANG: English
TYPE: Technical reports
ANNO: Criminal investigative analysis, formerly known as *profiling,* is a technique that might be applicable to computer criminals, although its usefulness may be limited if further research confirms studies indicating that these offenders are such an eclectic group that they cannot be clearly categorized.

Computer Crime—Piracy

ACCN: 082973
TITL: Security Officer's Role in the Legal Protection of Software
JCIT: Computer Security Journal, V 1, N 2 (Winter 1982), P 99–104
PAUT: Bigelow, R
PDTE: 1982 PAGE: 6 p CLSS: Article
ORIG: United States LANG: English
ANNO: Protecting proprietary rights in computer software is a complex and little understood area. Every data center should be aware of its obligations to protect the software of others that it uses under license.

ACCN: 101484
TITL: RICO (Racketeer Influenced and Corrupt Organizations Act), Modern Weaponry Against Software Pirates
JCIT: Computer/Law Journal, V 5, N 2 (Fall 1984), P 143–162
PAUT: Coolley, RB
PDTE: 1984 PAGE: 20 p CLSS: Article
ORIG: United States LANG: English
TYPE: Legislation/policy analysis
ANNO: With its provisions for mandatory treble damages, costs, and attorneys fees, the Racketeer Influenced and Corrupt Organizations Act (RICO) is an effective weapon against computer software pirates.

Electronic Funds Transfer Fraud

ACCN: 075719
TITL: Cashless Society—EFTS (Electronic Funds Transfer Systems) at the
        Crossroads
PAUT: Bequai, A
SALE: John Wiley and Sons, 605 Third Avenue, New York, NY 10016; BK
        Book.
PDTE: 1981   PAGE: 306 p
ORIG: United States   LANG: English
ANNO: A lawyer and former prosecutor discusses the technology of electronic
        funds transfer systems (EFTS) and the potential law enforcement and
        consumer problems and challenges EFTS pose.

ACCN: 083736
TITL: Computer Crime—Electronic Funds Transfer Systems and Crime
PAUT: Colton, KW; Tien, JM; Davis, ST; Dunn, B; Barnett, AI
CORP: Public Systems Evaluation, Inc., Cambridge, MA 02139;
SPON: US Department of Justice Bureau of Justice Statistics, Washington, DC
        20531;
SALE: National Institute of Justice/National Criminal Justice Reference Service
        Microfiche Program, Box 6000, Department F, Rockville, MD 20850;
        MF Microfiche. National Institute of Justice/National Criminal Justice
        Reference Service Paper Reproduction Sales, Box 6000, Department F,
        Rockville, MD 20850; DO Document.
PDTE: 1982   PAGE: 200 p
ORIG: United States   LANG: English
GNUM: 80-BJ-CX-0026
NOTE: Fifth in the Computer Crime Series.
ANNO: This document describes and analyzes potential criminal activity
        associated with electronic funds transfer systems and establishes
        definitions and classification schemes to be used in the measurement
        and analysis of such criminal activity.

ACCN: 092650
TITL: Electronic Fund Transfer and Crime
PAUT: Tien, JM; Fosque, GL; Cahn, MF; Colton, KW
CORP: Public Systems Evaluation, Inc., Cambridge, MA 02139;
SALE: National Institute of Justice/National Criminal Justice Reference Service
        Microfiche Program, Box 6000, Department F, Rockville, MD 20850;
        MF Microfiche. National Institute of Justice/National Criminal Justice
        Reference Service Paper Reproduction Sales, Box 6000, Department F,
        Rockville, MD 20850; DO Document.
PDTE: 1984   PAGE: 5 p
ORIG: United States   LANG: English
NOTE: Bureau of Justice Statistics Special Reports
ANNO: Despite the rapid proliferation of Electronic Funds Transfer Systems
        (EFTS), no system exists for measuring crime and abuse in this area.

ACCN: 099313
TITL: Electronic Fund Transfer Crime—An Overview
CORP: Hawaii Criminal Justice Data Center, Honolulu, HI 96813;
PDTE: 1985   PAGE: 60 p   CLSS: Document
ORIG: United States   LANG: English
NOTE: Research and Statistics Reports (CC01), August 1985
ANNO: Following a review of the current literature on electronic funds transfer
         (EFT) crime, this report examines technical computer crime methods
         that can be used in EFT fraud and assesses the nature and volume of
         EFT crime in Hawaii.

ACCN: 102822
TITL: Electronic Seal for Protection of Electronic Money in Sweden, Finland
         and Norway (From Electronic Crime Countermeasures, P 135–140,
         1986, John S Jackson, ed.—See NCJ-102815)
PAUT: Linden, C
SALE: University of Kentucky Office of Engineering Services Publications, 226
         Anderson Hall, Lexington, KY 40506; DO Document.
PDTE: 1986   PAGE: 6 p
ORIG: United States   LANG: English
TYPE: Program/project descriptions/evaluations
ANNO: A new security standard for the detection of criminal interference in the
         transmission or storage of electronic data processing based payment
         media and systems is being used by banks and corporations in Sweden.

ACCN: 122900
TITL: Electronic Funds Transfer: Oversight of Critical Banking Systems
         Should Be Strengthened
CORP: US General Accounting Office Information Management and
         Technology Division, Washington, DC 20548;
SALE: National Institute of Justice/National Criminal Justice Reference Service
         Microfiche Program, Box 6000, Department F, Rockville, MD 20850;
         DO Document. US General Accounting Office, Document Handling
         and Information Services Facility, PO Box 6015, Gaithersburg, MD
         20877; MF Microfiche.
PDTE: 1990   PAGE: 34 p
ORIG: United States   LANG: English
PNUM: GAO/IMTEC-90-14
TYPE: Program/project evaluations
ANNO: This examination of the adequacy of the regulatory structure and
         security measures for protecting the national and international systems
         for electronic funds transfers from misuse and abuse concludes that
         improvements are needed in oversight, management, and security
         measures.

Index